Early Child Development
in the 21st Century

Early Child Development in the 21st Century

PROFILES OF CURRENT RESEARCH INITIATIVES

EDITED BY
Jeanne Brooks-Gunn
Allison Sidle Fuligni
Lisa J. Berlin

Teachers College, Columbia University
New York and London

Published by Teachers College Press, 1234 Amsterdam Avenue, New York, NY 10027

Portions of Chapter 1 are reprinted with permission from "The Healthy Development of Young Children: SES Disparities, Prevention Strategies, and Policy Opportunities," by A. S. Fuligni and J. Brooks-Gunn, in *Promoting Health: Intervention Strategies from Social and Behavioral Research* (pp. 170–216), edited by B. D. Smedley and S. L. Syme. Copyright 2000 by the National Academy of Sciences. Courtesy of the National Academies Press, Washington, DC.

Library of Congress Cataloging-in-Publication Data

Early child development in the 21st century : profiles of current research initiatives / edited by Jeanne Brooks-Gunn, Allison Sidle Fuligni, Lisa J. Berlin.
   p. cm.
   Includes bibliographical references (p.   ) and index.
   ISBN 0-8077-4337-2 (cloth : alk. paper) — ISBN 0-8077-4336-4 (pbk. : alk. paper)
   1. Child development. 2. Early childhood education. I. Brooks-Gunn, Jeanne.
II. Fuligni, Allison Sidle. III. Berlin, Lisa.

LB1115.E27 2003
305.231—dc21   2002042986

ISBN 0-8077-4336-4 (paper)
ISBN 0-8077-4337-2 (cloth)

Printed on acid-free paper
Manufactured in the United States of America

10 09 08 07 06 05 04 03   8 7 6 5 4 3 2 1

Contents

List of Research Initiatives

Early Child Care

Welfare-to-Work

Neighborhood-Based Initiatives

Children with Special Needs

New National Longitudinal Surveys on Children

Acknowledgments

Support for this project was provided by the National Institute on Early Childhood Development and Education of the U.S. Department of Education; the Family and Child Well-Being Research Network of the National Institute for Child Health and Human Development; and the Office of the Assistant Secretary for Planning and Evaluation, U.S. Department of Health and Human Services.

We are grateful to our funders and wish to thank Naomi Karp, Jeff Evans, and Martha Moorehouse for their vision and support. We are grateful to the members of the Family and Child Well-Being Research Network for their assistance: Sandra Hofferth, Elizabeth Peters, Greg Duncan, Jay Teachman, Des Runyon, Kristin Moore, and Arland Thornton. Thanks also to our planning and advisory committee: Peg Burchinal, Natasha Cabrera, Martha Cox, Jane Knitzer, Marie McCormick, Kristin Moore, Suzanne Randolph, Faith Samples, and Martha Zaslow. Very special thanks are also due to Christy Brady-Smith, the project coordinator, Phyllis Gyamfi, and Amy Lowenstein for their efforts in organizing the project and finalizing the manuscript. Thanks also to Veronica Holly for her general support and good cheer.

CHAPTER 1

Themes in Developmental Research: Historical Roots and Promise for the Future

ALLISON SIDLE FULIGNI, JEANNE BROOKS-GUNN, AND LISA J. BERLIN

Over the past few decades, a great deal has been learned about how young children develop, about how their experiences in families and communities influence their development, about how families, preschools, and elementary schools contribute to their school readiness, and about the importance of health and developmental well-being for future engagement in learning. A series of national initiatives, both federally and foundation supported, have contributed to this knowledge.

Currently, the field of developmental research is receiving more attention than ever before. As is evidenced by the sheer number of research initiatives profiled in this volume, policy makers, child advocates, and researchers now have many resources to which they may turn to consider pathways of development. The current generation of research has resulted from the convergence of several streams of interest emerging over the past 25 years or so. First, there has been growing understanding of the importance of early development for later development; second, there has been an ongoing interest in enhancing development during early childhood through provision of early intervention and child care services; third, developmental theories increasingly consider the importance of the multiple contexts in which development takes place; and fourth, developmental research has increasingly become integrated with other fields of inquiry: developmentalists have begun to capitalize on research methods and resources traditionally utilized in other fields (e.g., sociology and economics) to address concerns about developmental processes, and social scientists from other fields have increasingly used developmental methods and studied children and families.

In this chapter, we outline the historical context for the current initiatives that are described in this volume. We take a look back at the research in developmental science to see what has been accomplished. The chapter uses the four themes listed above as a framework for understanding the contributions of previous research and the promise of current work for the future.

RECENT INTEREST IN THE EARLY YEARS OF DEVELOPMENT

Recent media and public policy have focused on the early years of life as a crucial period of development. The ill effects of early deprivation and neglect on children's later cognitive and emotional functioning have been demonstrated repeatedly (Shore, 1997). Concern about the experience of stress in the early years has been growing, as has the evidence linking stress to neuroendocrine functioning (Gunnar, 1998; Shonkoff & Phillips, 2000). At the same time, trends in maternal employment rates among the middle class, as well as new welfare reform requirements, are resulting in higher numbers of mothers working outside the home during the first few years of children's lives (Committee on Ways and Means, 1998; U.S. Census Bureau, 1999). Thus more very young children must be cared for by nonmaternal caregivers, often in settings outside the home. Studies of the quality of child care environments for children cared for outside the home have brought attention to the dangers of poor care environments, as well as the potential benefits of supportive, stimulating child care (Cost, Quality, and Child Outcomes [CQO] Study Team, 1995, 1999; Vandell & Wolfe, 2000; Whitebook, Howes, & Phillips, 1990). The role of paternal involvement in children's lives as well as the increase in shared caregiving also have been given heightened attention (Bianchi, 2000; Cabrera, Tamis-LeMonda, Bradley, Hofferth, & Lamb, 2000; Fuligni & Brooks-Gunn, 2002).

All of this research activity has been reflected in policy circles as well as reported by the media. In 1997, two White House conferences focused on early development: One addressed the importance of stimulation and relationships for early brain growth, and the second focused on the need for high-quality child care. Around that time, both *Time* and *Newsweek* magazines devoted entire issues to infants, and *Newsweek* published a second issue devoted to young children in 2000 (Nash, 1997; R. M. Smith, 1997, 2000).

In the following sections, we explore the well-being of young children through two perspectives. First, we address some of the ways that well-being has been defined and described by various investigators; and second, we discuss concerns about the well-being of children who are not developing in optimal settings, namely, children living in poverty.

Defining Healthy Development and Well-Being

National attention was focused on the concept of school readiness in 1994, when the federal government passed the Goals 2000: Educate America Act, adopting into law six national goals for improving the education system. The first of these goals states, "By the year 2000, all children in America will start school ready to learn" (National Education Goals Panel, 1998). School readiness has been defined broadly, to include five dimensions: physical well-being and motor development; social and emotional development; approaches toward learning; language usage; and cognition and general knowledge (Goal One Technical Planning Group, 1993).

Domains of child well-being are often conceived in different ways, though each of these conceptualizations emphasizes the importance of considering multiple domains of functioning when assessing health and well-being (Fuligni & Brooks-Gunn, 2000). Scholars and policy makers from a variety of disciplines have converged on broadening their definitions of child well-being: educators have recently added physical and emotional health; health scholars now include emotional health, communication, and relationships; economists also focus on these factors in addition to human capital indicators; and psychologists include more than cognitive, social, and emotional aspects of development.

Broad conceptualizations of healthy child development include domains that are usually considered under the rubric of health, defined by the World Health Organization (WHO) as being: "a state of complete physical, mental, and social well-being and not merely the absence of disease or infirmity" (1978). In addition to physical health, other competencies as well as liabilities or dysfunction are emphasized. Furthermore, competencies with social cognitive components are included, such as engagement, motivation, and curiosity. There is clearly a need for a balanced view of health and development that encompasses the absence of conditions that limit children's lives as well as the presence of factors and features that enhance their lives.

Regardless of debates about what constitutes a normal trajectory of development, researchers, practitioners, and policy makers alike have become alarmed in recent decades about the growing number of children who may be considered to be not following optimal developmental trajectories. As many as one-third of kindergartners are considered by their teachers to be not "ready for school" (Lewit & Baker, 1995; Rimm-Kaufman, Pianta, & Cox, 2000), and approximately one-quarter of all preschoolers are reported to have behavior problems (Richman, Stevenson, & Graham, 1975). One important factor affecting rates of school readiness is the number of children growing up in poverty.

Early Childhood Poverty and Its Effects on Development

The United States has witnessed considerable growth in early childhood poverty. Between 1979 and 1995, the proportion of American children under age 3 living in families with income below the official poverty line grew by 33% (National Center for Children in Poverty, 1996). After peaking at 26.2% for children under age 6 in 1993, poverty rates began to decline in the later 1990s to 22% in 1997 (National Center for Children in Poverty, 1997). This decrease was due in part to the effects of a robust economy, the rapid influx of single mothers into the workforce, high employment rate, and increases in the federal Earned Income Tax Credit (EITC; Eissa & Liebman, 1996; Primus & Porter, 1998).

Poverty compromises human life immediately and continuously. Low-income children are more likely to receive inadequate pre- and postnatal care, more likely to be of low birth weight, and more likely to die at birth or in childhood (Starfield, 1991). Poor children have higher rates of illness and physical health problems, are less likely to receive regular medical care and immunizations, and more likely to live in unsafe conditions (Brooks-Gunn, 1995b; Brooks-Gunn & Duncan, 1997; Brooks-Gunn, Duncan, & Aber, 1997a, 1997b; Duncan & Brooks-Gunn, 1997; Garbarino, 1990; Starfield, 1992). Early poverty has been associated with lower achievement test scores and higher incidence of behavior problems during childhood (Duncan, Brooks-Gunn, & Klebanov, 1994; Klebanov, Brooks-Gunn, McCarton, & McCormick, 1998; J. R. Smith, Brooks-Gunn, & Klebanov, 1997), and with lower rates of high school completion (Duncan & Brooks-Gunn, 1997; Haveman & Wolfe, 1994). These effects have been documented above and beyond the effects of co-occurring risk factors including (minority) ethnicity, single parenthood, and low parental education (Brooks-Gunn & Duncan, 1997; Duncan & Brooks-Gunn, 1997). It is notable, moreover, that income poverty during early childhood has been shown to exert greater effects than income poverty during later childhood (Duncan, Yeung, Brooks-Gunn, & Smith, 1998).

It is important to note, however, even as research illustrates the negative effects of early childhood poverty and other early hardships, that detrimental early experiences do not necessarily doom people to a lifetime of limited competence. The idea, rather, is that altering the life courses of people who have not had supportive early experiences is more difficult than providing these experiences in the first place (Furstenberg, Brooks-Gunn,

& Morgan, 1987; Shonkoff & Meisels, 2000). This is the rationale behind the development and provision of early childhood services, including early education intervention for children from poor families, as well as high-quality child care services to meet the needs of working parents and their children.

RESEARCH ON EARLY CHILDHOOD INTERVENTION PROGRAMS

During the 1960s, the War on Poverty spurred the creation of many programs attempting to reduce the generational spread of poverty and dependence by giving young children enhanced learning experiences and other forms of support. These experiences were intended to prepare them to enter school with the skills and motivation necessary to promote later academic success. Model preschool programs, such as the High/Scope Perry Preschool, and large-scale public programs, such as Head Start, are examples of the then-emerging focus on providing environmentally at-risk children with compensatory experiences before school entry. Since that time, numerous types of intervention services have been designed for young children considered to be at risk for poor school outcomes because of biological risk (e.g., premature birth or low birth weight), established disabilities (e.g., as Down syndrome or autism), or environmental risk (e.g., poverty and low maternal education; Guralnick, 1997; Shonkoff & Meisels, 2000).

Early childhood intervention programs for low-income children and their families aim to better these children's prospects by redressing the effects of poverty and co-occurring risk factors such as low birth weight, low parental education, and high levels of family stress. Program goals and activities include promoting family members' mental health and physical health practices, providing parents with information and/or social support, increasing parents' basic skills and economic self-sufficiency, enhancing parenting skills, and working directly with children to promote their physical, cognitive, languistic, and socioemotional development (Benasich, Brooks-Gunn, & Clewell, 1992; Berlin, O'Neal, & Brooks-Gunn, 1998; Guralnick, 1997; C. T. Ramey & Ramey, 1998; Shonkoff & Meisels, 2000; see Chapter 3, this volume).

Since the introduction of early models of intervention for disadvantaged children, numerous evaluations have been conducted assessing their effectiveness. Their findings are promising in the areas of effects across broad domains of children's development, as well as outcomes for parents. Several recent reviews summarize these results (Barnett, 1995; Brooks-Gunn, Berlin, & Fuligni, 2000; Bryant & Maxwell, 1997; Farran, 2000; Yoshikawa, 1995).

Cognitive Outcomes for Children in Early Intervention Programs

In the early generations of early childhood intervention, the key indicator of program success was participants' IQ or other assessments of intellectual functioning. IQ continues to be an important measure of program effects. Many programs have shown cognitive gains immediately following program participation compared with children who did not receive the intervention. Programs providing center-based services starting in infancy have documented the largest effects on IQ, ranging from ²/₃ to ¾ of a standard deviation (e.g., Brooks-Gunn et al., 1994; Campbell & Ramey, 1994; Infant Health and Development Program [IHDP], 1990; Karoly et al., 1998).

Center-based programs beginning later, at age 3 or 4, report smaller but significant effects on children's IQ scores, ranging from 1/3 to 1/2 of a standard deviation (Consortium for Longitudinal Studies, 1983). Model preschools have shown somewhat stronger effects than large-scale public programs (Barnett, 1995). Programs providing home-visiting services without a center-based early education component report the fewest effects on child IQ (Benasich et al., 1992; Gomby, Culross, & Behrman, 1999; Olds & Kitzman, 1993; Olds et al., 1999).

An important theme addressed in longitudinal follow-ups of intervention programs is that initial program advantages in IQ and achievement test scores have often been found to diminish over time (Royce, Darlington, & Murray, 1983). Some early childhood experts address this issue by posing the challenging question of how we can expect 1 or 2 years of high-quality intervention (often occurring for only a few hours per day) to offset the on-going effects of poverty, low parental education, poor housing, parental unemployment, and the many other experiences that combine to affect the functioning of economically disadvantaged children (Zigler, 1998). The so-called fade-out of intervention effects seems inevitable in many cases, given the fact that some attendees of preschool programs for poor children (such as Head Start) go on to attend schools of substantially lower quality than non–Head Start children (Currie & Thomas, 1995; Lee & Loeb, 1995).

On the other hand, some early interventions do report lasting effects. Some center-based programs beginning in infancy report continued IQ effects years after the intervention is concluded (Barnett, 1995; Campbell & Ramey, 1994; Garber, 1988; Karoly et al., 1998; McCarton et al., 1997). Several studies that have followed intervention children through the school years indicate that even when test scores become similar for program and control children, children who experienced early childhood intervention tend to be retained in grade and referred to special education less often, and graduate from high school at higher rates (Lazar & Darlington, 1982; Royce et al., 1983; Schweinhart, Barnes, Weikart, Barnett, & Epstein, 1993).

Social and Emotional Well-Being

As we discussed above, the first decades of early childhood intervention sought to break the cycle of poverty strictly through improving cognitive outcomes, which were hypothesized to foretell later success in school. Less attention was paid at that time to program effects on children's social and emotional development, as these outcomes were not considered to be related to children's school success. As a result, measures of noncognitive outcomes, such as behavior problems or emotional development, tended not to be included in the initial studies of center-based interventions.

Later studies of home-visiting programs reported short-term effects on infant and child behavior and quality of mother-child interaction (Gomby et al., 1999; Olds & Kitzman, 1993; Olds et al., 1999). The Infant Health and Development Program (IHDP) found significantly fewer mother-reported behavior problems among intervention children at 3 years, particularly when the mother had lower levels of education (IHDP, 1990). However, intervention effects on behavior problems were only marginally significant by the time the children were 5 years old (Brooks-Gunn et al., 1994).

Longer term follow-up studies of children who participated in the early model intervention programs have documented differences between program and control children in the areas of problem behavior and delinquency. For instance, the Perry Preschool study has now followed the participating children through age 27, and has documented positive effects of program participation for both cognitive and social-emotional outcomes. In addition to program effects on cognitive scores, grade retention, and special education, program children engaged in fewer delinquent behaviors at age 14 and were less involved with the criminal justice system at ages 19 and 27 (C. T. Ramey & Ramey, 1998; Schweinhart et al., 1993).

Such findings indicate the evolution of an increased emphasis on the importance of emotional well-being and the view that emotional security may be a foundation for cognitive development and other aspects of readiness for school and learning. Many current intervention programs profiled in this volume explicitly indicate social and emotional outcomes as program goals.

Factors and Pathways Affecting Program Success

Having found that some programs can make a difference in long-term outcomes for the children who participate, we must ask what it is about these programs that makes them successful. In fact, findings are hardly uniform. Program effectiveness frequently varies according to characteristics of the programs, its participants, and especially the match between program services and participant needs and the extent to which participants are fully engaged in treatment (Barnard, 1998; Berlin, Brooks-Gunn, McCarton, & McCormick, 1998). Increasingly, scholars are arguing that in addition to asking whether early interventions work, questions about for whom and under what circumstances services are most effective must also be addressed (Berlin, Brooks-Gunn, et al., 1998; Brooks-Gunn, Berlin, & Fuligni, 2000; Karoly et al., 1998; Reynolds, Mann, Miedel, & Smokowski, 1997). The early intervention literature, in fact, offers a growing body of information about the aspects of early intervention services, such as "two-generation" approaches (the provision of services to both children and parents), service intensity, and service integration (Berlin, Brooks-Gunn, et al., 1998; Brooks-Gunn, 1995b; Brooks-Gunn, Burchinal, & Lopez, 2001; Leventhal, Brooks-Gunn, McCormick, & McCarton, 2000; C. T. Ramey, Ramey, Gaines, & Blair, 1995; St. Pierre, Layzer, & Barnes, 1995; Yoshikawa, 1995). This information, in turn, informs early intervention practice as well as evaluation.

The type of services delivered by a program (e.g., home-visiting versus center-based interventions) may play a role in the domain of functioning they will affect. For instance, home-based services tend to target parental well-being and mental health, and improved parent-child relationships. This type of program may have stronger effects on parents (Yoshikawa, 1995). On the other hand, center-based programs, by providing educational services directly to children, are more likely have direct effects on children's cognitive and linguistic development. A review of 27 intervention programs found that 90% of center-based versus 64% of home-based programs resulted in immediate intervention effects on children's cognitive developmental outcomes; one year after the program had ended, the effects were maintained in 67% of center-based versus 44% of home-based programs (Benasich et al., 1992).

The quantity of services received can also make a difference. Most studies evaluating effectiveness of different "doses" of intervention find that higher frequency and duration of program participation is associated with positive effects on child IQ and school achievement, home environment, and parent-child interactions (Liaw, Meisels, & Brooks-Gunn, 1995; Ramey et al., 1992; Reynolds et al., 1997; Sparling et al., 1991).

Characteristics of program participants such as family and individual levels of risk also make a difference in program effectiveness. Vulnerable families appear to reap greater benefits from early intervention programs than do families with fewer risk factors, although families with extreme, multiple risk factors are less likely to benefit than families with moderate levels of risk. For example, the IHDP intervention was most effective for children with more environmental disadvantage (low maternal education and income), but less biological disadvantage (i.e., the heavier children in the low-birth-weight sample; Brooks-Gunn, Duncan, Leventhal, et al., 1997; Brooks-Gunn, Gross,

Kraemer, Spiker, & Shapiro, 1992; Brooks-Gunn, Klebanov, Liaw, & Spiker, 1993; Liaw & Brooks-Gunn, 1993). Initial intellectual disadvantage is also associated with greater benefits of intervention. Greater program effects have been found for families with low maternal psychological and cognitive resources or children who began with below-average intellectual abilities (Bryant & Maxwell, 1997; Garber, 1988; Klebanov, Brooks-Gunn, & McCormick, 2001; Olds et al., 1999).

Interactions between the program and participants may be the most critical factor in program effectiveness. It has been hypothesized that participants must be fully engaged in the program to benefit, and this engagement requires successful relationships between the participants and the program staff. For instance, IHDP analyses showed higher child IQ scores and higher home environment ratings among participating families in which both mother and child were rated as having "high" active participation in the program (Liaw et al., 1995). In addition, a match between participants' needs and program services is needed to ensure program relevance and active engagement of the participant. Ongoing program evaluation research is paying greater attention to characteristics of programs, participants, and their interaction, in order to more clearly assess the benefits of program participation (Love et al., 2001).

When considering how early intervention programs work to improve child outcomes, we must also consider the pathways through which such effects may take place. In particular, one reason that parenting and parent education components are included in many programs is because of the hypothesis that children will benefit indirectly from program effects on their parents. Indeed, Yoshikawa (1995) points out that among intervention programs with long-term positive effects on social outcomes, initial effects were found on children's cognitive and verbal abilities and parent's parenting skills, prior to the later social outcomes.

Many programs assume the child can be influenced indirectly through the mother. Therefore they seek to improve mother-child interactions and teaching skills, raise the mother's self-esteem and emotional functioning, promote her return to school or employment, and increase her knowledge about child development and child competence. Thus programs attempt to have a long-term impact on the family environment in which the child lives. Positive program effects have been found on maternal education, employment, mother-child interaction quality, and maternal knowledge and attitudes (Benasich et al., 1992; Brooks-Gunn, Berlin, & Fuligni, 2000).

Although programs may expect their parent-focused services to have indirect effects on child outcomes, only a few studies have explicitly tested this pathway (Brooks-Gunn, Berlin, & Fuligni, 2000). Some recent analyses have attempted to link intervention participation to child cognitive and social outcomes via program effects on maternal depressive symptoms and parenting practices (Brooks-Gunn, Berlin, & Fuligni, 2000; Burchinal, Campbell, Bryant, Wasik, & Ramey, 1997).

Conclusions

A survey of the numerous studies and reviews of early intervention programs suggests positive effects for children from low-income backgrounds. These effects include initial gains in intellectual and achievement scores, and longer term outcomes reflecting more successful school experiences (less special education placement, less grade retention, and higher graduation rates). Reduction of behavior problems and delinquency have also been reported.

Several reviewers of early intervention programs agree that certain characteristics of intervention are important. In terms of program characteristics, researchers note that in order to maximize the likelihood of improving children's intellectual and academic outcomes, services should be provided directly to the child; home-visiting services alone are more likely to affect parenting and home environment than child outcomes, though they may add to the effectiveness of center-based interventions (Barnett, 1995; Berlin, O'Neal, & Brooks-Gunn, 1998; Bryant & Maxwell, 1997; Gomby et al., 1999; S. L. Ramey & Ramey, 1999; Yoshikawa, 1995).

Thus the research on early childhood intervention over the past few decades has provided both researchers and practitioners with evidence that provision of intervention services can have lasting positive effects on children's social, emotional, and cognitive outcomes. It has also served to raise new questions about early intervention effects in terms of the types of services that can have the strongest impacts for different groups of families, the importance of considering program implementation and participation when evaluating effectiveness, and the added understanding of how interventions operate that may be gained from measuring both direct and indirect pathways of influence. In this volume we profile several current intervention programs that are breaking new ground in the early intervention field by incorporating the lessons learned over the past few decades of early intervention research.

STUDYING MULTIPLE CONTEXTS OF DEVELOPMENT

The current popular attention to the settings in which young children are developing is mirrored by the growing acceptance among researchers of theories specifying the influence of contexts, such as the ecological theory espoused by Bronfenbrenner (Bronfenbrenner, 1979, 1986; Bronfenbrenner & Crouter,

1983). According to Bronfenbrenner, early human development is a process occurring within four embedded contexts: "microsystems," the child's most immediate contexts including family and school; "mesosystems," contexts that have indirect effects on children's development via their influences on microsystems, such as parents' relationships with each other; "exosystems," larger institutions and community organizations; and "macrosystems," sociocultural practices, beliefs and values of a nation, region, or community, such as the acceptance of corporal punishment. Similarly, family systems theory (e.g., Sameroff & Seifer, 1983) guides much current research on child development, by considering the interrelations of proximal (e.g., family) and distal (e.g., community) systems influencing development. Thus developmental studies have expanded their focus to explore the effects of variation in many diverse contexts including family characteristics, the child care setting, and the neighborhood. The study of economic disparities, in particular, is enhanced by consideration of how socioeconomic variation affects each of these contexts. In this section we consider three environmental contexts in which the effects of living in poverty have been explored: the family, the child care setting, and the neighborhood.

The Family Context

It has long been noted that low family socioeconomic status (SES), in particular low family income and low parental education levels, is associated with poorer physical, cognitive, linguistic, social, and emotional outcomes in children (Brooks-Gunn & Duncan, 1997). However, the pathways linking family SES to child outcomes are not clear. For instance, low income and parental education may be associated with less-stimulating physical home environments as well as less cognitively enriching interactions between parents and children. Financial stress may contribute to poor parental mental health, which may result in less warm and more harsh parenting practices. It may be these home and parenting environments that negatively affect children's early development (McLoyd, 1990, 1998).

Recent research analyzing large and longitudinal data sets has been able to model some of these pathways for young children. Effects of low maternal education and income have been found on financial strain, maternal depressive symptoms, and home environment and parenting style, which in turn negatively affected preschoolers' cognitive scores (Jackson, Brooks-Gunn, Huang, & Glassman, 2000; Jackson, Tienda, & Huang, 2001; Linver, Brooks-Gunn, & Kohen, 1999; Yeung, Linver, & Brooks-Gunn, 2001). Similar pathways link family income, home environment, and parenting behaviors to preschoolers' problem behaviors (Jackson et al., 2001; Linver et al., 1999).

Child Care Settings

Moving beyond the scope of children's experiences within the home, a large and growing body of research links the quality of children's out-of-home care to their cognitive, linguistic, social, and emotional development. Research has shown that structural features of the care setting (ratio of children to adults, group size, education level of caregivers, adequate and stimulating materials), as well as process features (teacher-child interactions, teaching styles) have immediate and long-term effects on children's cognitive and social development (CQO Study Team, 1995, 1999; Whitebook et al., 1990; Zill et al., 1998).

The link between family socioeconomic status and the quality of out-of-home care is complex, however. When children receive care from relatives or in home-based arrangements, lower family income is associated with lower quality of these settings (Galinsky, Howes, Kontos, & Shinn, 1994; NICHD Early Child Care Research Network, 1997c). For children in center-based care, the associations are somewhat different: The quality of center-based care is higher for the lowest income families (below the poverty line), who receive subsidies for purchasing child care, and who may qualify for high-quality intervention programs, such as Head Start, than for less poor families (families with incomes above the poverty line). In fact, a curvilinear association is found—middle-income families receive lower quality center-based care than high- or low-income families (NICHD Early Child Care Research Network, 1997c; Phillips, Voran, Kisker, Howes, & Whitebook, 1994; Vandell & Wolfe, 2000). Many of the child care initiatives described in this volume are generating more information on how poverty and child care settings are related.

Studies of Neighborhood Effects on Development

A current school of thought on income disparities postulates that neighborhood-level SES may exert its own influence on neighborhood residents, separately from family-level SES. Neighborhood mechanisms that have been considered to influence relationships between neighborhoods and child outcomes include resources (availability of quality schools, child care, recreational activities, services, and opportunities); relationships (parental characteristics, support networks, quality and structure of home environment); and norms or collective efficacy (existence of formal and informal institutions to monitor residents' behavior, and the presence of physical risk to residents; Leventhal & Brooks-Gunn, 2000). For very young children, most effects are likely to be indirect, as parents control the child's access to neighborhood resources, relationships, and collective norms (Klebanov, Brooks-Gunn, & Duncan, 1994; Leventhal & Brooks-Gunn, 2000, in press).

Indeed, living in a poor neighborhood has been linked to less cognitively stimulating home environments for 3- to 4-year-olds in the IHDP and the National Longitudinal Survey of Youth (NLSY), and less maternal warmth in the IHDP (Klebanov, Brooks-Gunn, Chase-Lansdale, & Gordon, 1997; Klebanov et al., 1994), setting the stage for indirect effects on children through these parenting variables. Neighborhood effects on social support are curvilinear: Lower levels of social support are found among those living in low-income as well as affluent neighborhoods, relative to middle-income neighborhoods (Klebanov et al., 1997). These studies have also linked parenting characteristics (cognitively stimulating environment and maternal warmth) to preschoolers' cognitive outcomes. In both the IHDP and NLSY, living in a neighborhood with affluent neighbors was associated with higher verbal and ability scores as well as lower behavior problem scores for young school-aged children, and these effects were mediated by the cognitive stimulation parents provided in the home (Klebanov et al., 1997, 1998).

Again, we need to specify the processes through which neighborhood income operates to affect children's outcomes, or how neighborhood residence might influence parental provision of stimulating experiences, sensitivity, and warmth. For instance, institutional resources (the availability of learning, social and recreational activities, child care, schools, and health care services) may be of most interest regarding children's achievement outcomes, as the availability of libraries, museums, and learning programs in the community may affect parent's provision of such experiences outside the home and, in turn, children's school readiness and achievement. Social and recreational activities may affect children's physical and social development, and availability of quality child health care may affect parent's usage of health care services for their children and, in turn, children's physical health.

In terms of relationships, perhaps neighborhood poverty affects parental mental health, which influences parenting behaviors and, ultimately, child outcomes (Brooks-Gunn, Duncan, & Aber, 1997a, 1997b). Access to neighborhood sources of social support may help alleviate the stress of living in poor or dangerous neighborhoods, and this may reduce the negative effects of parent stress on child outcomes (Conger, Ge, Elder, Lorenz, & Simons, 1994; McLoyd, 1990). Parental warmth, sensitivity, harshness, supervision, and monitoring are all dimensions of parenting that could both be affected by neighborhood characteristics and affect child outcomes (Furstenberg, Cook, Eccles, Elder, & Sameroff, 1999).

The structural features of neighborhoods, such as income, residential stability, family stability, and ethnic heterogeneity, determine the extent to which formal and informal institutions are in place to monitor and socialize the behaviors of its residents. Kupersmidt and colleagues (Kupersmidt, Griesler, DeRosier, Patterson, & Davis, 1995) have found that living in a middle-SES neighborhood can help to protect poor black children of single parents from developing aggressive behavior, perhaps because of the higher prevalence of successful adult or peer role models outside the family.

The initiatives profiled in this volume reflect the growing interest in the influence of multiple environments on child development. Across a wide range of studies, measures include family processes, child care use and quality, and, in many current studies, measures of neighborhood-level characteristics. Additionally, intervention initiatives are beginning to have an expanded community-level focus, seeking to increase the social capital of a community by improving the number and quality of connections among residents and to indirectly affect individuals and families through their strengthening of the community (Berlin, Brooks-Gunn, & Aber, 2001; Brooks-Gunn, 1995a).

CONTEMPORARY LARGE-SCALE STUDIES OF DEVELOPMENT

The review above describes trends in developmental research that reflect the increased attention to well-being in the early childhood years, the commitment to providing effective intervention services for disadvantaged children and families, and the broadening scope of developmental research that considers multiple contexts of influence. Each of these themes has contributed to the increase in the number of large-scale research initiatives focusing on early development. Almost 10 years ago, a group of developmental psychologists asserted the importance of using large national and local data sets for secondary data analysis to address questions relevant to development (Brooks-Gunn, Phelps, & Elder, 1991). Previous to that time, the large and longitudinal studies had generally been designed and utilized by sociologists and economists to document labor market experiences, income and work, or educational achievement and attainment (Brooks-Gunn, Berlin, Leventhal, & Fuligni, 2000).

Large-scale longitudinal studies offer developmentalists an opportunity to explore many questions that cannot be addressed in smaller, cross-sectional or even short-term longitudinal studies. For instance, much of the research on the effects of parental characteristics on children has measured those characteristics at only one point in time. But parental characteristics and family circumstances do change over time, influencing how, where, and with whom children live (Duncan et al., 1998; Featherman, Spenner, & Tsunematsu, 1988; Hofferth, 1985). Furthermore, life events may have differential effects as a function of the life phase of the child, parent, or family. Analysis of longitudinal data sets may help to answer questions of relative impacts of life events occurring at different life phases, and whether prior events have persistent effects in later life phases (Brooks-Gunn et al., 1991). Such data sets may also facilitate analysis of intergenerational processes, including the consequences of multigenerational parenting for grandmothers and grandchildren, the costs and benefits of assuming parental roles the second time around (for grandparents), continuity of behavior and parenting style across the two generations, and satisfaction with assumed roles over time. Additionally, secondary data analyses of large-scale longitudinal data sets are particularly useful for the study of precursors of relatively infrequent events, such as criminal behavior or alcoholism (Robins, 1966; Vaillant, 1983).

A new wave of developmental studies has been launched within the last 5 years or so that builds upon the themes of the past 25 years. The growing number of children in poverty as well as the strong research base on the efficacy of some forms of early intervention has led to the continued development of early intervention programs that have evolved from the original programs of the 1960s and 1970s. These programs are contemporary in that they focus on a broader domain of child outcomes and seek to serve the child in the context of his or her life by supporting the whole family and even the community. The importance of the multiple settings in which children develop has been recognized, and developmental research is increasingly striving to incorporate methodology and theoretical approaches that can account for these multiple influences.

The primary questions being addressed by these current initiatives will help to fill out our broadening conceptions of developmental processes. The initiatives will serve multiple functions by also providing rich data from many sources and time points, making them ideal resources for secondary data analysis. As Chapter 2 will illustrate, this volume is devoted to describing several "families" of contemporary large-scale studies of early development.

The Profiles Project

ALLISON SIDLE FULIGNI AND JEANNE BROOKS-GUNN

The history and evolution of the field of early childhood research, as we have described in Chapter 1, has carried us to a point at which we know much about the importance of the early childhood period. Numerous studies have characterized this period as one of rapid development and suggested that it is a time when contexts of development may have great influence, potentially enhancing or restricting the course of development. At the beginning of the twenty-first century, policy makers and early childhood investigators alike are grappling with the realities of a growing population of children living in economically disadvantaged families, families headed by teen and single parents, and neighborhoods with dwindling social and material resources. Many questions remain about the nature of development in these diverse contexts, as well as about the most effective ways to provide needed social and educational services to families with very young children.

Many important questions about early childhood development have required the use of large data sets in order to determine the effects of age, genetic relatedness (e.g., twin, sibling, and adoption studies), life transitions, and family characteristics. Although research initiatives large enough to document these types of effects have existed for decades, especially in the fields of economics and sociology, studies with rich developmental data focusing on very young children have emerged only in the last 5 years or so (Brooks-Gunn, Berlin, Leventhal, & Fuligni, 2000).

OVERVIEW OF PROJECT

The Synthesis and Profiles of Research Initiatives on Early Childhood Education and Development Project was initiated to identify the current and ongoing large-scale research initiatives on early childhood education and development that are generating large data sets to help address many of these questions. The goal of the project was to bring together in a single volume detailed information about the many nationally representative or multisite longitudinal studies currently following young children and families. Each of these studies is breaking new ground as it contributes to an expanding base of research knowledge on young children and families in the twenty-first century. The findings of these studies provide information that will guide future thinking about early development; developmental research; and social policy, social service design, service delivery, and practice. Individually and collectively, these data will enable investigators to address several theoretical and policy issues that are on the forefront of current thinking about the situations of young American children at the beginning of the twenty-first century: early childhood interventions for economically disadvantaged children; neighborhood characteristics and residence patterns; the role of fathers; school readiness and the transition to school; and issues related to maternal employment, including child care and welfare reform (Brooks-Gunn, Berlin, Leventhal, & Fuligni, 2000).

All of the initiatives profiled in depth in this volume focus on the experiences of young children (generally under age 6 at the beginning of the study, although the studies focusing on neighborhoods and welfare-to-work programs tended to include older children as well). They are either nationally representative or follow large groups of children and families from multiple sites, with samples of at least 300 children and their families. Some studies are evaluations of large-scale intervention programs, whereas others document the experiences of different populations of young children, including those in families receiving welfare, children in child care, and children with special needs.

Among the studies assessing the efficacy of interventions, we include profiles of early childhood intervention programs, school transition programs, family support initiatives, pre- and perinatal health initiatives, and welfare-to-work initiatives. Other longitudinal studies include studies of child care patterns, influences of neighborhood residence, and studies with nationally representative samples of young children. The individual studies described in this volume are listed by topic in the List of Research Initiatives.

Twenty-eight studies are profiled in the following chapters. A group of authors who are involved in early childhood research was assembled to write profiles of these studies. In most cases, the profiles were written by persons other than the principal investigators of the studies. However, the principal investigators were consulted extensively to ensure the accuracy of the information presented here. Authors were asked to follow a standard format in the profiles, responding to the questions presented in the outline below.

HISTORY

- How did this initiative come about?
- Are there any articles or chapters that were critical in the evolution of the initiative?

GOALS

- What are the stated goals of the project?
- Are there other, secondary goals?
- What are the major research questions?
- For demonstration projects: What are the underlying principles of the program? Are they published anywhere?

CURRENT STATUS

- What is the current status of the project? (Which wave of data collection? Or, when will data collection begin?)
- Have any results been published or otherwise disseminated publicly?

THEORY OF CHANGE

- How does this initiative define and explain change? (in terms of improved outcomes or increased use of services)
- For demonstration projects: Is there a theory for how change occurs that guides the program?

DESIGN AND METHODS

- What are the years of birth of the children in the sample?
- At what ages do children provide data? (What is the frequency of data collection?)
- How is sampling done? (random? oversampling by family characteristics? poverty sample?)
- What are the inclusion/exclusion criteria?
- How many data collection sites? How many families per site?
- What are the data collection procedures?

- How is language use being addressed for participants who are Spanish-only speakers or other non-English speakers?
- What family structures are included? (Are fathers included? Single mothers living alone? Single mothers living with grandparents and/or boyfriends?)
- For demonstration projects: Is there a control group or baseline comparison?

MEASURES

- What information is collected on

    children?
    parents?
    family?
    peers?
    school?
    other?

- How are variables such as ethnicity, income, and poverty being measured and coded?
- Have measures been modified for cultural sensitivity? If so, how?
- How does the study deal with children with disabilities? Are they included/excluded? Are measures altered to accommodate disabilities?
- How is the home environment being assessed?
- How is the child care environment being assessed?
- Is the quality of child care being measured?
- How is health care being measured?
- Is the study collecting data on the use of social services? Is there information on direct service provision and/or referrals?
- How does the 1996 welfare bill affect the initiative? What steps, if any, are being taken to deal with that?

UNITS OF ANALYSIS

- What levels (e.g., individual, family, community, school) of data are collected?
- What data analysis approach is being used?

RESULTS/FINDINGS

- What preliminary results have been obtained, if any?
- If data on the primary research questions have been analyzed, what are the findings?

LIMITATIONS

- What aspects of the study limit its generalizability?

PUBLIC USE FILES

- Are the data available for public access?
- If not, when will public use files be available?

    In this chapter, we present very brief descriptions of the 28 studies profiled in this volume. These brief descriptions include information on the design, sample, measures, data collection procedures, principal investigators, funders, and related Internet sites. There are multiple purposes for bringing all of these research initiatives together in one volume. Taken together, the descriptions provide a rich picture of current approaches to studying the lives of young children and families in context and over time. Readers may observe the overlap and comparability across many of the studies, or locate data sets that may be useful for further secondary data analysis. Finally, we close the volume with a chapter synthesizing common findings, approaches, and themes across the studies, and identifying the implications of this rich array of research programs for researchers, practitioners, and policy makers.

SUMMARIES OF ALL INITIATIVES

EARLY CHILDHOOD INTERVENTION (Chapter 3)

Comprehensive Child Development Program (CCDP)

DESIGN	Longitudinal national study employing a randomized design with 2 conditions: CCDP group and a control group including eligible families who applied to CCDP at one of the 21 research sites (control group did not receive CCDP services but could receive other community services). Design includes an impact evaluation and process evaluation.
SAMPLE	The impact evaluation included 4,410 low-income families from 21 CCDP sites, 2,213 program fami-

lies and 2,197 control families. The process evaluation included 3,970 families from 24 sites.

MEASURES

Child: Health, motor, cognitive, language, social, and emotional development, including standardized assessments (e.g., Bayley scales, K-ABC, PPVT-3, CBCL) and child-parent interaction assessments (i.e., Nursing Child Assessment Satellite Training (NCAST) Teaching Scales [coded live]).
Mother: Household demographics, physical and mental health, child-rearing attitudes, home environment, economic self-sufficiency.
Parenting behavior (via observed child-parent teaching interaction): Includes ratings of parental sensitivity, responsiveness, social-emotional and cognitive growth fostering, and child's clarity of cues and responsiveness to caregiver.
CCDP services: Management of program staff and cultural appropriateness of early childhood services.

DATA COLLECTION

Between 1991 and 1998, children were assessed and parents interviewed when children reached 2, 3, 4, and 5 years of age. Some additional data were collected when children were 18 and 30 months old.

PRINCIPAL
INVESTIGATORS
AND FUNDERS

Principal investigators: For the impact evaluation, Robert St. Pierre, Jean Layzer, Barbara Goodson, and Lawrence Bernstein (Abt Associates); for the process evaluation, Jim DeSantis (CSR).
Funders: Administration on Children, Youth, and Families (ACYF).

INTERNET SITE

http://www.acf.dhhs.gov/programs/core/pubs_reports/ccdp/ccdp_intro.html

Early Head Start (EHS) Research and Evaluation Project

DESIGN

Seven-year national study employing a randomized design with 2 conditions: EHS program group and a control group including eligible families who applied to EHS at one of the 17 research sites (control group did not receive an offer of EHS services but could receive any other community services). Design includes (a) implementation study, (b) impact evaluation, (c) local research studies, (d) policy studies, (e) father studies, and (f) continuous program improvement activities.

SAMPLE

Approximately 3,000 low-income families from 17 local EHS sites with children born between September 1995 and September 1998.

MEASURES

IMPLEMENTATION STUDY

Parent services interview: Perceived needs and resources, employment, education, child care and home visits, health status/services, family support services.

Exit interview: Early Head Start program experiences.

Early Head Start ratings of program implementation: Consensus-based ratings of early child development and health services, family partnerships, community partnerships, staff development and management systems and procedures.

Early Head Start ratings of program quality: Quality of center-based care, aspects of home visits.

IMPACT EVALUATION

Child: Health, motor, cognitive, language, social, and emotional development, includes standardized assessments (e.g., Bayley scales, PPVT-3, CBCL) and videotaped child-parent interactions (e.g., Nursing Child Assessment Satellite Training [NCAST] Teaching Scales).

Mother: Household demographic information, education, employment, work and family issues, mental and physical health, the home environment, family routines and conflict, stress, social support, parenting attitudes and knowledge about child development, discipline, child care, parent-child activities, the parent-child relationship, and verbal ability.

Fathers: Fathers interviewed or interviewed and observed with the children.

Parenting behavior (via videotaped child-parent interactions): Includes ratings of sensitivity, intrusiveness, detachment, negative regard.

Neighborhood: Program coordination with other community service providers, parental perception of community services, qualitative descriptions of the community, and assessments of community child care quality.

Child care: Observations and provider interview in formal and informal settings.

DATA COLLECTION   From 1996 to 2001, children were assessed and parents interviewed when children were 14, 24, and 36 months old; parents were also interviewed at 6, 15, and 26 months after enrollment and when they exited the program. A follow-up study of the children and families is underway from 2001 through 2003. Public use files will be available in 2003.

PRINCIPAL   *Principal investigators*: John Love, Ellen Kisker
INVESTIGATORS   (Mathematica Policy Research), and Jeanne Brooks-
AND FUNDERS   Gunn (Columbia University); Helen Raikes, Rachel Chazan Cohen, and Louisa Tarullo were the project monitors for the national research; Esther Kresh was the project monitor for the local research studies.

Funders: Administration on Children, Youth, and Families (ACYF). ACYF, NICHD, and Ford Foundation for the father studies.

INTERNET SITE   http://www.mathematica-mpr.com/3rdLevel/ ehstoc.htm

TRANSITION TO SCHOOL (Chapter 4)

Head Start Family and Child Experiences Survey (FACES)

DESIGN   FACES is a longitudinal study designed to assess the success of Head Start in meeting its goal of promoting children's social competence. The project included a field study, conducted in spring 1997 with a follow-up in spring 1998, and a main study, which followed 3-, 4-, and 5-year-old children across at least one year of Head Start (beginning in fall 1997) and through the end of their kindergarten year. Data sources include child assessments, parent interviews, teacher reports, and Head Start classroom observations.

SAMPLE

The field study included 2,400 children from 40 Head Start programs in spring 1997. The main study sample was comprised of 3,200 children and families from the same 40 programs, beginning in fall 1997. The sample is nationally representative of the Head Start population. The sample is 37% African American, nearly 28% white, 24% Hispanic, 2% American Indian, and 1% Asian.

MEASURES

Child: Vocabulary; emergent literacy and numeracy abilities; memory, reasoning, and problem solving; gross and fine motor skills; social awareness, peer play, and child behavior.
Primary caregiver: Child's social-emotional development; child's positive and problem behaviors; household composition; parental education levels; parental employment status; household language use; family stressors (homelessness, exposure to crime); receipt of financial assistance; parental activities with the child; parental involvement with Head Start program; parental satisfaction with Head Start program; home environment; parent's mental health; parenting behaviors.
Teacher: Child's social-emotional development; child's positive and problem behaviors; child's musical ability and creativity; child's gross and fine motor skills.
Classroom observation: Classroom scheduling; early childhood and learning environment; caregiver behavior; children's social interaction with peers.

DATA COLLECTION

Field study: Data collection at the end of the Head Start program year in spring 1997 and follow-up in spring 1998 after either a second year of Head Start or one year of kindergarten.
Main study: Data collection at the beginning of the Head Start program year in fall 1997 with follow-up in spring of 1998, 1999, and 2000.

PRINCIPAL
INVESTIGATORS
AND FUNDERS

Principal investigators: Nicholas Zill (Westat, Inc.)
and David Connell (Abt Associates).
Funder: ACYF.

INTERNET SITE

http://www2.acf.dhhs.gov/programs/hsb/hsreac/faces/
index.html

National Head Start/Public School Early Childhood Transition Demonstration Study

DESIGN

The National Head Start/Public School Early Childhood Transition Study provides four types of services
to children and families from 31 sites throughout
the country to facilitate young children's transition
to public elementary school. The four components
of the intervention are: (1) developmentally appropriate learning experiences for children; (2) supportive social services for all families, including
special family workers to assist in family-school interactions and coordinate services across agencies;
(3) programs to increase parental involvement in
children's transition experiences; and (4) availability of physical and mental health services for children and families. The intervention is designed to
extend the types of services and supports provided
by Head Start programs through the first four years
of elementary school.

SAMPLE

The evaluation includes two cohorts of former Head
Start participants and their families. The first co-
hort entered kindergarten in the fall of 1992 ($N = 2,198$ demonstration families and 1,900 comparison families), and the second cohort entered kinder-
garten in the fall of 1993 ($N = 2,233$ demonstration
families and 2,070 comparison families). The sample
comprises 50% female-headed households, 40%
two-parent households, and small percentages
of families headed by grandparents, single fathers,
foster parents, or other relatives. The sample is a
poverty- or recent-poverty sample, as all children

were eligible for Head Start services in the preschool years.

MEASURES

Child: Vocabulary, reading and math achievement, school motivation and values, writing sample.
Primary caregiver: Household demographic, education, employment; motivation, expectations, values and social support; survival resources, security, and community context; social and health services in the community; family routines; parent's mental health; child's social skills and problem behavior; parenting; parent's involvement in children's learning; school climate.
Teacher: Child's social skills and problem behavior, school climate, child's health.
Principal: School climate and context.
Classroom observation: Learning environment and use of developmentally appropriate practices in the classroom.
School archival records search: Basic skills and school program context.

DATA COLLECTION

Data collection occurred for each cohort in the fall of the kindergarten year and the springs of kindergarten, first, second, and third grades.

PRINCIPAL
INVESTIGATORS
AND FUNDERS

Principal investigators: Craig Ramey and Sharon Landsman Ramey (Civitan International Research Center, University of Alabama).
Funder: ACYF.

INTERNET SITE

http://www.acf.dhhs.gov/programs/core/pubs_reports/hs/transition_study/trans_study.html

---

FAMILY SUPPORT (Chapter 5)

National Even Start Evaluation

DESIGN

The first 4-year funding cycle of the federal Even Start family literacy program was evaluated via two main sources: (1) a National Evaluation Information System (NEIS), an annual survey of program participants, which includes information on service participation, family characteristics, and parent and child outcome measures for all families participating in Even Start; and (2) an In-Depth Study, which provides more detailed information on programs, participants, and outcomes in ten Even Start sites, with a randomly assigned control group. The In-Depth Study included data from program observations, interviews with parents and program staff, and performance assessments of children and parents.

SAMPLE

The NEIS sample consists of 16,255 families, representing 270 out of 340 Even Start projects in 1992–93. The In-Depth Study includes 200 families with a child aged 3 or 4 years from ten Even Start sites, and 100 families with a 3- or 4-year-old child from five of those sites, randomly assigned to a control group.

MEASURES

Child: Receptive vocabulary (PPVT-R), school readiness, emergent literacy.

Parent: Adult literacy skills and their application, GED attainment, reading and writing activities in the home, locus of control, depressive symptomatology, child-literacy supporting activities and materials in the home, parent-child learning activities, parent's expectations for child's education, perceived social support, family resources, employment, income, perceptions of program impact.

Program: Number of participating families; cost per family; core and support services provided; recruitment strategies; barriers to implementation; staff type, duties, turnover, and training; funding sources; modes of service delivery; reasons for leaving program.

DATA COLLECTION

NEIS: Annual participant survey 1989 through 1992 program year.

In-Depth Study: Pretest data upon program entry, with follow-ups 9 and 18 months later.

PRINCIPAL INVESTIGATORS AND FUNDERS	*Principal investigator*: Robert St. Pierre (Abt Associates). *Funder*: Office of Policy and Planning, U.S. Department of Education.
INTERNET SITES	http://www.rmcres.com; http://www.abtassoc.com/

National Evaluation of Family Support Programs (NEFSP)

DESIGN	The National Evaluation of Family Support Programs is a 5-year project that includes a large review of research on individual evaluations of family support programs, a meta-analysis of these evaluations, and the design and implementation of several new prospective evaluations of the effects of family support programs. Seven individual family support programs were selected for evaluation, each with different designs and goals; four of these evaluations were completed. The evaluations were conducted in two tiers. Tier One evaluations were theory-driven, using individual program processes and goals to explicitly test hypothesized pathways of influence, with small samples and no traditional control or comparison groups; and Tier Two evaluations were experimental or quasi-experimental in design, comparing treatment families with control or comparison nontreatment groups.
SAMPLE	*Tier One*: Approximately 90 families in four different family support programs, with children ranging in age from 3 through 10 years. *Tier Two* (experimental and quasi-experimental studies varying in size across each of the four programs evaluated): Project Vision compares the entire middle school with comparable schools in other Florida school districts; FAST includes approximately 200 families of second- and third-grade children in each of the experimental and control groups; Cleveland Works compares state data on all graduates of the program to graduates of the Ohio JTPA program;

and the Iowa FaDSS Program follows a sample of 1,700 families who were randomly assigned to FaDSS or regular AFDC services in 1989.

MEASURES

Child: Parent/child relationship; parenting competence; family cohesiveness and communication; conflict resolution; parental support for education; emotional security; social support; community participation; impulse control; behavior problems; drug/alcohol use, sexual behavior, and delinquency; school attendance, achievement motivation, attitude toward school; self-esteem, peer relations, and problem-solving skills.

Parent: Parent/child relationship; parenting competence; nurturance; family composition and cohesiveness; home environment; family communication; conflict resolution; support for and involvement in children's education; emotional security; family resources; medical/dental care; social support; community participation; neighborhood support and cohesiveness; community services and resources; child's physical growth and nutrition; child's behaviors, reasoning, and language skills; child's drug/alcohol use, sexual behavior, and delinquency; child's school success.

Teacher: Family material resources; child's drug/alcohol use, sexual behavior and delinquency; child's school performance, attendance, and attitude toward school; child's problem behavior, self-control, social skills, and emotional development.

Program: Community characteristics and well-being; program activities and participation; staff interactions and behavior with families; program's "family supportiveness."

DATA COLLECTION

Data collection proceeds somewhat differently for each program being evaluated. Families are followed longitudinally for 1–2 years, with data collection occurring several times per year. The studies include both short-term and long-term follow-ups, as some programs are following families that were in the program over 10 years ago.

PRINCIPAL   *Principal investigators*: Jean Layzer (Abt Associates);
INVESTIGATORS   Sharon L. Kagan (Yale University).
AND FUNDERS   *Funder*: Administration for Children and Families.

INTERNET SITE   Not available

PRE- AND PERINATAL HOME VISITATION INTERVENTIONS (Chapter 6)

Nurse-Family Partnership (NFP)

DESIGN   The Nurse-Family Partnership (formerly the Nurse
                       Home Visitation Project) examines the efficacy of
                       nurse home visitation for improving child health and
                       development, as well as maternal life course, for at-
                       risk women. In three separate trials (Elmira, Memphis,
                       and Denver), women were randomly assigned to home
                       visitation (during pregnancy and, for some groups,
                       until the child's second birthday) or comparison
                       groups. Home visitors provide parent education, pro-
                       mote healthy behaviors, and assist women in meeting
                       education and employment goals. In Denver, home
                       visitation by nurses and paraprofessional is examined.

SAMPLE   The Elmira trial involved 400 primarily white moth-
                       ers living in a semirural area (4 treatment groups).
                       In Memphis, 1,139 primarily African American
                       women participated (4 treatment groups). A total of
                       735 women (primarily Hispanic and white) partici-
                       pated in Denver (3 treatment groups).

MEASURES   *Child*: Physical health and development, cognitive
                       development, social/emotional development, re-
                       ported maltreatment, criminal and antisocial behav-
                       ior (Elmira trial).
                       Mother: Physical and mental health, pregnancy out-
                       comes, intelligence, attitudes and coping, self-efficacy,
                       social support, program participation, labor force
                       participation, welfare use, parenting practices, arrests
                       and criminal convictions (Elmira trial).

Program implementation: Level and nature of program participation, client-helper relationship.

DATA COLLECTION   *Parent interviews*: During pregnancy and about every 6–12 months for first two years of child's life; follow-up interviews at 4–5 years of age and at age 15 (for Elmira trial).
Child: Child assessments approximately every year for first two years of child's life; child interview at age 15 (Elmira trial).
Medical and social service records: Accessed during pregnancy and throughout child's first two years, and at ages 4–5 and age 15 (Elmira trial).
Child Protective Service records/criminal arrests and convictions: Through child age 15 for mothers in the Elmira trial.

PRINCIPAL
INVESTIGATORS
AND FUNDERS

Principal investigator: Dr. David Olds, Department of Pediatrics, University of Colorado Health Sciences Center, Denver, CO.
Funders: Administration for Children and Families; Biomedical Research Support, the Bureau of Community Health Services, Maternal and Child Health Research Grants Division; Carnegie Corporation; Colorado Trust; Commonwealth Fund; David and Lucile Packard Foundation; Ford Foundation; Maternal and Child Health Bureau; Department of Health and Human Services; National Center for Nursing Research; National Institute of Mental Health; Office of the Assistant Secretary for Planning and Evaluation, U.S. Department of Health and Human Services; Pew Charitable Trusts; Robert Wood Johnson Foundation; U.S. Department of Justice; W. T. Grant Foundation; and Smith-Richardson Foundation.

INTERNET SITE   http://www.nccfc.org/nurseFamilyPartnership.cfm

Healthy Families America (HFA)

DESIGN   Forty-seven evaluations of HFA sites in the United States and Canada are currently under way or have been completed by a network of more than 50 researchers. HFA evaluations employ a variety of designs (randomized trial, comparison group, pre- and posttest of participants) to explore the effectiveness of the program for increasing parenting skills, decreasing child abuse and neglect, increasing child health and development, and increasing use of support programs. Three process studies investigate program implementation.

SAMPLE   Children born in each year since 1992 are included in the HFA evaluations. Sample size varies from less than 100 to more than 2,000.

MEASURES   *Child*: Physical growth and health, cognitive development, parent-child interactions, reported child abuse or neglect.
Mother: Depression, parent-child interactions, welfare utilization, parenting skills, child abuse potential, parenting stress, family conflict, family stress, home environment, participant satisfaction.

DATA COLLECTION   Data collection begins prenatally or at birth. At a minimum, participants are assessed either once during or at the completion of the program. Many studies collect data on a more regular basis, typically every 6 months.

PRINCIPAL   *Principal investigator*: Varies by site
INVESTIGATORS   *Funders*: Prevent Child Abuse America, Ronald
AND FUNDERS   McDonald House Charities, Carnegie Foundation, Freddie Mac Foundation, American Academy of Pediatrics, National Association of Children's Hospitals and Related Institutions, National Head Start Association, Cooperative Extension Service of the U.S. Department of Agriculture, local funders.

INTERNET SITE   http://www.healthyfamiliesamerica.org/

Healthy Steps (HS) for Young Children Program

DESIGN   Fifteen of the 24 Healthy Steps programs operating in the U.S. are participating in the national evaluation. Six sites employ random assignment and nine use a quasi-experimental design with matched comparison groups. A total of 5,565 families were enrolled in the evaluation which began in 1998 and was completed in 2001, when the children were age 3. Data about parenting practices, parent mental health, child physical health, child social and cognitive development, and health care program content and costs were gathered. Plans are under way for an age 5 followup.

SAMPLE

Sample includes 5,565 families, approximately 200 treatment and 200 control or comparison per site. Families represent a range of socioeconomic status, are ethnically diverse, and come from urban, suburban and rural locales.

MEASURES

Child: Physical health, cognitive development, socioemotional development.
Parent: Parenting practices, parental expectations, family routines, depression, service use and satisfaction.
Health care providers: Experiences, opinions, and satisfaction with health care and Healthy Steps program and services.
Key informants: Healthy Steps program implementation and experiences.

DATA COLLECTION

Parent questionnaire: Enrollment, then every 6 months.
Parent telephone interviews: 2- to 4-months and 30-months.
Child and parent-child interaction observations (2 sites): 16- to 18-months and 34- to 37-months.
Health care provider surveys: Annually.
Key informant interviews: Pre- and postparticipation.
Child medical records: Postparticipation.

PRINCIPAL INVESTIGATORS AND FUNDERS

Principal investigator: Dr. Bernard Guyer, Department of Population and Family Health Sciences, Johns Hopkins University Bloomberg School of Public Health.
Funders: Commonwealth Fund, local funding from managed care systems, hospitals, and community, state, and national foundations.

INTERNET SITE   http://www.healthysteps.org

CHILD WELFARE AND MENTAL HEALTH (Chapter 7)

Consortium for Longitudinal Studies in Child Abuse and Neglect (LONGSCAN)

DESIGN   The LONGSCAN Consortium is completing the 8th year of a 20-year project. Data have been collected across five sites (North Carolina, Chicago, San Diego, Seattle, and Baltimore).

SAMPLE   *The Capella Project (Chicago):* 180 maltreated infants whose families have been referred to Child Protective Services (CPS). A 6-month family intervention (*n* = 80) or usual CPS care (*n* = 100); 137 matched neighborhood controls.
The Stress and Social Support Study (Chapel Hill, NC): 221 high-risk infants at birth including 74 referred to CPS by age 4 years and 147 not referred to CPS by 4 years. Follow-up of infant sample; age of first cohort: 4–5 years old.
The Impact of Investigation Study (Seattle): 261 children judged to be at moderate risk following a report to CPS. Approximately 60% were later substantiated (*n* = 159), and 102 were not. Age of first cohort: 1–4 years.
The Foster Care Mental Health Study (San Diego): 320 maltreated children who have entered the dependency system and been put in out-of-home placement with a relative or foster family (50% returned home by age 4). Age of first cohort: 1–4 years.
Longitudinal Study of Child Neglect (Baltimore): 322 children from three Baltimore pediatric clinics for children with nonorganic failure to thrive (*n* = 123), children with prenatal drug use or an HIV-infected mother (*n* = 83), and low-income, inner-city children (*n* = 116). Age of first cohort: 4 years old.

MEASURES	Interviews and face-to-face assessments.
	Child: Demographics, birth weight, health/handicapping conditions, temperament, developmental status, intellectual functioning, adaptive behavior, behavior problems, aggressive behavior, affective symptoms, sexual behavior, perceived competence, peer status, social problem-solving ability, exposure to alcohol and illicit drugs, exposure to violence.
	Adult: Demographics, parent victimization history, parenting attitudes, substance use/abuse, mental health, physical health.
	Family measures: Family functioning, father involvement, spouse/parent relationships, daily stressors, home environment, services utilization, domestic violence, life events and witness violence, use of physical discipline, maltreatment of child index, family income, unemployment, neighborhood characteristics, school safety, social support, ethnic minority status, child's first language.
DATA COLLECTION	All children will have brief yearly follow-ups and extensive face-to-face assessments at ages 4, 6, and 8. However, sites have site-specific goals and will add unique measures to the common battery.
PRINCIPAL INVESTIGATORS AND FUNDERS	*Principal investigators*: Patrick Curtis, Mary Schneider (Chicago); Wanda Hunter, Jonathan Kotch, Desmond Runyon (Chapel Hill, NC); Diana English (Seattle); John Landsverk, Al Litrownik (San Diego); Howard Dubowitz, Maureen Black, Raymond Starr, Jr. (Baltimore).
	Funder: National Institute of Health.
INTERNET SITE	http://www.bios.unc.edu/cscc/LONG/longdesc.html

National Survey of Child and Adolescent Well-Being (NSCAW)

DESIGN	The NSCAW project is a 6-year contract with Research Triangle Institute and subcontracts from the University of California at Berkeley, University of

North Carolina at Chapel Hill, and Caliber Associates. The study is designed to collect longitudinal, state-level data on the experiences and outcomes of children and families who come in contact with the child welfare system.

SAMPLE

The sample includes about 6,700 children from 107 child welfare agencies ranging between 0 and 14 years of age. Children will be sampled within a year of entry into the child welfare system, and children who are presently not receiving services will also be included.

MEASURES

Annual telephone and face-to-face interviews. Interview question topics include health and physical well-being, cognitive development, academic achievement, and socioemotional adjustment. Administrative records will also be reviewed. Informants include custodial caregiver, noncustodial biological caregiver, child, caseworker, teacher, other agency personnel, and other service providers outside the child welfare system.

DATA COLLECTION

Data collection began in 1999 in the states of California, Florida, Illinois, Michigan, New York, Ohio, Pennsylvania, Texas, and 32 other states. Baseline data collection was completed in April 2001. Plans call for follow-up data collection at 12 and 18 months following the baseline assessment. There may be a 36-month follow-up as well.

PRINCIPAL
INVESTIGATORS
AND FUNDERS

Principal investigators: Paul Biener, Richard P. Barth, and Desmond Runyan.
Funders: Administration on Children, Youth, and Families.

INTERNET SITE

http://www.acf.dhhs.gov/programs/core/ongoing_research/afc/wellbeing_intro.html

Head Start Mental Health Research Consortium (HSMHRC)

DESIGN

Columbia University (CU): Preschool self-regulation was assessed in home visits with 850 4-year-old children who are part of the Project on Human Development in Chicago Neighborhoods (PHDCN) and who have been followed since birth.

University of New Mexico (UNM): Social-emotional skills curriculum was implemented in three Head Start classrooms for 12 weeks. Two additional classrooms served as a control.

University of North Carolina (UNC): Multimodal universal and indicated intervention was implemented in 22 Head Start classrooms. Fifteen classrooms served as a control.

University of Oregon (UO): Children from 41 Head Start classrooms were screened using the first stage of the Early Screening Project. Children who scored high on externalizing or internalizing behaviors, as well as a comparison group who did not score highly on either dimension, followed up using stages 2 and 3 of the ESP.

Vanderbilt University (VU): Children from Head Start classrooms were screened for language and behavioral problems. A subset of children identified as at risk participated in a communication and behavioral intervention (experimental group) or were assigned to the control group.

SAMPLE

CU: Approximately 850 4-year-old children from diverse economic and ethnic backgrounds.

UNM: 84 low-income, predominantly Hispanic, children participated in the study (53 in the experimental group and 31 in the control group).

UNC: Approximately 200 predominantly African American 4-year-olds from Head Start programs.

UO: 954 ethnically diverse children aged 3–4 from Head Start programs.

VU: 850 3-year-old children from predominantly low-income African American backgrounds participated in the screening study; 90 at-risk children (45 intervention and 45 control) participated in the intervention study.

MEASURES

Child: Social and emotional skills, behavior problems (internalizing and externalizing), ADHD symptoms, and functional impairment.

Family: Family context, parental depression, exposure to violence.
Classroom: Classroom quality.
Service use: Child and family service use, Program Information Reports.

DATA COLLECTION   *CU*: Data collection for 4-year-olds began in 2000 and continued through 2001 (Wave 3 of the PHDCN study).
UNM: Data gathered pre- and postintervention.
UNC: Data gathered pre- and postintervention (fall and spring of the 2 consecutive school years, 1998–2000).
UO: Children were screened in 1998–1999 and a second wave of children in 1999–2000.
VU: Four cohorts of children (1997–2000) were screened and followed through kindergarten or first grade. In addition, data were gathered for subsample of intervention study children immediately after completion of intervention, 6 months later, 1 year later, and 2 years later.

PRINCIPAL   *Principal investigators*: Jeanne Brooks-Gunn (Co-
INVESTIGATORS   lumbia University); Loretta Serna, Elizabeth Nielson,
AND FUNDERS   Steve Forness (University of New Mexico); Donna Bryant, Janis Kupersmidt (University of North Carolina); Edward Feil, Hill Walker, Herbert Severson (University of Oregon); Ann Kaiser, Michael Foster, Terry Hancock (Vanderbilt University).
Funders: Administration on Children, Youth, and Families and National Institute of Mental Health.

INTERNET SITE   http://www.acf.dhhs.gov/programs/core/ongoing_research/acyfnimh/acyfnimh.html

EARLY CHILD CARE (Chapter 8)

NICHD Study of Early Child Care

DESIGN   The NICHD Study of Early Child Care is a prospective, longitudinal study examining how variations in nonmaternal child care are related to children's social-emotional adjustment; cognitive, linguistic, and achievement performance; and physical growth and health. The design involves extensive direct observations of the home, child care, and school experiences, and multiple measures of children's adjustment.

SAMPLE

The sample is representative, with sites across urban, suburban, and rural areas of the country. Participants were recruited from 24 designated hospitals at 10 data collection sites in these states: Virginia, California, Kansas, Arkansas, Wisconsin, North Carolina, Pennsylvania, Washington, and Massachusetts.

Hospital screening: Every week, each site recruited approximately 20 newborn/mother dyads.

Two-week phone calls: A list of families is generated from the hospital screenings. Families are called from this list to determine eligibility and consent to participate.

One-month interview: Families who have successfully completed all data collection procedures to this point conduct the one-month interview and are officially enrolled in the study.

MEASURES

Measures captured child's experience in the home and family, in child care, and in school. Children's developmental status was assessed using measures of social-emotional, cognitive, linguistic, and academic development.

Child care environment: Quantity and stability of child care experiences, characteristics of caregivers, characteristics of the child care environment, and the characteristics of the before- or after-school child care environment.

School environment: Kindergarten and first grade. Teachers completed questionnaires on the student-teacher relationship. Classroom observations were done in first grade.

Home environment: Structural characteristics of the family, quality of the home environment, and parental characteristics.

DATA COLLECTION   Data collection is complete through second grade.
                     Third- and fourth-grade assessments are ongoing.

PRINCIPAL   *Principal investigators* (in alphabetical order): Vir-
INVESTIGATORS   ginia Allhusen, Mark Appelbaum, Dee Ann Batten,
AND FUNDERS   Jay Belsky, Cathryn L. Booth, Robert Bradley, Celia
                     Brownell, Donna Bryant, Margaret Burchinal, Bettye
                     Caldwell, Susan Campbell, Ana Mari Cauce, Alison
                     Clarke-Stewart, Martha Cox, Sarah Friedman, Ty
                     Hartwell, Kathryn Hirsh-Pasek, Aletha Huston, Eliza-
                     beth Jaeger, Deborah Johnson, Jean Kelly, Bonnie
                     Knoke, Nancy Marshall, Kathleen McCartney,
                     Marion O'Brien, Margaret Tresch Owen, C. Chris
                     Payne, Deborah Phillips, Robert Pianta, Suzanne
                     Randolph, Wendy W. Robeson, Susan J. Spieker,
                     Deborah Lowe Vandell, Kathleen E. Wallner-Allen,
                     and Marsha Weinraub.
                     Funder: National Institute for Child Health and
                     Human Development.

INTERNET SITE   http://www.nichd.nih.gov/od/secc/index.htm

Cost, Quality, and Child Outcomes (CQO) Study

DESIGN   The study consists of two phases. The first assessed
                     the relation between cost and quality, and the sec-
                     ond studied the longitudinal outcomes for children
                     in different quality child care centers. For the first
                     phase, for-profit and nonprofit child care centers
                     providing full-time, full-year care were randomly
                     selected in four states (CA, CO, CT, and NC). In-
                     fant/toddler and preschool classrooms in the selected
                     centers were then randomly selected for observation.
                     One boy and one girl in each class were randomly
                     selected for observation during a 2 day visit. The
                     longitudinal data for the second phase were collected
                     from up to 12 students in a stratified random sample
                     of the classroom observed in Phase 1. Data were
                     collected over 5 years, beginning when the children
                     were in their next-to-last year of preschool (time 1)

and ending when they were in the second grade (time 5). No data were collected from the children when they were in first grade (time 4).

SAMPLE

Phase 1: 228 infant/toddler classrooms and 521 pre-school classrooms from 401 child care centers.

Phase 2: 826 students from classrooms in 170 of the observed centers who were eligible for kindergarten in the fall of 1994, in the observed class during Phase 1, expected to continue attending the center the following year, and spoke primarily English at home. The sample dropped to 579 students in year 2, 451 in year 3, and 418 in year 5.

MEASURES

Child: Verbal, reading, and math skills, level of play, classroom behavior, and peer social relations.

Parents: Household demographics, family climate, parental beliefs and practices, valuing of different aspects of child care, perceptions of child care quality and classroom environment.

Teachers: Teacher involvement and sensitivity, teaching style, teacher responsiveness, teacher-child relationship, demographics, hours worked, and child care experience.

Child care center: Center costs, revenue sources, subsidies, center structure, program characteristics (total attendance, enrollment and capacity of the center, number of infants, toddlers, and so on), staff characteristics, staffing patterns, staff ratios, in-service training, quality of center leadership, and observational measures of classroom environment.

DATA COLLECTION

Phase 1: Observations were conducted in the spring of 1993.

Phase 2: Year 1 data was collected in the spring of 1993; Year 2 data in the spring of 1994; Year 3 data in 1995; and Year 5 data in 1997.

PRINCIPAL INVESTIGATORS AND FUNDERS

Principal investigators: Carollee Howes, Richard Clifford, Ellen S. Peisner-Feinberg, Mary L. Culkin, and Sharon Lynn Kagan.

Funders: Carnegie Corporation of New York, William T. Grant Foundation, JFM Foundation, A. L. Mailman Family Foundation, David and Lucile Packard Foundation, Pew Charitable Trusts, USWEST Foundation, an anonymous foundation, and the National Research and Development Centers Program administered by the Office of Educational Research and Improvement, U.S. Department of Education.

INTERNET SITE   http://www.fpg.unc.edu/~NCEDL/PAGES/cqes.htm

National Study of Child Care for Low-Income Families

DESIGN

The National Study of Child Care for Low-Income Families was initiated in response to the stated goals of welfare reform, where the anticipated result of welfare reform will likely increase the demand for child care. The design of the study requires a complex, multilevel data collection strategy with nested samples of counties within states, and families and providers within counties.

SAMPLE

Community level: A nationally representative sample of counties with above average poverty rates (17 states containing 25 counties).
Family level: A random sample of 5,000 low-income families with working parents and at least one child under age 13 (200 per county). A sample of 650 low-income parents who are receiving or have applied for child care subsidies.
Provider level: 650 child care providers linked to the sample of 650 families.

MEASURES

State level: Data are collected on child care subsidies policy, including subsidy rates, co-payments, proportion of child care subsidy funds from state sources, child care regulations and enforcement, and welfare policy.
Community level: Data are collected on community characteristics, including per capita income, child poverty rate, racial/ethnic mix, labor force partici-

pation, unemployment rate, household composition, supply of licensed child care, and supply of Head Start/preschool slots.

Individual level: Data are collected on families' use of center care, family child care, in-home care by nonparent, parental care, self-care, or no care (school only or mother does not work). In addition, data are collected on parents' perception of the availability, accessibility, and affordability of different care arrangements. The parent interview includes questions on family characteristics, characteristics of a focus child, parents' employment status and work history, knowledge and views about the child care market, and current child care arrangements for all children in the family.

DATA COLLECTION
Data collection began in 1999 and ended in 2001. Information on states and communities were collected twice: in 1999 and 2001. One-time survey in 2000 included information about the policies and programs that influence parents' decisions about child care, the stability and continuity of child care, the child care choices they make, and how these choices affect their ability to find and retain a job or participate in education or training programs.

PRINCIPAL
INVESTIGATORS
AND FUNDERS
Principal investigators: Abt Associates, Inc.
Funder: Administration for Children and Families in the U.S. Department of Health and Human Services.

INTERNET SITE
http://www.acf.dhhs.gov/programs/opre/childcar
.htm

Growing Up in Poverty (GUP) Project

DESIGN
The Growing Up in Poverty Project consists of four components: (a) repeated interviews with mothers, (b) home visits, (c) interviews with and observational assessments of child-care providers, and (d) direct child assessment of cognitive, language, and social development.

SAMPLE

Mothers: All 948 participants resided in one of five cities at entry: San Francisco, San Jose (CA), Manchester, New Haven (CT) or Tampa (FL). All participating women were eligible for welfare benefits, under State TANF rules (or old AFDC guidelines in the case of Connecticut). In Connecticut, single mothers were randomly assigned to an experimental group living under new welfare rules and a comparison group living under old AFDC rules.

Child care providers: Complete observation data (for CA and FL only) were collected on 292 child care providers, including centers, family childcare homes, and kith or kin arrangements, equaling 71% of all women who had selected a caregiver.

MEASURES

Home environments: Mothers were asked about the household social structure, the emotional character of the home, and their views of child rearing and children. Measures of four specific domains or maternal attributes were examined: (a) Household structure and cohesion, (b) the mother's linkage to information and community organizations, (c) the mother's level of social support, and (d) child rearing practices and the mother's views of the focal child. Family routines and stress, child development expectations, hunger and nutrition, and welfare involvement were also assessed.

Child care provider: For center-based care, the child's lead teacher was interviewed and observed. For family child care homes and individual kith or kin providers, the adult in charge was interviewed and observed. Two standard assessment tools were used to assess child care quality: (a) Early Childhood Environment Rating Scale (ECERS) for centers and the Family Day Care Rating Scale (FDCRS) for family and home arrangements, and (b) the Arnett Caregiver Scale. The Child Care Observation System (C-COS) was used to assess the frequency of both provider and child behaviors.

Child assessment: A basic assessment of the child's early language development and social skills was conducted.

DATA COLLECTION   Interview data from all participating mothers were collected three times at intervals spaced 18 months apart in 1998. The 90-minute interview was conducted at the welfare office or the home. Interviews with mothers entering welfare programs were conducted in 1998, and Wave 2 was conducted in 2000. Home visits and interviews/observations of child care providers were completed in 1999. Child assessments were conducted in 1998 and 2000.

PRINCIPAL
INVESTIGATORS
AND FUNDERS

Principal investigators: Bruce Fuller, University of California, Berkeley; Sharon Lynn Kagan, Teachers College, Columbia University
Funders: Packard, Spencer, and Casey Foundations, and the U.S. Department of Education, Child Care Bureau of the Department of Health and Human Services, Miriam and Peter Haas Fund, and Luke Hancock Foundation.

INTERNET SITE   http://pace.berkeley.edu/pace_growingup.html

WELFARE-TO-WORK (Chapter 9)

National Evaluation of Welfare-to-Work Strategies—Child Outcomes Study (NEWWS-COS)

DESIGN   The NEWWS Child Outcomes Study (NEWWS-COS) employs a random assignment design to examine the impacts of the JOBS Program on the well-being of children. This study is nested within three sites of the larger seven-site JOBS Evaluation: Atlanta, GA, Grand Rapids, MI, and Riverside, CA. Participants were randomly assigned to one of three groups. The design includes: (a) Child Outcomes Study (baseline, 2-year and 5-year follow-ups), (b) Descriptive Study (Atlanta only, 3 months post-baseline), and (c) Observational Study (Atlanta only, 4–6 months and 4½ years post-baseline).

SAMPLE   Families that had applied for or were receiving AFDC were randomly assigned to one of the following groups as part of the NEWWS Evaluation: (a) human capital development group, (b) labor force attachment group, or (c) the control group (free of the mandate to participate in the JOBS Program yet eligible for all AFDC benefits). Within these sites, families were included in the NEWWS-COS if they had at least one child age 3 to 5 at baseline. The total sample was 3,018 families at the two-year follow-up: 1,422 from Atlanta, 950 from Riverside, and 646 from Grand Rapids. The sample at the five-year follow-up was smaller (2,332 respondents). The sample for the Descriptive Study included 790 families from Atlanta.

MEASURES   *Child*: Cognitive development and academic achievement; physical health and safety; social development; and child adjustment and problem behaviors.
Family/mother: Household demographic information, employment, family economic status, maternal education, reading and math literacy, health, maternal psychological well-being, the home environment, parenting, children's experiences of child care, attitudes toward and experience of welfare, father involvement, child support.
Neighborhoods: Interviewer assessment of the street and exterior of homes.
Child care: Current child care use and history; teacher-student ratios, class size.
Teacher: Child's social development, adjustment, and academic progress; use of special services.

DATA COLLECTION   *Random assignment*: September 1991 (Riverside) through January 1994 (Atlanta and Grand Rapids).
Child outcomes study: 2-year follow-up ranged from the fall of 1993 (Riverside) through the spring of 1996 (Atlanta and Grand Rapids); 5-year follow-up

ranged from the fall of 1996 (Riverside) to the spring of 1999 (Atlanta and Grand Rapids).

Descriptive study (Atlanta only): March 1992 to December 1993.

Observational study (Atlanta only): 4–6 months after random assignment; 4½ years after random assignment.

PRINCIPAL
INVESTIGATORS
AND FUNDERS

Principal investigators: For Child Outcomes Study: Kristin Moore, Martha Zaslow, Sharon McGroder and Suzanne LeMenestrel, all of Child Trends; for overall NEWWS Evaluation: Gayle Hamilton, Manpower Demonstration Research Corporation.

Funders: U.S. Department of Health and Human Services, with additional support from the U.S. Department of Education. Observational Study funded by Foundation for Child Development, William T. Grant Foundation, George Gund Foundation, and an anonymous funder. Some funds for pilot work in the observational study also came from U.S. Department of Health and Human Services.

INTERNET SITE

http://www.childtrends.org and http://www.mdrc.org

New Hope Child and Family Study (CFS)

DESIGN

The New Hope Child and Family Study (CFS) is a substudy of the New Hope Project Evaluation. New Hope was a random-assignment demonstration experiment designed to test the effectiveness of an employment-based antipoverty program. Participants in the New Hope Demonstration received job-search assistance, wage supplements that raise income above the poverty threshold, and subsidies for health insurance and child care.

SAMPLE

New Hope Project Evaluation: 1,362 low-income adults age 18 or over were drawn from two inner-city areas in Milwaukee. Half were randomly assigned to a program group that could receive New

Hope benefits and services; the other half were assigned to a control group that could not. New Hope broadly targeted poor people who can work. Participants were eligible if they were willing and able to work at least 30 hours per week and had a household income at or below 150% of the federally defined poverty level. Participation in the program was voluntary.

New Hope CFS: 745 sample members (about 55% of the sample) had at least one child between ages 1 and 10 at baseline (927 children) and were included in the study of program effects on families and children. At the 2-year interview, 580 families (568 children) were included in the CFS sample. At the 5-year interview, 561 families were followed.

Ethnographic study: In-depth qualitative study of a subset of 44 families (program and control group) from the CFS that will continue for 3 years.

MEASURES

Children (ages 6–12): Activities, feelings, social behavior, and aspirations.

Parent: Employment, earnings, benefits, household income, economic well-being, health insurance coverage, child care arrangements, parenting and stress, parental and child time use, parent's psychosocial well-being, children's health and health care, discipline, the parent's relationship with the child, cognitively stimulating materials and activities available to the child, and parent's perceptions of child's characteristics and qualities; administrative and tax records.

Neighborhoods: Interviewer assessment of the street and exterior of homes.

Teacher: School progress and social behavior of a subset of CFS children.

DATA COLLECTION

Random assignment and baseline survey: August 1994 to December 1995.

Two-year survey: December 1996 through January 1998.

Five-year survey: December 1999 through January 2001.

Eight-year survey: In planning phase.

Teacher questionnaires: At 2-year and 5-year follow-ups.
Ethnographic study: Began in 1998 and will continue for 3 years.

PRINCIPAL INVESTIGATORS AND FUNDERS

Principal investigators: Robert Granger and Hans Bos, Manpower Demonstration Research Corporation; Aletha Huston, University of Texas.
Funders: John D. and Catherine T. MacArthur Foundation, W. T. Grant Foundation, and Annie E. Casey Foundation. The National Institute of Child Health and Human Development funds the 5-year follow-up.

INTERNET SITE

http://www.mdrc.org

Welfare, Children and Families: A Three City Study

DESIGN

Four-year study in Boston, Chicago, and San Antonio employing a rolling panel design; Cohort 1 includes two groups: families receiving public assistance and low-income working families; Cohort 2 includes low-income young families. Design includes (a) longitudinal survey, (b) embedded developmental study, and (c) comparative ethnographies.

SAMPLE

Cohort 1: 2,400 low-income families with children in either infancy/preschool (50% ages 0–4 years) or early adolescence (50% ages 10–14 years); Cohort 2: 1,250 low-income families with children in either infancy/preschool (ages 0–4 years) or early adolescence (ages 10–14 years).

MEASURES

Child: Physical, social, and emotional development; achievement assessments.
Mothers: Household demographic information, education, employment, work and family issues, family functioning, quality of family life, parenting, type and quality of child care/school, experience of welfare reform, use of social services, and children's daily experiences.
Fathers: Employment and earnings, physical and mental health, attitudes about family and parental

roles, problem behaviors, and experiences of welfare reform obtained via interviews with fathers.

Neighborhoods: Systematic social observations of neighborhood organizational features assessed in the ethnographies.

Child care: Child care provider and parent interview focusing on child care; child care observations for a subsample of families.

Services: Information from social service agencies and advocacy groups regarding the implementation of welfare reform at each site assessed via ethnography.

DATA COLLECTION The longitudinal survey, embedded developmental study (EDS), and ethnographies began in March 1999. Wave 2 of the survey and EDS began September 2000. Wave 3 began in March 2002.

PRINCIPAL *Principal investigators*: Ronald J. Angel, Linda M.
INVESTIGATORS Burton, P. Lindsay Chase-Lansdale, Andrew J. Cherlin,
AND FUNDERS Robert A. Moffitt, and William Julius Wilson.
Funders: NICHD; Office of Disability, Aging, and Long-Term Care Policy (ASPE, DHHS); Administration on Developmental Disabilities (DHHS); Office of Planning, Research, and Evaluation (ACF, DHHS); Office of Research, Evaluation, and Statistics (Social Security Administration); National Institute of Mental Health; Boston Foundation; Annie E. Casey Foundation; Edna McConnell Clark Foundation; Lloyd A. Fry Foundation; Hogg Foundation for Mental Health; Robert Wood Johnson Foundation; Joyce Foundation; Henry J. Kaiser Family Foundation; W. K. Kellogg Foundation; Kronkosky Charitable Foundation; John D. and Catherine T. MacArthur Foundation; Charles Stewart Mott Foundation; David and Lucile Packard Foundation; and Woods Fund of Chicago.

INTERNET SITE http://www.jhu.edu/~welfare

Project on State-Level Child Outcomes

DESIGN The Project on State-Level Child Outcomes was designed to measure child outcomes—particularly in the areas of health, school achievement, and social and emotional development—in the context of pre-PRWORA welfare reform programs in five states (Connecticut, Florida, Indiana, Iowa, and Minnesota). Welfare recipients were randomly assigned to treatment or control groups. Members of the treatment group were exposed to their state's particular welfare reform provisions that had been approved via the waivers process. Those in the control group may have been exposed to a contrasting program, received no program services, or no program requirements, depending on the state.

SAMPLE

For most states, the child well-being survey was introduced in the second or third wave of data collection of an ongoing evaluation of their demonstration programs. The initial, adult-centered interview was conducted via telephone or in-home interview. A "focal child" between the ages of 5 and 12 at the time of the interview was randomly selected from all children in the household. The areas represented in each state evaluation range from one county (Florida), to statewide (Indiana). Households sampled in each state range from 1,475 to 3,000.

MEASURES

Child: Engagement in school, school attendance and performance, hunger and nutrition, health, teen childbearing, accidents and injuries, behavior problems, arrests, social competence.
Primary caregiver: Household demographic, education, employment, income, family type, maternal depression, stability and turbulence in family life, absent parent involvement, use of state and federal benefits (food stamps, Medicaid, child care subsidy, medical care access), % of income spent on child care and rent, short version of the HOME scale, domestic violence, family routines, aggravation/stress in parenting, emotional support and cognitive stimulation provided to the child.
Child care: Child care type, extent of child care, quality of child care (parent report), child care history.

DATA COLLECTION

Connecticut: April 1999–June 2000; 2 counties.
Florida: August 1998–July 1999; 1 county.

Indiana: March 2000–November 2000; statewide.
Iowa: August 1998–August 1999; 9 counties.
Minnesota: August 1997–May 1998; 7 counties.

PRINCIPAL
INVESTIGATORS
AND FUNDERS

Principal investigators: For Minnesota, Florida, and Connecticut, Lisa Gennetian, Barbara Goldman, Pamela Morris, and Ginger Knox of MDRC; for Iowa, Christine Ross, Thomas M. Fraker, and Robin Dion of MPR; for Indiana, Erik Beecroft and David Fein of Abt Associates, Inc.; coordinators and technical assistants to the project include: the NICHD Child and Family Well-Being Research Network; Kathryn Tout, Sharon McGroder, Kristin Moore, and Martha Zaslow, all of Child Trends.
Funders: U.S. DHHS, ACF, ASPE, NICHD, Foundation for Child Development, Annie E. Casey Foundation, Edna McConnell Clark Foundation, George Gund Foundation, Smith Richardson Foundation, and John D. and Catherine T. MacArthur Foundation.

INTERNET SITE

http://www.childtrends.org; http://www.mathematica-mpr.com; http://www.abtassoc.com; http://www.mdrc.org

Assessing the New Federalism (ANF): National Survey of America's Families (NSAF)

DESIGN

National Survey of America's Families (NSAF) was implemented by The Urban Institute to act as a baseline in assessing family well-being as the responsibility for social programs changes hands with the passage of PRWORA. In order to track the changes occurring, NSAF looks across states, with a focus on low-income families.

SAMPLE

The NSAF administered telephone interviews to 44,461 households in the first wave of the study. Of these households, detailed information on 75,437 adults and 34,439 children (between the ages of 0 to 17) was collected. Households with low incomes were oversampled. Respondents represented 13 states that comprise more than half of the U.S. population (Alabama, California, Colorado, Florida, Massachusetts, Michigan, Minnesota, Mississippi, New Jersey, New York, Texas, Washington, and Wisconsin).

MEASURES

Economic security: Income, employment, welfare participation, child support, food security, housing and economic hardship, social service use.
Health and health care: Health status, health care coverage, use, and access.
Child: Education, school engagement, whether adult reads or tells stories to child, child care use, social and positive development, behavior and emotional problems.
Family: Family demographics and structure, household composition, stress and parent aggravation, parent's psychological well-being, participation in activities, attitudes on welfare, work, and raising children.

DATA COLLECTION

Wave 1: February 1997–November 1997.
Wave 2: January 1999–November 1999.
Wave 3: January 2002–November 2002.

PRINCIPAL INVESTIGATORS AND FUNDERS

Principal investigator: Alan Weil, Assessing the New Federalism, Urban Institute.
Funders: Annie E. Casey Foundation, W. K. Kellogg Foundation, Henry J. Kaiser Family Foundation, Ford Foundation, John D. and Catherine T. MacArthur Foundation, Charles Stewart Mott Foundation, David and Lucile Packard Foundation, Commonwealth Fund, Robert Wood Johnson Foundation, Weingart Foundation, McKnight Foundation, Fund for New Jersey, Stuart Foundation, and Rockefeller Foundation. Additional support is provided by Joyce Foundation and Lynde and Harry Bradley Foundation through grants to the University of Wisconsin at Madison.

INTERNET SITE

http://www.urban.org

NEIGHBORHOOD-BASED INITIATIVES (Chapter 10)

Project on Human Development in Chicago Neighborhoods (PHDCN)

DESIGN

Design includes components: (a) a longitudinal study (with an embedded intensive study of infants); (b) a community survey (with a repeated cross-sectional design); (c) an observational study of neighborhoods; (d) a neighborhood expert survey; and (e) administrative data. Neighborhoods were operationally defined as 343 clusters of city blocks from Chicago's 847 populated census tracts, and then census data were used to define two stratification variables: SES (three levels) and racial/ethnic composition (seven levels). Neighborhood clusters (NCs) were cross-classified by these two variables, and a stratified probability sample of 80 NCs was drawn for the longitudinal study.

SAMPLE

Longitudinal study (N = 6,234): Accelerated, longitudinal design with 7 cohorts from the prenatal period to age 18, who are separated by 3 year intervals (0, 3, 6, 9, 12, 15, 18; ages at Wave 1); each cohort has approximately 1,000 children, who are equally distributed by gender and of diverse racial and ethnic backgrounds.
Community survey (N = 8,782): Approximately 25 residents were interviewed from each of the 343 NCs with the number varying by whether the neighborhood was sampled for the longitudinal study (20 in nonsampled neighborhoods and 50 in sampled neighborhoods).
Observational study: Videotaped data of NCs (23,861 blocks) subsequently coded by trained observers.
Neighborhood expert survey: 2,820 interviews with six categories of experts.

MEASURES

Child: Exposure to violence, verbal IQ, reading achievement, behavior problems, efficacy and competence, provision of social relations, physical health and functional limitations, parent-child conflict, temperament, diagnostic interviews for depression, anxiety, and posttraumatic stress disorder, substance abuse, offending/delinquency.

Primary caregiver: Household demographic information, education, employment, partner/spouse conflict, family conflict and cohesion, physical and mental health histories, provision of social relations, parental monitoring, the quality of the home environment.

Neighborhood: Census demographic data, collective efficacy (social cohesion and informal social control), perceived violence, physical and social disorder, community organization and political activity, crime levels, morbidity and mortality rates.

Child care: Child care provider and parent interview focusing on child care; child care observations for a subsample of families; census demographic data on child care providers.

DATA COLLECTION   *Longitudinal study*: Wave 1 was conducted in 1995–1996, Wave 2 in 1998–1999, and Wave 3 in 2000–2001.
Community survey: 1995–1996 and 2001–2002.
Observational study: 1995–1996 and 2001–2002.

PRINCIPAL   *Principal investigator*: Felton Earls (Harvard Medi-
INVESTIGATORS   cal School).
AND FUNDERS   *Funders*: John D. and Catherine T. MacArthur Foundation, National Institute of Justice, NIMH, ACYF, U.S. Department of Education.

INTERNET SITE   http://phdcn.harvard.edu

Los Angeles Family and Neighborhood Study (L.A. FANS)

DESIGN   L.A. FANS is comprised of a longitudinal study (of adults and children) and a neighborhood expert survey. Neighborhoods in Los Angeles county stratified by income (very poor, poor, and nonpoor) and 65

neighborhoods (census tracts) randomly selected with
poor neighborhoods oversampled.

SAMPLE

Longitudinal study: A 4-year longitudinal study of
a representative stratified cluster sample of households in 65 randomly selected neighborhoods; average
of 41 households randomly selected per neighborhood with households with children under 18 years of
age oversampled (N = 2,700 households at Wave 1);
up to 2 children per household interviewed (N = 3,200
children); children and families followed if they move
out of a target neighborhood, and new sample of new
entrants into target neighborhoods obtained each
wave (N = 500 additional households with 1,000
children).

Neighborhood expert survey: Interview school principals, 8 key informants (e.g., teachers, small business owners, and religious and political leaders), and
10 family- and child-related services providers in 65
target neighborhoods; conduct systematic observations of neighborhoods.

MEASURES

Child: Woodcock-Johnson Battery (reading, verbal,
and math subtests), schooling, peer group, routine
activities, family relationships, behavior problems,
substance use, sexual activity, employment.

Primary caregiver: Household demographic information, education, employment, welfare use, residential
history, mental and physical health, efficacy, partner/
spouse conflict, family dynamics, social support,
children's schooling/child care, children's services use,
child behavior problems, parenting styles, family routines, and home environment.

Neighborhood: Census and L.A. County demographic data, social cohesion, informal social control,
safety, availability of community resources, and
physical and social disorder assessed via primary
caregiver interview, child interview, neighborhood
expert survey, and observation.

School/teacher: Characteristics of the school were assessed via child interviews and neighborhood expert
survey with school principals.

DATA COLLECTION   Data were collected in 2000–2002, and data collection is scheduled to continue until 2004.

PRINCIPAL
INVESTIGATORS
AND FUNDERS

Principal investigators: Anne K. Pebley (RAND Corporation and UCLA).
Funders: NICHD, with additional funding from ASPE, and Los Angeles County.

INTERNET SITE   http://www.lasurvey.rand.org

CHILDREN WITH SPECIAL NEEDS (Chapter 11)

National Early Intervention Longitudinal Study (NEILS)

DESIGN

NEILS is following a nationally representative sample of children from birth to 3 years old and their families through and after their early intervention experiences, with continuing periodic assessments through age 5. It is based on a conceptual framework identifying three key focal areas: (a) the characteristics of children and families served in early intervention; (b) early intervention services and service delivery; (c) the outcomes experienced by children and families who are served.

SAMPLE

A nationally representative sample of 3,338 children and their families from 94 counties in 20 states.
State sample: Included about 60% of the participants in Part C nationally, from the nine states serving the largest numbers of children under Part C. An additional 11 states were randomly selected from three regions, with probability proportional to the size of the states' birth-to-age-3 population. The identified target sample sizes for individual states ranged from 46 to 389.
County sample: Three to five counties were randomly selected for each state, with probability of selection being proportional to the size of the birth-

to-age 3 population in the county. The size of the sample allocated to individual counties ranged from 4 to 134.

Child sample: A total of 193 locations where families can enter early intervention recruited children for the study. Recruitment period for counties ranged from 2 to 15 months. Seventy-one percent of families invited to be in the study agreed to participate.

MEASURES

Enrollment data: A one-page form requesting child's date of birth, race/ethnicity, gender, whether there was a phone in the house, whether child is in foster care, whether family receives public assistance, the nature of the condition or delay for which the child is eligible for early intervention, and dates of referral and signing of the Individualized Family Service Plan (IFSP).

Family interviews: Computer-assisted telephone interviewing (CATI) guides the questioning sequence, and lasts an average of 38 minutes. Questions tap child's birth and demographic information and items related to child's development and behavior; health; and functioning with regard to vision, hearing, and mobility.

Service provider and program director surveys: This questionnaire to early intervention professionals asks about the number and kinds of clients with whom the respondent works, the types of services provided, the settings in which services are provided, perceptions of services in the area, and respondent's background, training, and experience. Program Director Surveys ask the number and types of employed and contracted personnel in early intervention, in addition to questions asked to service providers.

DATA COLLECTION

Data are being gathered at time of enrollment through child's third birthday via family telephone interviews, early intervention professionals, and mailed surveys.

PRINCIPAL INVESTIGATORS AND FUNDERS

Principal investigators: Kathleen Hebbeler, Donna Spiker, Sangeeta Mallik (SRI International); Susan Kinsey (RTI); Don Bailey, Lynne Kahn,

Robin McWilliam, Rune Simeonsson, Anita Scarborough (FPGCDC); Jay Chambers, JoAnne Lieberman (AIR).
Funders: Office of Special Education Programs (OSEP), Frank Porter Graham Child Development Center (FPGCDC), Research Triangle Institute (RTI), and American Institutes for Research (AIR).

INTERNET SITE   http://www.sri.com/neils

NEW NATIONAL LONGITUDINAL SURVEYS ON CHILDREN (Chapter 12)

Early Childhood Longitudinal Study—Birth Cohort (ECLS-B)

DESIGN

The ECLS-B is a longitudinal study of 13,500 nationally representative children born in the year 2001. Children will be followed from birth through first grade in order to assess their school readiness, as well as their growth and development in multiple domains (health, physical, gross and fine motor, cognitive, language, and socioemotional). Data about children's homes, communities, health care, nonparental child care, early childhood programs, schools, classrooms, and teachers will be gathered.

SAMPLE

Sample includes 13,500 nationally representative children identified through birth certificates. Asians, Pacific Islanders, and Native American Indians, moderately and very low birth weight infants, and twins will be oversampled.

MEASURES

Child: Physical growth, cognitive development, gross and fine motor skills, perceptual competencies, receptive and expressive language, temperament, behavior problems, behavioral self-control, attachment. *Mother*: Pregnancy and breast feeding experiences, household demographics and composition, education, employment, ancestry, country of origin, language, family composition growing up, receipt of public assistance growing up, school experiences, marital history, quality of current marriage or partner relationship, knowledge of child development, educational aspirations for child development, home learning environment, parenting behaviors and attitudes, child care arrangement, family health, neighborhood quality/safety, social support, community support, family routines, biological father information, public assistance, maternal teaching style.

Resident father: Activities with child, child's behavior and abilities, prenatal/neonatal experiences, knowledge about child development, discipline techniques, attitudes about being a father, separations from child, influence in child care decision making, current marital/partner relationship, marital and child bearing history, demographics, education, employment, health, family background, social support.

Child care provider: Caregiver background, program characteristics (staffing, program services provided, licensing, fees), type of care (length, time), other children in care, caregiver-child relationship, parental involvement, caregiver beliefs and attitudes, learning environment, caregiver health, caregiver income.

DATA COLLECTION   Scheduled for 9 months (2000), 18 months (2001–2002), 30 months (2002–2003), 48 months (2004), kindergarten (2005–2006), and first grade (2006–2007).

PRINCIPAL INVESTIGATORS AND FUNDERS

Principal investigator: U.S. Department of Education, National Center for Education Statistics (NCES).

Funders: In collaboration with NCES, additional funders include National Center for Health Statistics, National Institutes of Health (NIH), U.S. Department of Agriculture, Administration for Children, Youth, and Families, Office of Special Education Programs, Division of Nutrition and Physical Activity/Centers for Disease Control and Prevention, Administration for Children and Families, and Office of Minority Health. Within NIH, funding comes from National Institute of Child Health and Human Development, Office of the Director, National Institute of Mental Health, National Institute on Nursing Research, National Institute on Aging, and Office of Behavioral and Social Sciences Research.

INTERNET SITE   http://nces.ed.gov/ecls/Birth/agency.asp

Early Childhood Longitudinal Study—Kindergarten Cohort (ECLS-K)

DESIGN   Based on a nationally representative sample of approximately 22,000 kindergarten students who will be followed through fifth grade. Data at the child, family, and school levels are collected.

SAMPLE   The sample of approximately 1,000 schools is clustered in 100 Primary Sampling Units across the U.S. About 23 children in each school were sampled.

MEASURES   *Child*: ECLS-K assessments of reading, mathematics, and general knowledge, Peabody Achievement Tests, Woodcock-Johnson Psycho-Educational Battery, Peabody Picture Vocabulary Test, Primary Test of Cognitive Skills; height and weight; fine and gross motor development; teacher ratings of academic progress, classroom behavior, and approaches to learning; parent completion of the Social Skills Rating System and ratings of child's time use and activities during summer between kindergarten and first grade.
Parent: Household composition, parent education level, employment status, occupation, family income, and welfare status; home environment; aspiration for child's schooling and educational activities with the child; child care, history of child's preschool and Head Start attendance; food sufficiency; parenting styles; marital quality; mental health; information about nonresident biological parents.
School: Teacher-rated classroom characteristics and resources; services for low-performing children, grouping practices, instruction for LEP children, time

allocation; classroom management; school administrators' ratings of school and staff characteristics, policies in grouping; school record abstracts.

DATA COLLECTION Kindergarten data were collected in 1998–1999 and are being followed up in the first, third, and fifth grades. Public use files are available (see Internet site below).

PRINCIPAL
INVESTIGATORS
AND FUNDERS

Principal investigator: U.S. Department of Education, National Center for Education Statistics. Nicholas Zill is PI; Jerry West is the project officer.
Funders: In addition to NCES, U.S. Department of Education, ACYF, NICHD, U.S. Department of Agriculture.

INTERNET SITE http://www.nces.ed.gov/kindergarten/studybrief.asp

Fragile Families and Child Wellbeing Study

DESIGN Longitudinal design following a representative panel of children of unmarried and married parents (includes both mothers and fathers). Families drawn from 20 cities selected based on welfare and child support policies and labor market strength.

SAMPLE A hospital-based sampling procedure was used to enroll over 4,700 families, including approximately 3,600 unmarried couples and 1,100 married couples.

MEASURES *Child*: Health, cognitive, language, social, and emotional development.
Mothers and fathers: Mothers' prenatal care; parental health, education, employment, knowledge about local policies and community resources; mother-father relationship; attitudes about marriage and about fathers' rights and responsibilities; social support and extended kin.
Neighborhood: Census data and information on community resources and institutions (schools, day care facilities, churches, health and social services, neighborhood organizations).

DATA COLLECTION Between 1998 and 2002, parents were interviewed at the birth of their first child. Follow-up interviews with both parents are scheduled for when the child is 12, 30, and 48 months old.

PRINCIPAL
INVESTIGATORS
AND FUNDERS

Principal investigators: Sara McLanahan, and Irwin Garfinkel, Jeanne Brooks-Gunn, and Marta Tienda.

Funders: NICHD, National Science Foundation, DHHS, Ford Foundation, Robert Wood Johnson Foundation, William T. Grant Foundation, Public Policy Institute of California, California HealthCare Foundation, Hogg Foundation, St. David's Hospital Foundation, Commonwealth Fund, Fund for New Jersey, Healthcare Foundation of New Jersey, Foundation for Child Development, David and Lucile Packard Foundation, Kronkosky Charitable Foundation, A. L. Mailman Foundation, St. Vincent Hospitals and Health Services, William and Flora Hewlett Foundation, Christian A. Johnson Endeavor Foundation, Leon Lowenstein Foundation, A. L. Mailman Family Foundation, and Charles Stewart Mott Foundation.

INTERNET SITE http:// crcw.princeton.edu

Panel Study of Income Dynamics—Child Development Supplement (PSID-CDS)

DESIGN Longitudinal survey of a nationally representative sample of children and their families.

SAMPLE 3,563 children ages birth to 12 in about 2,394 families, with an oversampling of disadvantaged children; about 300 immigrant and 1,450 African American children.

MEASURES *Child*: Woodcock-Johnson Tests of Achievement—Revised, grade failure/progression, highest grade completed, verbal and math ability, literacy, self-esteem, behavior problems, physical health, temperament, and time use diaries of children's activities.

Mother: Employment and earnings, economic strain, physical and mental health, the quality of the home environment; parental monitoring, food security, child rearing values and rules, parenting styles, parent involvement in schools, and verbal ability.

Father: Employment and earnings, physical and mental health, attitudes about family and parental roles, and involvement with child.

Child care: Provider interview on classroom environment, teaching philosophy, child care characteristics, parent contact, time use diaries on child care activities, levels of learning strategies and literacy development, ratings of child behavior, and separate director interview.

School: Teacher interview on classroom environment, teaching philosophy, school characteristics, teacher preparation, parent contact, time use diaries on school activities, level of learning strategies and literacy development, ratings of child behavior, and separate administrator interview.

DATA COLLECTION Data collection was conducted in 1997; a follow-up is planned for 2003.

PRINCIPAL INVESTIGATORS AND FUNDERS *Principal investigators*: Jacquelynne Eccles; Frank Stafford, Greg Duncan, and Jeanne Brooks-Gunn are coinvestigators.

Funders: NICHD, U.S. Department of Agriculture, U.S. Department of Education, Annie E. Casey Foundation, William T. Grant Foundation.

INTERNET SITE http://www.isr.umich.edu/src/child-development/home.html

CHAPTER 3

Early Childhood Intervention Research Initiatives

LISA J. BERLIN, COLLEEN R. O'NEAL, AND JEANNE BROOKS-GUNN

The Johnson administration's War on Poverty in the mid-1960s ushered in the first large-scale early childhood intervention programs. The past 3 decades have witnessed not only a proliferation of early intervention initiatives but also the development of early intervention research. This research examines whether early interventions change the lives of young children and their families and, increasingly, *how* these programs work. In this chapter, we profile two initiatives in which early intervention services for low-income families began during pregnancy or in the infant's first year and continued at least through the child's second birthday. Both studies are contemporary federally funded early childhood intervention research initiatives: the Comprehensive Child Development Program (CCDP) and the Early Head Start (EHS) Research and Evaluation Project.

The Comprehensive Child Development Program consisted of 34 six-year comprehensive child and family development programs for low-income families with infants and young children. The first CCDP programs were funded between 1989 and 1993. The CCDP impact evaluation was a randomized trial in 21 of the first 24 sites (St. Pierre, Layzer, Goodson, & Bernstein, 1997). The CCDP process evaluation examined program families from the first 24 CCDP projects (Consulting Services and Research, Inc. [CSR], 1997). An evaluation of the second cohort of 10 CCDP projects also has been released (St. Pierre, McLaughlin, et al., 2000). The Early Head Start Research and Evaluation Project, which began in 1995, is an in-depth evaluation of the new Early Head Start program for low-income families with infants and toddlers.

Key forerunners of the CCDP and EHS programs that were operated under the aegis of the Administration on Children, Youth, and Families (ACYF) include the Head Start program, which has been serving low-income preschoolers since 1965; Migrant Head Start, which, in addition to preschoolers, has served infants and toddlers since its inception in 1969; the Parent and Child Centers, a small-scale initiative launched in 1967 to serve infants and toddlers; and the Child and Family Resource Program, an initiative funded by the Head Start Bureau from 1973 to 1978, which provided comprehensive services to low-income families with children from the prenatal stage to age 8.

Several other (nonfederal) large-scale intervention programs also helped set the stage for CCDP and EHS services and research. These include the Nurse-Family Partnership (see Kitzman, Olds, et al., 1997; Olds, Eckenrode, et al., 1997; Olds et al., 1999; see also Chapter 6, this volume); the Early Intervention Collaborative Study (see Shonkoff, Hauser-Cram, Krauss, & Upshur, 1992; see also Chapter 11, this volume); the Infant Health and Development Program (Brooks-Gunn et al., 1994; IHDP, 1990; McCarton et al., 1997); and the Center for Successful Child Development (the "Beethoven Project"; The Ounce of Prevention Fund, 1993). Lessons learned from each of these programs informed the development of both the Comprehensive Child Development Program and the Early Head Start Research and Evaluation Project.

COMPREHENSIVE CHILD DEVELOPMENT PROGRAM (CCDP)

History

In 1988, the U.S. Congress passed the Comprehensive Child Development Act to improve the prospects of children from low-income families. The act contained the following goals: (a) to prevent the academic failure of children from low-income families by addressing their educational, psychological, social, and medical needs from birth to age 5; (b) to decrease the likelihood that young children living in poverty will be caught in the cycle of poverty; (c) to prevent welfare dependency and promote self-sufficiency and educational achievement of all members of low-income families with young children. In response to this act, ACYF created the Comprehensive Child Development Program.

The CCDP reflected and integrated several trends and movements in the early intervention field. First, the CCDP reflected the trend toward a "two-generation" approach (see S. Smith, 1995). Second, CCDP reflected the "family support" movement, which viewed the whole family as the intervention target and developed multifaceted program models to meet various family needs (Kagan, 1996). Third, the CCDP reflected the trend toward service integration—toward increasing communication and collaboration among social service programs in order to provide children and families with a unified set of services (Kagan & Weissbourd, 1994).

ACYF funded a total of 34 CCDP projects between 1988 and 1992. The initial Comprehensive Child Development Act of 1988 authorized the establishment of 22 five-year CCDP projects to operate from fiscal years 1989–1993. The Augustus F. Hawkins Human Services Reauthorization Act of 1990 extended CCDP authorization through 1994. Two additional programs were funded in fiscal year 1990, and a second cohort of 10 programs was added in 1992. The Comprehensive Child Development Act of 1988 also mandated rigorous evaluation of CCDP. Accordingly, ACYF contracted with Abt Associates, Inc., to conduct an impact evaluation[1] and with CSR, Inc., to conduct a process evaluation.[2] Programs that applied to be CCDP sites were required to recruit more families than could be served and then to assign eligible families randomly to the program and control groups.

In 1994, Congressional reauthorization of the Head Start Act established a special initiative for ACYF to expand Head Start services for low-income families with infants and toddlers. A new program, Early Head Start, was launched. Funding for both CCDP and the Parent and Child Centers (PCCs) ceased, although some CCDPs and PCCs remade themselves into Early Head Start programs.

Current Status

The CCDP impact evaluation analyzed 21 CCDP projects (St. Pierre et al., 1997). The evaluation of the second cohort of 10 CCDP projects was published a few years later (St. Pierre, McLaughlin, et al., 2000). The CCDP process evaluation examined program families from the first 24 CCDP projects (CSR, 1997).

Goals

Goals of CCDP services. CCDP services began at birth and continued through children's fifth year. The CCDPs were intended to enhance children's physical, social, emotional, and intellectual development; to provide support to parents and other family members; and to help families become economically self-sufficient. Each CCDP also had five specific service mandates: (a) to intervene as early as possible in children's lives; (b) to involve the entire family; (c) to ensure the delivery of comprehensive social services to address the physical, social, emotional, and intellectual development of infants and children in the household; (d) to ensure the delivery of services to enhance parents' ability to contribute to the overall development of their children and to achieve economic and social self-sufficiency; and (e) to ensure continuous services until children enter school (St. Pierre et al., 1997).

Mandated core CCDP services included (a) developmental screenings, assessments, and referrals for children identified as at-risk or developmentally delayed; (b) the provision of developmentally appropriate "early childhood experiences" (services) for each CCDP family member under age 3; (c) health services such as health care and substance abuse services; and (d) parent education and adult education and training (CSR, 1997).

Early child development services for children from birth through age 3 typically took the form of biweekly, 30-minute, home-based child-parent activities conducted by case managers or by staff members with training in early child development. These activities usually followed or were adapted from an existing curriculum and focused on educating parents about infant and child development and on increasing parenting skills (St. Pierre & Layzer, 1999). By the time the CCDP children reached 4 and 5 years of age, at least half of them had enrolled in center-based early childhood education (St. Pierre & Layzer, 1999). Parenting education was also provided through classes and workshops, support groups, and the dissemination of written materials. In addition, programs connected or provided parents with child care on an as-needed basis. Child care services administered directly by CCDP projects were required to meet Head Start performance standards for education as well as the National Association for the Education of Young Children (NAEYC) guidelines for developmentally appropriate practices. Services available (either directly or by referral) to improve parents' economic self-sufficiency included adult education, vocational training, job training, job development and placement, life skills training, housing services, and income support services. Finally, each CCDP project was required to implement strategies to increase male (paternal) participation in program activities.

Goals of the CCDP impact and process evaluations. The CCDP impact evaluation aimed to examine four overarching issues: (a) the soundness of the theory and assumptions underlying the program; (b) the extent to which the program was adequately defined at the federal level; (c) adequacy of program implementation at the local level; and (d) the production of measurably positive effects (St. Pierre et al., 1997).

The principal research questions were as follows:

- What were CCDP's effects on the physical, social, emotional, and cognitive development of the children?

- What were CCDP's effects on mothers' parenting skills, education, training, reproductive behaviors, and economic self-sufficiency?
- Was there variation in CCDP's effects across sites?
- How did CCDP vary for subgroups of participants?
- Was CCDP more effective for families who remained in the program for longer periods of time?
- Did the monetary value of CCDP's benefits outweigh the costs of program services?

The CCDP process evaluation addressed the question of how and to what extent CCDP services actually addressed families' goals and promoted positive family development (CSR, 1997). There were seven specific research questions:

- What were the characteristics of CCDP families and how did they change over time?
- What was families' average length of tenure in CCDP and what were reasons for termination?
- What were the different levels of service use among CCDP families?
- What goals did CCDP families attain, and how long did it take them to attain their goals?
- What were the characteristics and quality of CCDP projects, and how have those characteristics changed over time?
- What impact did CCDP have on the community?
- What were the costs of CCDP?

Theory of Change

First, CCDP was predicated on the idea that services would be more effective if they targeted not just parents or children but the family as a whole. Children, in turn, would be best served *indirectly* by programs working with parents to improve family economic security, enhance family members' health and mental health, and improve parenting skills. A second key assumption centered on the accessibility of services for poor families. The CCDP viewed its target families as having multiple needs that could be addressed by *existing* social services if only these services were better coordinated and integrated. The CCDP thus assumed that the resources and services needed by poor families already existed in these families' communities and that a key problem for poor families was accessing these resources. A final set of assumptions referred to the timing of the program. Services were viewed as most likely to succeed if they were implemented as early as possible in children's lives and were provided for up to 5 years (St. Pierre et al., 1997).

CCDP projects, therefore, were designed to build on existing social services, although CCDP projects could also create new services when they were not available in the community or whenever it was necessary to ensure the provision of high-quality services. The resulting CCDP approach centered on case management. Case managers were required to visit families at least twice per month to refer families to services, broker families' receipt of services, and, in some cases, directly provide services including crisis intervention and parenting education.

Expectations about CCDP effects centered on short- and long-term benefits to both children and their families, all hypothesized to result from comprehensive case management. Specifically, case management was expected to result in children's receiving more health and developmental services, which in turn were expected to contribute to children's enhanced health and development. Children's enhanced health and development was hypothesized to lead to long-term benefits such as academic success. Case management was also expected to result in parents' receiving more health and parenting services as well as services to improve their economic self-sufficiency. These services were in turn expected to result in enhanced parental physical and mental health, more supportive parenting, greater economic self-sufficiency, and longer term parental self-sufficiency and child outcomes.

Design and Methods

Participants. To be eligible for CCDP services, a family must have had an income below the federal poverty line, included a pregnant woman or child under a year old, and agreed to participate in CCDP activities for 5 years. The impact evaluation, which was conducted in 21 of the first 24 CCDP sites, included 4,410 families recruited in 1990. There were 2,213 families in the program group and 2,197 families in the control group. Of the 4,410 families, 85% had a total income of under $10,000 at the time of recruitment. There were 43% African American, 26% Latino, 26 % white, 3% American Indian, and 1% Asian/Pacific Islander children. Eighty-four percent of the children in the sample spoke English as their primary language, and 14% spoke Spanish as their primary language. Thirty-five percent of the mothers in the sample were under age 18 when they gave birth to their first child. Fifty-one percent of the mothers had not graduated from high school when the CCDP began. The process evaluation examined only program families from the first 24 CCDP projects who had received three or more contacts with a case manager within 2 years of the family's enrollment in the CCDP ($N = 3,970$).

Procedures and measures. Data for the impact evaluation were collected annually over 5 years for each mother and focus child on the focus child's second, third, fourth, and fifth birthdays, with some additional data collected when the child was 18 and 30 months old. Data were collected principally during home visits consisting of 3-hour parent interviews and 1-hour child assessment sessions. The parent interviews for the impact evaluation addressed both child and family development. Mothers reported on their children's physical health and development and on their adaptive and problematic behaviors. Mothers also reported on their own physical and mental health, on their child-rearing attitudes, the quality of the home environment, and family economic self-sufficiency.

Direct child assessments included assessments of children's motor, cognitive, and language development using the Bayley Scales of Infant Development (Bayley, 1969, 1993), the Kaufman Assessment Battery for Children (K-ABC; Kaufman & Kaufman, 1981), and the Peabody Picture Vocabulary Test—Revised (PPVT-R; Dunn & Dunn, 1981).

When children were 3 years old, the quality of child-parent interaction was observed via a brief structured teaching assessment conducted according to the Nursing Child Assessment Satellite Training (NCAST) Teaching Scale (Sumner & Spietz, 1994). Live coding of the teaching assessments yielded scores on maternal "sensitivity to cues," "responsiveness to child's distress," "social-emotional growth fostering," "cognitive growth fostering," and on the child's "clarity of cues" and "responsiveness to caregiver."

Data were collected on 89% of the families at least once during the course of the evaluation. Seventy-four percent of the program families and 78% of the control group families participated in the final data collection when children turned 5 years old. The CCDP management information system (MIS) provided detailed information on services received by program families but not control families.

Data for the process evaluation drew on the MIS data. Additional data for the process evaluation came from qualitative ethnography reports and from cost case studies. The cost case studies focused on a subset of 10 of the first 24 CCDPs. For these case studies, raters evaluated the quality of three principal components of CCDP: administration, case management, and early childhood services. Specific indicators included ratings of the management of program staff, cultural appropriateness of services, and developmental appropriateness of early childhood services. It is important to note that these data were collected only for program families and thus did not allow for the analysis of differences in services received by program and control group families.

Units of Analysis and Findings

Program impacts. Looking across all CCDP projects, the impact evaluation revealed virtually no systematic program effects on children's physical, social, emotional, and cognitive development. Similarly, the impact evaluation revealed no program effects on parenting beliefs and attitudes, on the quality of the home environment, on observed parent-child interactions, on mothers' reproductive behaviors, or on indices of family economic self-sufficiency such as parental employment, household income, and welfare receipt.

Variation in program effects was seen by program site. One program, in particular, was distinguished by several significant program effects on children's cognitive development, on parenting attitudes, and on family self-sufficiency. Specifically, in the Brattleboro, Vermont, site, program children achieved significantly higher PPVT-R and K-ABC scores than comparison group children. Additionally, CCDP parents demonstrated more "empathetic awareness" of their children's needs and more "appropriate expectations" of their children than comparison parents. Finally, CCDP parents were employed for more time and received Aid to Families with Dependent Children (AFDC) and food stamps for less time than comparison parents, and CCDP families' total household incomes were higher than those of comparison families. Ready explanations for this site's success are not apparent. Possible explanations include the fact that this site's participants were at lower risk relative to other CCDP participants, the program's focus on early child development, and the strength of the program staff (St. Pierre et al., 1997).

No variation in CCDP effects was found for subgroups of participants defined in nine different ways (e.g., according to maternal age, maternal depressive symptomology, child sex). Yet an effect of duration of program enrollment did emerge. Specifically, for families who were enrolled in CCDP for 3 or more years, program children received higher scores on both the PPVT-R and the K-ABC than did control group children, and program families reported a higher household income than did control group families.

In addition to these (nonrandom assignment) "dose" effects based on duration of program enrollment, secondary analyses of CCDP data have begun to illustrate effects based on service intensity. Specifically, Brooks-Gunn, Burchinal, and Lopez (2001) divided CCDP programs into two groups according to average number of home visits received for the entire site: "more intense" parenting education and "less intense" parenting education. Children in the more intense parenting education sites achieved higher scores on the Bayley scales and the K-ABC than children in the less intense parenting education sites and in the control group. Additionally, growth curve analyses indicated that children in the more intense sites showed modest gains in K-ABC scores over time whereas children in the less intense sites showed modest declines. The children in more intense sites and in the control group also exhibited less decline in PPVT-R scores over time than did those in the less intense parenting education sites. Thus, looking more closely at program sites has revealed some promising effects as a function of the amount of parenting education sites provided.

Taken as a whole, then, the CCDP findings to date indicate a few scattered program effects. It is important to note that some generally positive trends in the well-being of *all* evaluation families were observed. These trends included increases in children's PPVT-R and K-ABC scores, increases in the proportion of working parents, and decreases in welfare receipt and in maternal depressive symptomology (St. Pierre et al., 1997). With some notable exceptions, however, these trends were *not* more likely among CCDP families than comparison group families, resulting in a generally disappointing answer to the question of overall program effectiveness. At the same time, the results from the Brattleboro site and from Brooks-Gunn, Burchinal, and Lopez's (2001) recent study illustrate that CCDP benefited children in some sites, especially when home-based parent education services were more frequent.

With respect to cost-effectiveness, the total cost of CCDP averaged $10,849 per family per year in 1994 dollars, excluding the costs of non-CCDP social services and of participating in the required research and evaluation activities (St. Pierre & Layzer, 1999). When the value of "donated" (e.g., no-cost) medical services are included, the total cost of CCDP averaged $15,768 per family in 1994 dollars (CSR, 1997). By way of comparison, as St. Pierre and Layzer (1999) point out, Head Start costs $4,500 per family per year, the Infant Health and Development Program for low-birth-weight infants and their families cost $10,000 per family per year, and the New Chance welfare-to-work demonstration for young mothers cost $8,300 per family per year (all in 1994 dollars). According to the Head Start Bureau, the average cost of Early Head Start programs was $9,646 per child in 2001. Thus the CCDP's average cost per family per year was high. Given the scarcity of positive program impacts, these costs appear to outweigh program benefits. The process evaluation report offers specific suggestions for reducing the cost of a replication of the CCDP (CSR, 1997).

The authors of the impact evaluation interpret the CCDP's findings in terms of problems in the theory and assumptions underlying the CCDP model (St. Pierre et al., 1997; see also Goodson, Layzer, St. Pierre, Bernstein, & Lopez, 2000). Specifically, it is not clear that the case management approach necessarily conferred more services on program families than on control group families. Services may have been too indirect and diluted to affect child and family development, at least according to the study's measures. The program's goals may have been too ambitious for the duration of the project and the available resources. The cost case study suggested that limited resources may have constrained some projects' abilities to serve all family members adequately, particularly in larger families (CSR, 1997). The authors of the impact evaluation also raised concerns about the quality of CCDP services. More recently, other scholars have suggested fatal flaws in program implementation as well as evaluation methods (Gilliam, Ripple, Zigler, & Leiter, 2000; see also Gilliam, 2000, and Goodson, Layzer, St. Pierre, & Bernstein, 2000, for a reply).

Process evaluation findings. The CCDP process evaluation indicated that the CCDP projects met the legislative goal of serving low-income families with young children in low-income rural and urban areas. As indicated by the impact evaluation, the process evaluation documented that African Americans comprised the largest percentage of participating families, and that a significant proportion of families were comprised of young, low-educated, and unemployed parents. The program also served a number of family members other than the primary caregivers and focus children, especially focus children's siblings and fathers (CSR, 1997). Over time, the characteristics of participating families changed somewhat, with more African Americans, single mothers, mothers with high school diplomas, and part-time workers enrolled in CCDP (CSR, 1997).

Ethnography reports indicated that the CCDPs experienced four major phases of program implementation: startup, growth, stabilization, and transition/institutionalization. Staff turnover and/or expansion was reported to play a key role in program operations. "Relatively smooth" program development was facilitated by such factors as a long-standing presence of the grantee agency in the community, compliance with performance standards, and the capacity to marshal resources. Stability in the project structure and environment was viewed as turning on three key factors: staffing (especially with respect to staff turnover), management (especially the extent to which there were "clear lines" of authority), and organizational framework (especially in terms of the program's relationship with the grantee agency).

Wide variation in CCDP families' participation rates was seen. Approximately one third of the families participated for the full 5 years. Among the 64% of the program group who left the program before the end of the demonstration, 48% of the families participated for 4 or more years, and 58% of the families participated for 3 or more years. The average length of families' participation in CCDP was 3⅓ years. Families' participation was terminated voluntarily and involuntarily. The principal reason for both voluntary and involuntary termination was "nonparticipation." "Change in lifestyle" was also a reason for a considerable proportion of voluntary terminations (CSR, 1997).

The process evaluation characterizes the service delivery model as a "unitary" model adapted over time by individual sites. Specifically, strong federal mandates and monitoring were in effect, which created similarities across projects. At the same time, the fact that case managers' principal goals were to help families access and integrate existing services meant that as long as community-based social services varied across CCDP sites, quantity and quality of services available to CCDP families also varied. In addition, the process evaluation indicates fluctuation in participants' service use, for example, as program implementation gelled, participants' service use increased (CSR, 1997). Intensity of service use was in turn related to participants' goal attainment.

CCDP families established a wide range of program goals for themselves, including bettering their housing, parenting skills, marriage, and child care. Strikingly low proportions of families reported attaining their goals. For example, the largest percentage of parents who reported attaining a specific goal (improved child care) was 40%. Twenty percent of all parents reported attaining the goal of improving their marriages, 13% of the parents reported attaining their goal of bettering their parenting skills, and 14% reported that their child's cognitive and social development had been enhanced. The length of time that it took families to achieve their goals (i.e., the number of days between setting a goal and attaining the goal) ranged from 416 days (1.13 years) for improving nutrition to 702 days (1.92 years) for improving parenting skills.

As mentioned above, as projects became more stable and "mature," goal attainment increased. Goal attainment, moreover, was positively associated with both duration of participation (defined according to number of days participating in the program) and service intensity, above and beyond the number of days that families took to achieve their goals.

The ethnographic data indicated that the CCDPs had positive effects on their communities, especially in terms of the integration and coordination of social services for young children and families. The CCDPs raised awareness about the importance and feasibility of providing coordinated services to low-income children and their families. The CCDPs also worked directly with other community service providers to improve and coordinate existing services and service systems including child care, education, and public health services/systems. Finally, CCDPs were viewed as increasing parental involvement and leadership in community organizations.

In sum, the CCDP process evaluation provided important information about CCDP services that complements the findings of the impact evaluation. The information on families' participation rates, service use, and goals, in particular, illustrates important variation in participants' experience *within* the program group. The CCDP process evaluation also illustrates program effects on the communities where the projects were housed.

Limitations

With respect to CCDP services, we agree with the authors of the impact evaluation that the case management model may well have resulted in services that were too indirect and diluted to affect child and family development significantly. With respect to the CCDP evaluations, we see one major limitation to the research design: The control group families were not part of the official process evaluation. Specifically, although the control group was not receiving CCDP services, control group participants may have been receiving other social and child development services. Information on control group members' service participation could have provided greater insight into the differences (and lack thereof) between the program and control group children and families. In addition, the process data that were collected did not include assessments of program implementation or program quality (e.g., quality of child care services provided to CCDP children). Again, information on what CCDP services actually entailed would have greatly informed the analysis of impact effects as well as provided important data in and of themselves (e.g., Leventhal et al., 2000).

Finally, the impact evaluation would have benefited from greater use of videotaped assessments of child-parent interaction. The parent-child relationship plays a key role in the development of children between the ages of birth and 5 years and videotaped observations provide a unique window into the dynamics of this relationship. Observational data may also be more sensitive to program impacts than interview or questionnaire assessments (see, e.g., Brooks-Gunn, Berlin, Aber, Carcagno, & Sprachman, 1996; Spiker, Ferguson, & Brooks-Gunn, 1993), and effects of CCDP services on parenting might currently be underestimated. These and other limitations of the CCDP service model and the CCDP evaluations were carefully considered in designing the Early Head Start program and the Early Head Start Research and Evaluation Project.

Public Use Files

The data from the impact evaluation of the CCDP and the CCDP MIS are available on-line (http://www.acf.dhhs.gov/programs/core/ongoing_research/hs/hs_data/hs_data_intro.html).

EARLY HEAD START (EHS) RESEARCH AND EVALUATION PROJECT

History

Two federal advisory committees convened in the early 1990s by U.S. Secretary for Health and Human Services Donna Shalala shaped the Early Head Start program. The committees included practitioners, researchers, policy makers, federal staff, and, on one committee, a Head Start parent. The first committee, the Advisory Committee on Head Start Quality and Expansion, charged Head Start programs to combat fragmentation of services and to expand services in several ways. One recommended expansion was to serve more families with infants and toddlers (U.S. Department of Health and Human Services, 1993). The second committee, the Advisory Committee on Services for Families with Infants and Toddlers, met three times during 1994. Together with federal staff who had conducted a series of focus groups with parents, practitioners, and researchers, this committee identified the following as characteristics of successful programs for infants and toddlers: (a) early prenatal services for expectant mothers; (b) a two-generation approach; (c) family-centered services that address self-sufficiency through the provision of social services and parent education; (d) high-quality child development services; (e) continuity of service delivery for children and families that ensures continuous support and provides for smooth transitions to other service systems; (d) continuity of caregivers; (e) intensity of services; and (f) integration of services (U.S. Department of Health and Human Services, 1994).

In 1994, congressional reauthorization of the Head Start Act established a special initiative for ACYF to expand Head Start services for low-income families with infants and toddlers. This initiative set aside 3% of the Head Start budget for the first Early Head Start programs. The next year, 68 programs across the country won competitive funds to launch Early Head Start programs. In the same year, Mathematica Policy Research and the National Center for Children and Families at Teachers College, Columbia University, became the national evaluators for the Early Head Start Research and Evaluation Project.[3] This project not only provides a detailed picture of some of the first Early Head Start programs but also generated unprecedented longitudinal data on approximately 3,000 low-income infants and toddlers and their families.

Current Status

The proportion of the federal Head Start budget set aside for Early Head Start programs has grown steadily since 1994. In 2002, 10% of the Head Start budget went to 664 Early Head Start programs across the United States serving 55,000 pregnant women and families with children under age 3.

The Early Head Start Research and Evaluation Project was funded from 1995 until 2002. The project focuses on 17 competitively selected sites from the first wave of (68) EHS programs. Programs were selected by the Head Start Bureau to represent a balanced distribution of program approaches, program histories, geographic locations (regions and rural/urban/suburban sites), and participant race/ethnicity. Selection criteria also included a commitment to participate in the Research and Evaluation Project, and a commitment from a local researcher to collaborate as a "local research partner," to serve as a liaison to the Research and Evaluation Project and to collect site-specific data. The 17 national research programs are located in rural, urban, and suburban communities across the United States and represent a wide range of populations and cultures.[4] These 17 programs are also broadly representative of all of the EHS programs funded in 1995 and 1996 (Kisker, Love, & Raikes, 1999). Data collection began in 1996. The interim impact report was released to Congress in 2001 (Love et al., 2001). The final impact report was released in 2002 (Love et al., 2002).

Goals

Principles and goals of Early Head Start services. Early Head Start services begin between the last trimester of pregnancy and children's 12th month. Services are provided through children's 3rd year of life. Several principles that have long guided Head Start programs informed the design of Early Head Start. These include (a) providing comprehensive services that are sensitive to the needs of low-income families and their children; (b) helping parents achieve and maintain self-sufficiency, and increasing parents' involvement in their children's education and development; and (c) serving as a national laboratory for policy-relevant program evaluation as well as child development research. Chief among these principles is Head Start's commitment to providing services that are sensitive to children's and families' needs. Head Start programs are permitted considerable flexibility to configure services according to perceived population needs. EHS programs were designed to be even more flexible and can provide home-based services, center-based services, or a mixed approach. At the same time, EHS programs are expected to follow nine principles and to address four service "cornerstones."

The Advisory Committee on Services for Families with Infants and Toddlers stated that the following nine principles would underlie EHS service provision: (a) high quality; (b) prevention and promotion ("early and proactive promotion of healthy development and healthy behaviors;" U.S. Department of Health and Human Services, 1994, p. 11); (c) positive relationships and continuity; (d) parent involvement; (e) inclusion; (f) culture (i.e., respecting families' existing cultures and cultivating a common culture); (g) comprehensiveness, flexibility, responsiveness, and intensity ("program resources of varied intensity will be marshaled to support the whole family in an individualized and responsive manner;" U.S. Department of Health and Human Services, 1994, p. 13); (h) transition (working to ensure that children make a smooth transition out of EHS services into a preschool program of equally high caliber); and (i) collaboration (working with other community service providers to establish an "integrated, community-wide response to families with young children;" U.S. Department of Health and Human Services, 1994, p. 14).

Four cornerstones. According to the Advisory Committee on Services for Families with Infants and Toddlers, EHS services should not only operate according to these nine principles but also address four key program "cornerstones": child development, family development, community building, and staff development.

- *The child development cornerstone.* EHS programs must aim to "enhance and advance" children's development by providing "individualized support." Supporting early child development, moreover, must be viewed as occurring via "positive parent-child interactions" and via enhanced parental knowledge about child health and development. Supporting early child development also must include providing comprehensive health and mental health services.
- *The family development cornerstone.* EHS programs must promote family development by supporting parental empowerment. EHS programs must provide opportunities for parental involvement in the program.
- *The community-building cornerstone.* EHS programs must build relationships with other community service "to mobilize community resources and energies on behalf of children and families" (U.S. Department of Health and Human Services, 1994, p. 18).
- *The staff development cornerstone.* EHS programs must recognize the critical nature of staff members' qualifications, especially in terms of their abilities to form supportive relationships with infants and toddlers. Ongoing staff training, supervision, and mentoring must be an integral part of EHS services.

Program guidelines reflecting these nine principles and four cornerstones were specified in the Early Head Start grant announcement issued in March 1995 and are stated in the Head Start Program Performance Standards issued in November 1996. The Head Start Program Performance Standards, in turn, guide the Head Start Bureau's monitoring of program implementation and quality.

Goals and research questions of the Early Head Start Research and Evaluation Project. The project had two overarching goals: (a) to understand the extent to which EHS services can be effective for low-income infants and toddlers and their families; and (b) to understand what kinds of programs and services can be effective for children and families with different characteristics living in varying circumstances and served by programs with varying approaches (Love et al., 2002). The project consists of an impact evaluation, an implementation study, local research studies, policy studies, and continuous program improvement activities. The *impact evaluation* was designed to analyze the effects of EHS services on children, families, communities, and staff. The *implementation study* was designed to examine service needs and use for low-income families with infants and toddlers and to assess EHS program implementation. The *local research studies* were site-specific investigations conducted by the local research partners in order to provide more detailed data on the mechanisms underlying program effects and child, family, staff, and community development. Cutting across the impact evaluation, implementation study, and local research studies were embedded *policy studies* that addressed emerging policy issues such as welfare reform, fatherhood, child care, and children's health. Finally, *continuous program improvement activities* referred to the feedback of information to EHS programs for ongoing formative evaluation.

The major research questions of the EHS Research and Evaluation Project were as follows:

- How do EHS programs affect child, parent, and family outcomes?
- How do different program approaches and community contexts affect these outcomes?
- How do program implementation and services affect outcomes?
- How do the characteristics of children and families affect outcomes?

Theory of Change

The EHS Research and Evaluation Project draws on several conceptual frameworks about program start-up and about child, family, community, and staff development, all of which highlight the role of relationships (e.g., parent-child relationships, staff-parent and staff-child relationships, family-community relationships; Mathematica Policy Research, Inc., 1995). Expectations for EHS effects on child development focus on the promotion of children's competence in terms of their "everyday effectiveness in dealing with their present environment and later responsibilities in school and life" (Zigler, 1973). EHS programs are hypothesized to promote children's competence directly (e.g., through center-based services) as well as indirectly through enhanced parenting and parent-child relationships (Love et al., 2002).

In addition to stating these expectations, the EHS Research and Evaluation Project made active dialogue about programs' theories of change an explicit, ongoing part of the project. As the project unfolded, members of the national research team, local research partners, and program staff engaged in numerous independent and collective discussions about the goals and expected outcomes of EHS services, and the mechanisms by which these outcomes are expected to be achieved (for details, see Kisker et al., 1999). This ongoing dialogue continually highlighted relationships as key outcomes as well as critical mechanisms underlying EHS effects on child, family, staff, and community development.

Design and Methods

Participants. Each of the 17 research sites began with 150 to 200 research participants (baseline N = approximately 3,000). Criteria for families' eligibility for the study included the following: First, families who had participated for 3 months or longer in the CCDP in the 5 years prior to application or families who had participated for 3 months or longer in Head Start, a Parent and Child Center, or a similar program in the year prior to application were *not* eligible. Second, families were required to have an income at or below the federal poverty level, a child under 1 year old born between September 1, 1995, and September 30, 1998, an understanding of random assignment procedures (described to many parents as a "lottery"), and an expressed willingness to participate in either the program or comparison group.

Sixty percent of the families enrolled before the target child reached the age of 5 months; 25% of the families enrolled when the primary caregiver was pregnant. Of those children born by the time of enrollment, 10% were born at low birth weight (under 2,500 grams) and an estimated 20% were at risk for a developmental disability.

The primary caregivers who applied with their children to the EHS research programs were predominantly single mothers. Ninety-nine percent were female, 39% were teenagers (under age 20), and 25% were married and living with their spouse. Primary caregivers were African American (34%), Latino (24%), white (37%), or of "other" race/ethnicity (5%). Twenty percent of the primary caregivers reported that their main language was not English. Fifty-two percent of the primary caregivers had graduated from high school. Twenty-two percent were in school or training at the time of enrollment, 23% were employed, and 55% were neither in school nor employed.

At the time of enrollment, primary caregivers identified a number of basic needs that were not being met, the most frequently mentioned of which was child care (mentioned by 34% of the primary caregivers). Other frequently identified needs included transportation (21%) and medical care (14%). Most of the families were receiving some kind of public assistance: 77% were receiving Medicaid, 88% Women, Infants, and Children (WIC) program benefits, 50% food stamps, and 36% cash assistance under the Temporary Aid to Needy Families (TANF) program. (This last figure may be somewhat misleading as some of the women who would be eligible for TANF when they became mothers were still pregnant with their first child at the time of EHS enrollment and thus not yet eligible for TANF benefits.)

Procedures and measures. Once a family's eligibility was determined, the principal caregiver was administered a baseline interview in order to collect basic demographic information such as family composition; parents' age, education, health, and pregnancy history; and children's special needs. The baseline interview also collected information on families' needs and resources.

Data for the implementation study were collected via extensive Parent Services Interviews (PSIs) and in-depth site visits to EHS programs. The PSIs were administered at three points determined by the duration of the target child's enrollment: after 6, 15, and 26 months and at program exit. An overview of the PSI assessments is available on-line (http://www.mathematica-mpr.com/3rdlevel/ehstoc.htm). PSIs were administered in English or Spanish. The PSIs addressed families' experiences in and satisfaction with a wide range of social services including EHS services, other child care and child development services, health care services, and services for basic needs such as public assistance services and housing, food, and transportation services. The PSIs also provided regularly updated information on family composition; families' needs, resources, and goals; parents' health, education, employment, and social support; and child care arrangements. Response rates for the 6-, 15-, and 26-month PSIs were 82%, 75%, and 70%, respectively.

The site visits consisted of three in-depth visits to each of the 17 sites over the course of the project conducted by members of the national evaluation research team. The site visits included interviews and focus groups with EHS program staff, parents, and other community service providers; observations of home visits and/or center-based activities; case reviews; and meetings with the local research partners. Additionally, at two of these three site visits, EHS program staff members completed in-depth questionnaires about their background, qualifications, education, training, and job satisfaction. Following each site visit, the site visitors wrote in-depth descriptive profiles of the programs and completed detailed checklists about the programs. These profiles and checklists became the basis for quantitative ratings of program implementation and quality.

Ratings of program implementation and quality were completed in the spring of 1997 and in the fall of 1999. Ratings of program implementation were completed by a panel of six people, four members of the national evaluation team and two outside experts. Ratings were based on program guidelines outlined in the Early Head Start grant announcement and in the Head

Start Program Performance Standards. Ratings tap program implementation in five service areas: (a) early childhood development and health services; (b) family partnerships; (c) community partnerships; (d) staff development; and (e) management systems and procedures.

In 1997, ratings of program quality focused on the quality of center-based child care for EHS children (child care provided directly by EHS programs or community-based child care attended by EHS children). Ratings were based on scores from the Infant/Toddler Environment Rating Scale (ITERS; Harms, Cryer, & Clifford, 1990) and the Family Day Care Environment Rating Scale (FDCRS; Harms & Clifford, 1989). For children in preschool settings, the Early Childhood Environment Rating Scale (ECERS; Harms, Clifford, & Cryer, 1998) was administered.

In 1999, ratings of program quality included ITERS, FDCRS, or ECERS scores as well as ratings of several other aspects of the quality of EHS center-based care such as the assignment of children to primary caregivers, the education and training of child care staff, and turnover rates for direct care staff. Additionally, ratings were made of several important aspects of home visiting including turnover rates for home visitors, the frequency of home visits, home visitors' case loads, and the extent to which home-based services are integrated with other EHS services.

For programs delivering home-based services, there were also descriptive reports completed by home visitors following each home visit. These reports assessed the substantive focus of the visits, the caregiver's or parent's interest and engagement in the home visit, and the child's interest and engagement in the home visit.

Data for the impact evaluation were collected at three points determined by the age of the focus child: 14, 24, and 36 months of age. An overview of all birthday-related assessments is available on-line (http://www.mathematica-mpr.com/3rdlevel/ehstoc.htm). Trained interviewer-assessors collected each set of data in 2-hour sessions in families' homes consisting of an extensive parent interview, the Mental Development Index (MDI) of the Bayley Scales of Infant Development (Bayley, 1969, 1993), and three videotaped child-parent interactions. Data on target children's child care experiences were also collected. All data were collected in English or in Spanish. The parent interview addressed such issues as knowledge of child health and development; values and beliefs about parenting; qualities of the home environment; parents' characteristics such as physical health, mental health symptoms, literacy, and cognitive abilities; the principal caregiver's relationship with the child's other parent and perceptions of that parent's relationship with the target child; family routines, conflict, and social support; children's health; children's language development; and child care use and quality. The Bayley scales yield mental development scores as well as ratings of children's test-taking behaviors such as their orientation toward the interviewer-assessor, engagement with the task, and arousal during the testing.

At each age point, the videotaped interactions included a free play assessment; a teaching assessment, and/or a challenge task. If a child or parent had a physical disability, the protocol was modified in order to collect as much data as possible. Coding of the videotaped child-parent interaction assessments focused on developmentally appropriate aspects of the parent-child relationship including parental sensitivity and insensitivity and child engagement of the parent, and sustained attention with objects (see Ware, Brady, O'Brien, & Berlin, 1998). The teaching assessments were coded according to the NCAST Teaching Scale (Sumner & Spietz, 1994).

Response rates for the 14-, 24-, and 36-month parent interviews were 78%, 72%, and 70%, respectively. Response rates for the 14-, 24-, and 36-month Bayley assessments were 63%, 59%, and 55%, respectively. Response rates for the 14-, 24-, and 36-month videotaped child-parent interaction assessments were 66%, 60%, and 55%, respectively (Love et al., 2002).

The impact evaluation also included visits to the child care providers of those target children experiencing 10 hours or more per week of nonmaternal care for interviews with child care center directors and caregivers, formal observations of the child care and (at 24 and 36 months) of the target child's specific experiences in child care. Assessments included the ITERS, FDCRS, or ECERS, the Arnett Scale of Caregiver Behavior (Arnett, 1989), and a Child-Caregiver Observation System scale (C-COS; Boller, Sprachman, & the Early Head Start Research Consortium, 1998).

Units of Analysis and Findings for the Implementation Study

The implementation study generated detailed information about programs' approaches and theories of change and about program implementation and quality.

EHS program approaches. EHS programs' approaches were characterized as "center-based" (center-based child care plus other activities), "home-based" (home visits plus other activities), or "mixed-approach"—some families receiving center-based services and some families receiving home-based services, all families receiving both types of services (the "combination option"), or all families receiving some other locally designed set of services (the "local design" option). When the 17 research programs were first funded, five were center-based, five were home-based, and seven were mixed-approach programs. By the fall of 1997, this distribution had shifted in response to funding decisions, perceived family needs, and technical assistance; there were four center-based, seven home-based, and six mixed-approach programs. By the fall of 1999, several programs had shifted (or shifted again), especially in response to families' changing needs brought on by the new welfare reform laws, with most home-based becoming mixed-approach programs (for details, see Kisker et al., 1999; Love et al., 2002).

EHS programs' theories of change. As already mentioned, an integral part of the EHS Research and Evaluation Project was its ongoing efforts to articulate programs' theories of change. A synthesis of meetings with program staff revealed enhanced parent-child relationships to be a key expected outcome *and* a critical mechanism through which EHS services were expected to affect child development. The theory of change meetings also highlighted the importance of specific aspects of parent-child relationships including a secure child-parent attachment, parents' knowledge of child development, and parenting stress. Programs also discussed expectations for family development, staff development, and community building (for details, see Kisker et al., 1999).

EHS program implementation and quality. The consensus-based implementation ratings identified three types of programs: "early implementers," "later implementers," and "incomplete implementers." The early implementers were the six programs that were rated as fully implemented both in the fall of 1997 and in 1999. The later implementers were the six programs that did not reach full implementation until after 1997. The five incomplete implementers did not reach full program implementation during the evaluation period.

With respect to the quality of EHS child care, the nine EHS programs that offered center-based services from the beginning received a "good to excellent" average rating of 5.6 (on a scale of 1 to 7) on the ITERS. By 1999, 12 of the 17 programs offered center-based services. The center-based programs generally offered full-time child care in small groups and with relatively small child-staff ratios. Staff members in most of the programs had either a Child Development Associate (CDA) degree or were working toward a CDA. Most of these center-based programs assigned children to a primary caregiver. Curricula used in these centers included the Creative Curriculum for Infants and Toddlers (Dombro, Colker, & Dodge, 1997), the Program for Infant/Toddler Caregivers (Lally, 1995), Partners in Parenting Education (PIPE; Butterfield, 1996), and Partners in Learning (Sparling et al., 1991).

The EHS program guidelines mandate that if EHS programs are not meeting families' needs for child care, the programs must help families find other child care that is of equal or higher quality. The quality of community-based child care received by EHS children, however, was found to vary considerably. In 1998–1999, the average ITERS and FDCRS scores for community-based child care centers attended by EHS children were "minimal to good." On a more positive note, these community-based programs were generally found to offer child care in relatively small groups and with relatively small child-staff ratios.

With respect to home-based services, in 1997 nine of the programs that provided home-based services were rated as providing "good" or "high" quality services. By 1999, 11 of the 13 programs providing home-based services received "good" or "high" ratings. Curricula used or adapted by EHS home visitors included Parents as Teachers (PAT; Wagner & Clayton, 1999), the Program for Infant/Toddler Caregivers (Lally, 1995), Partners in Parenting Education (Butterfield, 1996), and the Hawaii Early Learning Profile (HELP; Furuno et al., 1992).

The implementation study also offers detailed data on services in the family, staff, and community development cornerstones. For example, by 1997 all of the programs had established procedures for assessing family needs and for developing individual family partnership agreements (IFPAs), and ten of the programs offered special services for fathers and father figures. Twenty-four percent of all staff had a 4-year college degree and 20% had a graduate degree. All programs provided extensive training, supervision, and support for staff members working directly with children. The wages of these frontline staff members averaged $9.77 per hour. The programs that paid the highest average hourly wages ($12) to frontline staff were home-based programs that did not operate child development centers. Across all programs, there was a 20% rate of staff turnover. Programs formed many partnerships with other community organizations, especially Part C (early intervention/special needs) providers.

The rich descriptive information provided by the implementation study not only illustrated what EHS programs actually do but also contributed importantly to the impact evaluation, especially with respect to understanding how programs' approaches, implementation, and quality affected outcomes for children, parents, and families.

Units of Analysis and Findings for the Impact Evaluation

Effects of EHS services on children and families were reported at an interim point, after children's 24-month birthdays (Love et al., 2001), and in the final report, after children's 36-month birthdays (Love et al., 2002). At both points there were modest but consistent, statistically significant impacts overall, with effect sizes of 10% to 20%. In some subgroups there were much larger impacts, with effect sizes of 20% to 50%.

Impacts for all children. At both 24 and 36 months, there were positive impacts on cognitive, language, and socioemotional development. For example, EHS children scored higher on the Bayley Mental Development Index, and a smaller proportion of EHS children scored in the at-risk range (below 85). EHS children also scored higher on the Peabody Picture Vocabulary Test (PPVT-III) of receptive language, and again, fewer EHS than control children scored in the at-risk range. In videotaped interactions, EHS children were observed to engage their parents more, behave less negatively toward parents, and devote more attention to objects during play. They were also rated as lower in aggressive behavior by their parents than control children.

Impacts for all parents. At both 24 and 36 months, EHS parents were observed to be more emotionally supportive during play and to provide more support at home for language and learning than control parents. EHS parents were more likely to read daily to their children and less likely to demonstrate negative parenting behaviors during videotaped interactions. EHS parents also reported fewer instances of spanking their children and a wider range of discipline strategies, including fewer punitive strategies. EHS mothers were less likely to have subsequent births during the first 2 years after enrollment. After 26 months of enrollment, EHS parents were more likely than control parents to participate in education or job training and more likely to be employed (although they did not earn more income than control parents did).

Impacts for fathers. Twelve of the 17 sites collected supplementary data on fathering. EHS fathers reported spanking their children less often than control fathers. In videotaped interactions, EHS fathers were rated as less intrusive, and EHS children were observed to engage their fathers more and to devote more attention to objects during play.

Impacts in subgroups. Program impacts in some subgroups were larger than those in other subgroups. Subgroups were defined according to program characteristics and according to participant characteristics. Both made a difference in program effectiveness. For example, there were larger impacts (i.e., effect sizes of 20% to 50% across multiple outcomes) for participants in mixed-approach programs and for those receiving EHS services from programs that were fully implemented early. Mixed-approach programs that were fully implemented early conferred especially strong effects. Additionally, there were larger impacts for African American families, families who enrolled during pregnancy, and families who enrolled with a moderate number of risk factors, as opposed to families who enrolled with a "low" or "very high" number of risk factors.

Mediators of program effects. Consistent with the project's conceptual models and with programs' explicit theories of change, impacts on children at 36 months were associated with impacts on parenting at 24 months. For example, higher scores on the Bayley MDI were associated with greater parental emotional supportiveness during play and with more support at home for language and learning. Less child aggression at 36 months was associated with less spanking and less parental stress at 24 months.

Limitations

The impact evaluation revealed some limitations to EHS program effectiveness. For example, despite the fact that many parents reported symptoms of depression, there were no program effects on parents' receipt of mental health services or on parents' mental health per se. Another area requiring further attention is safety: EHS programs did not succeed in increasing parents' safety practices in the home or in their use of terms of infant car seats. The programs' requirements to address all four EHS cornerstones may have accounted for some of these limitations (i.e., the requirements may have been too demanding). These extensive demands may also account for the fact that some programs did not reach full implementation. They may have been working on addressing one cornerstone to the detriment of another.

It is also important to consider limiting factors in the research and evaluation project per se. Response rates are one such factor. Response rates declined over time, which makes it difficult to draw conclusions across the multiple data sources. For example, in the combined (program and control) sample, only 39% of the participants completed 14-, 24-, and 36-month videotaped child-parent interactions. Only 57% of the participants completed 14-, 24-, and 36-month parent interviews. Another limitation concerns the research design itself. Although participants were randomly assigned to the program or control groups, they were not randomly assigned to different types of programs, which makes it more difficult to draw firm conclusions about the effects of particular program approaches.

Public Use Files

Public use files are scheduled to be available in 2003.

NOTES

We thank the National Institute on Early Childhood Development and Education of the U.S. Department of Education; the Family and Child Well-Being Research Network of the National Institute for Child Health and Human Development (NICHD); and the Office of the Assistant Secretary for Planning and Evaluation, U.S. Department of Health and Human Development, for supporting the writing of this chapter. Thanks especially to Naomi Karp, Jeffery Evans, Martha Moorehouse, and the members of the SPEED consortium for insights and suggestions contributed along the way. We also thank Ellen Kisker, John Love, Helen Raikes, Louisa Tarullo, Rachel Chazan Cohen, and Esther Kresh for their leadership as well as their comments on earlier drafts of this chapter.

1. The CCDP impact evaluation was directed by Robert St. Pierre, Jean Layzer, Barbara Goodson, and Lawrence Bernstein (Abt Associates) and funded by the Administration on Children, Youth, and Families. For more information, see http://www.acf.dhhs.gov/programs/core/pubs_reports/ccdp/ccdp_intro.html on-line.

2. The CCDP process evaluation was directed by Jim De Santis (CSR) and funded by the Administration on Children, Youth, and Families.

3. John Love, Ellen Kisker (Mathematica Policy Research), and Jeanne Brooks-Gunn (Columbia University) are Co-Principal Investigators. The Administration on Children, Youth, and Families was the principal funder. For more information, see http://www.mathematica-mpr.com/3rdlevel/ehstoc.htm on-line.

4. The 17 EHS programs participating in the EHS Research and Evaluation Project are in the following locations, with local research partners listed in parentheses: Russellville, AR (Robert Bradley, Mark Swanson, & Leanne Whiteside-Mansell, University of Arkansas); Venice, CA (Claire Hamilton & Carollee Howes, University of California—Los Angeles); Denver, CO, 2 EHS programs (Robert Emde, Jon Korfmacher, Paul Spicer, JoAnn Robinson, & Norman Watt, University of Denver); Marshalltown, IA (Susan McBride & Carla Peterson, Iowa State University); Kansas City, KS (Jane Atwater, Judith Carta, & Jean Ann Summers, University of Kansas); Jackson, MI (Hiram Fitzgerald, Tom Reischl, & Rachel Schiffman, Michigan State University); New York, NY (Mark Spellmann & Catherine Tamis-LeMonda, New York University); Kansas City, MO (Mark Fine, Jean Ispa, & Kathy Thornburg, University of Missouri at Columbia); Pittsburgh, PA (Carol McAllister & Robert McCall, University of Pittsburgh; Beth Green, NPC Research, Inc.); Sumter, SC (Richard Faldowski , Medical University of South Carolina); McKenzie, TN (Mathematica Policy Research, Inc.); Logan, UT (Lisa Boyce & Lori Roggman, Utah State University); Alexandria, VA (Shavaun Wall, Catholic University of America); Kent, WA (Kathryn Barnard & Susan Spieker, University of Washington School of Nursing); Sunnyside, WA (Eduardo Armijo & Joseph Stowitschek, University of Washington College of Education); and Brattleboro, VT (Catherine Ayoub, Barbara Pan, & Catherine Snow, Harvard University).

CHAPTER 4

Initiatives on the Transition to School

ALLISON SIDLE FULIGNI AND CHRISTY BRADY-SMITH

In recent years there has been growing general concern about our educational system's success in providing necessary skills to students. In particular, the growing number of students who do not complete high school and who reach adulthood without basic literacy or other job-related skills has prompted concerned educators, researchers, and policy makers to take a closer look at the early school years to determine what experiences may lead to these outcomes and what steps may be taken to alter children's educational paths. At least two current policy-practice issues have led to a focus on the transition into elementary school.

One issue has to do with the concept of school readiness. Although traditional conceptions of school readiness have focused on cognitive skills that children are expected to have upon school entry, current thinking has broadened this definition to include not only children's skills, backgrounds, and experience, but also schools' ability to serve children with diverse backgrounds and needs (Powell, 1995). The sources of "readiness" are not only the child's emotional, cognitive, linguistic, and social abilities, but also the contexts in which children live and the adults with whom they interact (parents, grandparents, teachers, recreation staff, and other community members; Kagan, 1992; Love, Aber, & Brooks-Gunn, 1994).

Current research on the transition to schooling has emerged in the context of the National Education Goals 2000, particularly Goal Number One: "By the year 2000, all children in America will start school ready to learn" (National Education Goals Panel, 1998). Children enter school with varying levels of experience in classroom settings, familiarity with academic subjects, and awareness of academic discourse styles. When they enter school, they may find the new environment supportive of their individual educational needs and consequently achieve early success, which will put them on a path toward continued educational success and attainment. On the other hand, if children find the school setting to be both unfamiliar and unsupportive of their needs, early difficulties can result in placement of the child in lower academic tracks or special education programs and set the stage for possible long-term difficulties, disengagement, or failure (Alexander & Entwisle, 1996; Entwisle & Alexander, 1994).

Because educational research has not traditionally focused extensively on children of school-entry age, little is known about the nature of the transition process generally, nor the circumstances that ease school entry. Several current large-scale research projects have been undertaken that begin to answer questions about the experiences children have as they enter and progress through elementary school, and illuminate multiple pathways of influence. Research on the transition to schooling tends to adopt an ecological approach (e.g., Bronfenbrenner & Crouter, 1983) by exploring the multiple settings that interact to affect children's experiences and outcomes.

Another policy-practice issue has also informed the development of current initiatives. Research on the effects of preschool intervention programs for economically disadvantaged children has documented early cognitive, social, and emotional gains related to participation in such programs. However, these seem to diminish (and sometimes disappear) by the middle of elementary school. In particular, research has found that while there seem to be immediate positive and educationally meaningful effects related to children's participation in Head Start, by first grade the differences between Head Start children and control group children are smaller (Barnett, 1995; Currie & Thomas, 1995; McKey et al., 1985). Common lines of reasoning used to explain the fade-out of early intervention effects are the fact that interventions are short in duration (e.g., one year for Head Start) and therefore not sufficient to sustain effects several years after the support services have ended, and the existence of continued differences between the quality of schooling and the home environment after intervention periods end (Kagan, 1991b; Lee, Brooks-Gunn, Schnur, & Liaw, 1990; Zigler & Styfco, 1996). One study examined the middle schools of 25,000 eighth grade students and found that children who had attended Head Start were in poorer quality middle schools than those who had either attended no preschool or another form of preschool. Differences in middle school quality were associated with decreases in the long-term cognitive benefits from participating in Head Start (Lee & Loeb, 1995). Therefore, it is argued, young children who are at risk of poor adaptation to schooling may benefit from longer-term support provided both before and during the transition into elementary school (Kennedy, 1993; Zigler & Styfco, 1993, 1996).

In this chapter, two major research initiatives on the transition to schooling are profiled, the Head Start Family and Child Experiences Survey (FACES), and the National Head Start/Public School Early Childhood Transition Demonstration Study. Both focus specifically on children who have experienced early education intervention (Head Start), and follow them as they make the transition to formal schooling. One provides continued services to the children and their families in an attempt to maintain and enhance the effects of the early intervention and evaluates the effectiveness of these services. Both studies place children's educational experiences and outcomes in the context of their families, schools, and communities, and collect contextual information on all of these levels of influence.

HEAD START FAMILY AND CHILD EXPERIENCES SURVEY (FACES)

History

Demands for accountability in federally funded programs for disadvantaged children and families have grown, as is illustrated by the recent history of Head Start.[1] The Advisory Committee on Head Start Quality and Expansion recommended, and legislation mandated, the development of an extensive outcome-oriented evaluation of the Head Start program (Section 641A[b] of the Head Start Act [42 USC 9831 et seq.] as reauthorized in 1994, and the government Performance and Results Act [GPRA] [PL 103-62]).

The Head Start Program Performance Measures Initiative is the broad name given to the multiple activities that have been launched in order to respond to this mandate. As the name suggests, specific measures have been designed to assess the processes by which Head Start programs attempt to meet their goals, and their success in meeting them. Important activities that led to the design of the Head Start Program Performance Measures include the 1993 report of the Advisory Committee on Head Start Quality and Expansion, *Creating a 21st Century Head Start* (U.S. Department of Health and Human Services, 1993), and a consensus-building process which took place in 1995 between Head Start staff and parents, early childhood experts from many fields of research and practice, and Head Start Bureau representatives. This process resulted in a report outlining the original Head Start Program Performance Measures and available data sources (Administration on Children, Youth, and Families, 1995). The principal source of data used in this initiative is the Family and Child Experiences Survey (FACES), which is described in detail in this profile. FACES is conducted by a team of researchers from Westat, Inc., Abt Associates, Ellsworth Associates, the CDM Group, Inc., and the Administration on Children, Youth, and Families (ACYF). This longitudinal initiative focuses on 3- to 5-year-old children who were in Head Start in 1997.

Current Status

FACES began with a field test in which 3- to 5-year-old children were assessed at the end of the Head Start program year in spring 1997, and followed up in the spring of 1998 after either one more year of Head Start or one year of kindergarten. Results from the field test have been analyzed and disseminated by the ACYF (Zill et al., 1998).

The main FACES study was continued with a national sample of Head Start children who were 3 through 5 years of age when assessed in the fall of 1997. Follow-up data were collected in the springs of 1998, 1999, 2000, and 2001. A new national sample was launched in the fall of 2000. Results are disseminated as they become available.

Goals

Program goals. The Program Performance Measures Initiative was designed to assess the success of Head Start programs in achieving their goals for children and families. The overarching goal of Head Start, to promote the social competence of children, is conceptualized as being supported by the following five objectives:

- Enhance children's healthy growth and development
- Strengthen families as the primary nurturers of their children
- Provide children with educational, health, and nutritional services
- Link children and families to needed community services
- Ensure well-managed programs that involve parents in decision making

Together, these five objectives encompass outcomes for children (Objective 1) and families (Objective 2), as well as process goals for Head Start programs (Objectives 3 through 5). Head Start seeks to achieve these goals through the provision of services to members of two generations—parents and young children. Children receive direct services of the Head Start preschool, and families receive an array of family support services.

Each of the objectives listed above has been operationalized as a set of performance measures. For example, under Objective 1, Enhance Children's Growth and Development, one performance measure is "Head Start children demonstrate improved emergent literacy, numeracy, and language skills." This performance measure can then be assessed using specific indicators from evaluation data. For the above example, data are compiled from child assessments, parent interviews, and teacher ratings to assess the percent of change in Head Start children's emergent literacy, language skills, and numerical skills over time.

Evaluation goals. The Program Performance Measures Initiative undertakes the assessment of the objectives listed above to provide information that can be used by all levels of Head Start administrators, from the federal government to local programs. Goals of this evaluation include the following:

- Establish an ongoing system of data collection
- Develop a communication plan
- Institute a feedback loop for policy and resource decisions
- Promote uses of the data by local programs

The FACES project was established to begin to address these goals. In addition, longitudinal data from the FACES study are supplemented with information from the School Readiness Component of the 1993 National Household Education Survey (NHES), which allows for comparison of Head Start and low-income non–Head Start children. Existing Head Start data sources providing information are the Program Information Report (PIR), and the Head Start Monitoring Tracking System (HSMTS).

The FACES studies address four principal research questions:

- Does Head Start enhance children's development and school readiness?
- Does Head Start strengthen families as the primary nurturers of their children?
- Does Head Start provide children with high-quality educational, health, and nutritional services?
- How is classroom quality related to child outcomes?

Theory of Change

The Program Performance Measures Initiative has developed a conceptual framework that guides its activities, and specifies the expected links between the objectives listed above (see "Program goals"). For example, Head Start children's competence is conceived to be specific to their developmental stage—at age 5, it includes the concept of "school readiness," or the set of skills, knowledge, and behavior that will promote functioning in the new elementary school environment. School readiness, then, includes the domains of physical well-being and motor development, social and emotional development, approaches to learning, language usage and emerging literacy, and cognition and general knowledge (Goal One Technical Planning Group, 1991, 1993).

The interrelatedness of these developmental domains is considered in the conceptual framework, which is designed as a pyramid with children's social competence as the pinnacle (see Figure 4.1). Child and family outcomes (Objectives 1 and 2) represent the next tier on the pyramid—the outcomes Head Start is aiming to achieve. Thus, family outcomes, side by side with child development outcomes, are expected to affect children's social competence. Below these are the process objectives (3 through 5), representing the necessary program characteristics for achieving the desired child and family

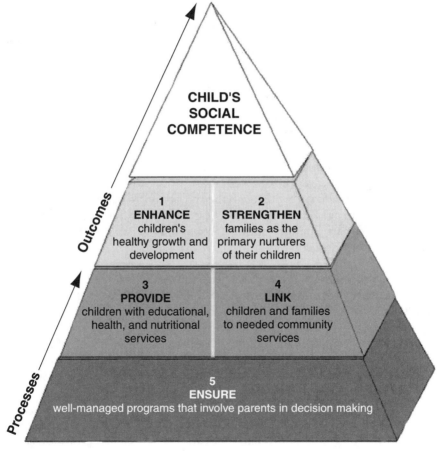

Figure 4.1. Head Start program performance measures: Conceptual framework.

outcomes. Provision of direct services to children is represented as adjacent to provision of links with community services, illustrating how these two sources of service may work together to support families. Finally, the base of the pyramid lists the objective of ensuring well-managed programs with parent involvement in decision making. A hallmark of the Head Start program is its commitment to parent involvement. Programs must both be well-run and include parent involvement in order to support successfully the objectives in the pyramid above.

Design and Methods

The primary FACES study is longitudinal, with a nationally representative sample of Head Start programs, classrooms, teachers, parents, and children. A field test collected data on 3- to 5-year-old Head Start children at the end of the Head Start year in spring 1997, again after one or two years of Head Start, and yet again in the spring of their kindergarten or first-grade years. Data sources include child assessments, parent interviews, teacher reports, and Head Start classroom observations. A new national cohort began in fall 2000, with a national probability sample of 2,400 children from 40 new Head Start programs representing the national population of Head Start families.

Sample children. Children in FACES were born in 1992 to 1994. In the main study, they ranged in age from 3 to 5 years at the first wave of data collection (fall 1997), and were followed across at least one year of Head Start and each subsequent spring through the end of their kindergarten year. Thus those who were age 3 in 1997 were assessed at the end of each of two years of Head Start participation (spring 1998 and 1999) and at the end of kindergarten in spring 2000.

Sampling procedures. The FACES field study included 2,400 children from 40 Head Start programs in spring 1997. The FACES main study included 3,200 children and families from the same 40 programs in fall 1997, and is nationally representative of the Head Start population. Three stratification characteristics were used in sampling Head Start sites: (a) region of the country in which the program was located (Northeast, Midwest, South, or West); (b) urban versus rural location; and (c) whether or not the program served a predominantly minority population.

Data collection. The FACES data collection includes direct child assessments of cognitive, physical, emotional, and social development. The assessment battery is comprised of both published, nationally normed scales and specially tailored questionnaires. Assessments, normally requiring 30–40 minutes per child, are conducted by specially trained assessors in a quiet space in the Head Start center. Parents are interviewed to provide data on the family, as well as on their satisfaction and experiences with Head Start, their ratings of their child's development, and their own economic and social self-sufficiency goals. Teacher interviews provide additional information on child development and classroom information. Classroom observations are conducted by trained observers to assess classroom environments and processes, as well as to assess the behavior of target children. Programs provide information via staff interviews and review of family records.

Characteristics of sample families. The families in the study represent the Head Start population. They include families headed by two parents, divorced or separated parents, and those who were never married. The individual who responded to the parent interview was the target child's primary caregiver— 94% were the parents of the Head Start child; 88% the child's biological mother. The sample is 37% African American, 28% white, and 24% Hispanic (also 2% American Indian and 1% Asian). Seventeen percent of parents were interviewed in a language other than English, with Spanish being the most prevalent non-English language spoken in the home. Most of the primary caregivers were in their twenties or thirties at the time of the interview, born in the United States, and living in a household of four or five people. Fifty-one percent were married; 21% separated, divorced, or widowed; and 36% had never been married. About 72% of the primary caregivers had completed high school or a GED High School Equivalency Diploma; 9% had completed an associate's or higher college degree. In spring 1998, 55% of the primary caregivers held full-time or part-time jobs. Most families received some form of financial or other outside support (e.g., Medicaid, food stamps, WIC, AFDC/TANF). Although most primary caregivers reported that their neighborhood was a good place to raise a child, almost one-third of the families had seen or heard violent crime in their neighborhoods. Seventeen percent of the children had been a witness to a crime or domestic violence.

Measures

Measures of child growth and development were conducted via direct child assessments, completion of standardized scales by parents and teachers, and direct observation of the classroom and children's social play by trained assessors. Child development measures included standardized cognitive tests assessing language, literacy, and numeracy, as well as an assessment developed by the FACES team that involved tapping practical knowledge such as the child's ability to say his or her name and birthday and understand emergent literacy concepts. Teachers provided ratings of the child's behavior and accomplishments, and parents reported on their activities with their child, experiences with Head Start, family characteristics, and child behavior.

Parents reported the ethnicity of their children, categorized as white, African American, Hispanic, American Indian, and Asian. Several indicators of poverty were assessed among this low-income sample. Parent's employment status, receipt of government assistance, and type of housing represent some of the more direct measures. Other indicators associated with family well-being were assessed, including parental educational attainment, families' experiences with violent crime in their neighborhoods (either as a witness or victim), domestic violence, and arrests or incarceration of family members.

Cultural relevance. The child assessments used in the study were chosen primarily for their widespread use in other studies of children and low-income populations to enable comparisons with previous large-scale studies. Specific attention to cultural relevance of the measures was less of a focus than the desire to measure skills that were currently expected of children in the schools they were entering following Head Start. However, classroom observation measures included scales of how well diversity of cultures, language, and family life were represented in classroom materials and activities. Parents reported on how well Head Start programs served non-English speaking children and families.

Children with disabilities. As Head Start is mandated to reserve a portion of its spaces for children with disabilities, the sample included children with a range of disabilities. Over 17% of the children in this sample had some kind of physical or emotional disability, including speech/language impairments, emotional or behavioral disorders, and chronic health impairments such as cerebral palsy, asthma, and seizures. Measurement of how well Head Start serves children with disabilities came from PIR and HSMTS data, as well as from classroom observations.

Measures of the environment, social service, and health care use. The home environment was assessed completely via parent interviews. No observational methods were used. However, several portions of the parent interview included indicators of the home environment, including parent-child activities, type of housing, and household composition. The quality of the Head Start environment is central to this study and was assessed via extensive classroom observation and the use of several widely used and validated observational measures.

Parents and staff reported whether children had an ongoing, continuous source of health care, and parents reported whether they themselves had such a source of health care. Parents reported whether they were covered by Medicare/Medicaid. Data from the PIR and HSMTS included the number and percent of Head Start children who received needed medical services. The linkage of families to needed social services is an important goal of Head Start programs. Parent interviews assessed the extent to which parents received needed social services such as child care, WIC, housing assistance, and GED classes. The PIR also provided the ratio of the total number of Head Start families to the number of family service workers.

Implications of the 1996 welfare bill. Many Head Start families were affected by the changes in welfare regulations that occurred in 1996. Among FACES Head Start parents, from fall 1997 to fall 1998, there was a 14% decline in the receipt of TANF. There was also a small (2%) increase in the number of primary caregivers who were employed, an increase reflecting primary caregivers entering full-time jobs.

Units of Analysis

Data were collected at multiple levels in this initiative: from individual children, families, classrooms, and Head Start programs. The sample was created to enable analyses at the individual, classroom, and program levels. Data were analyzed by several policy-relevant family characteristics, such as parent education level, household composition (family size and one- versus two-parent families), parent employment status, home language use, and household income.

Findings

Data from the 1997 field study and from the FACES main study have been analyzed. Extensive reports are available from the U.S. Department of Health and Human Services (Zill et al., 1998) or on-line (http://www.acf.dhhs.gov/programs/hsb). Findings addressed each of the four principal research questions and are summarized below.

Does Head Start enhance children's development and school readiness? Typical Head Start children demonstrated many important skills relevant to school readiness. For example, they were able to tell their full name and address, identify 10 basic colors by name, solve simple addition and subtraction problems, and answer simple factual questions about a story that was read to them. A majority also demonstrated many social skills required in kindergarten, such as following the teacher's directions, using free time in acceptable ways, and helping in putting work materials away. Some skills that a majority of Head Start children did *not* show at the end of the program year, however, were the ability to identify most letters of the alphabet, know that English text is read from left to right and top to bottom, and social skills such as accepting classmates' ideas for play or inviting others to join in activities very often.

Head Start children showed important gains on standardized tests during the program year. At program entry in the fall, 82% of the children had writing skills below the low-average to average range, and 75% had vocabulary skills below the low-average to average range. By the spring, the proportion of Head Start children approaching the national mean on the Peabody Picture Vocabulary Task (PPVT-III) increased from 25% to 34%, with a mean standard score of 88.8. The proportion of Head Start children approaching the national mean on the Woodcock Johnson—Revised (WJ-R) Dictation Writing Task increased from 18% to 31%, with a mean standard score of 88.1. Other studies that have focused on children from low-income families have found lower scores on the PPVT-R and similar tasks, ranging from 82 to 85 (e.g., Duncan et al., 1994; McKey et al., 1985; J. R. Smith, Brooks-Gunn, & Klebanov, 1997). Thus, these Head Start 4-year-olds are scoring at least ¼ of a standard deviation higher than might be expected.

Greater gains (at ½ to ⅔ of a standard deviation) were seen among English-speaking children who began Head Start with initially lower skills, and among all Spanish-speaking children. By the spring, Spanish-speaking children were able to perform some tasks, such as stating their name and address, equally well in English and Spanish.

Socially, over the course of the Head Start year, the percentage of time that the children spent "uninvolved" (not playing alone or with others) decreased and the percentage of time in play with peers increased. Head Start children also demonstrated gains in specific social skills such as teacher-rated peer competence and social problem solving. Greater gains were seen among children who began Head Start with initially lower social skills.

Finally, children who were assessed at the end of Head Start and at the end of kindergarten were shown to continue to make significant strides during kindergarten. For example, at the end of kindergarten, the PPVT scores of the Head Start graduates were almost 20 points higher than they had been one year prior, with a mean standard score of 93.5. Eighty-three percent of the Head Start graduates could identify most or all letters of the alphabet, and all could write their first names. Their mean standard score on the WJ-R Dictation Writing Task was 97.

Does Head Start strengthen families as the primary nurturers of their children?

Most parents reported being involved in many different Head Start activities, such as receiving home visits from Head Start staff, observing in their child's classroom, attending parent-teacher conferences, and volunteering in the classroom. Parent involvement in Head Start activities was related to parents' education, marital, and employment status. The four most common barriers to parent participation were work schedules, child care needs, transportation needs, and school or training schedules. Parents reported very high levels of satisfaction with Head Start services and rated their own and their child's experiences in Head Start very highly. Forty-one percent of the parents reported that Head Start had taught them a new way to discipline their child, and there was a significant decline in the use of spanking. Parents reported gains in their own accomplishments during the Head Start year including a 9% increase in the number of primary caregivers who obtained a license, certificate, or degree, and a significant increase in parents' self-reported sense of control over their lives.

Does Head Start provide children with high-quality educational, health, and nutritional services?

Head Start class size averaged 14 children with 5 to 6 children per adult, numbers which are better than those mandated by Head Start monitoring standards and NAEYC accreditation standards. Overall, Head Start classrooms fell in the "good" range, with an average score of 4.9 out of 7 points on the Early Childhood Environment Rating Scale (ECERS; scores on this scale are classified as follows: 1 = inadequate; 3 = minimal; 5 = good; and 7 = excellent). No classrooms received an overall score of 1 or 2 (indicating "inadequate" learning environments), and 19% of the classrooms received an "excellent" (or near-excellent) score of 6 or 7. These ratings were slightly higher than those found for a sample of 183 child care center classrooms in the Cost, Quality, and Child Outcomes Study, which averaged 4.3 on the ECERS, with 11% scoring an "inadequate" 1 or 2 (CQO Study Team, 1999). The FACES study also found that lead Head Start teachers had good teaching qualifications, 68% having some college experience or a college degree. Classroom quality was found to be consistent over 2 years and to increase slightly over the Head Start academic year.

Average ECERS scores in the FACES study have been compared with ECERS ratings in several other studies that have assessed the quality of Head Start and other preschool classrooms in school-based, nonprofit, and for-profit centers (CQO Outcomes Study Team, 1995; Layzer, Goodson, & Moss, 1993; Scarr, Eisenberg, & Deater-Deckard, 1994; Whitebook, Howes,

& Phillips, 1989). This sample of Head Start classrooms was of equivalent or higher quality than the classrooms in those studies (see Figure 4.2 for a comparison).

How is classroom quality related to child outcomes? Classroom quality was related to children's vocabulary scores and social behavior in the classroom. Classrooms that received higher scores on language learning opportunities and classrooms that had lower adult-child ratios had children with higher vocabulary scores. In addition, children in Head Start classrooms that were rated higher in learning environment materials spent more time in play and less time "uninvolved." Classroom quality was also related to home activities. In centers where teachers received more training in child development and engaged children in academic activities more often, there were greater increases in parents' reports of educational and recreational activities at home.

Limitations

The main strengths of the FACES study are that it provides longitudinal data on a large sample of Head Start children from many sites as they proceed through Head Start into school, and that it collects program process data as well as outcome data. However, it does not include a comparison group of children who are not attending Head Start, so its generalizability is limited to the populations of Head Start children and Head Start classrooms. Find-

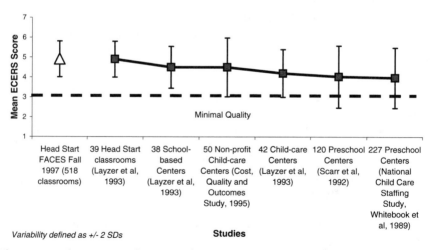

Figure 4.2. Classroom quality in Head Start versus other preschool centers. Reprinted from Zill et al., 1998.

ings may not be generalized to preschoolers nationally, nor to the population of low-income preschoolers. Use of other nationally representative studies of low-income children provides some remedy to this problem, but does not substitute for randomly assigned control groups.

Public Use Files

Data are not yet available for public use, but may become available. Updated information is available on-line (http://www2.acf.dhhs.gov/programs/hsb/ hsreac/faces/ index.html).

NATIONAL HEAD START/PUBLIC SCHOOL EARLY CHILDHOOD TRANSITION DEMONSTRATION STUDY

History

Research on the diminution of effects of early childhood intervention over time (e.g., Barnett, 1995; Brooks-Gunn, 1995b; Lee, Loeb, & Lubeck, 1998) has resulted in recommendations from researchers and educators that support services for disadvantaged children and families be extended beyond the preschool years.[2] The Head Start Transition Project Act, passed in Congress in 1991, authorized funding for a demonstration project to extend the types of services and supports provided by Head Start programs through the first 4 years of elementary school. Thus, the National Head Start/Public School Early Childhood Transition Demonstration Project was created. This intervention program is a multiyear program with two cohorts of participants, conducted at 31 local sites in 30 states and the Navajo Nation.

The 1991 legislation for the demonstration project required two forms of evaluation: Each of the 31 project sites was to conduct individual evaluations of program impacts on children, families, schools, and communities, as well as participate in the National Transition Demonstration Study. The national evaluation is a standard, cross-site evaluation of program implementation and impacts. The 1994 Head Start Reauthorization Act provided for the continuation of this demonstration project and its evaluation, conducted at the University of Alabama at Birmingham.

Current Status

The demonstration project enrolled two cohorts of participants—a group of former Head Start children who entered kindergarten in the fall of 1992 and their families, and a group of former Head Start children who entered kindergarten in the fall of 1993 and their families. The program provides for transition services from kindergarten through third grade; thus the second cohort of participants finished their final year of participation in the 1996–97 school year.

Data collection occurred during each year of participation. The final wave of data for Cohort 2 was completed in spring of 1997. Analysis of early data has been conducted to answer questions about program implementation, family characteristics, and early adjustment to school (using kindergarten data). These findings have been reported in an interim report (Head Start Bureau, 1996). Ongoing data analyses assess longer term program implementation and impacts.

Goals

Program goals. The Head Start Transition program was designed to provide ongoing services to children and families who formerly participated in Head Start programs, as the children entered kindergarten. The demonstration was a 4-year project, extending through the child's 3rd-grade year. Each local Head Start Transition Project was expected to include a comprehensive set of components to support children and families, including the following: programs to increase parent involvement in school activities; establishment of local governing boards of parents, school, and community representatives; facilitation of positive family-school interactions; individualized family needs assessments and family support plans; mental and physical health services; developmentally appropriate classroom services; partnerships between Head Start programs and public schools; individual child transition plans; inclusion activities for children with disabilities; and activities to promote cultural relevance and recognition of school and community diversity. Three major activities were expected of each local program:

- To develop successful strategies in which Head Start programs, parents, local education agencies (LEAs), and other community agencies would join together to plan and implement a coordinated and continuous program of comprehensive services for low-income children and their families, beginning in Head Start and continuing through the first four grades of public school
- To develop effective strategies to support the active involvement of parents in the education of their children
- To test the hypothesis that the provision of continuous, comprehensive services would maintain and enhance the early benefits attained by Head Start children and their families (Head Start Bureau, 1996)

Each demonstration project represented a partnership among three local groups: Head Start programs, public schools, and universities or other non-profit research organizations. This partnership ensured that ongoing research would be built into the program activities.

Evaluation goals. The first step in creating the Head Start Transition programs and designing their evaluation was establishing a definition of successful transitions that could be applied to programs and participating families. The National Transition Demonstration Consortium, an interdisciplinary group of researchers and local program administrators and agency representatives, agreed upon the following set of defining features of successful transitions:

- Children have positive attitudes toward school, and are motivated to do well in school.
- Children maintain and enhance their physical, social, emotional, and intellectual development (such as showing good health, progress in the acquisition of new academic and social skills, and an eagerness to learn in many areas).
- Parents and other key adults in young children's lives display positive attitudes toward their children's school program and are active partners (along with school personnel) in promoting children's learning.
- Teachers and principals recognize individual differences in children's academic and social-emotional maturity, positively value cultural and linguistic diversity, and provide developmentally appropriate experiences within the class and school setting.
- Positive and mutually supportive relationships occur among families, school personnel, social and health service providers, and communities concerning the well-being and education of young children. (Head Start Bureau, 1996)

The main goals of the National Transition Demonstration Study were to evaluate the processes that projects used in implementation, and to assess the outcomes for children, families, schools, and communities. The primary research questions guiding the evaluation were as follows:

- How has the National Head Start/Public School Early Childhood Transition Demonstration Project been implemented?
- To what extent have comprehensive, continuous Head Start–like services been provided to participating children and families?
- What have been the barriers and difficulties encountered in implementing the transition demonstration programs?

- What characteristics of local sites are associated with more (or less) successful implementation of the transition demonstration programs?
- As a result of the National Head Start/Public School Early Childhood Transition Demonstration programs, what institutional and systemic changes are evident at local sites?
- To what extent do families participating in transition demonstration programs show expected positive outcomes?
- To what extent do children in transition demonstration programs show expected positive outcomes?
- Are there some identifiable families and children who appear to benefit more from participating in the transition demonstration programs than do others? If so, what are the likely mediating processes?
- Which families and children appear more likely to have poor transition experiences during the transition years?

Theory of Change

The conceptual framework for the Head Start Transition program was based on the importance of multiple functional domains of influence on child adaptation and development. The framework draws on social ecology, systems theory, and research on early intervention, and is described in detail elsewhere (Head Start Bureau, 1996; S. L. Ramey & Ramey, 1992). The primary reasoning behind the Head Start Transition program is that a successful transition to school involves both children and parents, and is determined by many factors in addition to cognitive abilities, including family resources and characteristics, school and classroom culture and environment, families' access to social and health services, and community-level supports for children and parents.

As described above, successful transitions to school influence not only children, but families, schools, and communities as well. Positive child outcomes are considered to be embedded within family contexts. In addition, positive outcomes are related to eight identified domains of functioning: family survival resources; health and nutrition; safety and security; self-concept; educational values and motivation; social support for the school transition; communication skills; and basic academic, social, and work skills. Initial status in these domains, and the extent to which these domains were affected by the intervention were expected to affect program impacts.

The conceptual model hypothesized inputs from child characteristics, family characteristics, and community supports and services feeding into transactional processes (including the receipt of comprehensive Head Start–like services through the first years of elementary school). These processes in turn affect children's successful transitions and have an impact on child and family development, as well as change in schools and communities.

Design and Methods

The evaluation was a multisite, longitudinal trial randomized by site, designed to answer the research questions described above. Two independent cohorts of families were enrolled in the study, with no restrictions on the types of former Head Start families who could participate. The demonstration program provided transition supports and services to all children in the classroom, regardless of whether or not they were formerly in Head Start. The subset of children receiving services who were enrolled previously in Head Start and whose parents consented to participate in the study comprised the treatment sample. For each cohort there was also a comparison group of families and children not receiving Head Start transition services. Cohort 1 included 2,198 demonstration families and 1,900 comparison families. Cohort 2 included 2,233 demonstration families and 2,070 comparison families.

The design of the evaluation allowed for estimation of program effects through comparisons between treatment and comparison group children, as well as longitudinal comparisons within groups.

Sample children. Sample children entered kindergarten in 1992 and 1993, so their years of birth were approximately 1986–1988. Data were collected in the fall and spring of kindergarten, and in the spring of first, second, and third grades.

Sampling procedures. The evaluation was a randomized trial conducted at each site. Randomization was achieved on a project level: In each local site, two clusters of Head Start/elementary school units were identified that served comparable types and numbers of children and families; one of these was randomly assigned to receive the demonstration treatment and the other became the comparison group receiving typical services. Schools in the comparison group were *not* prohibited from implementing new initiatives or strengthening supports for the children and families they served.

At the intervention sites, sample children included former Head Start service recipients who subsequently received the special transition support services provided by the project. Comparison group children were former Head Start children who attended the comparison schools. Inclusion in the study, therefore, was based primarily on inclusion criteria for the Head Start program and attendance at a school that was selected for the study. At the time of their Head Start participation, the children came from families with incomes below the poverty line.

Data collection sites. The demonstration project included 31 local sites that were involved in the national evaluation. Local sites recruited samples that ranged from 70 to 624 families. The number of families involved in the demonstration group within the research sample was smaller than the number of families receiving transition services at each site because the research sample included only former Head Start children (although all children in the classroom received the transition services); some eligible families declined to participate in the research; and the size of the local program differed considerably so that it was not always feasible to enroll all former Head Start children in the national study.

Procedures. Multiple data-collection procedures were employed to measure program implementation and effects on children, families, schools, and communities. These included interviews with family members by specially trained community members; direct child assessments by trained child examiners; teacher ratings of children, classrooms, and school environment; principal reports on school climate and transition services; classroom observations; local site visits by a multidisciplinary team to assess implementation, challenges, and accomplishments; record-data collection (child school records and program documentation); and collection of community-level data from public sources.

Characteristics of sample families. All types of family structures that occur among Head Start families were eligible to participate in the study. The most common structure for these families was children living with their mother but not father (50% of the sample, although 40% of these families include some other adult living in the household); 40% lived with both mother and father. A small percentage of families were headed by grandparents, single fathers, foster parents, or other relatives.

The total sample included over 8,400 former Head Start children and families. About 40% of these former Head Start families received AFDC, and 13% received Supplementary Security Income (SSI). Almost 20% of these families reported annual incomes above $18,000, and almost half of the primary caregivers were employed, with about one-third employed full-time (Head Start Bureau, 1996).

Primary language spoken was not a factor in study eligibility. However, the vast majority of families in the study spoke primarily English at home (87%); Spanish was the primary language for 7% of the families. Despite the prevalence of English and Spanish, some sites had great linguistic diversity, serving over 20 different linguistic groups within a single school district. In terms of service delivery, an attempt was made to meet the linguistic needs of the family by providing a family service coordinator who could use a case management and referral approach to connect families to appropriate community services. Many staff members were recruited because of their bilingual capabilities. Generally, sites recruited staff who reflected the cultural diversity of participants.

Program implementation and process variables. The main research question of the National Transition Demonstration Study was how transition support services affected children's adaptation to schooling; additionally, while children in demonstration schools received special services expected to have an impact on their success, comparison schools were not prohibited from instituting their own forms of educational reform. Therefore, the actual experiences of children in their schools were measured in order to determine the effects of developmentally appropriate curricula and comprehensive support services, and whether these were provided by demonstration or comparison schools. In order to consider the effects of program implementation and processes, data were collected on school and classroom context from parents, teachers, principals, and direct classroom observations.

Measures

Data were collected from children, parents, teachers, school administrators, and through classroom observations. Measures included a large number of previously published and validated scales, as well as scales that were specifically developed for the transition study. Child outcomes assessed directly included standardized tests of vocabulary, reading, and mathematics achievement, as well as school motivation and self-concept. Parents and teachers provided reports on children's social skills, problem behaviors, and health. Parents reported on family background and demographic characteristics, depression, family resources, routines, and activities. Extensive data on school context and climate were collected via classroom observation, interviews with teachers and principals, and review of school records.

The study sample was, by definition, a poverty or recent-poverty sample, since all children were eligible for Head Start services in the preschool years. Information on family economic situations was obtained from parents, who described their employment status, income, and public assistance sources.

Cultural relevance. The measures chosen and designed for the national study were chosen in part because the National Transition Demonstration Consortium deemed them to be culturally appropriate for use with the diverse

Head Start population. For the great majority of participants, instruments and interviewers were available to conduct the interview in the respondent's native language. Standardized translations of the interview were available in Spanish, Hmong, and Vietnamese; for other native languages, interpreters were used. Child assessments used English and Spanish versions of the PPVT-R.

Children with disabilities. The progress of children with disabilities was followed in this study. Interviewers were trained to be conscious of children's special needs, and indicated on the interview form whether the child used a speech or hearing device.

Home and child care environment. Home environment was assessed via extensive parent interview (including family involvement, family resources, and family routines). No home observations were conducted. While the child care environment outside of schooling was not a focus of this study, elementary school and classroom environments that children experienced were essential to the investigation. Therefore, the school environment was assessed through parent interviews, teacher and principal reports, and direct school observations.

Role of fathers. In the design of the Head Start Transition program, fathers were encouraged to participate as much as possible, such as by being part of the governing board which requires 51% parent representation. Some individual sites developed their own father involvement projects. In the National Transition Demonstration Study, fathers were similarly encouraged to participate in the family interview, though it was up to the family to determine who would respond to the interview. In most cases, the child's mother was the respondent (87%). The family interview included measures of whether the father lives in the child's home, and whether he is active in the child's life or responsible for child care on a regular basis.

Health care. The evaluation assessed families' satisfaction with their health care, their source of health insurance (Medicaid, employer, individual, and none), the consistency of care (extent to which care is provided by the same health care provider), and health of both the child and the primary caregiver.

Social services. The extent to which family service coordinators linked families to appropriate social service agencies was an important measure of transition program processes. Individual site evaluations tracked information such as the caseloads of family service coordinators, the integration of the coordinators within the schools, and the types of support provided (e.g., assistance finding safe housing; referrals to employment assistance agencies, clothing and food banks, and legal assistance; and direct services, such as tutoring, counseling, and parent education).

Units of Analysis

The evaluation study measured multiple levels of influence. Data were collected on individual children, their caregivers and family environments, classroom and school contexts, and community settings. The basic research questions were designed to explore how these different levels of influence are related to the provision of transition services and children's subsequent transition outcomes. Data will be analyzed according to each research question.

Because programs conducted at different sites vary in the ways the transition services were provided, site-level analyses will be an important component of implementation and outcome analysis. In addition, subgroup analyses will be performed with attention to ethnic groups and children with disabilities, in particular.

Findings

Data from the first years of the National Head Start/Public School Early Childhood Transition Demonstration Project have been analyzed, and an interim report details the findings from some of the kindergarten data (Head Start Bureau, 1996). In particular, the interim report details some of the findings describing program implementation and characteristics of the children in the sample. A brief sample of these findings is reported below.

Program implementation. Annual site visits from the first 2 years of the demonstration project provided information on the diversity of programs. In general, most local projects were found to be meeting the following goals:

- Developing programs that adhere to a common framework while still reflecting the unique condition of individual communities
- Implementing activities that simultaneously address the needs of children, families, schools, Head Start programs, and local community service providers
- Meeting the needs of families and children (such as health, social services, housing, parenting education, literacy, substance abuse, transportation) by coordinating local services, educating parents about how to access services and be advocates for themselves and their children, and participating in local planning efforts for service delivery and reform
- Creating meaningful continuities in the child's everyday schooling experiences, for example, by encouraging teachers at different grades to

communicate about individual children and to better coordinate their classroom practices so that children's learning can be continuous
- Seeking ways to ensure that the effective components of the transition demonstration programs can be replicated in other schools and communities and that their own communities find ways to sustain ("institutionalize") these programs (Head Start Bureau, 1996)

Furthermore, the most successful programs were found at sites that provided supports for the teachers and principals as well as the children and families they served. Successful program sites seemed to be those that used creative problem-solving and program-design approaches, created support services that were individually tailored to the needs of participants, and created local governing boards that were involved in all aspects of program implementation.

Health and development of sample children and families. Health care was generally consistent and reliable for 80% of the families. Just over half the families were covered by Medicaid, and 20% had employer-provided health coverage. A very small percentage of primary caregivers reported having a major health condition affecting their ability to care for their child, but a large proportion (about 50%) reported experiencing depression for 2 or more weeks in the past year. In general, the health of the children was good, with about 7% having a major health condition that placed limitations on their activities. Approximately 10% of the former Head Start children were enrolled in special education programs during kindergarten.

Parents reported high expectations for their children as they entered kindergarten, with almost half of the parents anticipating that their children would not experience problems during the kindergarten year. About 20% of the parents were concerned that their children might experience social problems during the transition, and just over 10% worried about their children's academic or behavioral readiness for school. Most families reported strategies they used to help their children adjust to kindergarten, such as showing interest in school and learning at home, establishing routines, helping with homework, talking about expectations and the value of education, providing support in developing their children's social and behavioral skills, and working to create linkages between the home and school. Approximately 50% of the parents reported being in contact with their child's teacher once a week and 85% had contact with the teacher at least once a month.

Both parents and children reported that the children were adjusting well to kindergarten. Parents believed their children enjoyed school and put great effort into doing well at school. Children reported liking school, getting along with peers and teachers, and being motivated to do well in school.

The data analyses released to date provide the baseline measures for children and families as the children enter kindergarten, and descriptive information on early program implementation and early transition experiences. Further data analyses addressing the primary research questions regarding how the transition services and supports received by children and families affected their transition experiences have been conducted, but not yet released by ACYF.

Limitations

The National Transition Demonstration Study is a study of former Head Start children and their families. The study obtained a rich array of data on children's family, school, and community settings, measuring their progress longitudinally, and providing a comprehensive set of services to these families and recording their impact. However, the implications of the findings will be limited to children whose families were below the poverty level when the children were of preschool age, and who participated in Head Start before school entry. A complementary study is being conducted of non–Head Start children at 19 of the local sites that will enable comparison of Head Start and non–Head Start children in their responses to the transition intervention. This complementary sample is relatively similar demographically to the Head Start sample (they attend the same elementary schools), but is not nationally representative of kindergarten children.

The evaluation component of the national study has as its primary focus the comparison of children from demonstration schools with those from comparison schools. However, the investigators acknowledge that not only is it possible that comparison schools may institute similar services (in fact there is an expected community-level "spillover effect" of the demonstration program), but wide variation exists in levels of program implementation across demonstration sites. Therefore, additional analyses will be required that take into account the actual experiences of children at each school, whether a demonstration or comparison school.

Public Use Files

At the end of the contract period, all data files will be turned over to ACYF, at which time they will be made available for public access.

NOTES

We would like to thank Robin Gaines Lanzi for providing helpful information on the Head Start Transition program. We are also grateful for the support of the

MacArthur Network on the Family and the Economy, and the Administration on Children, Youth, and Families and National Institute for Mental Health Research Consortium on Mental Health in Head Start. Christina Borbely provided helpful editorial assistance.

1. Principal investigators of Head Start FACES are Nicholas Zill (Westat, Inc.) and David Connell (Abt Associates). The project is funded by the Administration on Children, Youth, and Families (ACYF). For more information regarding this initiative, see http://www.acf.dhhs.gov/programs/hsb on-line.

2. The principal investigators of the study are Sharon Landsman Ramey and Craig T. Ramey (Civitan International Research Center, University of Alabama at Birmingham). The project is funded by the Administration on Children, Youth, and Families (ACYF). For more information regarding this initiative, see http://www.circ.uab.edu on-line.

CHAPTER 5

Family Support Initiatives

ALLISON SIDLE FULIGNI AND JEANNE BROOKS-GUNN

The term *family support* has been used to describe an approach in service provision that conceptualizes the whole family as a system that can benefit from multiple types of support. Thus, rather than designing programs to serve a single member of a family (the mother or the preschool child, for instance), family support programs strive to meet the needs of children and parents by offering a number of diverse services. A traditional family support program includes a child component (often some form of early childhood education), an adult education component, and a parenting education component based on the belief that family outcomes can be affected by improving the nature of parent-child interactions within the family.

Family support approaches have evolved out of the understanding that the social support networks that families often relied upon in past generations are no longer as extensive and available to families today. The changing economic structure of our country has affected family life in many ways: Families are often headed by two working parents or a single working parent; job relocations mean that families move away from extended family and familiar neighborhoods; joblessness and other hardships are associated with greater numbers of families with children living in poverty, being troubled by addiction, and living in communities plagued with crime, deteriorating housing, and other stressors. Even families who do not live in extreme poverty conditions may benefit from family support—all parents need advice on parenting issues, contact with other adults who are in similar situations, and assistance in locating the services they and their families require. The philosophy guiding family support programs recognizes that individual families have unique sets of strengths that can be built upon by providing appropriate supportive services, and that there are many stresses in daily life that can hinder optimal family functioning.

Traditionally, family support programs were community-based efforts designed to offer a broad array of support and information that could be accessed on a voluntary basis by all families in the community. This model is called the "universal access" model, because the programs are designed for all families, not targeting a special population. However, because of the growing crisis among certain groups of families, family support programs have emerged that are specifically designed for families that are considered to be "at risk" for one reason or another. The populations that have been the focus of such specialized efforts include families who are environmentally at risk because of low income or low education of the parents, or families with children who are biologically at risk due to conditions such as premature birth, low birth weight, or developmental disability (Barnes, Goodson, & Layzer, 1995).

Because of their definition as grassroots, preventive efforts to serve the individual needs of families, family support programs are actually quite variable in the design of their programs and the services they provide. What these programs have in common is the goal to serve the family as a system: to serve multiple members of the family with appropriate educational services, to help empower family members to achieve their personal goals by giving them relevant skills and strategies, to bring families together to share common problems and solutions, and to provide links to other social services available in the community as needed. Programs go about these goals in many different ways, some offering home-visiting services, while others are primarily center based. All programs seek to improve the lives of children and families by improving parents' education and resources, parents' understanding of child development and parenting skills, and the resources available to children in the home, as well as improving the care and education they receive outside the home.

The term *family support program* is descriptive of the philosophy of the programs rather than the mode of service delivery. Family support programs may utilize many of the design features of some of the other initiatives profiled in this volume. For instance, many family support programs serving families with infants use a home-visiting approach. What they have in common is a focus on improving child outcomes by serving the family through multiple services. Services may focus on the mother or family, seeking to influence child outcomes indirectly. In addition, some programs such as the federal Even Start family literacy program, also include direct early childhood services.

In this chapter, two research efforts related to family support are profiled in depth. The first is the National Even Start Evaluation, an evaluation study of the federal Even Start family literacy program. This is an evaluation of a national demonstration program designed to improve the literacy outcomes of families using a family support model targeted at low-income families. Begun in 1990, this is one of the earliest of the initiatives reviewed here. The second detailed profile describes the National Evaluation of Family Support Programs (NEFSP). This initiative was begun in 1994, and is an ongoing evaluation of a number of different family support programs seeking to provide a broad understanding of the effects of and approaches to providing family support. These and other evaluations of family support programs serve to broaden understanding about how this model of service provision affects the families who are served. This type of research is especially challenging to conduct because of the multiple domains in which effects are expected (e.g., child cognitive and socioemotional functioning; parent educational attainment, employment, and literacy practices; parenting styles and expectations; and home environments), and the studies presented below represent noteworthy approaches to assessing these effects.

NATIONAL EVEN START EVALUATION

History

The concept of "family literacy" programs emerged in the late 1970s and early 1980s, bringing together previous learning from intervention and early literacy programs. The family literacy approach sought to combine early childhood education, adult education, and parenting education in an attempt to bring literacy skills to the entire family. Even Start is the federal family literacy program instituted in 1989.[1]

In 1988, Congress amended the 1965 Elementary and Secondary Education Act with the Hawkins-Stafford Elementary and Secondary Improvement Amendments, and in 1991 with the National Literacy Act. This Act calls for the integration of early childhood and adult education into a unified program utilizing existing community resources and creating new services.

Even Start was created as a demonstration program to carry out the new family literacy legislation. The original demonstration program was implemented in 1989 at 76 sites utilizing $14.5 million in demonstration grant funds. The program grew to 340 projects, with $70 million in federal funds, when it became a state-run program in 1992. By the 1994–95 program year, there were 513 local projects, serving approximately 31,000 families. In 1999–2000, Even Start provided $135 million to more than 800 projects. Proposed legislation would almost double this amount.

Current Status

The first national evaluation of Even Start was conducted independently by Abt Associates and RMC Research Corporation. The contract for the evaluation was awarded in 1990 by the Office of Policy and Planning in the U.S. Department of Education. The evaluation described characteristics of the Even Start projects that were first funded in the years 1989, 1990, 1991, and 1992, and provided impact data from the 120 projects funded in the first 2 years (1989 and 1990). This evaluation has been completed, and the final report was delivered to Congress (St. Pierre, Swartz, et al., 1995).

Evaluation for the subsequent 4-year period (1993–1996) was conducted by Fu Associates, with a subcontract to Abt Associates. Interim (Tao, Swartz, St. Pierre, & Tarr, 1997) and final reports (Tao, Gamse, & Tarr, 1998) are available from the Department of Education. The Department of Education has funded a third national evaluation (to Abt Associates with a subcontract to Fu Associates). An interim report from that evaluation was released in 2000 (St. Pierre, Ricciuti, et al., 2000). A summary of Even Start research and policy issues was prepared and is available from the Department of Education (St. Pierre, Gamse, Alamprese, Rimdzius, & Tao, 1998).

Goals

Program goals. Even Start programs focus on the entire family, rather than just the child or just the parent. Thus the following three goals guide the program:

1. To help parents become full partners in the education of their children
2. To assist children in reaching their full potential as learners
3. To provide literacy training for parents

Following from these general goals are a number of positive outcomes for parents and children that are expected to result from Even Start participation. It is hoped that parents will increase their literacy behaviors through sharing literacy events with their children, increasing the number of literacy resources in their home, and increasing their use of literacy materials. Parenting education is expected to promote positive parent-child relationships, help parents create a home environment that will foster child development, and encourage parents to hold positive expectations for their children and provide adequate supervision. The adult education component of Even Start is also designed to improve outcomes specific to the adults: to increase their basic skills and English language ability, enable their higher educational attainment, and improve job skills and employment status, as well as increasing parents' self-esteem, self-efficacy, and personal well-being. It is also hoped that participation in Even Start will increase parents' involvement in schools and access to social services.

The early childhood and adult components of Even Start are also expected to improve child outcomes. Possible positive outcomes for children are school readiness (age-appropriate cognitive, language, and social skills), better performance in school, improved school attendance, and lower incidence of special education, remedial placement, and retention in grade.

The program is based upon the basic notion that appropriate services provided to parents and their young children can improve both parents' education and parenting and children's school readiness and achievement. Even Start programs are allowed great flexibility in designing projects and activities to achieve their goals. Programs are encouraged to use existing services as well as to provide their own direct services. For this reason, individual Even Start programs vary widely in the ways they provide services to participating families. However, all programs are designed to provide each of the following core services:

- *Early childhood education.* Services to enhance development and school readiness for children from birth to 8 years of age
- *Adult education.* Basic educational and literacy instruction for the adult, including adult basic education, adult secondary education, English as a Second Language (ESL) instruction, or preparation to attain a General Education Development (GED) certificate
- *Parent education.* Services to help parents understand and support their child's growth and development and to enhance parent-child relationships

Families are eligible for Even Start if they have an adult who is eligible for adult basic education programs, a child less than 8 years of age, and live in a Chapter 1 elementary school attendance area. Participating families are expected to utilize all three core services.

Evaluation goals. The first national evaluation of the Even Start program was conducted by Abt Associates. The evaluation was designed to address the following questions:

- What are the characteristics of Even Start participants?
- How are Even Start projects implemented and what services do they provide?

- What Even Start services are received by participating families?
- What are the effects of Even Start projects on the participants?

The second evaluation, by Fu Associates, addressed similar questions, but with a less-rigorous methodology for assessing program effects (see below, "Design and Methods"). The primary research questions for the second evaluation were:

- Who is served by the program, and what services do they receive? Is the program reaching the appropriate target population?
- How is federal funding spent on the program? How many of the projects are well implemented?
- How well does the Even Start basic model work? Do participants perform better on key measures than similar persons who do not participate?
- What are effective practices and programs?

The third national evaluation, funded in the fall of 1997, updated the national reporting system, which was renamed the Even Start Performance Information Reporting System (ESPIRS). Improvements to the reporting system included the addition of a new section asking parents to report the types of literacy-related activities and behaviors in which they and their children engage as well as the kinds of literacy-related tasks that their children can perform; a more detailed set of forms for collecting data on the amount of time that families participate in Even Start; and an updated project profile system that was developed in the second national evaluation.

A second component of the third evaluation, the Experimental Design Study (EDS), was included to provide an assessment of program impacts in 20 projects. The EDS used a research design in which families that wanted to take part in Even Start were randomly assigned to begin the program right away (intervention group) or to wait for one year (delayed intervention or control group).

Theory of Change

The Even Start program is designed to affect both parents and children, as described above. These expected outcomes are part of a general conceptual model proposing that program processes are influenced by several contextual variables, including population demographics, family resources and support, the community context (affecting the self-esteem, depression, self-efficacy and aspirations of its members), and the service context (including the availability of early childhood education services, adult basic education,

ESL instruction, and an appropriate site location). According to the Even Start conceptual model, these context variables influence the program processes directly as well as indirectly, through their effects on the availability of Even Start and local funding, the formal and informal guidance received by the programs, and the experience and training of Even Start staff. Program processes, such as design characteristics, services available, service delivery mechanisms, and actual services received, are in turn expected to influence parent and child outcomes. Thus the overall conceptual model proposes that the population, community, and service contexts affect inputs to program processes as well as the creation of program processes directly, and that the processes of each Even Start program directly affect parent and child outcomes and indirectly affect child outcomes through their effects on parents (see Figure 5.1).

Design and Methods

The first national evaluation of the Even Start program was designed to answer the research questions stated above through four different evaluation components:

- National Evaluation Information System (NEIS)
- In-Depth Study
- Individual Even Start project evaluations
- Recognition in the National Diffusion Network (NDN)

First, all Even Start projects participated in an annual survey called the National Evaluation Information System. The first 4 years (1989–1992) of program implementation were evaluated with the NEIS. This system provided annual data to answer research questions about who participated in Even Start programs, the services received, and child and adult literacy outcomes. Baseline data were collected on each family participating in Even Start, and outcome data were collected at the end of each program year for families who remained in the program ($Ns = 2,461$ for year 1, 6,726 for year 2, 9,701 for year 3, and 16,255 for year 4). This component of the study provides longitudinal data comparing baseline measures with short-term follow-up measures.

The second major component of the evaluation was the In-Depth Study. This component provided more detailed information about a subset of ten Even Start projects. The ten sites used for the In-Depth Study were selected based on certain criteria including location, willingness to participate, and having a fully operational program. Five of the evaluation sites randomly assigned families to participate in Even Start or to be members of a control

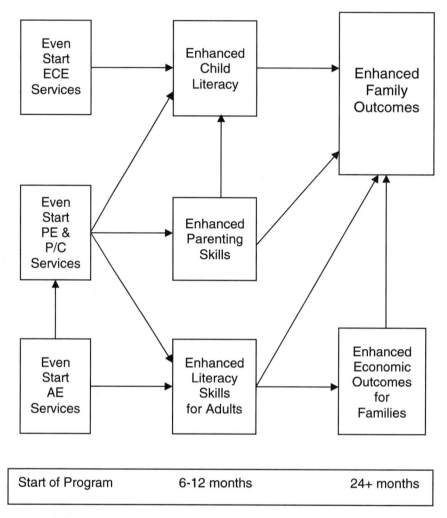

Figure 5.1. Even Start conceptual model. "ECE" indicates early childhood education. "PE" indicates parenting education. "P/C" indicates parent/child. "AE" indicates adult education. Reprinted from St. Pierre, Ricciuti, et al., 2000.

group; in the other five sites where random assignment was not feasible, no control group existed. These sites provided descriptive and cost data only. The In-Depth Study sample included about 200 Even Start families and 100 control group families, each with children 3 or 4 years old. Baseline measures of the outcomes of interest were taken on program and control group families prior to entry into the program, when the average age of the children was 4 years. Outcome data were then collected after 9 months and again 18 months after entry. These assessments were made on each control group and program family, regardless of whether an Even Start family dropped out of the program or a control group family began to receive similar services from another source. This component of the evaluation was designed to enable estimation of the effectiveness of the program based on comparisons of Even Start families with similar families not receiving Even Start services.

Two other types of evaluation activities took place, both involving individual sites. First, individual Even Start projects were free to conduct their own local evaluations with approval from the Department of Education. Second, individual sites could apply for recognition as a program worthy of emulation in the National Diffusion Network, resulting in eligibility for additional dissemination funds. In these local evaluation activities, individual sites could compare their within-project gains to control families and to national norms in order to determine exemplary project models.

The second national evaluation, conducted by Fu Associates, resembles a continuation of the NEIS component, without the In-Depth Study component. This evaluation comprised two parts: the Universe Study, which provided annual data from all programs on implementation and participants, and the Sample Study, a subsample of 57 projects providing outcome data. Outcome effects were based on pretest-posttest comparisons. Thus the second evaluation measured program implementation and effects, but without including a comparison sample. The third evaluation is ongoing. The interim report is soon to be released, but it does not focus on the experimental portion of that evaluation. For the sake of clarity, and because it is the only evaluation with program impact results from a controlled study, the remainder of this profile describes the methods and findings from the first (Abt) evaluation only.

Sample children. Data for the NEIS represents information on all Even Start families. Because Even Start is designed to provide early childhood services, each participating family had to include at least one child who was 7 years old or younger at the time of service receipt (1989–1992). This translates into years of birth for sample children ranging from 1982–1992. The In-Depth Study focused on children who were 3 and 4 years of age in the 1991–92 service year, who therefore were born in 1987 and 1988.

The NEIS was an annual survey of program participants, so children provided data during their years of participation, with ages ranging from 0 to 7 years. The In-Depth Study included pretest child data at age 3 or 4, and follow-up data 9 months and 18 months later.

Sampling procedures. The NEIS reflects the total sample of Even Start families and projects. Inclusion in Even Start is based on adult literacy needs (eligibility for basic education programs), child age (at least one child 7 years old or younger), and residence in a Chapter 1 elementary school attendance area.

Families in the In-Depth Study sample were selected through two non-random recruitment procedures. First, ten project sites were selected based on a number of criteria including geographic location, willingness to participate, and level of service provision. Next, families at these sites were recruited for participation if they had a child 3 or 4 years of age. Once these families were recruited, they were randomly assigned (at five of the sites) into Even Start and control groups.

Data collection. The NEIS data come from a total of 450 Even Start projects and 16,518 families (an average of 61 families per project site). The In-Depth Study provides data from ten sites. From five of these, there are 20 Even Start families and 20 control group families, and the remaining five sites contributed 20 Even Start families each, with no comparison group. Thus, the In-Depth Study, with 200 Even Start families and 100 control families, represents a very small sample relative to the NEIS and the total Even Start population. The ten program sites participating in the In-Depth Study were: Birmingham, Alabama; Phoenix, Arizona; Golden, Colorado; Indianapolis, Indiana; Waterville, Maine; Billings, Montana; Albuquerque, New Mexico; Reading, Pennsylvania; Estill, South Carolina; and Richmond, Virginia.

The NEIS survey was conducted every year for the first four cohorts of Even Start programs (first funded in 1989–1992). The first two cohorts (1989 and 1990) provided data by responding to survey questions on scanable forms for project-level information. Parent interviews, testing of children and adults, and recording of service receipt were all done by specially trained local Even Start staff. Training and technical assistance in the data collection were provided by Abt and RMC. For the 1991 and 1992 cohorts, the scanable answer forms were replaced by software allowing direct data entry onto a formatted diskette.

The In-Depth Study required more extensive data collection from a small subset of Even Start projects and comparison families, focusing on short-term outcomes of program participation. Data on participant and program characteristics and child and adult performance at pre- and posttest were collected through observations, interviews with parents and program staff, and administration of performance tests.

Characteristics of sample families. Through the NEIS, data were collected on all families that participated in Even Start services. In the 1992–93 service year this included two-parent families, single-parent households, households with extended family members, blended and stepparent families, and children under the care of their grandparent(s) or other guardians. The primary language spoken by adults participating in Even Start is English for a majority of adults. Spanish is primary for 26%, and 8% of the families report another language as primary, including Hmong, Vietnamese, Chinese, Creole, and French. Among those adults who are not native speakers of English, 78% claim to understand English "somewhat" or "very well," and 22% understand English "not at all." Some Even Start programs focus services on Limited English Proficient (LEP) adults, and others do not.

Children with disabilities, including learning problems, hearing or vision impairment, physical disability, emotional problems, physical disabilities, mental retardation, and others, comprised 7% of sample children in the 1992–93 service year.

Program implementation and process variables. The NEIS provides data on the first four cohorts of Even Start projects in terms of how projects were implemented. Projects identified recruitment strategies, core and support services provided, cooperative arrangements with outside agencies, and staffing details (see "Measures" below for a more detailed description).

In addition, levels of participation in Even Start were measured in multiple ways. First, an annual in-person interview with an adult family member (usually the mother) provided information on whether or not the family actively participated in each of the three core services during that year. Project staff maintained ongoing "contact logs" for each family, recording hours of monthly participation in each core service. These sources provide information on the number of families participating in each type of service, as well as the amounts of participation per family. These data are also analyzed by project, to determine participation variation across sites; and longitudinally, to assess multiyear participation. Reasons for families discontinuing participation in Even Start are also recorded when possible.

Measures

Data were collected from children, adults, and program directors to answer the main research questions of the evaluation. Children's language development, literacy, and school readiness were assessed directly. Parents were interviewed and assessed as well, providing information on their own literacy development, educational attainment, and literacy activities in the home; depression and locus of control; parent-child learning activities; and family context and resources. Even Start program directors were interviewed regarding patterns of service delivery, and program staffing and needs. Program records were reviewed for data on family participation in each type of service.

The sample is considered to be a low-income sample based on the eligibility criteria for receipt of Even Start services. Data were collected to assess variations in families' income level and sources, government support, and employment status.

Cultural relevance. The measures used in the evaluation were chosen to be meaningful for the general Even Start population. For example, literacy outcomes in adults were measured via GED attainment (a reasonable goal for some participants), Comprehensive Adult Student Assessment System (CASAS) scores, and literacy activities and materials in the home (including practical activities like check writing and list making). When possible, respondents were interviewed in their native languages. Some of the outcome measures have Spanish-language alternatives, which were used when appropriate (e.g., Peabody Picture Vocabulary Test—Revised and Pre-School Inventory), but respondents with other native languages had to provide data in English or not at all. Service providers had varying levels of fluency in and familiarity with the languages and cultural backgrounds of the families served.

Children with disabilities. Children with disabilities were included in the sample to the extent that they could provide data using the standard measures.

Home and child care environment. Data on home environment were collected as outcome measures of the literacy environment. In-person interviews with parents (for both the NEIS and the In-Depth Study) asked questions about parent-child reading and teaching activities, toys parents provide for learning, and books for the child in the home. In addition, families in the In-Depth Study participated in a storybook reading task in which parent-child interaction was live-coded by a trained observer.

Early childhood education was one of the core services provided by the Even Start projects. However, projects varied in the ways they provided this service—either directly by Even Start staff, or indirectly through cooperating agencies. Even Start project directors reported the types of early childhood services provided. For preschool children, these included enrolling children in Head Start, a Chapter 1 prekindergarten program, or providing another preschool option. Some Even Start projects provided a kindergarten program, and school-aged children were served in some projects when Even Start projects participated in joint planning activities with public schools. Beyond determining these categories of service, the evaluation did not measure the quality of these services. Although child care was also provided by 82% of Even Start projects as a support service to enable families to participate in other core services, the quality of this service was not assessed in the national evaluation.

Both project directors and Even Start staff reported on staff characteristics for the NEIS. Therefore, data are available on the percentage of Even Start staff providing early childhood education in the roles of coordinator, instructor, and aide; rates of staff turnover; percentage of early childhood education providers from collaborating agencies; work experience and educational backgrounds of Even Start staff providing early childhood education; and the frequency of in-service and staff development trainings.

Health care and service use. Access to and use of health care by Even Start families were not assessed in the national evaluation. The provision of "health care assistance" as a support service was measured on the project level: 77% of projects provided this type of assistance either directly (7%), through a cooperating agency (40%), or from both Even Start and cooperating agencies (30%).

Families' general access to and use of social services were not assessed in the national evaluation. The extent to which individual projects provided additional social services such as family advocacy assistance, counseling and mental health services, referrals for employment, child protective and domestic violence services, chemical dependency treatment, and referrals for services for the disabled (directly or through collaborations with other agencies) was recorded by the NEIS. Across all of these types of services, an average of 69% of projects provided some form of access to support services.

Implications of the 1996 welfare bill. The new welfare legislation has possible implications for Even Start service delivery and participation. As more parents are required to work as part of the welfare requirements, this may affect their availability to participate in Even Start core services. The current evaluation will be able to focus on and possibly document some of these effects.

Units of Analysis

Data were collected on individual children, parents, and families, as well as on each Even Start program. Analyses are conducted both across and between sites. Although the Even Start conceptual model proposes community context effects on program processes, there are no community-level data or analyses.

Data were analyzed according to each of the major research questions. Family income was treated as an outcome variable only, and other family contextual variables, such as race/ethnicity, parent educational background, and language in which testing was administered, were used as moderating variables of parent and child outcomes.

Findings

Evaluation data have been analyzed according to the four original research questions. The findings have been published and presented to the Department of Education (St. Pierre, Swartz, et al., 1995). A brief summary of the results is presented below:

Characteristics of Even Start participants (based on 1992–93 program year; N = 16,518). Even Start adults generally did not complete high school (79%), have total family annual incomes under $10,000 (66%), and speak English as their primary language (66%). Another 26% of adults speak Spanish as their primary language. The racial/ethnic background of Even Start adults is as follows: 40% are white, 26% African American, 22% Hispanic, 4% Native American, and 8% Asian or Pacific Islander. Fifty percent of Even Start families are two-parent families, 37% are headed by a single parent, and 13% live in extended family or other living arrangements. Families are almost evenly split between those earning job wages (46%) and those receiving government assistance (49%) as their primary source of income.

The average age of children receiving Even Start services was 4.3 years in the 1989–90 service year, and dropped to 3.7 years in 1992–93. The average PPVT-R score for 3- and 4-year-old Even Start participants was in the 9th percentile. Seven percent of children had an identified disability.

Implementation of Even Start projects. Early childhood services are provided in a number of different ways by Even Start projects. Head Start services are available in 67% of the projects, Chapter 1 prekindergarten programs are available at 50% of the projects, and 87% offered some other type of preschool program. Even Start projects also collaborated with public schools to provide services to school-age children, resulting in 78% of the projects providing kindergarten, and 70% providing some other early childhood education services through the public schools to school-age children under age 8.

The most common form of adult education is GED preparation instruction, which is offered by 93% of the projects. In addition, projects provide adult basic education (85%), adult secondary education (81%), and ESL instruction (61%).

In the area of parenting education, Even Start programs often help families make use of other parenting services available in the community, as well as offering advice and instruction in the areas of child development, the role of parents in children's education, child behavior management, health, and nutrition. Programs also work on building parents' self-esteem and orienting parents and children to school routines.

In addition to the three core services, many Even Start projects offered home-based instruction, services to parents and children together, and support services. More than 90% of the projects report delivering core services to parents and children together, such as reading and storytelling, developing readiness skills, development of gross motor skills, social development activities, and play. Over 80% of the projects report providing support services in order to enable families to better participate in Even Start activities. These include transportation, child care, nutrition, family advocacy assistance, and counseling.

A further requirement of Even Start programs is that they establish cooperative arrangements with other community service agencies. In the 1992–93 program year, programs averaged 20 cooperative arrangements with public school departments and programs; local, county, state or tribal agencies; and postsecondary institutions.

Even Start services received. The number of families served by Even Start projects increased from 2,500 families in the 1989–90 school year to 30,000 families in 1993–94. Most families participated for 2 years or less—only 10% of the families that began Even Start in 1989–90 participated in the full 4 years of the program. Reasons for ending participation include completing the planned educational objectives (24%), moving out of the program's catchment area (24%), lack of interest (13%), family crisis (12%), and change in eligibility status (10%).

All Even Start families are required to participate in each of the three core services. For early childhood education, participation rates have been at 97% or higher since the 1990–91 school year (including Head Start, Chapter 1 prekindergarten, other preschool, kindergarten, and primary school services). Parenting education has lower rates of participation, ranging from 88% in 1989–90 to 95% in 1992–93. The lowest rate of participation is in the area of adult education, which has been due to confusion regarding appropriate adult education services as well as to difficulty getting regular adult participation. In 1989–90, participation in adult education services was only 54%, but had risen to 86% by 1992–93.

Duration of participation in Even Start services averages 7 months. Overall, families average 107 total hours of adult education, 58 hours of parenting education, and 232 hours of early childhood education. This translates into monthly averages of 13.5 hours of adult education, 6.5 hours of parenting education, and 26 hours of early childhood education. The age of the child is related to the amount of early childhood education received: infants under 12 months received 15.5 hours per month, 2-year-olds received 20 hours per month, and 4-year-olds received 35.5 hours per month.

When participation rates are compared with baseline rates before entering Even Start and with data from other related studies, it appears that Even Start does increase the amount of services received in each of the three core areas. Adult education is received by 91% of Even Start families, but only 30–40% of comparison families; participation in parenting education is 95% for Even Start families and estimated to be 8% without the program, and 98% of children in Even Start families participate in early childhood education compared to approximately 60% without Even Start.

Effect of Even Start on children. Effects on school readiness were assessed using Pre-School Inventory scores. In the NEIS, 2,730 children were pre- and posttested on the Pre-School Inventory. Based on normal development, children's scores are expected to increase by .40 items per month. Even Start children's scores increased by .91 items per month, which is over twice the expected rate. This translates into an average effect size (based on the average 8-month participation rate in Even Start) of .56 standard deviations over what would be expected due to normal development alone. In the In-Depth Study, Even Start children (n = 74) gained more than control group children (n = 68), but control group children caught up at the 18-month posttest, likely due to 80% enrolling in preschool or kindergarten programs themselves. After the second posttest in the In-Depth Study, the program effect size on the Pre-School Inventory was .15 standard deviations.

The Peabody Picture Vocabulary Test—Revised (PPVT-R) scores of children on entry to Even Start indicated that children's receptive vocabulary scores were at the 9th percentile nationally. NEIS data (n = 3,119) revealed that upon posttest, Even Start children scored at the 19th percentile, indicating an improvement during the time they participated in the program. On average, this program effect was .48 standard deviations. However, in the In-Depth Study, both Even Start (n = 76) and control group (n = 70) children gained about .4 standard deviations on the PPVT-R, with no significant program effects. Other aspects of emergent literacy, such as print awareness, letter recognition, and understanding of the purposes of reading, were assessed in the In-Depth Study using the Child's Emergent Literacy Test, and although gains from pretest to posttest were statistically significant (nearly 3 points on a 16-point scale), the Even Start and control groups had similar scores at both time points.

Regression analyses on 614 families with valid data for family background, participation, and child outcomes revealed significant associations between these variables. The amount of time children spent in early childhood education was significantly positively related to receptive vocabulary (PPVT-R) posttest scores, and the amount of time parents spent in parenting education through Even Start positively contributed to PPVT-R scores beyond the effects of early childhood education. These participation variables were stronger predictors of receptive vocabulary scores than demographic variables such as family income or the number of children's books in the home.

Effect of Even Start on parental literacy. One of the goals of many parents in Even Start programs is to attain a GED, and it appears that Even Start is successful in helping them reach that goal. NEIS data (n = 12,481) reveal that 8.3% of all adults who did not have a GED or high school diploma did achieve one while participating one year or less in Even Start adult education services. When this analysis was restricted to those adults who had at least a ninth-grade education at entry to Even Start and who participated in the program for at least 3 months (a subsample more likely to be able to attain the GED in less than a year), the figure rose to 14.1% GED attainment (n = 5,172). The In-Depth Study shows that 22.4% of Even Start adults versus only 5.7% of control group adults attained a GED. Based on the Comprehensive Adult Student Assessment System, adults who participated in at least 70 hours of adult education in Even Start gained about $1/3$ of a standard deviation in their CASAS reading scores (n = 1,751). The In-Depth Study revealed statistically significant gains in reading scores for both the Even Start group (n = 64) and the control group (n = 53), with no significant program effect.

NEIS analyses showed a significant positive relationship between hours of adult education instruction and gains on the CASAS. While the effect size for adults receiving 1–69 hours of instruction (n = 2,029) was .20, it was .29 for those receiving 70–200 hours (n = 1,206), and adults with over 200 hours of instruction (n = 578) had CASAS scores improve by .34 standard deviations.

Effect of Even Start on parenting skills. Data from the In-Depth Study did not reveal any program effects on levels of depressive symptomatology or locus of control in participating parents. The NEIS showed small but significant changes in the measures of learning activities in the home (such as frequency of story reading, and numbers of books and play materials for the child), parenting and parent-child interactions (reading activities, play materials available, parent teaching, and parent participation in learning activities), and the Parent As A Teacher Scale (parents' values and attitudes toward children's learning and behaviors) (n's 4,062–4,401; effect sizes .02–.63). The In-Depth Study found only one difference in the home learning environments of program versus control group families: Even Start families showed a greater increase in the number of reading materials for children in their homes. Even Start families (n = 84) had a statistically significant 16.9% increase in reading materials, whereas control group families (n = 73) had a nonsignificant

6.4% increase (effect size = .40). No difference between program and control families was found on any of the measures of parent-child reading interactions. Even Start parents in the NEIS showed higher expectations for how their children would do in school (n = 3,884; effect size = .20), and for the likelihood of their children graduating from high school (n = 4,219; effect size = .10). In the In-Depth Study both Even Start (n = 75) and control group (n = 58) families had statistically significant gains in their expectations for their children, with no significant program effect.

Effect of Even Start on families. No program effects from the NEIS were reported on family income level, perceived social support, adequacy of family resources, or employment status. However, focus group participants in the In-Depth Study describe a number of positive qualitative effects, including achieving adult educational goals, getting a job, being a better parent, and noticing improvements in children's verbal, social, and organizational skills.

Limitations

While the design of the evaluation allows for reasonable and conservative estimates of the effects of Even Start participation, it does limit the generalizability of the findings. The In-Depth Study includes a control group, with families randomly assigned to either the control or program groups. However, once these groups are assigned, there is no control for the services received in either group; therefore, families in the Even Start group may terminate their participation in the program, but they remain in the dataset, as do control group families who receive similar services from another source (e.g., Head Start services). Findings from the In-Depth Study may not apply to all Even Start families, regardless of length of time in the program; because they are based on only five programs and have a small sample size, their generalizability may be limited.

The other major component of the evaluation, the NEIS, provides data from all Even Start projects, but only for families who remained in the program long enough to be posttested. Therefore, these findings reflect the effects only of longer term participation in the program, which may be subject to selection bias regarding families who stay in the program. Furthermore, as there is no comparison group for this component of the evaluation, conclusions should be drawn only about how much participating families gained, not whether or not similar gains would have occurred without Even Start services. It is this component of the evaluation that has been continued in the second evaluation by Fu Associates. Therefore, ongoing evaluation does not include a randomly assigned comparison group.

Public Use Files

Data from the Abt Associates/RMC evaluation are now available in public use files, through RMC (http://www.rmcres.com).

NATIONAL EVALUATION OF FAMILY SUPPORT PROGRAMS (NEFSP)

History

The National Evaluation of Family Support Programs is a 5-year project designed to bring together the knowledge that has been accumulated through individual evaluations of family support programs, to identify gaps in the knowledge, and to conduct a number of new evaluations of the effects of family support programs.[2] The project is funded by the Administration for Children and Families, with the goal of documenting and assessing the implementation and impact of family support programs, including but not limited to those that have been funded under Title IV-B, Subpart 2, "Family Preservation and Support Services." In particular, the question is whether family support programs might prevent family problems (which could eventually lead to the break-up of the family), and might improve the life chances of low-income families and children. The Administration for Children and Families awarded a contract to carry out the evaluation to Abt Associates (with a subcontract to Yale University) in 1994.

Current Status

The first phase of this project was a comprehensive literature review compiling the available research evidence on the effects of family support programs. This review has been completed (Barnes et al., 1995). Based on the conclusions and questions raised from this first phase, the second phase of the project was devoted to the design and implementation of several new evaluations of family support programs, and a meta-analysis of research on the effects of family support. The meta-analysis involved review of 900 studies of two-generation family support programs varying in their levels of "family supportiveness." Of these, 665 studies representing 260 programs were selected for coding. A final report for the meta-analysis has been released (Layzer, Goodson, Bernstein, & Price, 2001). For the prospective evaluation studies, seven diverse family support programs were chosen for evaluation after an extensive selection process. The plan for this innovative evaluation project was outlined in a study design document (Abt Associates, 1996). The programs were selected in 1994–1995, and the first waves of data collection began in the fall of 1995.

Goals

Program goals. The individual programs to be evaluated were selected through a careful process that began with nominations from experts in the field of programs that use best practices and that also meet ACYF's selection criteria. (Programs had to be mature and well-implemented, have a well-articulated theory, and primarily serve at-risk families.) From an initial pool of 36 nominated programs, programs were excluded if they were currently or recently involved in an evaluation, served 20 or fewer families at a single site, or were unstable due to funding problems or other changes. Final program selection considered factors such as geographic location, characteristics of the population served, and the level of prescriptiveness of the program model (in order to have a range of levels of prescriptiveness). Seven programs, each with different designs and goals, were ultimately selected for evaluation (Layzer, Goodson, Creps, Werner, & Bernstein, 2001):

- *Families and Schools Together (FAST).* Madison, Kenosha, and Racine, Wisconsin, and New Orleans, Louisiana. FAST is a program that is implemented in schools, focusing on the early school years. Originally, it was a substance abuse prevention program, but it has also been funded as a school failure prevention program, and in California it is funded as a child abuse prevention program. Following the original program model, the program is offered to families with children who are beginning to show difficulties with school. In school districts where all students are considered to be at risk because of a high proportion of families in poverty, all families in the school are eligible. The program consists of eight one-hour family meetings with structured content, held at the school. Following the 8-week program, parents meet monthly in a less-structured follow-up group for 2 years. The FAST program includes a parent self-help group, alcohol and drug abuse education, family interaction and parent-child play activities, and other family events. Studies took place in schools in Wisconsin from 1996 to 1997 and in New Orleans from 1997 to 1999. Both sites focus on families with children in grades 2 and 3 and serve a primarily African American urban population.
- *Project Vision at the Holley-Navarre Intermediate School.* Pensacola, Florida. Project Vision is an advanced version of a Florida Full Service School, offering a variety of social services at the school location. Twenty-one different social services are available through the school location for families with children in the school, including academic, behavioral, and health screenings; counseling and referrals for all family members; parenting classes; and home visits. For children who are specifically referred to the program, a coordinated case management approach is utilized. In addi-

tion, two special classrooms target fourth and fifth graders at risk of dropping out of school. The program serves a rural, white population of families with third-, fourth-, and fifth-grade children.

- *Family Development Program (FDP)*. Albuquerque, New Mexico. This program serves low-income families through home visits for families with infants and toddlers; a center-based preschool incorporating parent involvement and parent teaching activities; and a program for school-age children using center-based activities, home visits, and teacher conferences. In addition, counseling and referral services are available when needed. The strongest component of the program is the center-based preschool program. FDP serves an urban Hispanic population. FDP was dropped from the evaluation plan due to difficulties obtaining critical data from the school district.
- *Parent Services Project (PSP)*. San Jose, California, and New York, New York. The Parent Services Project serves existing preschool or day care programs by adding a parent-directed parent involvement component. Funds are provided for parenting classes and family events, and the formation of parent support groups and parent decision-making committees. The program originated in California, but has spread to sites in many other states, including many Head Start programs that have purchased the PSP training. The San Jose site serves urban Hispanic families, and in New York City, two Head Start centers run PSP programs that serve urban African American and Hispanic families. PSP was dropped from the evaluation after the first year of data collection because another evaluation being conducted in four Head Start Centers in New York City found no PSP/control group differences in parent activities or parent participation.
- *Cleveland Works*. Cleveland, Ohio. This program, primarily serving urban African American mothers on AFDC/TANF, adds family support services to a job-training program. The theory behind this program is that the additional services will increase the likelihood that clients will obtain and keep jobs that pay a living wage and provide benefits. The program has been replicated in several cities in Ohio, Washington State, and Orange County, California.
- *Iowa Family Development and Self-Sufficiency Program (FaDSS)*. FaDSS also falls in the category of adding family support elements to programs that focus on moving families to economic self-sufficiency. FaDSS is a state initiative with a large sample of approximately 1,700 AFDC recipients who were randomly assigned to a program or control group in the period 1989–1993. FaDSS provides home visits and family support as well as employment-related services to welfare recipients in 39 rural sites and serves a primarily white clientele.
- *Home Visitation 2000*. Denver, Colorado. The evaluation of the Nurse-Family Partnership being conducted by David Olds (profiled in Chapter 6

of this volume) received additional funding from the National Family Support Evaluation to collect data and assess program effects on families and children through the first 24 months of the child's life. The Nurse-Family Partnership provides home visits during the first 2 years of the child's life to educate parents on parenting and child development, and give referrals to social services. The population served is low-income and includes African American, Hispanic, and white families. This evaluation is ongoing and not reported further here.

Evaluation goals. The primary goal of the project is to inform Congress about the impact of family support legislation. To do this, two main research questions were identified:

- How effective are family support programs?
- What is the differential effectiveness of different family support programs for children and families with different characteristics, needs, and circumstances?

In order to address these questions, the project used three sources of information: existing studies of family support programs and their impact, current evaluations of state family resource initiatives, and new prospective studies on impacts of family support programs. The meta-analysis combines the data from all of these sources to estimate the size of the effects of family support programs.

Theory of Change

Central to the evaluation approach used by this project is a well-specified set of theories about how family support programs influence participating families and communities. Determining the effects of family support programs is challenging, because by definition they offer a wide variety of services that are often specific to individual family needs. In addition, families receive varying levels of support from programs, depending on their needs, motivation, barriers to participation, and other factors. Therefore, measuring effects of program participation may be enhanced by determining levels and qualities of services received, rather than simply comparing participation to nonparticipation.

The investigators conducting this project have created a conceptual model of family support that is based on the initial phase of the project—with information from intensive discussions with family support program staff, advice from researchers in the field of family support, and extensive literature review. The model proposes that family support programs are guided by a set of principles determining the nature of the activities and services they offer to families. Program activities are expected to lead to outcomes for families, communities, and ultimately (through families and communities), for children. These effects are moderated by contextual characteristics of families and communities.

The types of outcomes that are expected to be influenced by family support programs are many, and include enhancing community, family, and child well-being. For example, family outcomes may include additional adult education; improved adult coping, self-concept, and self efficacy; improvement of parent-child relationships; provision of a safe home environment; reduction of risk behaviors; increased income, health care, and other material resources; high-quality child care; and increased participation in community and schooling. Children may benefit by experiencing improved physical growth and nutrition; healthy emotional, cognitive, and social development; improved school grades and attendance; reduction of needs for special educational services; and healthy lifestyle behaviors (Abt Associates, 1996).

In addition to the general conceptual model described above, individual program evaluations are guided by tailor-made conceptual models, which serve to specify the variables of importance and the hypotheses to be tested for each family support program.

Design and Methods

The set of new evaluation studies being conducted for the National Evaluation of Family Support Programs follows a two-tiered design. In the first tier, studies used a theory-driven evaluation design, in which individual programs' treatment processes and expected outcomes were explicitly laid out into a conceptual model, and the hypothesized pathways of influence were matched against actual family patterns of change. For these evaluations, extensive data were collected on a small number of families at each site. In these studies, no traditional control or comparison groups exist. In the second tier, studies implemented more traditional experimental or quasi-experimental designs, in which outcomes for families receiving family support services were compared with those for an appropriate group of families not receiving those services. For each program evaluated, individual experimental or quasi-experimental studies were designed to provide a more rigorous test of the effects of family support programs.

Sample. The samples for each of the second-tier program evaluations are as follows:

- *Project Vision.* This program is a school-level intervention, so it is not possible to randomly assign children to schools or schools to the program, so an experimental study is impossible. In addition, no second middle school exists in the district that could serve as a valid comparison school. Instead, several comparable schools from other districts in Florida are being compared to the Holley-Navarre school population with respect to data that the state has been tracking, including attendance, standardized test scores, and grades. Students who were in the Holley-Navarre schools before Project Vision was implemented also serve as a nontreatment comparison group. Data include up to 6 years of information from before the program began and all years thereafter. In 1995–1996 the Holley-Navarre schools served 2,600 students from kindergarten through eighth grade.

- *FAST.* A pilot study was conducted in one school in Madison to test the feasibility of conducting random assignment. Based on the pilot study, a randomized design was put into place in nine schools in New Orleans. In each school, teachers were asked to refer twice as many students to FAST as are needed to fill a program, and those families who agreed were randomly assigned to FAST or a control group. Across the schools, the study had a sample size of 207 families in the program group and 200 families in the comparison group. Children were in second and third grade at the beginning of the study. Data were collected at baseline, at the end of the 8-week program, and one year later.
- *Cleveland Works.* This study is a longitudinal follow-up study of economic outcomes for Cleveland Works graduates ($N = 580$) compared with graduates of Ohio JTPA participants ($N = 407$) 3 to 5 years after program entry. Data have been obtained from the State on AFDC/TANF participation, employment, and wages for the period, fall 1993–fall 1998. Families in the sample are mostly female, urban African Americans.
- *Iowa FaDSS Program.* A longitudinal follow-up study was conducted of the original sample of families randomly assigned to FaDSS ($N = 899$) or regular AFDC services ($N = 799$) in 1989. Economic outcomes were compared, as well as data from child protective services. Families in the sample are white, rural women at risk of long-term welfare dependency.

The evaluations were done on programs that serve children of different ages. Families were followed for varying lengths of time, ranging from 12 months in the FAST program to 8 years in the FaDSS program.

Sampling procedures. As indicated in the brief sample descriptions above, most of the evaluation studies rely upon the total population of families who participate in the various programs, or subsamples of volunteer families. Random assignment to program versus comparison groups occurs in only two of the studies: the Iowa FaDDS program and the FAST evaluation; in the latter, students who were referred to the program because of behavioral or academic problems are randomly assigned to be in the program or the comparison group. In the other studies, comparison groups are composed of volunteer families participating in similar programs in similar locations that are not part of a family support program. These sampling procedures enable description of the types of families that participate in these family support programs, but generally do not provide samples representative of other larger populations.

Data collection. Across the studies, there are approximately 20–25 individual sites, with 10–50 families participating in the studies per site.

- *Project Vision.* The Holley-Navarre School in Pensacola, Florida; multiple comparison middle schools in Florida for database comparisons
- *FAST.* Schools in New Orleans, Louisiana, implementing the FAST program
- *FaDSS.* Eleven AFDC sites in Iowa
- *Cleveland Works.* One program in Cleveland and comparison families in the state JTPA program, which involves multiple job-training projects.

Data collection measured each of the main domains identified in the family support conceptual model described above (see "Theory of Change"). Therefore, evaluations assess community and family contexts and characteristics; program principles, activities, and processes; and family, community, and child outcomes. Program variables were assessed through on-site observations of activities and interactions, discussions with program staff, and reviews of program records of services and family participation. Parents were interviewed extensively about their own and their children's well-being, and children in fourth grade and higher were given a Student Interview. Teacher ratings indicated behavior of both preschool and school-age children, and children's school records were reviewed for child school performance.

Characteristics of sample families. All family structures that occur naturally in the sample of families are included in the studies. The adult family member who responds to the Parent Interview may be the child's mother, father, grandparent, legal guardian, or other relative. The interviews have English language and Spanish language forms so that parents and children can be interviewed in their primary language.

Program implementation and process variables. Program processes are central to the theory-driven evaluation studies. Therefore, extensive data on program philosophy, activities, and participation were collected, using multiple methods. Program records were examined to extract information on family participation in various program activities, and parents were asked directly about the quantity and quality of their own participation and their perceptions of the program process. In addition, new information was collected from the program sites through direct observation of program activities and informal discussion with program staff. For most of the program activity and participation variables, project-specific indicators were used. In addition, a standard measure of programs' levels of family supportiveness was developed using the 10 principles of family supportiveness described by the Family Resource Coalition. This Family Supportiveness Profile was used to assess the "family supportiveness" of all programs included in the meta-analysis. The 10 principles incorporated into the profile are the following:

- Building parenting skills and support
- Promoting child development
- Mobilizing informal and formal resources for families
- Helping build and strengthen the neighborhood and community
- Promoting voluntary participation by families
- Building on individual and family strengths
- Involving families as active, competent collaborators
- Responding to individual needs
- Reflecting sensitivity to participants' cultures
- Reflecting family support principles in all aspects of program operation, such as staff relationships. (Abt Associates, 1996, p. 4)

Measures

Instruments for the prospective studies have been created specifically for this investigation, drawing on a number of existing measures whenever possible. Four different interviews were designed to provide data on family and community context, program activities and processes, and outcomes for children, families, and communities. These include two parent interviews, the Family Well-Being Interview, which provides information on family relationships, parenting, resources, and social support; and the Child Well-Being Interview, with information on the child's physical growth and nutrition, behavior, language, and reasoning skills. Children in fourth grade and higher complete the Student Interview, providing information on their attitudes, family environment, social support, behaviors, and school performance. Teachers complete the Teacher Questionnaire—Pre-K and School-Age, which provides information on children's school performance, behaviors, and attitudes. Data on program processes, activities, participation, and staffing are collected from program records and program observation.

Family income and employment. Most of the families served by these programs are low-income families. To measure family resources, the Parent Interview includes a series of questions about the responding parent's employment, work hours, actual income, employment benefits, and employment history over the last year. If the respondent indicated living with a partner, either the parent or the partner also responded to questions about the partner's education, employment, and benefits. Respondents indicated total household income for the previous year. In addition, parents rated the adequacy of a number of family resources, including food, housing, money, clothes, utilities, employment, medical care, public assistance, transportation, sleep, child care, and many other resources.

Children with disabilities. Children are not excluded, nor really identified, based on disability status. In programs in which children with disabilities were referred to the program by their teacher, they were included in the evaluation. None of the prospective studies involved child testing, so there was no need to modify measures in order to include children with disabilities.

Home and child care environment. The quality of the home environment is assessed primarily through the Family Well-Being Interview. Parents reported on family composition and stability, family routines, family cohesiveness and communication, conflict resolution, their own parenting attitudes and behaviors, and the learning environment in the home. No additional observational measures of home environment were conducted.

The child care environment was extensively measured using data from multiple respondents and observational measures (see above "Design and Methods"). For child care arrangements that are not part of the family support programs being evaluated, the only source of information is from the Parent Interview. A series of items in the interview asks about parents' perceptions of their child's school or child care center's quality, safety, and philosophy, and their own participation at the child's school.

Health care. In the Parent Interview, parents report on the adequacy of their family's medical and dental care, the type and continuity of medical care family members receive for routine and sick care (whether it is at a doctor's office or clinic, company or school clinic, hospital outpatient clinic, migrant clinic, other clinic, hospital emergency room, walk-in emergency care center, rural health center, HMO or prepaid group, or other), and health care coverage (Medicaid, private insurance or HMO, payment with family's own money, other government assistance, or another source), and barriers to arranging health care for the children (such as not having a doctor, being unable to miss work or school, child care problems, problems scheduling an appointment, transportation problems, language barriers, or communication problems with the doctor or nurse).

Social services. The Parent Interview includes a section on the community environment, which has questions about the availability of a number of community services and resources (such as a community family health service or counseling center, supermarket, bank, library, police station, after-school programs, community day care, summer recreational programs, literacy/ GED/tutoring programs, scouting or other youth clubs, family planning clinic, employment office, or other organized centers or programs); whether or not family members use such services; problems or barriers to using services; parents' perceptions of the quality of services like schools, parks, recreational services, mental health and counseling; and whether over the last 3 years services have gotten worse, stayed the same, or improved.

Impact of the 1996 welfare bill. Welfare reform is not of central relevance to this study, although many of the sites serve families who are affected by welfare reform. In particular, Cleveland Works and the Iowa FaDSS programs serve welfare recipients and focus on job training and moving families to economic self-sufficiency.

Units of Analysis

These program evaluations have been designed to provide data from multiple sources on multiple levels. These include child-, family-, program-, neighborhood-, and community-level data. In addition, data are available at multiple time points. Research questions focus on both individual or family-level outcomes as well as descriptions of programs themselves. This design offers the possibility that data could be analyzed by site, as well as pooled and analyzed across sites. In fact, existing data sets were pooled in the meta-analysis, and findings across studies were compared. In assessing the effects of family support programs, characteristics of families and communities are hypothesized to be important factors mediating final outcomes, so variables such as race, ethnicity, and income guide much of the analysis.

Findings

Final reports have been issued for the meta-analysis (Layzer, Goodson, Bernstein, & Price, 2001) and the prospective evaluation studies (Layzer, Goodson, Creps, Werner, & Bernstein, 2001). The main impact findings for each of the four completed program evaluations are as follows:

- *FAST.* A small number of significant program effects 1 year after completion of the program were found. Program children had more positive ratings of their behavior on parent ratings, but not on teacher ratings, and there was no effect of program participation on school grades. Participating families were more likely to engage in community volunteer work and to be in a leadership position, but the program did not influence the family environment, parenting outcomes, or school-family connections.
- *Iowa FaDSS Program.* Longitudinal follow-up of the program and control welfare recipients found no program impacts on the amount of welfare payments received annually; payments decreased over time in both groups. Similarly, employment rates increased over time in both groups through the 7th year after random assignment. A small program impact on reduction of the proportion of children victimized by child abuse or neglect was found through the 8th year following random assignment. Generally, the addition of family support services for welfare families did not add to the economic self-sufficiency gains experienced by families in welfare-to-work programs.
- *Project Vision.* Tests of fifth-grade students revealed higher reading comprehension and vocabulary scores, higher math computation concepts and application scores, and higher scores on three different language subtests for Project Vision students compared to comparison group students, although at second grade their scores were either equivalent to or lower than those of comparison students on these tests. Growth-curve analyses suggest that for particularly at-risk students, the language benefits may be expected to persist beyond the fifth grade.
- *Cleveland Works.* The addition of family support services was found to be positively related to employment and earnings in the 3 years following program participation. Cleveland Works participants were more likely to be employed and earned, on average, $6,400 more over the three years than did the JTPA participants. Over the 3-year follow-up period, the program impacts on employment and earnings decreased.

Limitations

The major limitations of the prospective studies are their small sample sizes (with the exception of FaDDS) and, for some, nonrandom assignment. However, the studies have a somewhat unique strength in that their smaller scope allows for the formation of project-specific, theory-driven hypothesis generation and, in some cases, testing. In addition, the prospective studies were conducted within the context of the larger project that has included many other project evaluations to which the current studies can be added and compared.

The measures developed for the prospective studies include a compilation of numerous existing instruments that have been extensively tested for external validity. Therefore, an additional strength of this initiative is its measurement of the constructs of interest.

Public Use Files

Public use data files will be available for the impact studies (FaDSS, FAST, Cleveland Works, Holley-Navarre) and from the meta-analyses.

NOTES

We would like to acknowledge the support of the MacArthur Network on the Family and the Economy, the Administration on Children, Youth, and Families, and the National Institute for Mental Health Research Consortium on Mental Health in Head Start. The authors would also like to thank Robert St. Pierre, Barbara Goodson, and Fumiyo Tao for verifying information on the Even Start and the National Evaluation of Family Support Programs, and Christy Brady-Smith for editorial assistance.

1. The first National Even Start Evaluation was conducted by Abt Associates under contract with the Office of Policy and Planning, U.S. Department of Education. For additional information regarding this initiative, see http://www.abtassoc.com/reports/paper5.pdf on-line.

2. The National Evaluation of Family Support Programs is being conducted by Abt Associates under contract with the Administration for Children and Families. Principal investigators are Jean Layzer (Abt Associates) and Sharon L. Kagan (Yale University).

CHAPTER 6

Pre- and Perinatal Home Visitation Interventions

LISA MCCABE AND JEANNE BROOKS-GUNN

An estimated 3,244,000 cases of suspected child abuse and neglect (1,396 child abuse fatalities) were reported to Child Protective Service (CPS) agencies in 1999 (Peddle & Wang, 2001). At the same time, juvenile crime and antisocial behavior is a significant problem in the United States, and has been the focus of much recent media attention. These facts, coupled with many parents' desire for more information about child rearing, have propelled the creation of programs to assist new parents and to improve child health and developmental outcomes. Across these programs, home visiting (in which a professional who is knowledgeable about early childhood parenting visits parents and children in their homes) has emerged as a promising intervention technique. Typically, the home visitor provides parenting education and serves as a link to other services in the community. Professional background of the home visitor (e.g., nurse, child development specialist, paraprofessional) varies depending on particular program philosophies and goals. In some programs, home visiting is targeted for at-risk families, while in others these services are more generally available.

In this chapter we highlight three home visiting programs that focus on reaching families either before or soon after a child is born. The Nurse-Family Partnership (NFP) (formerly known as the Nurse Home Visitation Project) involves three trials of a program for at-risk families that has been underway for more than 20 years. We next provide a detailed description of the national Healthy Families America (HFA) program. Finally, we describe the Healthy Steps (HS) for Young Children Program, a multisite intervention program linked to traditional pediatric care. In each of these programs, design and implementation efforts are accompanied by evaluations of the efficacy of the program.

NURSE-FAMILY PARTNERSHIP (NFP)

History

Program development, implementation, and evaluation of the Nurse-Family Partnership project has spanned more than 2 decades.[1] Established in 1977, the NFP project began in Elmira, New York, as a program to improve pregnancy outcomes, child development, and family economic self-sufficiency. Based on theories of human ecology (Bronfenbrenner, 1979), human attachment (Bowlby, 1969) and self-efficacy (Bandura, 1977), the program employed nurses as home visitors to first-time mothers beginning during pregnancy and continuing through the child's second birthday. During regular 75–90 minute visits, nurses promoted health-related behaviors during and after pregnancy (e.g., reducing cigarette, alcohol, and illegal drug use), educated mothers about appropriate physical and emotional care of their infants, and encouraged maternal personal life course development (e.g., family planning, educational achievement, and employment).

Promising results from this first randomized trial of the program made it important to test its generalizability to other communities and populations. Thus a second trial (in Memphis, Tennessee) was designed specifically to address concerns about the efficacy of the nurse home visitation program for families living in urban areas. This replication of the program, with predominantly African American families, once again demonstrated the effectiveness of the program for improving maternal and child outcomes.

In each of these trials, nurses were deliberately chosen for the role of home visitor because of their expertise with women's and children's health issues, familiarity with the health care system, and experience in managing complex situations. Yet, despite the success of the Elmira and Memphis trials (with nurses representing a key element of the program), similar programs with paraprofessionals playing the role of home visitors were being implemented. Would a paraprofessional home visiting program be as successful as the nurse home visitation model? Home Visiting 2000 (HV 2000) was designed to answer this empirical question. Begun in 1994 with funding primarily from the Colorado Trust, HV 2000 (the Denver trial) seeks to examine the unique contributions that can be made by nurse and paraprofessional home visitors.

Current Status

A 15-year follow-up of the Elmira sample has been completed. Results from this trial have been widely published (see Eckenrode et al., 2000; Olds, Henderson, Tatelbaum, & Chamberlin, 1986; Olds, Eckenrode, et al., 1997; Olds et al., 1998).

In Memphis, a 3-year follow up of the program has been completed and findings published (Kitzman et al., 2000). With funding from the National Institute of Mental Health, more long-term follow-ups are currently underway.

Data collection for the initial HV 2000 study is now complete. Results exploring the differences between nurse and paraprofessional home visitation have been published (Korfmacher, O'Brien, Hiatt, & Olds, 1999). More general findings have also been published (Olds et al., 2002). These findings include initial results, as well as follow-up data from when the children were 2-years-old.

Funding has also been obtained from the Robert Wood Johnson Foundation to support carefully monitored national replication of the Nurse-Family Partnership.

Goals

Concerns about poor birth outcomes (e.g., low birth weight, preterm delivery, fetal impairment), child abuse and neglect, and welfare dependence are at the heart of the NFP program. As such, the program's goals are threefold. First, the program attempts to improve pregnancy outcomes. Second, the program seeks to improve the quality of parental caregiving in order to ultimately promote positive child health and developmental outcomes. Finally, the program aims to improve maternal life course development by encouraging education, employment, and family planning.

Theory of Change

As mentioned at the outset, three psychological theories (human ecology, attachment, and self-efficacy) offering different ideas about human development shaped the design of the NFP program (for a more detailed description of the theory of change underlying the NFP project, see Olds, Kitzman, Cole, & Robinson, 1997). Based on the theory of human ecology, which emphasizes the role of social context in human development, the NFP program operates assuming that behavioral change is influenced by familial, neighborhood, and cultural factors. For this reason, the program emphasizes maternal support networks, the use of community services, and attention to culture. Also following this theory, the NFP program focuses on first-time mothers based on the assumption that these women are undergoing an "ecological transition" and will be more receptive to services designed to increase positive pregnancy, child, and maternal outcomes.

Attachment theory emphasizes the importance of early relationships, especially the child-parent attachment, for later development. Consequently, the NFP program includes parent education components that promote the development of sensitive and responsive caregiving techniques.

Finally, self-efficacy theory contends that an individual's beliefs about his/her own abilities shapes behavior. This theory thus forms the basis for the third major component of the NFP program: the identification of maternal goals, and strategies for reaching those goals. It is assumed that in meeting these goals, mothers will gain the confidence necessary to make similar decisions in the future.

Design and Methods

The Elmira trial involved 400 mothers who were recruited through prenatal care facilities between April 1978 and September 1980. Participants were primarily white (89%) and lived in a semirural area. A special effort was made to recruit adolescent mothers, single parents, and mothers from lower socioeconomic status. Thus, the vast majority (85%) were at-risk in that they were unmarried, adolescent mothers, and/or low-income.

The mothers were randomly assigned to one of four groups. The first two served as control groups. Group 1 received sensory and developmental screenings for the children at 12 and 24 months of age and referrals to treatment and clinical evaluations when necessary. Those in the second control group also received screenings and referrals, but in addition were given free transportation for prenatal and well care up to 24 months of age. The second two groups made up the program groups. Both received the screening and transportation services available to the control groups. In addition, nurses made regular home visits during pregnancy in one group, while in the other program group nurse home visits continued through the child's second birthday.

In the Memphis trial, recruitment focused on women with overlapping risk factors. Thus women needed to have at least two of three sociodemographic risk conditions to be included in the project: unmarried, less than 12 years of education, or unemployed. A total of 1,139 women, recruited from an obstetric clinic between June 1990 and August 1991, met these criteria and were enrolled in the study. Women were primarily African American (92%) and low-income (85%). Sixty-four percent were 18 years old or younger.

As a replication of the original Elmira study, the Memphis trial also involved random assignment to one of four treatment conditions. The first group received free transportation to scheduled prenatal care visits. Group 2 was provided developmental screenings and referral services in addition to transportation to prenatal care visits. Group 3 received the same services as Group 2, plus nurse home visits during pregnancy and two postpartum visits (one in the hospital before discharge and one in the home). Finally, women in the last group were provided all services offered to Group 3, and nurse home visits continued until the child was 24 months old.

In HV 2000, 735 women (recruited from prenatal clinics between March 1994 and June 1999) participated in the project. For this trial, women were again randomly assigned, but this time to one of three treatment groups. Two groups received home visiting beginning in pregnancy and continuing until the child was 2 years of age. In one, home visits were conducted by nurses and in the other by paraprofessionals. The third treatment group received routine community care, but no home visits. All women were also provided with developmental screenings and referral services when the child was 6, 12, 15, 21, and 24 months of age.

Respondents for the Denver trial were similar to those in the first two trials in that they were typically unmarried (84%) and young (mean age 19.76 years), and had less than a high school degree. However, these respondents came from more diverse racial and ethnic backgrounds (45% Hispanic, 34% white, 16% African American, 4% American Indian, 1% Asian).

Data collection for each of the three trials was similar. Individuals involved in data collection were always blind to the women's treatment conditions. Interviews with mothers occurred when they registered for the program, at 28 and 36 weeks of pregnancy (Memphis and Denver only), and when children were 6 months, 1, 2, and 4–5 years old. Observations of parenting and the home environment were made over the course of the child's first two years of life. Child developmental assessments (including cognitive, language, and mental development) were conducted around ages 1 (Elmira only) and 2. Medical and social service records provided a wealth of data from the prenatal period through early childhood.

For the Elmira study, additional data has been gathered as part of a 15-year follow-up. When the children were 15 years old, 324 of the mothers were reinterviewed, adolescents were interviewed, Child Protective Service records and records of arrests and criminal convictions (for mothers) were accessed, and probation and family court data (for adolescents) were reviewed.

Program implementation was also evaluated through a variety of qualitative and quantitative techniques. Home visitors tape recorded narrations of their work and kept track of contacts and visits with families through "encounter" forms. Weekly logs and notes on program processes were made by home visiting supervisors. Drop-out rates in program participation and turnover in home visitation staff were also recorded.

Measures

Extensive data have been gathered across the three home visitation trials. Using a wide variety of measures, child physical, cognitive, and social and emotional development were assessed. Information about maternal physical and mental health, intelligence, attitudes and coping, self-efficacy, labor force participation, welfare use, and social support was also gathered. In addition, measures of parenting, the home environment, and neighborhood safety were included. Finally, program processes and implementation were investigated through interviews and reviews of program records.

Units of Analysis

Data have been gathered on individual children, mothers, and families. Analyses thus far have therefore predominantly examined the effects of home visitation on child and maternal outcomes. Program implementation variables have also been the focus of recent analyses.

Findings

Given that the Nurse-Family Partnership has been underway for more than 2 decades, extensive findings and results are available. Here, we provide a brief overview of the major findings.

Results from both the Elmira and Memphis trials suggest that the Nurse-Family Partnership leads to a wealth of positive outcomes for both children and their families. Specifically, the program has been successful at improving maternal life course (fewer subsequent pregnancies and births, increased time between births, decreased welfare use; Kitzman et al., 2000; Olds et al., 1999) and in decreasing the dysfunctional care of children (decreased rates of childhood injuries and ingestions associated with child abuse and neglect; Kitzman, Olds et al., 1997; Olds, et al., 1999).

In addition to these overlapping findings, other positive results have also been reported for individual trials. In Elmira, women who received home visiting services demonstrated a decrease in cigarette smoking and alcohol or illegal drug use, fewer arrests, improved diet, increased birth weight (for children of women less than 17 years old), and increased cognitive development in children (for children of smokers; Olds et al., 1999). At age 15, children of women who experienced home visiting were less likely to run away; had fewer arrests, convictions and violations of probation; had fewer sex partners; and drank less alcohol and smoked cigarettes less frequently (Olds et al., 1998). Home-visited children were also identified less often in child maltreatment reports. Similarly, their mothers were less likely to be identified as the perpetrator of child maltreatment (although this positive effect was not true for mothers who experienced domestic violence; Eckenrode et al., 2000; Olds, Eckenrode, et al., 1997).

In Memphis, additional positive findings have also been reported. For example, home-visited women showed a decrease in pregnancy-induced hypertension and vaginal yeast infections, attempted breast feeding more frequently, and demonstrated more positive mother-child interactions (e.g., greater empathy, fewer unrealistic expectations, and less support for physical punishment; Kitzman, Olds, et al., 1997; Olds et al., 1999). Differences in positive outcomes for the two trials most likely stem, at least in part, from differences in the two populations served. For example, smoking was much less common among the primarily African American women from an urban setting (Memphis) than it was for semirural white women from Elmira. Therefore, positive effects from decreased smoking were much less likely in Memphis (Kitzman, Olds, et al., 1997; Olds et al., 1999).

The NFP project has also evaluated program implementation in particular. For example, a recent report by Hiatt, Sampson, and Baird (1997) outlines the difficulties involved in employing paraprofessionals as home visitors, while Kitzman, Cole, Yoos, and Olds (1997) describe challenges faced by home visitors when implementing the program. Korfmacher and colleagues (1999) present findings from a comparison of nurse and paraprofessional home visitors. According to their research, nurses completed more home visits than paraprofessionals, but paraprofessional visits tended to be longer in length. The specific content of the visits also differed depending on the background of the home visitors. Nurses spent more time on physical health and parenting issues, while paraprofessionals tended to focus on environmental health and safety. Turnover was also greater among the paraprofessional staff than among the nurse home visitors. NFP researchers have also examined how intervention processes (e.g., number of visits, nature of the relationship between home visitor and parent) affect outcomes among participants (Korfmacher, Kitzman, & Olds, 1998).

Limitations

Two of the greatest challenges inherent in research that examines program efficacy are questions about replication and consistency of program implementation across sites or individuals. The NFP project has addressed each of these concerns. First, the program has now been replicated in three sites with women from diverse locales and racial/ethnic backgrounds. Thus researchers can effectively speak to issues of replication with very different populations. Second, the NFP project has made a great effort to track details about program implementation so that analyses may examine how differences in intensity, content, or procedure may affect the outcomes of interest.

Public Use Files

There are currently no plans to make data from any of the Nurse-Family Partnership trials public. Those interested in projects that would involve use of the data should contact David Olds directly.

HEALTHY FAMILIES AMERICA (HFA)

History

The Healthy Families America[2] initiative was established in 1992 by Prevent Child Abuse America (PCAA)[3] as a program to combat child abuse and neglect. HFA promotes positive parenting and child health and development through voluntary home visits with new parents. Home visitors provide a variety of services, including parenting education and referrals to other assistance programs, training, and employment opportunities for up to 5 years.

The establishment of the HFA initiative is grounded in research findings from two primary sources. First, the Carnegie Corporation's *Starting Points* report (Carnegie Corporation of New York, 1994) highlighted the importance of the first three years of a child's life as a foundation for future development. This report, combined with the realization that most physical abuse and neglect occurs among children younger than 2 years of age, encouraged HFA founders to create a program for parents with very young children. Second, preliminary evaluations of Hawaii's Healthy Start Program pointed to the success of home visiting as an effective intervention. Based on these promising results, the HFA program adopted home visiting as its primary strategy for decreasing rates of child maltreatment.

Current Status

In 1994, Prevent Child Abuse America created a network of researchers, currently comprised of over 50 researchers from state agencies, universities, and private evaluation firms, to evaluate the effectiveness of the HFA program. To date, 47 studies have been conducted or are under way within the HFA Research Network to evaluate the 420 HFA sites in 39 states, the District of Columbia, and Canada. Results in key areas from 17 studies with preliminary or final results have been published by Daro and Harding (1999). In addition, PCAA is currently conducting a 13-state study (funded by the Packard Foundation and the Gerber Foundation) to examine program implementation.

Goals

Broadly defined, the goal of HFA is to promote positive parenting and child health in order to decrease child abuse and neglect and other negative child outcomes. To meet this goal, HFA adheres to a set of "critical elements" that focus on service initiation (e.g., prenatally or at birth), service content (e.g., long-term and culturally sensitive), and staff characteristics (e.g., providers selected based on ability to establish trusting relationship) and are needed for successful implementation of a home visiting program.

The major research questions, then, focus on how effective the program is for (a) promoting positive parent-child interaction; (b) reducing reported child abuse or neglect cases; (c) increasing positive child health indicators (e.g., child immunizations and well-child visits); (d) increasing positive child development outcomes (e.g., early identification of developmental delays, greater vocabulary); (e) increasing the identification and use of sources of support; and (f) promoting better maternal life course choices (e.g., decreased substance abuse).

Theory of Change

Home visits, the primary component of the HFA program, are based on attachment theory, which focuses on the importance of early parent-child relationships. HFA also expects that change is most likely when interventions are targeted both at the individual and the community. For this reason, HFA not only implements home-visiting services for individual families, but it also aims to increase support for this kind of preventive effort in the community by, for example, improving coordination among the wide variety of family support services available. In addition, HFA advocates that effective intervention must provide a universal base of support that includes varied service options to meet the needs of individuals. Finally, HFA suggests that replication procedures that maintain quality standards and yet are flexible enough for implementation in diverse communities are essential to effective intervention.

Design and Methods

The 47 HFA evaluations employ a variety of study designs including randomized trial (9 studies), comparison group (11 studies), and examination of a single group pre- and post-HFA (27 studies). In addition, 3 process studies examine engagement and retention of overall program implementation.

Children born in each year since 1992, the start date for the first evaluations, have been included in the HFA evaluations. All studies begin data collection prenatally or at birth and, at a minimum, assess HFA participants once either during or at the completion of the program. Many studies collect data on a regular basis, typically every 6 months, but in some cases as often as every 2–4 months (depending on the particular measures used).

The number of sites included in each evaluation ranges from 1 to as many as 57. Fifteen states have undertaken statewide evaluations of HFA. Sample size also varies widely, from less than 100 to more than 2,000. Within each evaluation, all HFA participants are recruited to participate. Methods for recruiting comparison groups, however, differ across studies. In most cases, families who meet eligibility criteria but live outside the service area are included as a comparison group. In other studies, the comparison group is made up of families who choose not to participate or families who drop out of the program.

Data collection methods differ by study design, with randomized control and comparison group studies tending to use research staff, and pre/post studies tending to use home visitors or other program staff. Most often, data are collected from the mother or primary caregiver and target child by the home visitor or assessment worker during the home visit. In some instances, parents come to program offices or other "neutral ground" for data collection.

In some evaluations, program implementation and processes are assessed. For example, in one evaluation, participants were interviewed about their perceptions of the program. Other sites have examined engagement and retention, cost effectiveness, or worker satisfaction through the use of archival program records. Three studies focus exclusively on program processes and implementation (e.g., McCurdy & Daro's, 2001, multisite study of engagement and retention).

Measures

Most of the 47 investigations evaluate similar outcomes such as child health and development, home environment, parenting knowledge and practices, maternal life course, and social support. The specific measures used, however, vary by study. Some of the most commonly used measures include the following: Ages and Stages Questionnaire (Bricker & Squires, 1999), the HOME Inventory (Caldwell & Bradley, 1984), the NCAST Feeding and Teaching Scales (Barnard, 1978), the Child Abuse Potential Inventory (Milner, 1986), and the Maternal Social Support Index (Pascoe, Loda, Jeffries, & Earp, 1981). In addition, evaluations typically collect administrative data on reported abuse and neglect.

Unit of Analysis

Typically, data are collected, and therefore analyzed, at the individual and family level. In a few cases, multisite analyses (usually within one state) that examine participant, provider, program and/or community variables are under way.

Findings

Results from the 17 completed or ongoing program evaluations with preliminary data suggest several key findings, some more promising than others. On the positive side, HFA participants were more likely to provide routine medical care (e.g., immunizations and well-baby visits) for their children than were nontreatment families. In addition, better parenting skills and less stress associated with parenting were observed in treatment families when compared to control and comparison groups. Finally, HFA families demonstrated a decreased dependency on government programs such as AIDC (now known as Temporary Assistance for Needy Families) and food stamps (Daro & Harding, 1999).

The effectiveness of HFA for other outcome measures has been less encouraging. For example, there is some evidence to suggest that children whose families participated in HFA were not significantly different from control children in terms of their cognitive development (Daro & Harding, 1999). HFA families also did not demonstrate an increase in the use of social supports (Daro & Harding, 1999).

Results about child abuse and neglect are mixed. In some studies, participation in the HFA program was associated with a decreased potential for child abuse and neglect, as demonstrated by lower reported maltreatment rates for HFA families than for comparison families (Daro & Harding, 1999). In contrast, the three randomized trials that examined child maltreatment as an outcome did not find a significant difference between the home-visiting and the control groups. Also, Daro and Harding (1999) caution against using reported abuse and neglect as an indicator of program success because low base rates of child abuse, small sample sizes, difficulties identifying abuse in infants, and increased chances for observing abuse in home-visiting participant families make finding statistically significant differences in the desired direction difficult to observe.

An important part of any program evaluation is an examination of whether some participants benefit more than others. Findings regarding the effectiveness of HFA for participants with particular characteristics have not been consistent. For example, in some studies teenage mothers were more likely to benefit from the program, while in others, older mothers were easier to engage. Similarly, program characteristics such as point of engagement (prenatally or at birth) and service intensity, did not consistently predict better outcomes.

Limitations

Two limitations should be kept in mind when considering results from the HFA evaluations. First, most of the evaluations to date compare HFA participants to populations matched on key demographic characteristics. Without random assignment and a control group, the possibility of self-selection factors playing a role in outcome measures cannot be ruled out. Second, use of program staff, who are presumably invested in the program and not blind to family participation status, as evaluators calls into question the validity of some of the outcome data collected. Currently, efforts are being made to track how the specific implementation of individual measures (e.g., who implements, when implemented, training needed to implement) affects results.

Public Use Files

Although public files for research from the HFA Research Network are not currently available, reports detailing research activities and findings can be obtained from PCAA (www.preventchildabuse.org/program/hfa.html). Data from one study, a randomized trial in Hawaii, may be available from PCAA in the next year.

HEALTHY STEPS (HS) FOR YOUNG CHILDREN PROGRAM

History

The Healthy Steps for Young Children Program was initiated in late 1994 to help parents of young children foster the emotional, cognitive, and social development of their children through the use of expanded pediatric health care services.[4] The program aims to provide a more comprehensive approach to traditional pediatric health care by linking child development professionals, called "Healthy Steps Specialists," to pediatric services. Healthy Steps Specialists, modeled after the "Development Specialists" piloted with two pediatric practices by Zero to Three (Eggbeer, 1995), offer a variety of services to parents including home visits, a telephone information line, parent support groups, and enhanced well-child visits conducted jointly or consecutively with the child's pediatrician. In addition, the Healthy Steps program offers child development assessments beginning at 6 months of age, written informational materials emphasizing preventive care for parents, and links to community resources.

The development of the Healthy Steps program was informed by extensive research about parents and children, including a review of child development and parent education programs (Brooks-Gunn, Fuligni, Barth, & Young, 1997). Especially informative were the results from the Survey of Parents of Young Children, a national telephone survey of 2,017 mothers and fathers with children between the ages of 0 and 3. This investigation revealed two important findings: (a) Parents want more information about child discipline and how to encourage learning in young children, and (b) pediatricians typically do not provide child development guidance as part of well-child care (Healthy Steps for Young Children Program, 1997; McLearn, Zuckerman, Parker, Yellowitz, & Kaplan-Sanoff, 1998; Young, Davis, Shoen, & Parker, 1998). These findings, combined with recent evidence that the quality of early experiences have a powerful influence on brain development (Carnegie Corporation of New York, 1994), and that financial strain and stress associated with juggling work and family responsibilities have made child rearing especially challenging for many of today's parents (Healthy Steps for Young Children Program, 1997), led the Healthy Steps planning committee to conclude that pediatric practices should serve both parents and children and that parents need closer relationships with pediatric health care professionals. Thus creation of the Healthy Steps Specialist role, designed to make child development knowledge more accessible to parents through their pediatric care provider, is firmly rooted in research findings.

Current Status

Healthy Steps programs are currently in operation or have completed their participation in 24 pediatric and family practices throughout the United States. A national evaluation, directed by Dr. Bernard Guyer from the Department of Population and Family Health Sciences at the Johns Hopkins University Bloomberg School of Public Health, is being conducted at 15 of these sites. Data collection for this multiyear study began in 1996 and was completed in 2002. Evaluation findings have been presented at national conferences and reported in pediatric journals (Caughy, Miller, Genevro, Huang, & Nautiyal, 2001; Guyer, Caughy, & McLearn, 1998; Guyer et al., 2000; Markowitz, 1998; Minkovitz et al., 2001). References (including links to references) and project updates, with current news about the Healthy Steps for Young Children Program, are available through the project website (http://www.healthysteps.org).

Goals

The goal of the Healthy Steps program is threefold. First, the program aims to promote the healthy physical, emotional, and intellectual development of children in the first three years of life. Second, Healthy Steps seeks to increase parents' knowledge, skills, and confidence in child rearing. Finally, with managed care systems impeding pediatricians' ability to spend time discussing developmental issues with new parents, Healthy Steps attempts to expand pediatric services by adding a child development professional to pediatric teams, in order to better meet the needs of families with young children.

With these goals in mind, the national evaluation focused on assessing whether and how participation in HS led to improved outcomes for children, parents, and pediatric practices. Thus several components were included within the national evaluation: a process evaluation, an outcome evaluation, an economic analysis, and an assessment of the program's potential for institutionalization. Specifically, the national evaluation investigated whether children in Healthy Steps programs demonstrated fewer behavior problems and increased language abilities. Additionally, the investigation explored the effectiveness of the program for increasing parenting skills and confidence, as well as parents' satisfaction with and use of pediatric care. The evaluation also examined the cost effectiveness of HS versus traditional pediatric practices. Finally, the evaluation assessed the potential for program implementation in other pediatric practices across the country.

Theory of Change

Healthy Steps practitioners and researchers expected change to occur through the promotion of a close partnership between health care professionals and parents. Routine use of pediatric care makes pediatric settings ideal for providing information and support to parents, which in turn facilitated positive child outcomes through increased parenting skills and confidence.

Design and Methods

Fifteen Healthy Steps sites around the country participated in the evaluation. At six of these sites (those with the largest number of pediatric patients), families were randomly assigned to treatment or control groups. At the remaining nine sites, a quasi-experimental design, in which information was gathered from Healthy Steps families and from a matched comparison group, was employed.

A total of 5,565 families (approximately 200 treatment and 200 control/comparison at each site) enrolled in the evaluation between September

1996 and November 1998. Families with children 28 days old or less were eligible to participate, with minimal exclusion criteria.[5] Because eligibility restrictions were kept to a minimum and because the 15 sites come from diverse geographic locations, the Healthy Steps sample includes ethnically diverse families from urban, suburban, and small town locales, with a wide range of incomes.

Families were followed through November 2001, when the last of the enrolled children turned 3 years old. Frequency of data collection depended on the type of data collected. Parent questionnaires were administered at enrollment and every 6 months during office visits (when children were 6, 12, 18, and 24 months old). Telephone interviews with parents were conducted twice, once when the child was 2–4 months of age and again when the child was 30 months old. The child's medical records were reviewed at the end of the families' participation. Key informants also were interviewed at the beginning and end of the evaluation, and providers filled out annual surveys.

In addition, an embedded study that included direct observation and assessment of child behavior and parent-child interactions (measures not feasible for inclusion in the larger study) was conducted at 2 randomized sites. Data were gathered when children were 16–18 months and again at 34–37 months of age.

Measures

Computer-assisted telephone interviews were used to gather demographic information about the family and to survey parents about their child's development, concerns about child development or behavior, and referrals for behavioral or developmental problems. The phone survey also asked about parent-child activities, family routines, engagement in safety activities, parenting behaviors and knowledge (e.g., parents' expectations of their children and their nurturing activities), and parental depression. Finally, the interview assessed the extent to which families received developmentally related services from the pediatric practice and their satisfaction with the care they received. Data on hospitalizations, injuries, immunizations, and emergency department care came from parent self-report and the children's medical records.

Key informant interviews conducted by telephone with the lead physician, site administrator, and HS Specialists at baseline and 30 months post-implementation, were designed to document the degree to which the HS sites incorporated the program into the practice; to understand how sites may have modified the program; and to record the site's experience in implementing the program. A self-administered survey of all clinical and nonclinical staff in regular contact with pediatric patients provided information about their experience and personal satisfaction during the years that HS was implemented, their opinions of the value of particular services to parents, and their views of the HS program and its services. These data, along with program documents, will be the primary source of information used to explore the feasibility of implementing HS on a wide-scale basis.

The embedded study used direct observational measures, such as the Home Observation for Measurement of the Environment scale (HOME; Caldwell & Bradley, 1984) and the NCAST Teaching Scale (Barnard, 1994; Sumner & Spietz, 1994).

Unit of Analysis

The ultimate goal of the analysis of data from Healthy Steps is to obtain an overall estimate of the effectiveness of the Healthy Steps program among parents, children, and providers. The quasi-experimental and randomization sites are treated separately because of their different sampling structures. Analyses are examining how covariates at the practice level affect outcomes at the individual level. The evaluation will also study the effects of HS among subgroups, for example, low-, middle-, and high-income families.

The HS researchers use an "intention to treat" strategy (i.e., the inclusion of all participants enrolled in the intervention group, even those known to have received less than the full intervention or who dropped out). Thus the researchers will be able to evaluate the effectiveness of the HS program on a population of families who have differing service needs and different patterns of utilization, who are exposed to different clinical styles, and who experience different tenures in care. Analyses will therefore reflect a "real-world" evaluation and be useful for potential program replication efforts in the future.

Findings

Results to date indicate that HS had a positive impact on receipt of developmental services by families, parents' perceptions and expectations for care, and parenting safety practices (Hughart & the Healthy Steps Evaluation Team, 2002; Minkovitz et al., 2001). A greater percentage of intervention families than control/comparison families reported receiving four or more developmental services, having a home visit, and discussing five specific topics (calming baby, sleep position, routines, solid foods, and car seats) with their child's provider around 2–4 months. Intervention families were more than twice as likely as control families to be satisfied with their pediatric practice at 2–4 months, as measured by someone at the practice going "out of their way for them". Further, at 6 months, Healthy Steps families were more likely than control families to seek advice from someone at the practice. Finally, at 2–4 months, intervention families demonstrated better safety practices than control families; they were 25% less likely than control families to place their baby on his or her stomach to sleep, a position that has been associated with Sudden Infant Death Syndrome (SIDS).

In addition, early results from the embedded study indicate that HS had a modest impact on discipline strategies. Intervention mothers were less likely to use physical discipline than control mothers.

In the process study (Hughart & Healthy Steps Evaluation Team, 2002), physicians implementing the program consistently rated the HS Specialists as the most valuable component of the program. Not only did the Specialists lead to improved ability for clinical staff to address children's developmental and behavioral needs, but the program benefited practices in a more general sense as well. For example, the HS program was used as a marketing tool by participating practices. The process study also tracked challenges in implementation, such as relationship building between HS Specialists and other clinic staff.

Future analyses will examine the effects of the program on child injuries, hospitalizations, vaccination rates, and health care utilization, in addition to longer-term impacts on parenting knowledge and practices, child health and development, and provider attitudes and practices. Analyses will also evaluate the program's cost-effectiveness and potential for replication and institutionalization in general pediatric care.

Limitations

Results from the Healthy Steps evaluation are limited by the fact that the pediatric practices included in the study were not randomly selected. In fact, the 15 practices were intentionally selected to be representative of the best quality in pediatric care in order to determine if the program significantly adds to high-quality care already in place. Should HS prove to be an effective program, results from this study may not be applicable to lower quality practices, where implementation may be more difficult and outcomes may not be so positive.

Another limitation, one that plagues multisite evaluations in general, is uneven program implementation among the 15 sites. Although all the sites in this evaluation implemented all the components of the HS intervention, there were variations across sites in factors that contributed to the ease or difficulty of implementation (Women's and Children's Health Policy Center, 1999b). To address this issue, the Healthy Steps evaluation researchers will conduct qualitative analyses of the importance of these factors in implementation. Moreover, a parsimonious group of practice-level variables will be developed from process data and incorporated in the analyses of HS effects. Analyses for the Healthy Steps evaluation will thus be able to investigate difference in outcomes across sites, in addition to evaluating multisite data while taking into account variations in program implementation.

Public Use Files

HS evaluators intend to make the data available for public use once the project is further along in the evaluation process.

NOTES

The authors would like to thank the Administration on Children, Youth, and Families and the National Institute of Mental Health for providing funds for the writing of this chapter. We also wish to express our gratitude to Kathryn Harding (Healthy Families America), Peggy Hill (Nurse-Family Partnership), and Nancy Hughart (Healthy Steps) for providing up-to-date information about the projects profiled in this chapter and for extensive editing assistance. We are also grateful to Rebecca Fauth, Christy Brady-Smith, and Phyllis Gyamfi for editorial assistance.

1. The Nurse-Family Partnership (formerly known as the Nurse Home Visitation Project) is directed by David Olds (University of Colorado). Funders included the Colorado Trust, the Administration for Children and Families, and the Robert Wood Johnson Foundation. For more information see www.nccfc.org/nurseFamilyPartnership.cfm on-line.

2. Healthy Families America involves numerous evaluations across the country and is directed by multiple site-level project directors. Funders include Ronald McDonald House Charities and the Carnegie Foundation. For more information see http://www.healthyfamiliesamerica.org on-line.

3. PCAA, a nonprofit organization formerly known as the National Committee to Prevent Child Abuse, was founded in 1972 to increase public awareness of the problem of child abuse and the services available to prevent child abuse.

4. Healthy Steps is a program of the Commonwealth Fund, local funders, and health care providers. It is cosponsored by the American Academy of Pediatrics and was developed in collaboration with a multidisciplinary team from Boston University School of Medicine. The program evaluation is directed by Dr. Bernard Guyer (Johns Hopkins University). For additional information regarding this initiative, see http://www.healthysteps.org on-line.

5. Children were excluded from eligibility only if (a) their parents planned to move within 6 months; (b) their custodial parent did not speak English or Spanish fluently; (c) they were to be adopted or placed in foster care; or (d) they were too ill to make an office visit within the first 28 days of life.

CHAPTER 7

Child Welfare and Mental Health Initiatives

JANIS KUPERSMIDT, LISA MCCABE, AND DONNA BRYANT

Despite a universally perceived need for more information about young children's mental health, research initiatives on the mental health status, service use, and treatment of young children have lagged behind projects on older children and adolescents. The relative paucity of studies in this area has been attributed, for the most part, to both methodological and developmental reasons. First, the diagnostic systems developed for the assessment of psychiatric functioning may not adequately describe the behavior of young children; thus diagnostic instruments may not address psychiatric symptoms appropriately, in terms of type, quantity, intensity, or duration. Second, young children are more limited in their cognitive and communication skills, which presents a unique challenge for using them as informants about their own behavioral, emotional, or social functioning. Third, young children change so rapidly; this relative instability presents a significant challenge for evaluating the psychiatric meaning of behavior. Despite these issues, several ambitious and important research initiatives have been conducted or are currently being conducted to improve the mental health and welfare of young children.

In this chapter, three major research initiatives will be discussed in detail. First, we describe the five-site Consortium for Longitudinal Studies in Child Abuse and Neglect (LONGSCAN).[1] The second major research project is entitled the National Survey of Child and Adolescent Well-Being (NSCAW),[2] which involves a nationwide sample of children living in out-of-home placements. Finally, we highlight the Head Start Mental Health Research Consortium (HSMHRC),[3] a five-site initiative. These projects have in common the fact that they are basic research, multisite projects that were developed in response to research priorities identified by the federal government and are supported by the National Institute of Health and other agencies.

CONSORTIUM FOR LONGITUDINAL STUDIES IN CHILD ABUSE AND NEGLECT (LONGSCAN)

History

The U.S. Advisory Board on Child Abuse and Neglect (U.S. ABCAN, 1990, 1995) has reported on several occasions that the prevalence of child maltreatment has been reaching the point of a national emergency. In 1994, more than 2.9 million reports on 1.9 million children were made to Child Protective Services (CPS) agencies in the United States, and more than 1 million of these reports were substantiated by investigators (U.S. Department of Health and Human Services, 1996). Despite the increasing and large numbers of children referred to CPS, there are still many unreported cases of maltreatment. The negative ramifications of maltreatment for the child, family, and community are well known, and the consequences are also expensive. This crisis situation has resulted in a call for theoretically grounded longitudinal studies that explore the antecedents and consequences of child abuse and neglect (National Research Council, 1993). The LONGSCAN Consortium resulted from a Request for Applications (RFA) from the National Center on Child Abuse and Neglect (NCCAN). This RFA outlined the criteria for the program that included the development of a coordinating center as well as satellite centers that develop common protocols within a set of longitudinal studies to examine the antecedents and consequences of child maltreatment. The University of North Carolina at Chapel Hill was selected as the Coordinating Center for the project. Five sites were selected for the individual study sites: the UNC School of Public Health; Juvenile Protective Association of Chicago; Department of Health and Social Services in Seattle, Washington; San Diego State University; and Department of Pediatrics, University of Maryland at Baltimore.

Current Status

The LONGSCAN Consortium is completing the 10th year of a 20-year project. Extensive data that begin to address both the short- and long-term objectives of the consortium have been collected across the five sites. For example, LONGSCAN investigators have completed all age-4 baseline interviews and will submit their data to be archived. The North Carolina site has gathered data at birth and again at ages 1, 2, 3, 4, 6, 8, and 12. Telephone interviews have been completed for 5-, 7-, 9-, 10-, and 11-year-olds. The Baltimore, San Diego, and Seattle sites have completed data collection through age 8.

Goals

The overarching goals of the LONGSCAN Consortium are threefold: (a) to assess the negative outcomes associated with child maltreatment; (b) to evaluate the effects of societal interventions for families with suspected or substantiated child maltreatment; and (c) to examine possible moderators of the effects of child maltreatment on children's adjustment. The development of some common procedures and a common battery of measures allow for more powerful studies across samples. All children will have brief yearly follow-ups and extensive face-to-face assessments will be conducted at ages 4, 6, and 8. Sites have site-specific goals discussed below, and therefore each has some unique measures added to the common battery.

Theory of Change

LONGSCAN researchers attempt to examine child maltreatment using an ecological-developmental framework (Bronfenbrenner, 1993). Thus these empirical studies go beyond main effect models and instead investigate more complex interactions in the antecedents and consequences of child maltreatment (including an examination of the child in various social systems such as family and the larger culture; Runyan et al., 1998).

Design and Methods

Some of the design features of LONGSCAN are as follows:

- A developmental focus throughout childhood and adolescence
- The selection of samples of children from along the continuum of child protection, including at-risk, reported for maltreatment, substantiated for maltreatment, receiving family treatment for maltreatment, and in foster care as a consequence of maltreatment
- Use of a common battery of measures
- Use of a common data center
- The development of a governance structure to best utilize the diverse expertise of each of the disciplines represented among the sites

Some of the unique activities of the Coordinating Center include providing technical assistance to promote uniformity of method across the five sites;

conducting data analyses regarding outcomes of maltreated children; conducting case-control analyses comparing results across sites; and supporting site-specific analyses. In 1999, the North Carolina site inaugurated data collection with a set of new child self-report measures of maltreatment history with 12-year-olds in the longitudinal sample. An audio computer-assisted self-interview (ACASI) format was used in order to provide subjects with the highest possible level of privacy.

Each of the five sites that compose LONGSCAN addresses a slightly different aspect of child maltreatment using different populations. Table 7.1 describes the samples and research foci of each of the five sites. At the Chicago site, major data collection efforts are conducted using the LONGSCAN age-4 and 5 protocols. Off-year tracking interviews are conducted for 3- and 5-year-olds. A face-to-face interviewing format is used for both yearly tracking visits and major data collection points. At the North Carolina site, home visits were made to interview mothers of newborn children. Mothers were reinterviewed when their child reached one year of age. Subsamples of the original population of mothers were also interviewed yearly after the age-1 interview. This site joined the LONGSCAN Consortium after the age-3 interviews were completed. Additional telephone interviews were conducted at ages 5, 7, 9, 10, and 11. Now at age 12, new computer-assisted self-interviewing methods are being used. At the Seattle site, families were recruited at baseline between infancy and 4 years of age. Data were collected on 4-, 5-, 6-, 7-, and 8-year-olds and interviewers are currently in the field with protocols for data collection at ages 9 and 10. The San Diego site is conducting face-to-face interviews with children, youth, and caregivers. The LONGSCAN assessments were conducted on children removed from their homes before 3½ years of age and baseline assessments were conducted at ages 4 or 6. Finally, at the Baltimore site, baseline LONGSCAN child interviews began at age 4, followed by home visits with extensive data collection from mothers and father figures at age 5. A subset of the original sample of children was reinterviewed at age 6.

Measures

Cross-site measures involve the assessment of individual child, parent, and environmental factors. For example, information about children's temperament, intelligence, health, behavior problems, competence, and exposure to substance abuse or violence is gathered. For adults, parental attitudes, mental and physical health, victimization, child maltreatment, and substance abuse, among other things, are assessed. Assessments of the environment are conducted at the micro, exo and macro level and include measures for characteristics of the home environment, spousal/partner relationship, family

Table 7.1. Description of Samples Used in Five Sites of the LONGSCAN Project

Project	Principal Investigators	Sample	Age of First Cohort	Primary Research Foci
Chicago: The Capella Project	Mary Wood Schneider and Patrick Curtis (Juvenile Protective Association, Chicago)	180 maltreated infants whose families had been referred to CPS for either 6-month family intervention ($n = 80$) or the usual CPS care ($n = 100$) and 137 matched neighborhood controls	Infancy	1. Parent-infant attachment and maltreatment 2. Effects of clinical intervention on maltreated children
Chapel Hill: The Stress and Social Support Study	Jonathan Kotch (Department of Maternal and Child Health, UNC-CH, Chapel Hill, NC)	221 high-risk infants at birth, including 74 referred to CPS by age 4 and 147 not referred to CPS by age 4	4–5 years old (follow-up of infant sample)	1. Family stress, parental attitudes and behavior, and social support as predictors of child abuse 2. Social support as moderator of maltreatment
Seattle: The Impact of Investigation	Diana English (Department of Social and Health Services, Seattle)	261 children judged to be at moderate risk following a report to CPS [a]	1–4 years old	1. Effects of risk on child outcomes 2. Impact of investigation on substantiated and unsubstantiated cases
San Diego: The Foster Care Mental Health Study	John Landsverk and Alan Litrownik (San Diego State University, San Diego)	320 maltreated children who had entered the dependency system and been put in out-of-home placement with a relative or foster family [b]	1–4 years old	1. Predictors of successful vs. unsuccessful reunification of families 2. Impact of service intervention
Baltimore: Longitudinal Study of Child Neglect	Howard Dubowitz, Maureen Black, and Raymond Starr, Jr. (Department of Pediatrics, University of Maryland, Baltimore)	322 children from three Baltimore pediatric clinics for children with nonorganic failure to thrive ($n = 123$), children with prenatal drug use or HIV-infected mother ($n = 83$), and low-income inner-city children ($n = 116$)	4 years old	1. Ecological determinants and outcomes of neglect 2. Predictors of CPS involvement

[a] Of these 261 reports, 159 were later substantiated, and 102 were not (60 and 40%, respectively).

[b] Fifty percent returned home by age 4.

functioning, service use, neighborhood setting, school safety, language, and ethnicity of child. Data are gathered through parent and teacher reports and child assessment/interviews.

Units of Analysis

The main level of analysis is the individual child. For the multisite study, broad-scope analyses included examination of the child, the primary female caregivers, fathers or father figures in the child's life, and archival data. Also, each of the five sites will be conducting site-level analyses reflecting the principal investigator's (PI) specific interests including neglect, attachment, stress and social support, parent-child interaction, and the role of the father in his child's life. Main analyses will be conducted both within and across sites. Cross-site analyses will be useful when invariant processes are hypothesized across groups (e.g., relations between family stress and support as a protective factor among maltreated children). The cross-site analyses may include up to 1,400 subjects, a sufficient sample size to examine the moderating effects of protective factors, as well as the person-process-context models. Also, data will be analyzed by sex, race, low birth weight, relationship to child, caregiver, education level, marital status, and welfare support (socioeconomic status).

Findings

The LONGSCAN project has published several papers (see Black, Dubowitz, Hutcheson, Berenson-Howard, & Starr, 1995; Black, Howard, Kim, & Ricardo, 1998; Harrington, Black, Starr, & Dubowitz, 1998; and Kotch, Browne, Dufort, Winsor, & Catellier, 1999). Some of the most important findings, based upon baseline assessments of children, suggest that these children are exhibiting serious developmental and behavioral problems. For example, for the children older than infancy, 25–40% exhibited behavior problems in the clinical range and 66% had at least borderline developmental deficits.

One of the unique aspects of LONGSCAN is that maltreatment status is measured through the use of multiple methods and multiple informants. Using this method of measurement, approximately one-fifth of the children with a history of maltreatment reports have been reported three or more times at the North Carolina and Seattle sites. This suggests that for a subsample of maltreated children, the maltreatment is ongoing. Also, child neglect reports were found to be underrepresented in the Central Registry (at the North Carolina site), and many of the referrals for physical or sexual abuse were classified as neglect by the parent, suggesting a misclassification of the child's maltreatment experience.

The sites also examined predictors of maltreatment and found that poverty, maternal depression, high numbers of children in the household, and low maternal education significantly predicted reports of maltreatment. In addition, children whose mothers were currently experiencing domestic violence were also at high risk for child abuse and neglect. Maternal alcohol use was less consistently associated with child maltreatment reports. Protective factors against maltreatment were also examined and only caretaker's social support emerged as a significant factor.

With regard to the father's involvement in the family, a father's positive contribution to parenting and finances, as well as his presence in the home, can significantly lower the incidence of child maltreatment. In turn, when a father is less nurturing, less involved with the household tasks, and demonstrates a lower sense of being an effective parent, the occurrence of child maltreatment is likely.

These findings have direct implications for the design of preventive intervention programs. Some possible components include increasing social support services and stress reduction methods for at-risk mothers, introducing means for increasing family income, providing family planning services for high-risk mothers, acquiring a better understanding of the factors contributing to a father's involvement in the family unit, and creating family-centered social and economic policies.

Predictors of unintentional injury (e.g., burns, poisoning, falls) to infants were also examined. The best predictors were family conflict, number of siblings in the home, and maternal unemployment. Use of social support among highly stressed mothers was associated with fewer unintentional injuries.

Risk and protective factors for at-risk children were also examined in analyses of the data. At-risk children had more positive outcomes if there were indices of higher social capital available to the family, including caretaker's social support, neighborhood support, regular attendance at religious services, presence of a two-parent family, and fewer siblings. Aggressive behavior in at-risk children was predicted by a history of neglect, witnessing community violence, harsh discipline, and maternal depression.

Many children were reported for exposure to maltreatment to social service agencies. However, all reports of maltreatment were not substantiated after investigation by a caseworker. The Seattle site examined predictors of substantiation and reported that perceived dangerousness of the alleged act, amount of supervision of the child, and substance abuse in the home were the best predictors of substantiation. In addition, caretaker social support, caretaker history of domestic violence, the child's being an only child, and recognition of the problem were associated with rereferral for maltreatment.

One of the important implications of LONGSCAN is that involvement with Child Protective Services is often associated with contact with other needed services for preschool children. These findings suggest that other non-CPS professionals involved with preschool children, such as day care providers and physicians, should be more actively involved in referring children and families to services.

Limitations

LONGSCAN is using current advances in theory and computational statistical methodology in an attempt to decrease problems related to the use of longitudinal data and is able to describe patterns of change and to examine multiple outcome variables. The strategies used include structural equation modeling (SEM), generalized estimating equations (GEE), hierarchical models, and multiple regression techniques. These analytic approaches reduce limitations found in prior studies.

Public Use Files

The 4-year-old interview data, which is the common set of data, is archived at the National Data Archive of Child Abuse and Neglect at Cornell University. Additional data from the multisite study is expected to be archived as well. For more information, visit the Web site (www.ndacan.cornell.edu).

NATIONAL SURVEY OF CHILD AND ADOLESCENT WELL-BEING (NSCAW)

History

Little national research examines the long-term outcomes for children who come in contact with the child welfare system and the specific links between child welfare systems and services to child and family outcomes. Serious concerns exist about Child Protective Service agencies and their ability to meet the needs of children who come to their attention. Specifically, more information is needed about the benefits of kin versus nonkin placements of children, the benefits of long-term foster care versus more permanent guardianship or adoption, the benefits of institutional placement versus family-based placement, and the effects of family disruption on children during critical developmental periods as well as ways to ameliorate potentially harmful effects of disruption and placements. In general, more information is needed so that services provided will better match the child's needs.

The NSCAW project developed in response to a congressional directive to the Secretary of the Department of Health and Human Services (DHHS), which led to an RFA to conduct a national study of children who are at risk for abuse or neglect or are involved with the child welfare system. The NSCAW includes the collection of longitudinal data on different types of abuse or neglect, agency contacts and services, and out-of-home placements. The results of this study are designed to yield reliable state-level data. Title V, section 429A, in the amendments to Title IV-B of the Social Security Act, authorized the Secretary of DHHS to conduct a "National Random Sample Study of Child Welfare" and the Administration on Children, Youth, and Families has undertaken this project. The study offers an opportunity to expand the knowledge base about the characteristics of children and families who come to the attention of the child welfare system, to understand the agency and court decisions affecting these children and families, to understand their service experiences, and to chart the outcomes that result for these clients.

The national study is being conducted through a contract with Research Triangle Institute (RTI) and with subcontracts to the University of California at Berkeley (UCB), the University of North Carolina at Chapel Hill (UNC-CH), and Caliber Associates. The project has 2 advisory groups. The first advisory group is a Federal Steering Committee (FSC), which includes representatives from the Administration on Children, Youth, and Families (ACYF), the Administration for Children and Families (ACF), the Children's Bureau, the Office on Child Abuse and Neglect (OCAN), and the Office of the Assistant Secretary for Planning and Evaluation (ASPE). The second advisory group is a Technical Work Group (TWG), which includes experts on child welfare agencies and systems, social welfare policy, and child youth development. These advisory groups provide advice and consultation to the Federal Project Officer (FPO) and the project team on policy and research issues, research design, methods, operations, instrument development, sample design, and priorities and strategies for dissemination of results.

Current Status

The project team began working together in 1997 and expects to continue until 2003. Major activities completed include (a) obtaining cooperation from remaining states and agencies; (b) negotiating details of sampling and data collection with local agencies; (c) obtaining Office of Management and Budget review and approval; (d) obtaining approval from individual Institutional Review Boards; (e) hiring and training field staff; (f) finalizing English and Spanish versions of all instruments; (g) beginning data collection; and (h) preparing the second annual report. Pretesting occurred in August and September of 1999. The first wave of data collection began in October of 1999 and continued through September 2000. Another round of data was collected in September 2002. For annual reports, see http://www.2.acf.dhhs.gov/pro-grams/hsb/core/dox/ann_sum.htm on-line.

Goals

The primary goals of the project are to describe the outcomes experienced by children and families and to gain an understanding of the factors that contribute to these outcomes. Specifically, the NSCAW aims to describe the children and families who come in contact with the child welfare system, the pathways and services children and families experience while in the child welfare system, and the short- and long-term outcomes for these children and families. The short-term goals focus on developing an understanding of the characteristics of children and families most likely to come into and stay in care, the characteristics of children who come to the attention of the child welfare system, as well as the characteristics associated with coming versus not coming into care, the service needs of children and families, and the kinds of services *actually* provided to children and families entering the system and what determines the kinds of services provided. The long-term goals are to describe the kinds of services or interventions associated with different out-comes, and how children and families change over time.

There are several secondary goals including intensive substudies, with samples selected from the core study. The issues to be addressed include collecting in-depth information about the nature and costs of the services provided, a follow-up of children already in foster care at the outset of NSCAW, the responsiveness of agency practices, policies, and services to the developmental needs of infants and young children in the child welfare sys-tem, the developmental outcomes for children in the child welfare system, identifying children at-risk or those who have a history of maltreatment and who *have not* come in contact with the system, and changes in "system chil-dren" over time. The implementation of these substudies will be dependent on the continued availability of funding.

Theory of Change

The research attempts to examine the effects of various child and family services (including foster care placement) on child development. Researchers take into account child, family, and service characteristics in examining these associations.

Design and Methods

The sample contains children between the ages of 0 and 14 years of age, including children who are and who are not presently receiving services from the child welfare system. Four annual rounds of face-to-face interviews with children and caregivers will be conducted between November 1999 and September 2003.

Approximately 6,700 children from 107 child welfare agencies, who entered the child welfare system within a one-year period beginning in September 1999, were sampled. There were approximately 5,400 children who entered the study through the investigation sampling procedures, 600 through other gateways, and 700 through out-of-home placements. Approximately 4,200 children will participate in ongoing services, and, along with 600 recruited through other gateways, there will be 3,230 in the home and 1,570 in out-of-home placements. Data collection sites are in California, Florida, Illinois, Michigan, New York, Ohio, Pennsylvania, and Texas, as well as in 32 other states, and will be completed over a 3-year period. An additional 700 children who have been in out-of-home placement for one year will also be assessed.

These children were selected from 100 primary sampling units (PSUs) in 107 counties nationwide. For the most part, a PSU is a county; however, in a few instances, a PSU represents a region within a county or a group of counties. The sampling plan considered variations among child welfare agencies and the potential contributions of those variations to child and family outcomes. Also, oversampling strategies were used to ensure that an entering cohort of children represents all of the major service conditions of interest.

Measures

Data are collected across many different informants and domains of interest including children's health and physical well-being, cognitive developmental and academic achievement, and social-emotional adjustment. The family and child's experiences with the child welfare system are also reviewed. Concurrent life experiences and child outcomes are assessed. Spanish versions of all measures were created. This study is a direct result of the 1996 Personal Responsibility and Work Opportunity Reconciliation Act (PRWORA). Therefore, all data collected will reflect family circumstances and experiences post-PRWORA. Informants include the custodial caregiver, the noncustodial biological caregiver, the children in the welfare system, their teachers, their caseworkers, other agency personnel, review of administrative records, and service providers outside the child welfare system. Each child is interviewed in person annually.

Units of Analysis

The child and the family are the units of analysis.

Findings

Data collection is ongoing; no results are available yet.

Public Use Files

Data collection has not yet been completed. Plans are for the data to be archived for public use.

HEAD START MENTAL HEALTH RESEARCH CONSORTIUM (HSMHRC)

History

Little research exists about the prevalence of mental health problems in very young low-income children. In particular, not much is known about how identification rates in Head Start programs (where emotional and behavioral disorders are rarely diagnosed and speech and language impairments are more prevalent) compare to those in the general population. In addition, few studies have examined the trajectory of social and emotional development of young low-income children, in spite of evidence for their increased exposure to risk factors (such as violence and abuse) associated with problematic behaviors.

These gaps in our existing knowledge base, combined with the fact that Head Start serves as one of the earliest mechanisms for identification of and intervention with low-income children and families, prompted the creation of the Head Start Mental Health Research Consortium in 1997. Through a joint effort, ACYF and NIMH awarded five research grants to begin a new young children's mental health research initiative. Recipients of these grants included Columbia University (in partnership with Harvard University), University of New Mexico, University of North Carolina, University of Oregon, and Vanderbilt University.

This research consortium built upon previous work examining mental health in a Head Start context, including (a) the Task Force on Head Start and Mental Health (supported by the American Orthopsychiatric Association), (b) the Descriptive Study of the Head Start Health Component, (c) the Head Start Performance Standards, and (d) *Lessons from the Field: Head Start Mental Health Strategies to Meet Changing Needs* by Yoshikawa and Knitzer (1997). With guidance from program officers Kimberly Hoagwood and Peter Jensen at NIMH and Michael Lopez and Louisa Tarullo at ACYF, three of the five sites (University of New Mexico, University of North Carolina, and Vanderbilt University) implemented and evaluated mental health intervention programs for children in Head Start. Two sites (Columbia University and University of Oregon) focused their efforts on the development of new assessments appropriate for use with diverse groups of low-income children.

Current Status

The HSMHRC concluded its fifth and final year in 2002; therefore each of the five individual grantees recently completed data collection on intervention and assessment efforts that focused on mental health issues in low-income children. Analyses are currently under way at each of the five sites. Possibilities for cross-site analysis and future collaborative work are under discussion.

Goals

The HSMHRC aimed to further advance our understanding of and ability to provide high-quality identification, prevention, and intervention services for improving the mental health of low-income children in Head Start programs across the country. This focus translated to three broad research questions:

- What are the prevalence, types, and severity of emotional, behavioral, and language problems among Head Start children in multiple communities, and how can these problems be identified effectively and reliably in real-world settings?
- What types of mental health–related services are available to Head Start children with emotional, behavioral, and language problems and to their caregivers in multiple communities?
- What is the impact of home-based, classroom-based, and skills instruction interventions on the emotional, behavioral, and language problems of Head Start children, and how does the impact vary across different types of interventions and/or across different settings? (Boyce, Hoagwood, Lopez, & Tarullo, 2000, p. 9)

Theory of Change

Research in the HSMHRC was based on the theory that early identification and primary prevention better promote and facilitate long-term positive mental health outcomes (Coie et al., 1993). Screening young children for problematic behaviors allows researchers and practitioners to intervene early on with children who may have behavioral or language difficulties and thus prevent more severe mental health problems in later childhood, adolescence, and adulthood.

The projects in this consortium also operated under the assumption that the Head Start program provides a unique venue for screening young children and implementing mental health interventions for a number of reasons (Lopez, Tarullo, Forness, & Boyce, 2000). First, Head Start is a federally funded program that reaches large numbers of low-income children and their families. Second, as a comprehensive program, it provides an ideal setting for multifaceted interventions to take place. For these reasons, the HSMHRC focused its efforts on Head Start programs nationwide.

Design and Methods

Three of the five sites worked on the development of comprehensive interventions for improving young children's mental health. At the University of North Carolina, a multimodal intervention provided both a universal and an indicated intervention curriculum that included classroom management, literacy enhancement, social skill development, parent education, and home visiting. Two cohorts of children (a total of nearly 200 four-year-olds) from 37 Head Start classrooms participated in the project. Children (approximately 50% boys) were predominantly African American. Twenty-two classrooms served as the experimental group ($N = 103$). Within these classrooms, children (about 50%) identified as having problems with aggression and noncompliance received the indicated intervention. All children in the experimental classrooms received the universal intervention. An additional 15 classrooms (with both indicated and nonindicated children; $N = 90$) served as a control group.

At Vanderbilt University, four cohorts of 3-year-old children ($N = 850$) from Head Start programs in the Nashville area were screened by parents and teachers for behavioral problems and communication deficits. These children were then followed through kindergarten or first grade (depending on the cohort). A subset of 45 of these children, identified as at risk for developing conduct disorder on the basis of these screenings, took part in a communication and behavior focused intervention consisting of (a) parent training, (b) classroom intervention, and (c) maintenance training and transition support. A second group of 45 at-risk children comprised the control group. Children (approximately 50% boys) were primarily low-income African Americans.

At the third intervention site, the University of New Mexico, a self-determination curriculum was implemented for 12 weeks in three Head Start classrooms. The curriculum was later expanded to 16 weeks. Two additional classrooms served as a control group. This intervention taught social-emotional skills (e.g., direction following, sharing, and problem solving) through the use of stories, games, and songs. Additionally, a parent training program was also offered. Three classes (held every 4 weeks during the intervention) introduced parents to skills related to communication with community agencies and problem solving in order to help them better advocate for and support their children. In order to encourage parents to reinforce at home the behaviors taught to their children in the classroom, these sessions also informed parents about the curriculum being taught to their children in Head Start.

At the University of Oregon site, the goal was to further develop and test the Early Screening Project (Feil & Becker, 1993; Feil et al., 1995), a tool that uses a multiple-gating procedure to screen children for externalizing and internalizing behavior problems. Approximately 1,000 children (N = 954; 47% female) from 41 Head Start classrooms throughout the state of Oregon were screened with the Stage 1 teacher ranking procedure (the first "gate" of the ESP). Children were 3 or 4 years old at the time of assessment and represented diverse ethnic and racial backgrounds including white, Hispanic, Asian American, African American, and Native American. A subset of 90 children who ranked high on externalizing or internalizing behaviors (and who had parental permission to participate), along with a comparison group of 36 children who did not rank high on either externalizing or internalizing, were subsequently followed up with ESP Stage 2 and Stage 3 measures in addition to other commonly used mental health measures for children (e.g., the Child Behavior Checklist).

Finally, the fifth site (Columbia University/Harvard University) focused on the assessment of self-regulation, a process thought to underlie the development of mental health. Numerous tasks based on the work of researchers such as Kochanska (Kochanska, Murray, & Coy, 1997; Kochanska, Murray, Jacques, Koenig, & Vandegeest, 1996) and Diamond (Diamond & Taylor, 1996), as well as psychological batteries (e.g., the Leiter International Performance Scale—Revised; Roid & Miller, 1995, 1997), have been adapted and developed for use with both individuals and groups of preschoolers in homes and classrooms. Tests were conducted with 115 low-income, English- and Spanish-speaking children from a variety of racial and ethnic backgrounds. A subset of these assessments was selected for inclusion in the third wave of data collection for the birth cohort of the Project on Human Development in Chicago Neighborhoods (for more information, see Chapter 10, this volume). More than 850 four-year-olds, followed since birth, were assessed in their homes using four measures that tap delay of gratification, motor control, and sustained attention. Children come from diverse ethnic and economic backgrounds and speak English, Spanish, or Polish (for details, see Chapter 10, this volume).

Measures

Measures varied across the five sites. However, given the common focus on young children's mental health, there was significant overlap in the constructs assessed. The majority of sites gathered information about children's social skills, behavior problems, attention deficit/hyperactivity disorder (ADHD) symptoms, and functional impairment. Typically, multiple sources (including parent and teacher report and direct child assessments) were employed in order to obtain these data. Information on family context, exposure to violence, classroom quality, and service use was also common across sites. In many cases, efforts were made to develop "cross walks" across sites by using identical measures at similar time points.

Unit of Analysis

The individual child is the primary focus of analyses at each site. Where applicable, child-level cross-site analyses will be conducted. In addition, the three intervention sites are examining program implementation effectiveness. The University of Oregon and Columbia University will also assess the cross-cultural validity and psychometric properties of newly developed assessment procedures.

Findings

Results from individual sites have been presented at various conferences (e.g., Lopez, 1999, 2000; Lopez & Boyce, 2002; Tarullo, 2000) and in a special issue of Behavioral Disorders (Kauffman & Brigham, 2000). Preliminary findings suggest that there are high rates of aggression in preschool and Head Start classrooms (Kupersmidt, Bryant, & Willoughby, 2000) and that these behavior problems often co-occur with language delays (Kaiser, Hancock, Cai, Foster, & Hester, 2000). Preliminary findings also suggest promising results for the intervention work being conducted in Head Start programs. At the University of New Mexico site, children in the experimental classrooms demonstrated significant improvements on adaptive behavior, social interaction, and attentional skills when compared to children in control classrooms (Serna, Nielsen, Lambros, & Forness, 2000). Analyses of the efficacy of other intervention approaches are currently underway at the University of North Carolina and Vanderbilt University.

Results from work on the development of new assessment techniques show promise as well. The ESP was used successfully across four of the sites (Oregon, North Carolina, New Mexico, and Vanderbilt). Preliminary findings suggest that it is an effective, easy to use, and cross-culturally appropriate screening instrument (Feil, Walker, Severson, & Ball, 2000).

Findings from Columbia University demonstrate the potential for using self-regulation assessments in homes and classroom and with individuals or groups of young low-income children (McCabe, Hernandez, Lara, & Brooks-Gunn, 2000; McCabe, Rebello-Britto, Hernandez, & Brooks-Gunn, 2003). A variety of measures, either adapted from laboratory or clinical assessments, or newly developed, have worked well in more ecologically valid settings. Results of the associations among self-regulation and individual, family, and neighborhood characteristics are forthcoming.

Limitations

One of the greatest challenges to evaluating new interventions is taking into account how well a program is implemented across sites or classrooms. Systematic records of program fidelity enable researchers to assess how well the "same" intervention is implemented across sites. Gathering these kinds of data, however, is time consuming and costly (and sometimes premature for a new program that is constantly developing and changing), and therefore was done on only a limited basis in these projects.

Another challenge across these projects was participant recruitment. Because of the sensitive nature of gathering information on children's mental health and the potential for stigmatization, some parents were reluctant to participate in the studies. In their second cohort of children, the University of Oregon chose to invite all parents and children to participate (instead of selecting participants based on early screenings). This practice resulted in increased costs for the researchers, but did increase the participation rate.

Public Use Files

Decisions about public use of the data have not yet been made.

NOTES

We would like to thank Jennifer Resnick, Kimberly Hoagwood, Joan Luby, Desmond Runyan, Wanda Hunter, Robert McMahon, and Michael Willoughby for their help in preparing this chapter. Lisa McCabe would also like to acknowledge Susan Kinsey and Kristen Siebenaler at the Research Triangle Institute for providing information for this chapter, and the Administration on Children, Youth, and Families and the NIMH Head Start Mental Health Research Consortium for funding. The authors are grateful to Phyllis Gyamfi, Sandra Lara, and Christina Borbely for their editorial assistance.

1. Janis Kupersmidt is the primary author of this section of Chapter 7. Principal investigators are Desmond Runyan, Wanda Hunter, Patrick Curtis, Mary

Schneider, Jonathan Kotch, Diana English, John Landsverk, Alan Litrownik, Howard Dubowitz, Maureen Black, and Raymond Starr. The National Institute of Health is the funder. For more information see http://www.bios.unc.edu/cscc/ LONG/longdesc.html on-line.

2. Janis Kupersmidt is the primary author of this section of Chapter 7. Principal investigators are Paul Biener, Richard Barth, and Desmond Runyan (University of North Carolina). The funder is the Administration on Children, Youth and Families. For more information see http://www.acf.hhs.gov/programs/core/ongoing_research/ afc/wellbeing_local_child/wellbeing_local_execusum.html on-line.

3. Lisa McCabe is the primary author of this section of Chapter 7. Principal investigators are Jeanne Brooks-Gunn, Loretta Serna, Elizabeth Nielson, Steve Forness, Donna Bryant, Janis Kupersmidt, Edward Feil, Hill Walker, Herbert Severson, Ann Kaiser, Michael Foster and Terry Hancock. This study is funded by the Administration for Children, Youth, and Families of the U.S. Department of Health and Human Services and the National Institute of Mental Health. Additional information may be obtained from http://www.acf.dhhs.gov/programs/ core/ongoing_research/acyfnimh/acyfnimh.html on-line.

CHAPTER 8

Early Child Care Initiatives

PART I: THE NICHD EARLY CHILD CARE RESEARCH NETWORK
PART II: PHYLLIS GYAMFI, NATASHA CABRERA, AND JODIE ROTH

During the past 25 years a dramatic change has taken place in the early experiences of the youngest children in the United States. In 1975, 39% of
married mothers with children under 6 years of age worked outside the home;
today, 64% do so (U.S. Bureau of Labor Statistics, 1997). This increase in
employment among mothers of young children is the result of both economic
conditions (Oppenheimer, 1973, 1982) and the changing role of women in
the family and society (Danziger & Gottschalk, 1986; McCartney & Phillips,
1988; Silverstein, 1991). The change in child care patterns in the United States
is related primarily to this change in employment patterns. As a result, by
1990 more than 50% of infants under 12 months of age were being cared
for on a routine basis by someone other than their mothers (Hayes, Palmer,
& Zaslow, 1990; Hofferth, Brayfield, Deich, & Holcomb, 1991).

The dramatic increase in the number of infants receiving nonmaternal
care has generated fundamental scientific and social policy questions about
the effects of early child care experiences on children's development (Booth,
1992; Fox & Fein, 1990). Some argue, for example, that any and all child
care poses risks for infants because healthy development requires continuous caregiving by one person, usually the mother (Hojat, 1990; Leach, 1994;
White, 1985). Others contend that child care, as experienced in the United
States, is problematic primarily when it is extensive, defined as more than
20–30 hours per week (Belsky, 1988, 1990). Still others assert that very young
children can thrive in child care arrangements if the quality of care is high
(Clarke-Stewart, 1987; Field, 1991; McGurk, Caplan, Hennessy, Martin, &

Moss, 1993; Phillips, McCartney, & Scarr, 1987). Finally, some argue that early experiences do not alter developmental trajectories unless they are characterized by extreme deprivation, as in the case of abuse and neglect (Scarr, 1992).

In this chapter, four early child care initiatives are detailed. In Part I, the NICHD Study of Early Child Care[1] examines the relation between child care and children's development over the first seven years of life. Part II profiles the Cost, Quality, and Child Outcomes (CQO) Study,[2] which examines the interaction between quality and the cost of providing child care services for children, and also provides briefer profiles for two early child care initiatives related to welfare reform, the National Study of Child Care for Low-Income Families,[3] which explores the structure and sufficiency of child care markets for low-income families in the era of welfare reform, and the Growing Up in Poverty (GUP) Project,[4] which tracks the effects of welfare reform on children.

Part I. NICHD Study of Early Child Care: Contexts of Development and Developmental Outcomes over the First Seven Years of Life

NICHD Early Child Care Research Network

The NICHD Study of Early Child Care is a natural history study that describes the family and child care/school contexts of development in the first 10 years of life and examines the associations between variations in such contexts and the developmental outcomes of children from different parts of the country. The developmental outcomes studied are in the social-emotional, cognitive, linguistic, achievement, and physical growth and health domains. The NICHD study is the most comprehensive study to date about the relation between child care and children's development over the first ten years of life.

CURRENT STATUS

Families with newborn infants were recruited during 1991 from 10 sites. Phase III of the study is currently being conducted to follow over 1,100 of the children to 2005 through their sixth year in school.

Numerous articles have been published on the Phase I data (e.g., NICHD Early Child Care Research Network [ECCRN], 1992, 1996, 1997a, 1997b, 1997c, 1998a, 1998b, 1999a, 1999b, 1999c, 2000). The findings presented can be classified into four categories. First, reports describing the nature of the sample and the child care that children receive were published. These include an examination of regulatable characteristics of care (e.g., adult-to-child ratio and caregiver education and training), patterns and predictors of child care usage during the first year of life, and child care for children in poverty. Second, the role of the family for children in child care has been reported. Third, the relations between child care and children's relationship with their mothers when the children were 6, 15, 24, and 36 months of age, after controlling for family characteristics, have been explored. Finally, the relations between child care and children's development, with controls for the influence of the family environment, have been examined. Specifically, we have examined relations of child care in the first three years of life to cognitive and language development, security of mother-child attachment, peer relations, and children's compliance, self-control, and problem behaviors. We have also examined the association between indices of quality of

This study is directed by a Steering Committee and supported by NICHD through a cooperative agreement (U10), which calls for scientific collaboration between the grantees and the NICHD staff. The participating investigators are listed in alphabetical order with their institutional affiliations designated by number: Virginia Allhusen (10); Mark Appelbaum (11); Jay Belsky (1); Cathryn L. Booth (19); Robert Bradley (9); Celia Brownell (15); Peg Burchinal (13); Bettye Caldwell (9); Susan Campbell (15); Alison Clarke-Stewart (10); Martha Cox (13); Ganie DeHart (7); Sarah L. Friedman (4); Kathryn Hirsh-Pasek (8); Aletha Huston (16); Elizabeth Jaeger (6); Jean Kelly (19); Bonnie Knoke (5); Nancy Marshall (21); Kathleen McCartney (3); Marion O'Brien (14); Margaret Tresch Owen (17); C. Chris Payne (14); Deborah Phillips (2); Robert Pianta (18); Suzanne Randolph (12); Wendy Wagner Robeson (21); Susan J. Spieker (19); Deborah Lowe Vandell (20); Kathleen E. Wallner-Allen (22); Marsha Weinraub (8). The institutional affiliations, in alphabetical order, are Birkbeck College, University of London (1); Georgetown University (2); Harvard University (3); National Institute of Child Health and Human Development (4); Research Triangle Institute (5); Saint Joseph's University (6); State University of New York at Geneseo (7); Temple University (8); University of Arkansas at Little Rock (9); University of California, Irvine (10); University of California, San Diego (11); University of Maryland at College Park (12); University of North Carolina at Chapel Hill (13); University of North Carolina at Greensboro (14); University of Pittsburgh (15); University of Texas–Austin (16); University of Texas–Dallas (17); University of Virginia (18); University of Washington (19); University of Wisconsin–Madison (20); Wellesley College (21); Westat (22). We wish to express our appreciation to the study coordinators at each site who supervised the data collection, to the research assistants who collected the data, and especially to the families and child care providers who welcomed us into their homes and workplaces with good grace, and cooperated willingly with our repeated requests for information. Correspondence concerning this article should be addressed to NICHD Early Child Care Research Network, OEP, Office of the Director, NICHD, 6100 Executive Blvd., 4A05, Rockville, MD 20852.

care that can be regulated (e.g., adult-to-child ratio) and the social and cognitive development of children.

GOALS

The primary purpose of the NICHD Study of Early Child Care is to examine how variations in nonmaternal care are related to children's social-emotional adjustment, cognitive, linguistic, and achievement performance, and physical growth and health. Nonmaternal care is defined as regular care by someone other than the child's mother. Nonmaternal care can be provided by a relative (including the father) or by a nonrelative. It can be provided in the child's home, in someone else's home (e.g., a child care home), or in a child care center. Children's social-emotional adjustment is measured in terms of the quality of their relationships with parents, care providers, and peers; their social competence in various settings; the extent to which they have behavioral problems; and their self-concept and identity. Cognitive performance reflects children's knowledge about the world and their ability to attend to information, abstract it, and use it in a variety of ways (e.g., reasoning or problem solving). Language performance is indicated by children's comprehension of language and their ability to express themselves verbally. Achievement includes academic knowledge and skills needed for school, primarily literacy and numeracy. Physical growth is measured by height and weight, and health is measured by assessing the presence of chronic disease such as asthma and the frequency of minor illnesses such as ear infections, upper respiratory infections, and gastrointestinal infections.

Two conceptual frameworks guide the study. The ecological conceptualization takes into account the complex interactions of nonmaternal care experiences with home and family conditions, parenting practices, and child characteristics, and attempts to place individuals and families in a larger social, cultural, and economic context. The developmental/life-course approach focuses attention on the timing of events in the lives of children and their families. Both approaches drive the longitudinal design of the study because they emphasize the importance of time in understanding variations in psychological outcomes.

Because this is a prospective, longitudinal study, the data are well suited for the evaluation of four models pertaining to the ways in which early child care experiences may be related to development: Model 1: Child care contributes cumulatively to developmental outcomes, and its effects increase gradually over time or exposure; Model 2: Child care's effects on developmental outcomes are durable and continue even when the child is no longer in child care; Model 3: Child care does not have concurrent effects on development, but effects appear at a later point in time; and Model 4: The effects of child care on developmental outcomes are transient and fade over time. In addition to testing these developmental models, data from the study are used to examine the relation between child care experiences and concurrent psychological and health outcomes.

The research plan also includes several other, less central goals:

- To examine how the home environment influences child outcomes. Factors such as the quality of parenting and the quality and stability of the home environment are being examined.
- To examine the demographic and family characteristics that are associated with different patterns of child care usage. The quantity and quality of nonmaternal care experienced by an infant or young child are largely dependent on family circumstances, parental characteristics, and parental choices. The relations between family variables and nonmaternal care are of interest in their own right. Understanding these relations contributes to knowledge about the total ecology of the young child's environment and has direct implications for child care policy.
- To provide a longitudinal description of the variety, stability, and change of children's experiences in care over time. Such experiences include the number of hours in care and the quality of care.
- To provide information about the patterns of employment for mothers and about experiences of parents with nonmaternal care over time. Such information gives a picture of the nature of parenting in the 1990s that is quite different from that obtained from cross-sectional studies.
- To examine the relation between the child's experiences in child care and parent-child interactions.

THEORY OF CHANGE

Major constructs in the study are *trajectories* of development in three major domains (cognitive, social-emotional, and health), the *contexts* that both influence and are influenced by these trajectories, and *time*. Bronfenbrenner's ecological framework has guided the investigators' conceptualization of contexts, leading to inclusion of family, child care, school, out-of-school settings, parents' work, and socioeconomic factors as contexts with potential influences on development (Bronfenbrenner, 1979). Bronfenbrenner's recent addition of time to his ecological model, the "chronosystem," emphasizes the importance of tracking developmental trajectories in the context of historical, biological, social, and cultural transitions (Bronfenbrenner & Morris,

1998). Life course theory (Elder, 1998) provides a useful and complementary way of conceptualizing developmental processes because it also incorporates contextual influences in a framework that includes time. Although ontogenetic change is not denied, time-based contextual influences such as life events and transitions are emphasized. This framework leads to the examination of the timing of particular contextual influences and the differential effects of events based on age of experience. Some experiences are normative in that they occur at particular ages for most people (e.g., school entry), and some are nonnormative in that they are not expected nor associated with a specific age (e.g., parental divorce, change in child care arrangement, family relocation). In short, the ecological model and life course theories together provide a framework for conceptualizing the relations of both normative and individual contextual influences to developmental trajectories.

A central focus of the study is the interplay between early and concurrent experience in varied contexts and developmental trajectories from birth to later points in development. Several models can be explicitly tested using data from this study. The *primacy of early experience* model has been at the heart of much developmental theory (Bowlby, 1969; Grusec, 1992; Maccoby, 1992). In this model, the contexts to which a child is exposed early in development may have continuous and long-term influences that outweigh many of the influences of concurrent contexts. For example, one could speculate that early socialization experiences in family and child care may create secure child-parent relationships and social competencies that will buffer the child against psychopathology even when she or he confronts a later family crisis like divorce or parental remarriage. The *contemporaneous effect* model makes the opposite prediction. It suggests that the concurrent context has a stronger influence on developmental status than earlier environments do. These two models were supported in different domains of development in our analysis of child care contexts and children's cognitive and language development. Language stimulation provided in child care at age 2 predicted children's language competence at age 3 better than did such stimulation in concurrent child care settings. By contrast, concurrent child care characteristics accounted for the relations of child care to school readiness skills at age 3 (NICHD ECCRN, 2000).

More interesting, and probably more likely, are models that incorporate contemporaneous influences with the early experiences the child brings to a context. In an *incremental* model, early exposure produces effects on early development that are maintained, enhanced, or deflected by exposure to later contexts. Contextual change adds incrementally and independently to the prediction of developmental outcomes. A variation on this model posits the *magnification of small differences*. The initial effects of early environments may be small, but are magnified as children get older. Entwisle,

Alexander, and Olson (1997) use this model to explain the increasing discrepancy of school performance over time associated with socioeconomic status. Another model posits that contexts at particular ages or junctures in development will have particularly important effects. Events or contextual changes that are associated with major transitions, for example, may be more important than those that occur at other times (e.g., a parental divorce as the child is starting school; a family move when the child is in the process of gaining initial competence in reading).

DESIGN AND METHODS

The NICHD Study of Early Child Care can be characterized by its breadth, detail, and complex design. Among the unique features of this investigation are (a) extensive direct observation of home, child care (6 months to 54 months), and school (beginning in first grade) experiences; (b) multiple measures of social-emotional development, cognition, language, achievement, and physical growth and health; (c) a sample sufficiently large to permit reasonably precise estimation of effect sizes; and (d) sites located across major regions of the country in urban, suburban, and rural areas. Within sites, the sample is representative of families and children eligible to participate in the study. The different geographic locations represent not only different populations and subcultures, but also widely varying state regulations concerning child care. Ethnic-minority, single-parent, and low-education families were included at every site. Additionally, children are followed from birth through a wide range of child care experiences rather than being identified through child care centers or home-care settings. As a result, the study addresses informal and formal family care as well as center care. The longitudinal design permits assessment of combinations or changes in child care arrangements over time. Multiple measures of the child care environment allow comparisons of quality-of-care indices: individual children's observed experiences, observed global quality of the care setting, and structural features (e.g., ratios, caregiver training).

Enrollment

Participants in the study were recruited from 24 designated hospitals at 10 data collection sites. The sites are in the vicinity of Charlottesville, Virginia; Irvine, California; Lawrence, Kansas; Little Rock, Arkansas; Madison, Wisconsin; Morganton, North Carolina; Philadelphia, Pennsylvania; Pittsburgh, Pennsylvania; Seattle, Washington; and Wellesley, Massachusetts. Factors such as location, availability, previous working relations with the site investigators, and the nature of the patient load contributed to the selection of hospitals within sites.

Enrollment into the study consisted of three stages: (a) a hospital screening of newborn/mother dyads within 48 hours following birth; (b) a 2-week phone call to a subset of the mothers found to be eligible at screening; and (c) a 1-month interview with families who were eligible after the 2-week phone call, agreed to the 1-month interview, and kept the appointment. Recruitment was accomplished during the first 11 months of 1991, resulting in the screening of 8,986 dyads.

A total of 1,364 families with healthy newborns were enrolled in the study, with an approximately equal number of families at each site. The enrolled families included mothers who planned to work full-time (53%), part-time (23%), and not at all (24%) during the child's first year. The enrolled families came from a wide range of socioeconomic and sociocultural backgrounds, as well as from diverse family arrangements (24% ethnic-minority children, 11% mothers who did not complete high school, 14% single mothers; these percentages are not mutually exclusive).

Hospital Screening

On a weekly basis, each site was expected to screen a minimum of 20 newborn infant/mother dyads in the participating hospitals for potential enrollment to the study. This screening was to net 10 or more eligible dyads at each site per week for a 2-week phone call. For each newborn infant/mother dyad, the hospital screening consisted of two steps. First, information available in the hospital (without contact with the mother) was reviewed with respect to the study exclusion criteria. If the dyad met any one of the exclusion criteria at this step, no contact with the mother was required.

The exclusion criteria for the hospital screening were the following: (a) the mother was under 18 years old; (b) the mother did not speak English; (c) the family planned to move from the area within one year; (d) the infant had serious medical complications or was born to a mother with known or acknowledged substance abuse; (e) the mother was too ill; (f) the mother was placing her infant for adoption; (g) the mother refused to do the 2-week phone call; (h) the mother lived more than an hour from the lab site; (i) the family was enrolled in another study; (j) the mother lived in a neighborhood (generally high rise projects) deemed by police too unsafe for visitation; (k) the mother refused the hospital interview; and (l) other. For each dyad that was eligible based on the available information in the hospital, the screening process proceeded to the second step with an in-hospital visit to the mother. The hospital visit with the mother was used to further assess the eligibility (as defined by the exclusion criteria above) and to collect the following additional background information: the child's gender, the child's weight, the mother's ethnic/racial identification, the mother's age, the mother's education, whether the partner was present in the home, the partner's education, the mother's employment status during the past 6 months, the mother's plans to return to work or school in the child's first year, and the infant's gestational age.

Two-Week Phone Calls

The Data Coordinating Center used the screening data to generate calling lists of eligible families for the 2-week phone calls. The 2-week phone calls included additional exclusion criteria: (a) the infant was hospitalized for more than 7 days following the birth; (b) the family planned to move from the area within 3 years; (c) there were three unsuccessful calls to reach the family; (d) the mother refused to participate; and (e) other.

Specific characteristics of the enrolled families were monitored and adjustments were made at the Data Coordinating Center to the order of the calling list for each site to increase the opportunity for adequate representation of various subgroups. Each site's enrollment was expected to have the following marginal constraints: at least 10% single-parent households; at least 10% mothers with less than a high school education; and at least 10% ethnic-minority mothers. The enrolled families at each site were to split approximately 60%, 20%, and 20% on the mothers' plans to return to work full-time, part-time, and not at all during the child's first year, respectively. This approximate distribution occurred naturally without further conditioning on the calling list order.

One-Month Interview

Families were officially enrolled in the study upon successful completion of all data collection through the one-month interview. For any family that had agreed to the interview but did not keep the appointment, the site was to select additional families on the current week's calling list.

Retention

Subject retention has been good. Of the original 1,364 families, only 131 families (9.6%) had dropped out of the study by the time the child was 36 months old. As of fall 1999 (when most of the children were entering third grade), 133 additional families had dropped out of the study, leaving a sample of 1,100 families. This translates into a retention rate of 80.6% from the time of recruitment 8 years earlier.

Assessments

The study was funded and conducted in phases; Phase I covered the children's first 36 months and Phase II from age 37 months through the end of first grade. The major face-to-face assessment points occurred when children were 1, 6, 15, 24, 36, and 54 months of age and when they were in first grade. Children were observed in the home, laboratory, child care setting (if in care for more than 10 hours per week), and in school (first grade). In addition, data were obtained between major assessments using telephone interviews and questionnaires. During Phase I, phone calls to families were made every 3 months. During Phase II, calls were made every 4 months until the child entered school. When the child entered kindergarten, calls were made approximately every 6 months, once during the fall semester and once during the spring semester. To ensure reliable administration of all measures and guard against site difference in administration practices, data were collected by centrally trained and certified individuals. Table 8.1 outlines the data collection schedule. Specifics of the study procedures can be found in the operation manuals for the study (http://secc.rti.org).

With additional funding during Phase I from the U. S. Department of Health and Human Services, 6 of the 10 sites (Arkansas, California, Kansas, North Carolina, Pittsburgh, and Wisconsin) expanded the study to include direct measures of fathers' attitudes and perceptions. This added component was designed to examine (a) how marital quality and paternal attitudes contribute to families' child care choices and to time use during nonworking family time in families with employed and nonemployed mothers; (b) how

Table 8.1. Timing and Location of Assessments for NICHD Early Child Care Study

Assessments	Child's Age							
	1 mo.	6 mo.	15 mo.	24 mo.	36 mo.	54 mo.	K	1st grade
Home	✓	✓	✓	✓	✓	✓	✓[a]	✓
Laboratory			✓	✓	✓	✓		✓
Child Care		✓	✓	✓	✓	✓		✓[a]
School							✓[a]	✓
Phone[b]	✓	✓✓	✓✓✓	✓✓✓	✓✓✓✓	✓✓✓✓	✓✓✓	✓✓

[a] Mail contacts only.

[b] Multiple checks indicate the number of contacts following the previous major assessment point.

marital quality and paternal attitudes influence the quality of mother-child relationships in families with employed and nonemployed mothers; (c) the extent to which maternal employment and reliance on child care may affect the quality of the marital relationship; and (d) the direct and indirect influences of father involvement on children's development in households with employed and nonemployed mothers.

MEASURES

Experience during early development was assessed through a diverse array of measures designed to capture the child's experience in the context of home and family, in child care, and in school. Measures of social-emotional, cognitive, linguistic, and academic development and physical growth and health were used to assess children's developmental status. Selection of measures was based on: (a) the child's developmental level; (b) the psychometric properties of the measure; (c) the applicability of measures to children and families varying in ethnicity and socioeconomic status; (d) the amount of time needed to complete the measure; (e) the relations among the different measures planned for each visit; and (f) the results of pilot testing. Two criteria were considered in selecting specific child outcomes to be assessed: (a) that the developmental importance of the outcome construct was well documented in previous research and theory; and (b) that there was reason to hypothesize that children's development in a particular domain would be affected by early child rearing environments.

Insofar as possible, each construct was evaluated with multiple measures and at each assessment point. For example, child care quality was measured by both structural indicators, such as the ratio of caregivers to children, and process variables, such as the frequency and quality of interactions between caregiver and child. This approach allows the investigation of the empirical relation between theoretically related measures, some of which are easy to employ for regulation and accreditation of child care settings. Multiple measures were also used to assess developmental outcomes because such a strategy increases the reliability and validity of the findings.

Table 8.2 presents an overview of the child care, school, and home and family constructs as well as the child outcome constructs along with the corresponding ages of assessment. Information on some of the constructs presented in Table 8.2 was supplemented with data collected during the periodic telephone interviews with the mother. Lists of all the measures used in Phase I and Phase II of the study can be obtained at http://secc.rti.org on-line.

Table 8.2. Constructs for Phase I and Phase II of NICHD Study of Early Child Care

	Child's Age							
	1 mo.	6 mo.	15 mo.	24 mo.	36 mo.	54 mo.	K	1st grade
Child care environment								
Structural regularities	✓	✓	✓	✓	✓	✓	✓	✓
Quantity	✓	✓	✓	✓	✓	✓	✓	✓
Stability	✓	✓	✓	✓	✓	✓		✓
Quality	✓	✓	✓	✓	✓	✓		✓
Caregiver characteristics	✓	✓	✓	✓	✓	✓		✓
School environment								
Structural context							✓	✓
School curriculum							✓	✓
Child's perceptions								✓
Home/family environment								
Structural context	✓	✓	✓	✓	✓	✓	✓	✓
Quality of home life		✓	✓	✓	✓	✓		✓
Parent characteristics	✓	✓	✓	✓	✓	✓	✓	✓
Social-emotional development								
Quality of relationships		✓	✓	✓	✓	✓	✓	✓
Adjustment		✓	✓	✓	✓	✓	✓	✓
Self-concept and identity								✓
Cognitive development								
Global intellectual functioning			✓	✓		✓		✓
Knowledge and achievement					✓	✓	✓	✓
Cognitive processes			✓	✓	✓	✓	✓	✓
Language development			✓	✓	✓	✓	✓	✓
Health	✓	✓	✓	✓	✓	✓	✓	✓

Child Care Measures

Child care environment. At each major assessment point, each child who was in a child care arrangement for 10 or more hours per week during Phase I or 8 or more hours per week during Phase II was observed in his or her primary arrangement. During Phase I, the primary child care arrangement was the one in which the child spent the most time or, if the child spent equal time in two settings, the arrangement that was more formal. During Phase II, the primary arrangement was, in general, the arrangement that was more formal. Priority was given to settings in which there were other preschool children aged 2–6 years who were not siblings of the target child and settings in which the caregiver was not the mother or father.

Both distal and proximal characteristics of the child care environment were assessed with observations, interviews, and questionnaires. The distal characteristics that were assessed in the child care setting are those that are not experienced directly by the child, yet are believed to influence the day-to-day experiences of children in child care (e.g., caregivers' education level, years of experience in providing care, attitudes about raising children, and wages and fees). Proximal characteristics included (a) features of the setting (e.g., the cleanliness and safety of the setting, the degree to which learning materials were available, number of adults per child, group size) and (b) aspects of individual children's experiences (e.g., age of entry into child care, number of hours per week in child care, number of child care arrangements experienced, and the interactions between target children and their caregivers). These distal and proximal characteristics provided information about both structural and human interaction dimensions of child care. The data were collected through interviews with caregivers and with parents and through observations in child care settings.

Quantity and stability of child care experiences. Information on the number of hours per week each child spent in child care (quantity) and the stability of care (number of child care arrangements started and stopped) was obtained during periodic phone calls to the mother.

Characteristics of caregivers. Caregivers were asked to provide basic demographic data such as age, education, and ethnic identity, as well as information about the length of their experience as child care providers, their training, and their wages. Caregivers' professionalism was assessed in a brief interview concerning their attitudes toward their job, reasons for providing care, plans for the future, participation in professional activities, and so on. Caregivers' attitudes toward child rearing were measured using the Modernity Scale (Schaefer & Edgerton, 1985), which provides an estimate of how traditional (strict, conservative) vs. modern (progressive) adults' attitudes are toward child rearing.

Characteristics of the child care environment. Type of care, group size, and adult-to-child ratio were observed in the child care settings that were visited. When access to child care could not be obtained, the information was obtained through interviews with mothers or, in the case of center care, through interviews with directors. Data about other child care features such as staffing patterns, number and ethnicity of children in the care arrangement, wages, and fees were obtained from caregiver and/or director interviews.

The child care environment was observed and coded using instruments that describe the setting available to all children in it and instruments that focus on the specific interactions of the target child with his or her caregivers. During Phase I, observations of the settings were coded with a child care version of the Home Observation for Measurement of the Environment (HOME) Inventory (Caldwell & Bradley, 1984) developed for the current project and with an adaptation of the Assessment Profile for Early Childhood Programs (PROFILE) (Abbott-Shim & Sibley, 1987, 1993; Abbott-Shim, Sibley, & Neel, 1992). The HOME Inventory was used in all home-based settings (i.e., the target child's home or another person's home) and was designed to measure the quality and quantity of stimulation and support available to a child in the child care environment. Two different versions of the PROFILE were used, one for centers and one for home settings (care in a home that was not the child's residence). In Phase II (when the children were 54 months old), a new Physical Environment Checklist was developed for the study in lieu of the PROFILE used in Phase I. The Checklist was developed to reflect important aspects of the setting: health and hygienic practices, safety, organization, and stimulation. Some of the items were selected from the PROFILE; some were adapted from scales in the ECERS (Harms & Clifford, 1990); and others were added on the basis of our own piloting. For each scale in the Checklist, there is also an overall summary rating of the dimension being assessed.

For the purpose of assessing the interaction of caregivers and children, the investigators of the NICHD Study of Early Child Care developed the Observational Record of the Caregiving Environment (ORCE). This instrument provides two types of data: frequency counts (called Behavior Scales) of specific caregiver and child behaviors, and ratings (called Qualitative Ratings) of caregivers' behaviors that take into account the quality of the caregiver's behavior in relation to the child's behaviors. The ORCE method for observing the care of 6-month-old infants is described in NICHD ECCRN (1996).

During Phases I and II of the study, the ORCE was designed to measure the frequency and quality of caregivers' behaviors. Because the exemplars of positive caregiving differ by age, the ORCE was systematically adapted to the age of the children at the time that the observations were made.

For the 54-month assessment, the Classroom Practices Inventory (CPI; Hyson, Hirsh-Pasek, & Rescorla, 1990) was also used to assess quality of center-based (or formal preschool) settings. The CPI is an observation instrument based on the National Association for the Education of Young Children guidelines for developmentally appropriate practices for 4- and 5-year-old children. It consists of items that index both the academic activity focus and the emotional climate of the program. The items are rated on the basis of several hours of direct observation.

Characteristics of the before- or after-school child care environment. In first grade, the child's primary before-school or after-school care arrangement was evaluated using questionnaires to the care provider and interviews with the mother and the child. The child's primary arrangement was any non-parental arrangement (including self-care) that was at least 5 hours per week. If time spent in two different arrangements was similar, the primary arrangement was the one that was more formal. If the duration of the nonparental arrangement was less than 5 hours per week, then parental care was the primary arrangement. Information was collected on the aspects of context that can be regulated, type of care, quantity and stability of care, caregiver characteristics, and perceptions of care quality and satisfaction. Measures of the mother's and child's satisfaction with care were used because they have been found to be related to observed quality of care. The mother's satisfaction with the child's primary before- or after-school arrangement was assessed using a scale developed for this study that was based on scales by O'Connor (1991) and Rosenthal and Vandell (1996). The child's satisfaction was assessed using a modification of the After School Questionnaire (ASQ; Rosenthal & Vandell, 1996). This questionnaire, which was given in the form of an interview, focuses on children's feelings of support from peers and caregivers in their after-school settings, as well as their general feelings about the arrangement.

School Measures

Kindergarten. When children were in kindergarten, teachers completed a questionnaire pertaining to the child's classroom, the instructional program, and the supports and challenges individual teachers experienced within the school. Included were questions about the teacher's and any aide's backgrounds. The teacher also completed a questionnaire on the student-teacher relationship (Pianta, 1992). Items in this questionnaire are derived from attachment theory and the Waters and Deane Attachment Q-Set (Waters & Deane, 1985) as well as from a review of the literature on teacher-child relations. The items involve the respondent's feelings and beliefs about his or her relationship with the student, and about the child's behavior toward the teacher.

First grade. In first grade the school environment was assessed through a classroom observation, a recess observation, teacher-completed questionnaires, and school records. Information was obtained on school and teacher characteristics, teacher-student relationships, and parental involvement.

An observation system called the First Grade Classroom Observation System (COS-1) was developed for the purposes of this study; it required approximately 2.5 hours of classroom observation time. The COS-1 is a multiconstruct, multilevel observational system containing both frequencies of discrete behaviors or conditions and global seven-point rating scales. The frequency data are focused on four categories: (a) *activity*, the situation or activity in which the target child is involved; (b) *content*, the content of the activity; (c) *teacher behavior*, a variety of behaviors (not mutually exclusive) directed at the target child; and (d) *child behavior*, behavior toward the teacher and peers and child engagement. Observations are based on a 30-seconds-on (observe) and 30-seconds-off (record) schedule across 10-minute blocks.

The global ratings capture classroom-level and individual-level factors. Classroom-level ratings include scales such as climate and classroom management strategies. The individual-level ratings capture the teacher's behavior toward the child and include scales such as teacher sensitivity and intrusiveness/overcontrol.

A recess observation was conducted to assess peer interaction using the First Grade Unstructured Peer Interaction Observation System. This measure was modeled on the ORCE and the COS-1 and was developed for this study. Predetermined behaviors observed during 30-second time windows were recorded and rated. The method also captured information about the settings in which behaviors were seen. The behaviors recorded were in the areas of activity, teacher behavior, child's behavior with peers, and child engagement. The rating scales were used to record the child's negative affect, positive affect, prosocial behavior, and assertiveness, as well as the teacher's monitoring and involvement.

Home and Family Measures

Measures of the home/family context are designed to assess structural characteristics of the family, quality of home life, and parent characteristics.

Structural characteristics of the family. In phone and face-to-face interviews, information was collected frequently and on a regular basis about who lived in the child's household. Mothers were also asked if the child had alternate custodial arrangements on a formal or informal basis. Information was obtained about the child's father and/or the mother's partner and, when a father was not in the home, the child's contact with the father.

Mothers reported on both maternal and paternal employment. Because many mothers and fathers have multiple jobs, information was collected about each job currently held by each parent, including the number of hours, income, start and stop dates, times of day worked, and hours of the paid job performed at home. Information about the parents' school enrollment, hours devoted to school, and class schedules was also obtained.

Quality of the home environment. The quality of the home environment was assessed using information about (a) parental attitudes and perceptions of socialization; (b) observed parental sensitivity, stimulation, and quality of assistance; and (c) observed parental involvement.

During Phase I, parents were asked about their attitudes toward raising children to determine parenting style using the Modernity Scale (Schaefer & Edgerton, 1985). During Phase II, parents were asked about parental discipline strategies using a scale called Raising Children (Posner & Vandell, 1994), which was modified from the Raising Children Checklist (Greenberger & Goldberg, 1989). Parents also completed a modified version of the Maturity Demands Scale (Greenberger & Goldberg, 1989).

Sensitivity, stimulation, and quality of assistance were observed using ratings of the quality of the parents' interaction with the target children during videotaped mother-child and father-child interaction tasks. The tasks provided a context for assessing age-appropriate qualities of supportiveness, intrusiveness, positive regard, hostility, and quality of instruction in both mother-child and father-child interaction.

The HOME Inventory (Caldwell & Bradley, 1984) was used to assess the quality of the family environment. The HOME Inventory consists of direct observation and a semi-structured interview with the mother and is designed to measure the quality and quantity of stimulation and support available to a child at home. Parental involvement was assessed with questionnaires designed to assess the relative roles of fathers and mothers in caring for the target children and the extent to which parents have contact with caregivers or teachers, as well as the amount of involvement each parent has in the child's schooling.

Parental characteristics. Mothers' and fathers' health, depression, social support, life stress, job stress, financial stress, and marital quality were measured in interviews and questionnaires at multiple time points throughout the study. During the telephone interviews, mothers were asked about their general health status and were asked to describe the health of their husband/partner. During the home visits, mothers and fathers/partners completed self-report measures on these constructs.

Child Outcome Measures

Measures of child outcome were designed to assess social-emotional functioning, cognitive development, and health. Social-emotional constructs included (a) quality of relationships (with mother, father, friends, caregivers, and teachers), (b) adjustment (emotional adjustment, social competence, behavior problems, and self-regulation), and (c) self-concept and identity. Cognitive constructs included (a) global intellectual functioning, (b) knowledge and achievement (school readiness and literacy), (c) cognitive processes (attention, problem solving, and memory), and (d) language development. Constructs from the health domain included health (status, illnesses, injuries, health-care usage) and growth (height and weight).

Information also was obtained regarding children's school attendance, referral to special services (e.g., speech/language, tutoring, and gifted/talented), and grade retention.

UNITS OF ANALYSIS

The NICHD Study of Early Child Care was designed as a study of the development of children in contexts over time. These children were to be the primary research participants in the study and all information that was collected about the contexts of development was about the contexts in which the research participants were reared. Multiple assessments of the family, the child care setting, kindergarten, school, and after-school settings were collected. Some involved the experiences of the target child in the setting, including the interaction of the target child with others. Other assessments focused on the household (e.g., income, number of people), the parents (e.g., education, employment, attitudes), the household setting (e.g., availability of books), the child care provider (e.g., education, experience, attitudes), the teacher, the child care setting (e.g., adult-to-child ratio, group size, licensing), and the school setting. Because data were collected about the child from multiple contexts (home, child care setting, school) and different people (parents, child care providers, teachers), data can be analyzed separately from the target child in order to answer questions pertaining to these contexts and categories of people. However, in most analyses conducted to date and planned for the near future by the investigators of the study, the unit of analysis is the individual child.

RESULTS

In this section, we briefly summarize the results, to date, of the NICHD Study of Early Child Care. During the children's first year of life, there was high reliance on infant care, very rapid entry into care post-birth, and substantial instability in care. By 12 months of age, 84% of the infants in the study had entered some form of nonmaternal child care, with the majority starting care before age 4 months. When they first entered care, 25% of the infants were cared for by their father or their mother's partner, 23% were cared for by other relatives, and only 12% were enrolled in child care centers. Over the first year of life, the majority of children in nonmaternal care experienced more than two different child care arrangements, and more than one-third experienced three or more arrangements.

Economic factors were most consistently associated with the amount and nature of nonmaternal care infants received. For example, mothers with higher incomes and families that were more dependent on the mother's income placed their infants in child care at earlier ages. Maternal personality and beliefs about maternal employment also contributed. For example, mothers who believed that maternal employment has positive effects on children put their children in nonmaternal care for more hours. Poor families were less likely than affluent families to use child care, but poor children who were in care averaged as many hours as children from other income groups.

Observations of the quality of care at 6 months indicated that more positive caregiving occurred when children were in smaller groups, child-adult ratios were lower, caregivers held less authoritarian beliefs about child rearing, and physical environments were safe, clean, and stimulating. Observed quality of care for poor children was generally lower than for nonpoor children when they were cared for by an unrelated caregiver, with one exception: Poor children in centers received better quality care than near-poor children, perhaps because they were more likely to be in subsidized (and therefore perhaps more regulated) settings. Evaluation of child care centers in relation to guidelines recommended by professional organizations for child-staff ratios, group sizes, teacher training, and teacher education indicated that most classes observed in the study did not meet all four of these guidelines.

Analyses of the effects of family and child care on child outcomes indicated that, in general, family characteristics and the quality of the mother's relationship with her child were stronger predictors of child outcomes than were child care factors. Family factors predicted child outcomes even for children who spent many hours in child care, and statistically significant child care effects were relatively small in size. One family predictor of child outcomes (in addition to income level, education, attitudes, and behavior) was maternal depressive symptoms. Children whose mothers reported feeling depressed performed more poorly on measures of cognitive-linguistic functioning at 36 months and were rated as less cooperative and more problematic. However, depression effects on expressive language and ratings of cooperation were moderated by maternal sensitivity, with sensitivity predicting better outcomes more strongly among children of depressed mothers.

Analyses controlling for nonrandom use of child care by families of different socioeconomic backgrounds revealed that among the aspects of child care studied, a relatively consistent predictor of child outcomes was the observed quality of care. When observed quality of caregivers' behavior was high,

children had better cognitive and linguistic abilities, showed more cooperative behavior with mother during play, and had fewer behavior problems. For
children in center care at 36 months, children had fewer behavior problems
and higher scores on language comprehension and school readiness when
classes met more of the guidelines recommended by experts for ratios, group
sizes, and teacher training and education. Higher quality child care was also
associated with higher quality mother-child interaction among the families that
used nonmaternal care. Additionally, poor-quality child care was related to
an increased incidence of insecure infant-mother attachment at 15 months, but
only when the mother was also relatively low in sensitivity and responsiveness.

Overall, type of child care by itself appeared to have relatively limited
impacts on child outcomes. At age 3, greater *cumulative* experience in center care and *early* experience in child care homes were both associated with
better performance on cognitive and language measures than other forms of
care, assuming comparable quality of caregiving environment. Experience
with group care (settings with at least three other children, not counting siblings), whether in centers or child care homes, made some difference in several
social-emotional outcomes at ages 2 and 3. Children with more cumulative
experience in group care showed more cooperation with their mothers in the
laboratory at age 2, less negative laboratory interaction with their mothers
at age 3, and fewer caregiver-reported behavior problems at both ages.
However, higher amounts of group experience before 12 months were associated with more mother-reported behavior problems at age 3, suggesting
that benefits from group care may begin in the second year of life.

The quantity of nonmaternal care was also a statistically significant
predictor of some child outcomes. When children spent more hours in child
care, mothers were less sensitive in their interactions with their children (at
6, 15, 24, and 36 months) and children were less positively engaged with
their mother (at 15, 24, and 36 months, the ages at which child engagement
was assessed). In addition, analyses of infant-mother attachment security at
15 months show that children who spent more hours in child care *and* had
mothers who were relatively insensitive and unresponsive were at heightened
risk for insecure mother-infant attachment.

LIMITATIONS

The sample is not nationally representative, but it was designed to include
families from diverse geographic regions, economic backgrounds, and ethnic
groups. It was also designed to include families with diverse plans for maternal employment during the child's first year of life. These design features, together with the detailed characterization of both the family and child care

environments, represent a great improvement over previous psychological research about the relations among family background, child care experience, and children's psychological development. Despite our goal of having a diverse sample, our sample did not include enough children from some ethnic groups to allow us to describe developmental trajectories for these children. More specifically, while we have a sizable African American subgroup, we have too few Latino/Hispanic, Asian American, or Native American children.

Despite the inclusion and exclusion criteria that guided the recruitment of research participants (see above, "Design and Methods"), the sample characteristics were surprisingly similar to those of families with young infants residing in the communities from which the research participants were recruited. We compared demographic characteristics of families in our sample with United States Census Tract data and found that on most demographic variables, our sample was very similar to families from the areas in which we recruited. However, parents in the sample of the NICHD Study of Early Child Care had higher education levels; more families in the study's sample were on public assistance; and the study sample had slightly lower household incomes relative to families in the same Census Tract (but higher relative to others in the same state or the United States). Because the study sample included only mothers who were at least 18 years old at the time their child was born, the percentage of participants in the workforce was higher than in Census Tract data, which include individuals as young as 16 years old.

PUBLIC USE FILES

The data from Phase I of the study (birth to 36 months) were released in January 2000. The data for Phase II of the study (37 months to first grade) were released in November 2002.

PART II. THREE EARLY CHILD CARE INITIATIVES

Phyllis Gyamfi, Natasha Cabrera, and Jodie Roth

COST, QUALITY, AND CHILD OUTCOMES (CQO) STUDY

History

Much of the care children receive in centers and in family child care does not promote their cognitive, social, and physical development (CQO Study Team,

1995). Except for poor children who are enrolled in Head Start (as documented in FACES, see Chapter 4), low-income children tend to receive poor quality care (NICHD ECCRN, 1996). Embedded in the discussion about quality care is the issue of cost and its link to supply and demand of services. Prior to the Cost, Quality, and Child Outcomes Study, little was known about the interaction between quality and costs of care, particularly with respect to differences between types of provider. Nonprofit centers may provide higher quality care (but at higher cost) as compared to centers run for profit (Kagan, 1991a); cost and quality are related (e.g., Phillips, Mekos, Scarr, McCartney, & Abbott-Shim, 1995). However, the CQO Study Team (1995) reports that the economics literature has paid little attention to cost functions in the industry—the explicit associations between types of inputs and costs, the effects of substitution between inputs on cost and quality, the extent of economies of scale, the association of additional cost with better care, and differences in the relation of costs to quality at various kinds of centers (for example, see Blau, 1991; Maggenheim, 1990). In short, there is little data to permit an analysis of the relation between production of quality and amounts and qualities of inputs.

The Cost, Quality, and Child Outcomes Study was designed to fill the gaps in the literature by addressing the interaction between quality and cost of providing child care services. To this end, the study combines the expertise of child development professionals and economists in measuring quality and cost. Additionally, this study provides critically important information to help policy makers make decisions affecting the future of children in this country. For policy makers and participants in the child care market, knowledge of the cost-quality relation in child care is a key consideration in designing policy concerning the financing of child care: How much does care cost? Which factors determine cost? And how likely is it that these factors will persist into the future? The CQO study was funded by a group of foundations intent on helping policy makers make difficult decisions in the face of rapid change in family structure, the role of women in the work force, and the child rearing practices.

The main purpose is to examine the intersection between cost and quality care. This focus requires addressing two sets of issues: (a) the economic principles relevant to the child care industry structure and competitive environment and (b) the conceptual structure of the process of producing quality services and of the linkage between this process and children's development.

Economic principles. The CQO Study Team's (1995) economic analysis of early child care markets suggests that the child care market is:

- Made up, at the local level, of a heterogeneous group of providers (e.g., child's own parents, nannies, mixed markets of for-profit, pri-

vate, nonprofit, and public centers) with different ownership structures and objectives and a differentiated set of services provided; or
- Growing rapidly and highly competitive and unstable; or
- Segmented, with several submarkets, each with different types of pro-
ducers serving different clientele; or
- Characterized by monopolistic competition, where each provider has
a tiny bit of monopoly power, but no two providers supply exactly
the same services; or
- Characterized by an inadequate supply of good-quality services, leading to market inefficiencies that could raise cost and lower quality,
such as uninformed consumers, externalities (child care services provide external benefits to those who do not directly receive these services and do not have to pay for them), and monopoly power; and
- Differentially regulated at the state, county, and municipal levels.

Theoretically, profit-oriented centers should respond to the market and
try to minimize costs in order to maximize their profits. However, consumers' values and lack of knowledge may lead to poor-quality services maximizing profits. On the other hand, for-profit centers may react to consumer
demand by providing innovative programs and efficient cost-saving procedures.
Nonprofit and public agencies may be organized for altruistic purposes based
on ideological commitments. When this is true they may emphasize producing good-quality services, affordable care, or services to low-income families.
The possible negative consequence of the nonprofit organization, however, is
inadequate attention to minimizing costs.

Increasingly, child care services are becoming a market commodity
bought and sold more or less according to principles of market supply and
demand. With the exception of providing care in certain geographic locations, for infants and toddlers, and for families with special needs (care in
the evening or on weekends and sick care; Hofferth, 1991), early childhood
care markets are meeting the increasing demand. For instance, center fees
have not increased in real terms since 1975 (CQO Study Team, 1995, p. 9).
However, the stable cost may hide higher prices per level quality and lower
overall quality (Walker, 1991). Although increasing demand may not be
exceeding supply, the quality of care may have declined over time (Whitebook
et al., 1989). This suggests that markets have met increased demands at the
expense of quality.

Before presenting the conceptual framework for this study outlining
the relations between cost and quality of early child care services and the
development of the children receiving the services, a brief account of what
quality is, as conceptualized for this study, follows. Three interrelated types
of quality have been identified for centers: structural (quality of resources

used), process (quality of services), and child outcomes (the effect of these services on the children). Some of the attributes of structural quality are easily observable, measured, and state regulated (e.g., staffing ratio, group size, staff education, training and experience, and physical aspects of the center itself). Process qualities refer to the general environment and the social relationships in the center (e.g., a well-articulated program of care, developmentally appropriate activities for children, nurturing staff members who interact with children, and a stimulating and challenging physical environment). Child outcomes refer to the observable levels of cognitive and social functioning of the children, as well as outcomes related to the children's success in school, and the potential long-run effects on the children's success as adults. The effects of such services on parents, although not addressed in this study, are also another important set of outcomes (Brooks-Gunn, Berlin, & Fuligni, 2000).

Current Status

The study was initiated early in 1993, with the first of four waves of data collection. In the first phase, quality and cost data were collected and analyzed during 1993 and 1994. The initial reports were released in 1995 (CQO Study Team, 1995). Child outcomes data were collected each spring, beginning in 1993, when children were in their next-to-last preschool year in child care and continuing until 1997, when children were in second grade. Data collection is complete. Several publications have been generated (e.g., CQO Study Team, 1999; Helburn & Howes, 1996; Howes, 1997; Peisner-Feinberg & Burchinal, 1997; Tietze, Cryer, Bairrao, Palacios, & Wetzel, 1996).

Goals

This study examines the relation between the cost and quality of early child care and early learning in centers providing full-time services, and how these factors relate to children's development, including their school readiness and performance. This study was designed to fill an important gap by creating a data set that permits analyses of the relation between the cost and quality of early childhood center services for typical children from a wide variety of family backgrounds. It helps explain the effects of competition on the delivery of early care and education services. An interesting feature of this study is the measurement of administrative effectiveness and the impact of management on the quality of services. The conceptual structure reflects this approach by providing a way to look at these internal feedback mechanisms.

Research Questions

The questions addressed by this study include the following:

- Does quality differ by sector and auspice? Is there evidence that non-profit centers provide better quality and are cost effective?
- Are early childhood care markets segmented into sectors serving children of different socioeconomic status? If so, how does this affect the costs and quality of services provided to different groups of children?
- How is the early childhood care market affected by public intervention? What is the impact of state licensing regulations on the quality and cost of services provided, as well as their availability? What is the impact of subsidies, both public and private, on the cost and quality of services?
- Are parents fully informed consumers? Much of current public policy is based on the assumption that parents are informed consumers when they elect child care for their children.
- How do labor market operations and personnel policies of centers affect the cost and quality of child care? To what extent is relatively unskilled staff being used? How much evidence is there of the dependence of the industry on foregone wages of highly qualified staff members to maintain some level of quality of care and still contain costs? How do wages affect quality?
- What public policies are suggested by these findings?

Design and Methods

This study examined the relation between cost and quality of early childhood care and education programs and the developmental outcome of children enrolled in the programs in four states: California, Colorado, Connecticut, and North Carolina. The research was designed to provide an intensive, on-site study of centers in four fairly representative states with varying licensing standards and demographic and economic characteristics.

Sample. Children were selected for participation in the study at two separate times—for the cost and quality phase of the study (Phase 1) and for the longitudinal outcomes phase of the study (Phase 2). The children were born in 1988 and 1989.

Phase 1. First, detailed information about cost and quality was gathered from 401 randomly selected child care centers in four states. The participating states represented the diversity of early care and education programs found within the United States as well as differing regional and demographic characteristics. Child care regulation in these states was generally representative of the spectrum of licensing criteria from low to high. The sample of early childhood programs included in the study was drawn from subregions within the four states. In California, centers were selected from Los Angeles County; Colorado's centers were located from Colorado Springs through Denver, Boulder, Fort Collins, and Greeley; centers in Connecticut were in the Hartford-New Haven corridor; and North Carolina's centers were in the Piedmont Triad area between Graham/Burlington and Winston-Salem. All areas within the states were chosen to represent the diversity in minority population, city size, geographic location, and economic characteristics.

Data were collected on a stratified random sample of 100 programs in each participating state, with approximately equal representation of for-profit programs and nonprofit programs. The sample was stratified on this variable because of the demonstrated importance of this structural feature in predicting quality and because of the differing structure of each type of program. Two randomly selected groups of programs were created: for-profit and non-profit. Of the 200 for-profit programs in the four states, 48 were centers from corporate systems.

In each classroom observed for this phase of the study, two unidentified children, a girl and a boy, were randomly selected by data collectors as target children to be observed during the collection of program quality data. The boy and girl were observed to assess level of play that took place in the classrooms. No other information was collected on these children.

Phase 2. Once the cost and quality data collection had been completed, children were selected for developmental assessment as part of the longitudinal outcomes phase. Children were recruited from participating centers for this phase of the study if their observed preschool class enrolled children who would be eligible to enter kindergarten in the fall of 1994 (i.e., children who were in their next-to-last year of preschool). Before centers were recontracted for this part of the study, they were stratified by quality ratings and proportion of children served who were receiving subsidies from the data that were gathered in the first component. Stratification assured inclusion of programs of varying quality and child composition. Within the strata, programs and the order in which they were to be contacted were randomly selected. In each selected program, all classrooms observed in the first phase of the study were randomly selected to be representative of each program, one from the older groups (children from 30 months or older, but not school-aged) and one from the younger groups (children less than 30 months) to ensure representation of the age range of children in care. All eligible children in the selected class-rooms were invited to participate, and up to 12 children were randomly se-lected from those with parent permission to participate in the longitudinal phase of the study. Within each of the four states, researchers were to con-tact centers until approximately 200 children had been seen. In all, 826 chil-dren were initially recruited.

Data collection. Data were first collected from children in the spring of 1993, when participants were in their next-to-last year of child care, with an aver-age age of 4.3 years. Outcome data were collected annually for 2 consecu-tive years, when the participating children were in their last year of child care (average age of 5.1 years) and kindergarten (average age of 6.0 years), and again in year 5, when the children were in Grade 2.

Only programs that were listed as child care facilities by the state licens-ing agencies were included. All programs in the sampling areas were num-bered, and a table of random numbers was used to select each for possible inclusion. Only early childhood programs that served infants, toddlers, and/or preschoolers were included; no family child care homes or programs that served only school-aged children were used. Generally, developmental day care programs that served only children with disabilities were excluded, al-though three developmental day care programs were sampled because the nature of these programs was not apparent until observers visited the class-rooms. Programs that mainstreamed children with disabilities were included. Programs had to provide care for at least 30 hours a week, 5 days a week, for the program to be included in the sample. Part-day Head Start programs were included in the pool if a wraparound child care option was provided so that they met the criteria for full-time care. The sample was limited to pro-grams that were conducted in English, although some programs did serve children for whom English was not the primary language. Finally, newly opened centers were not sampled. Only centers that had been in operation long enough to have one full fiscal year of operating data were included.

Children were eligible for inclusion in Phase 2 of the study if they were of kindergarten entry age for the fall of 1994, had been enrolled in the target classroom during the classroom observation phase, expected to continue attending that center the following year, and spoke primarily English at home. This study is based on 228 infant/toddler classrooms and 521 preschool class-rooms in 401 child care centers selected during the spring of 1993. The ini-tial sample of 826 preschool children attended these centers. The sample of children dropped to 579 during the second year of data collection for the longitudinal outcomes phase of the study because only initial participants who stayed in the same child care center for the second year of data collection were invited to remain in the study. Data were collected from 451 children in year 3 (kindergarten), and 418 in year 5 (second grade).

A letter and a brief phone interview with administrators of all programs in the sample were used to recruit centers for the study. When the administrator gave permission for the center to take part in the study, data collectors made an appointment for 2 days of visits.

Cost and quality component. Data were collected by a team of six to eight data collectors in each state. Interrater reliability in the use of the cost and quality instruments was assessed through both in-state and between-state tests at about the midpoint in the data collection process. Comprehensive financial data was collected, as well as detailed information about the early child care program, including administrative style and management strategies to gather cost information.

Data were collected on structural characteristics for both the overall center and the individual classroom. Process quality data (e.g., ratio, group size, global measures of classroom quality, specific measures of adult-child interactions, types of children's activities, and teaching style), parent's assessment of the quality of their children's early childhood programs, and their value ratings for the aspects of care they evaluated were collected for each classroom.

Developmental outcomes components. Data collection was initiated after the majority of cost and quality data had been completed. Data for the outcomes component were gathered by a team of three to six assessors in each state.

Developmental outcomes were based on individual child assessments, teacher ratings, and parent reports. Information was gathered from children about cognitive developmental status (verbal ability, prereading, and premath skills), their self-perceptions of competence, and attitudes about their child care environment. From teachers, ratings of the children's social skills and teacher-child relationships were obtained. Parents provided demographic information about their children and families, including questions about family structure, family composition, income, occupations, child care history and update, health status, and parental beliefs. Only English-speaking participants were included in the sample.

Measures

Child. Data on children's cognitive and social functioning was collected from individual assessments in years 1, 2, 3, and 5. The Peabody Picture Vocabulary Test—Revised (PPVT-R; Dunn & Dunn, 1981) was used to measure receptive language ability. The letter-word recognition and applied problems subtests of the Woodcock-Johnson Tests of Achievement—Revised (WJ-R; Woodcock & Johnson, 1989, 1990) were used to measure academic skills. Level of children's play was observed using the Peer Play Scale (Howes, 1980), which assesses the complexity of children's play with peers. This was used as an index of social competence.

Teachers rated children's classroom social and cognitive skills using the Classroom Behavior Inventory (CBI; Schaefer, Edgerton, & Aaronson, 1978). In second grade, teachers also completed the Teacher Assessment of Social Behavior (Cassidy & Asher, 1992), which measures peer relations.

Parents. Parents completed surveys each year. In addition to a variety of demographic and family climate questions, such as parent education, family income, marital status, and measures of parental beliefs and practices, the parent questionnaire asked how parents valued different aspects of child care that are associated with child care quality by professionals. They were asked about their perceptions of the quality of their children's classrooms. Parents were also asked to complete the Early Childhood Environment Rating Scale Parent Questionnaire (ECERS-PQ) (Harms, Clifford, & Cryer, 1998) and/or the Infant/Toddler Environment Rating Scale Parent Questionnaire (ITERS-PQ) (Harms, Cryer, & Clifford, 1990).

Family. Participants are asked about who is the head of the household and the number of adults and children, and their ages, living in the household.

Peers. Second grade teachers assessed social behavior.

Teachers. Teacher involvement and sensitivity was measured using the Caregiver Interaction Scale (CIS; Arnett, 1989), which measures teacher sensitivity, harshness, detachment, and permissiveness. Teaching style (didactic versus child-centered) was assessed using the UCLA Early Childhood Observation Form (ECOF; Stipek, Daniels, Galuzzo, & Miburn, 1992). Teacher responsiveness to children was measured using the Adult Involvement Scale (AIS; Howes & Stewart, 1987). Teacher-child relationship was also measured, using the Student-Teacher Relationship Scale (STRS; Pianta, 1992), which yields scores on closeness, conflict, and overdependency. In addition, a staff survey/questionnaire collected data about staff demographics, including marital status, race, age, hours worked, and child care experience.

Child care center characteristics. Data on center costs, revenue sources, subsidies, and center structure were collected for descriptive and econometric and other statistical analyses. Complete financial information was compiled using a questionnaire that was piloted in this study and used during the interview with the director. In addition, the interview included questions on program characteristics such as total attendance, enrollment and capacity of the center, number of infants and toddlers, and so forth. Data were also collected on staff characteristics, staffing patterns, benefits, and so forth. During the interview, data on standard structural measures of quality were collected (e.g., staff ratios), as well as on some nonstandard structural measures (e.g., cost or value of inservice training for staff) and on overt conditions of the building.

Information required to calculate staff to child ratios and group size was collected five times throughout the observation day in the sampled classrooms. Data on the quality of leadership at each center were collected through two versions of an Administrative Questionnaire, one completed by the director and the other by the teachers. Poverty of children and their families was not measured, but income was measured in a questionnaire that asked for income levels in increments of $2,000–$4,000. No modifications were made for relevance across cultures.

Children with disabilities. Generally, developmental day care programs that served only children with disabilities were excluded, but three developmental day care programs were sampled because the nature of these programs was not apparent until observers visited the classrooms. Programs that mainstreamed children with disabilities were included.

Home assessment. Parents filled out the Home Screening Questionnaire that was mailed to them. Observations in the home were not conducted.

Child care environment. In the first year of the study, four observational measures were used to assess quality. Three measures involved rating of the global classroom environment. The classroom environment was measured using the Early Childhood Environment Rating Scale (ECERS; Harms & Clifford, 1990) and its infant-toddler version, the Infants/Toddler Environment Rating Scale (ITERS; Harms et al., 1990). These scales comprehensively assess the day-to-day quality of care provided for children by examining the developmental appropriateness of classroom practices by assessing routine care needs, furnishings and display, activities and experiences related to motor, language, cognitive, and social development, and adult provisions. As mentioned above, teacher sensitivity was assessed using the CIS (Arnett, 1989), teaching style was measured using the UCLA ECOF (Stipek et al., 1992), and teacher responsiveness was assessed using the AIS (Howes & Stewart, 1987).

Health care assessment. There are no detailed data on this variable; however, parents were asked to rate the health status of their children.

Units of Analyses

The sampling design involved random selection of 50 for-profit and 50 non-profit centers in each state. Accordingly, there were two stages of analyses:

- Analysis determined whether there were significant state or sector differences in the measures.
- Analysis tested whether or not there were differences in means based on the three program scope variables. These scope variables were selected because they represent important dimensions of the center programs.

The findings of this study reflect descriptive analyses of center structure; staff policies and characteristics; classroom process and classroom structure; costs, revenue, and subsidies; preschool children's developmental outcomes; parents as child care consumers; and sector comparisons and the effect of public funding. There are also analytic analyses of the three major sets of relations among cost, quality of child care, and children's concurrent cognitive and social development. In terms of the conceptual structure depicted in Figure 8.1, associations between the Finances and the Classroom Quality domains, between the Classroom Quality and Classroom Structure domains, and among the Classroom Quality, Children, and Family domains are examined. Included in the specifications of each of these models are variables related to the Center Structure domain to control for state, sector, auspice, and scope of the center programs. Site-level analyses were presented only on a descriptive level.

There are descriptive analyses of variables such as ethnicity of children and staff. Ethnicity was coded as white, Asian, black, and Latino.

Results

The analysis of these data:

- Provides insights into the dynamics of the market that inhibit centers from providing better care
- Compares the performance of both for-profit and nonprofit centers
- Describes a competitive industry with low profit margins and with little financial incentive to improve quality
- Explains why the quality of most care is inadequate and points to ways in which investment can improve the developmental outcomes of young children to help ensure their ability to begin school ready to learn

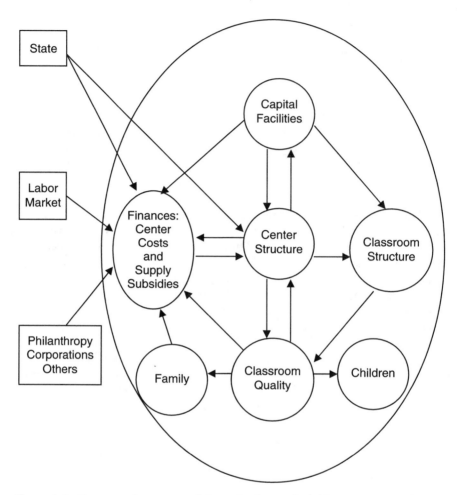

Figure 8.1. Conceptual structure of Cost, Quality, and Child Outcomes Study.

Two main sets of findings have been reported. The first set, from the first phase of the study, focuses on the child care environment. A detailed review of these findings can be found in the introductions to Parts 2 and 3 and the chapter summaries of the technical report (CQO Study Team, 1995). Papers on teachers' background, relationship between structural features of child care and process quality, parents as child care consumers, and child care experiences and concurrent child development have been published (see Helburn & Howes, 1996; Howes, 1997; Peisner-Feinberg & Burchinal,

1997; Tietze et al., 1996). In addition, a report on the longitudinal outcomes was recently released (CQO Study Team, 1999) and is available at http://www.fpg.unc.edu/~NCEDL/PAGES/cqes.htm on the Web. Below is a brief presentation of the major findings.

The findings on quality are as follows:

- Child care at most centers in the United Stares is poor to mediocre, with almost half of the infants and toddlers in rooms of less than minimal quality.
- Across all levels of maternal education and child gender and ethnicity, children's cognitive and social concurrent development are positively related to the quality of their child care experience.
- The quality of child care is primarily associated with higher staff to child ratios, staff education, staff wages, administrators' experience and curriculum support, and teacher turnover. In addition, certain characteristics discriminate among poor, mediocre, and good-quality centers, the most important of which are teacher wages, education, and specialized training.
- States with more demanding licensing standards have fewer poor-quality centers. Centers that comply with additional standards beyond those required for licensing provide higher quality services.
- Centers with access to extra resources that they use to improve quality provide higher than average overall quality.

The findings on costs, revenues, and subsidies are as follows:

- Center child care, even mediocre-quality care, is costly to provide. Even so, donations and foregone wages are large, accounting for more than one fourth of the full cost of care.
- Good-quality services cost more, but not a lot more.
- There are economies of scale in providing child care.
- Cash payment from government and philanthropies represent 28% of center revenue overall and demonstrate a social commitment to share the expenses of child care.

The findings on sector differences and economic environment are as follows:

- Differences between for-profit and nonprofit sectors exist. Overall quality of services, however, is not significantly different between the two sectors except in the one state with very lax licensing standards.

- Characteristics of the market setting for child care—notably, market competition and subsidy dependence—affect center finances. For-profit and nonprofit centers face different competitive conditions that can affect their performance.
- Consumer information is inadequate, which creates market imperfections and reduces incentives for some centers to provide good-quality care.

The second major release of findings focuses on the relation between child care quality and children's development from the preschool years through second grade, taking into account family background differences. The longitudinal findings on outcomes are as follows:

- Children who attended higher quality child care centers performed better on measures of both cognitive skills, such as math and language abilities, and social skills, such as interactions with peers and behavior problems, in child care and through the transition into school. This finding held for children from various family backgrounds.
- Child care quality continues to impact children's cognitive and behavioral skills, such as thinking/attention skills, sociability, problem behaviors, and peer relations, in the classroom at least through kindergarten, and in many cases, through the end of second grade.
- Children whose mothers had lower levels of education were more sensitive to the negative effects of poor-quality child care and benefited more from high-quality care than other children. These findings persisted through second grade.
- The quality of the child care classroom practices was related to children's cognitive development, and the closeness of the child care teacher–child relationship was associated with social development through second grade.

Limitations

This study was based on a sample of child care centers covering a range of quality from low to high. The findings are most relevant for full-time center-based care; part-time center-based or Head Start care that did not have wraparound care were excluded from the study. A potential limit to its generalizability is the nature of the sample. It excluded non-English speaking children and parents' who could not communicate in English. Children, particularly infants and toddlers, are increasingly experiencing multiple child care arrangements; the effects of this on children's development are not captured in this study. It is also likely that centers with very low quality refused to participate in this study; hence nonparticipation is probably not random. The sample of poor and ethnic families was small, and attrition was greatest in these subgroups. Centers with "middle" quality were the largest group; this could be an artifact of sampling or a true representation of the quality of centers.

Public Use Files

The data for the first phase of the study are available to the public. For more information see http://www.fpg.unc.edu/~NCEDL/PAGES/cqes.htm on-line.

NATIONAL STUDY OF CHILD CARE FOR LOW-INCOME FAMILIES

History

This initiative was created in response to the dearth of information available on how low-income families with children under 5 years of age negotiate demands of family and work. Questions raised include: (a) To what extent can states and communities meet the demand for child care for families moving off welfare into work? What are the child care needs of the working poor and of families with other special needs? (b) What types of child care do low-income families use? What are the factors that influence their choice of care, and to what extent does it meet their needs? (c) What are the challenges that low-income parents face in balancing the demands of work and care for their children? (d) What are the characteristics of family child care providers, the services they provide, and their relationships with the families to whom they provide these services?

Current Status

The National Study of Child Care for Low-Income Families will provide policy makers with much-needed information on the effects of federal, state, and local policies and programs on the child care market at the community level and on the employment and child care decisions of low-income families. The first wave of data collection began in 1999 and ended in 2001. Information about the policies and programs that influence parents' decisions about child care, the stability and continuity of child care, the child care choices they make, and how these choices affect their ability to find and retain a job or participate in education or training programs was collected through a one-time survey in 2000. More information on families that use family child care, their providers, and the experiences of children in family child care will be collected over 6 data collection points over the 2½-year duration of the study. No results have been published or disseminated publicly as yet.

Goals

The following objectives guide this study:

- To develop an understanding of state child care and welfare policies and how these are implemented at the community-level
- To develop an understanding of how other community-level factors (e.g., the community poverty rate, labor market, and the nature and scope of institutions related to child care) affect the way that communities are organized to help low-income families address work and child care needs
- To examine the effects of child care and welfare policies and community-level factors on the demand for and the supply of child care, and on the types of child care arrangements that low-income parents make
- To examine changes in policies and programs over time and the effects of these changes
- To examine and model the child care decisions of low-income families and the role of child care subsidies in decision making
- To conduct an in-depth examination of family child care used by low-income families, including the role of family child care in helping poor families manage the competing demands of work and child care, and children's experiences in the care environment

Design and Methods

To address the objectives listed above, the researchers have designed a study that requires a complex, multilevel data collection strategy. Data will be collected at three levels, with nested samples of counties within states and families and providers within counties. The first level is a sample of 17 states containing 25 counties that were selected to be a nationally representative sample of counties with above average poverty rates. At the family level, the study includes several samples:

- A random sample of 5,000 low-income families with working parents and at least one child under age 13 for whom they use nonparental child care, that will be selected in the 25 counties (200 per county).
- A sample of 650 low-income parents who are receiving, or have applied for, child care subsidies, and who are using family child care at

the start of the study will be used to examine the experiences of low-income families.

- At the provider level, data will also be collected from the 650 family child care providers linked to these 650 families.

Sample. The sample consists of 25 counties. The primary reason for using counties is the availability of benchmark data at the county level from the National Child Care Survey (NCCS) and the Profiles of Child Care Settings (PCCS) studies conducted in 1990 in a nationally representative sample of counties. The goal was to select a sample that would be representative of where low-income children live. Starting with the NCCS/PCCS sample of 100 counties/county groupings, 80 counties/county groupings with a 1993 poverty rate for children greater than 13.8% have been identified. These 80 counties/county groupings, once properly weighted, represent more than 90% of poor children in the United States. The sample of 25 counties was selected to be a representative sample of these 80 counties/county groupings.

Selecting families for the community survey in 25 counties. The primary objective of the community survey is to provide information on the demand for child care among low-income working parents in each of the 25 counties included in the study. A random digit dialing (RDD) telephone survey will be conducted in each of the 25 counties. The household screening will include households with children under age 13, a mother working or in school, using some form of nonparental child care, and family income below 200% of the federal poverty line. The screening process will be done until 100 families in each county using work or education-related child care are identified. Across the 25 counties, the sample will include a total of 2,500 such families. This sample will include some families that are receiving subsidies, some that are on waiting lists to receive subsidies, as well as families who are eligible for, but have not applied for subsidies. In addition, it will include some families whose income places them just above the eligibility limits. At the family level, this sample will also be used to address questions regarding parents' choice of child care arrangements and the effects of child care and subsidy policies (as well as welfare policies) on this choice.

Selecting a subsample of five counties for the in-depth study of family child care. An in-depth examination of low-income families using family child care will be conducted in a subsample of 5 of the 25 counties. The 5 counties to be included in the subsample will be selected to represent the following: same geographic distribution, variation in state regulatory and subsidy policy, variation in other policy-relevant indicators, variation in urban versus rural location, different concentrations of poverty populations, ethnic mix within the community, and factors facilitating implementation of the study (e.g., cooperation of local and state personnel). In addition, the counties needed to include a sufficient number of subsidized families to provide an adequate sample for the in-depth examination of family child care.

Selecting a sample of 650 low-income parents using family child care in the five counties. The sample of 650 low-income working parents with children in family child care will include 130 families in each of the 5 counties. All of the families included in this sample will be eligible to receive child care subsidies at the time of sample selection. This sample will be stratified by subsidy status and age of child. The method of selecting families differs for subsidized versus unsubsidized families. Families selected will be followed over the 2½-year data collection period regardless of any changes in their child care arrangements.

In each of the counties, 98 families receiving child care subsidies for family child care (for a total of 490 subsidized families) will be selected. These families will be drawn from state subsidy lists. Each of the five states included in this part of the study is able to provide lists of families receiving child care subsidies. The process of identifying and recruiting unsubsidized children to participate in the study is complex. Since there are no lists of children in child care who are eligible for but are not receiving child care subsidies, the plan is to use "snowball sampling." This involves asking families on the child care subsidy lists to identify families in their neighborhood that are similar to their own family, but who do not receive child care subsidies. This will be done as part of the screening interview for families receiving child care subsidies.

For the in-depth examination of family child care, it is also necessary to gain the cooperation of linked family child care providers. Based on previous research, researchers expect that 56% of their linked family child care providers will also agree to participate. The initial sample for family child care users will be increased to allow for noncooperation on the part of linked providers.

Measures

This study will provide information on the effects of federal, state, and local policies and programs on the child care market at the community level, and on the employment and child care decisions of low-income families. To this end, it will collect data at the state, individual, and community levels. The instruments include interviews with key informants at the state and community levels; community survey of low-income working parents; focus groups with parents and parent interview; community survey of low-income working parents; interviews with child care providers and in-care observations; and interviews with school-age children. Information will be gathered on child care subsidies at the state level; community characteristics such as per capita income and child poverty rate at the community level; and parents' use of child care, such as center-based, in-home, self-care, or no care at the individual level.

Measures such as ethnicity will be coded using the standard categories determined by the Census Bureau. Income is coded as total household income in whichever way the respondents provide this information. The study will use federal poverty levels, which are adjusted by household size.

In addition to collecting the information in Spanish, survey instruments will be translated into Spanish. However, the HOME inventory, used to assess the quality of the home environment, will not be modified to take into account cultural/ethnic differences. The study will include children with disabilities, but instruments will not be altered. The organization of the home environment will be assessed using the HOME.

The child care environment will be assessed using a variety of instrument/ approaches including survey and in-person interviews with family child care providers and observations in the family child care setting and interviews with older children. The in-person interviews with child care providers will obtain information about the providers, including education, household characteristics, reasons for becoming a child care provider, views on child rearing and the role of the child care provider and her relationship with the parents. In-care observations will be used to describe children's experience in child care. Interviews with school-age children will be conducted in the child's own home and will include questions about the number of other children in the care arrangement, the number of caregivers and other adults present, activities while in care, and satisfaction with the child care arrangement.

Site-level analyses will be conducted and the data will be analyzed by policy-related variables such as race, ethnicity, and income.

Results

No results are available yet.

Limitations

A limitation of the study is that it does not collect child outcome data.

Public Use Files

The data will be available to the public in 2003.

GROWING UP IN POVERTY (GUP) PROJECT

History

The primary aims of the Growing Up in Poverty Project are to learn how the welfare reform law may alter the upbringing and development of children, and to examine whether the goals of welfare reform are being carried out. Furthermore, as a result of the new law, about one million additional children have entered child care, resulting in many more single parents seeking child care. Several crucial questions about child care cost and quality have been raised. GUP is one project that begins to find answers to some of these questions.

Current Status

In the summer of 1998, single mothers with preschool-aged children entering new welfare programs were invited to participate in this 4-year study in five cities: San Francisco and San Jose, California; Manchester and New Haven, Connecticut; and Tampa, Florida. In terms of state welfare requirements, local labor demands, ethnic composition, and community infrastructure, these cities are quite diverse.

Women in California and Florida had been enrolled for up to 6 months in new welfare programs. Connecticut participants were divided into experimental (new programs) and control (old programs) groups that were compared after 18 months. Wave 1 data collection on 948 families is complete and results have been disseminated to the general public. Wave 1 data collection included child care provider observations and direct child assessments. The summary of findings can be found in the Wave 1 report: *Remember the Children: Mothers Balance Work and Child Care Under Welfare Reform* (Fuller et al., 2000). Wave 2 data collection was completed in 2000 and included home visits and direct child assessments. The summary of findings can be found in the report *New Lives for Poor Families?* (Fuller et al., 2002).

The project's main research questions are framed in the context of examining children's lives as their mothers move out of welfare and into the workforce, and exploring how mothers meet work requirements and make ends meet. Specific questions examined are the following:

- What are the variations in children's home environments as mothers spend more time in welfare-to-work activities?
- What kinds of child care arrangements are available to mothers, and does the quality of these settings help or harm children's early development?

- What kinds of social support (either from welfare agencies or household and family members) do mothers obtain?

Goals

Though proponents of reform are interested in improving the lives of families and children through increases in tax benefits and expanding family supports such as child care, the goals of this study go far beyond examining the economic incentives of welfare reform. GUP has four main objectives:

- To sketch the varied and complex lives of welfare recipients
- To inquire about households, sources of support, and degree of isolation
- To assess the nature and quality of new child care settings

Design and Methods

In order to assess the above stated objectives, the researchers of GUP have designed the study to consist of five components:

- Repeated interviews with mothers
- Home visits
- Interviews with and observational assessments of child care providers
- Direct child assessments of cognitive, language, and social development

Wave 1 data were collected in Connecticut, California, and Florida. All participants in the project in California and Florida had recently entered a new welfare program. These participants were recruited from welfare orientation sessions after their eligibility was determined. Data in these two states were collected during the first 2 to 6 months in the program. Participants sampled in Connecticut are taking part in a random assignment experiment. Half of the Connecticut participants were randomly assigned to the state's new welfare program (Jobs First), while the other half formed a control group, living under the old AFDC welfare rules. These mothers were interviewed and child care settings were assessed 18 months after entering the experiment.

Measures

Data were collected on the home environment, child care provider, child care setting, and children's development via interviews, direct observations, and direct child assessments. Mothers were interviewed for about 2 hours and information was collected on the following topics:

- A demographic profile, including school attainment, age, ethnicity, marital and fertility history, and household composition
- Prior work experience and involvement with welfare and family support programs
- Parental role strain and quality of life with household members
- Parenting practices, including disciplinary approaches and learning activities with child
- Sources of social support
- Maternal and child health
- Engagement in welfare-to-work activities
- Prior use of child care
- Maternal reports on child's language and social development and behavior problems

Child assessments were conducted as follows:

- The MacArthur Communicative Development Inventory was used to assess early language.
- The Emotionality, Activity, Sociability, and Impulsivity Scale (EASI) was used in assessing young (12–23 months) toddlers' social development. The Child Behavior Checklist (CBCL) was used for the older (24–42 months) preschoolers.
- Maternal reports were used to assess children's word comprehension and production.

Assessments of child care use and quality included the following:

- The Early Childhood Environment Rating Scale (ECERS) or the Family Day Care Rating Scale (FDCRS) were used to assess indicators such as teacher/provider attributes, space, basic furnishings, personal care routines, language-related materials and disciplinary strategies employed by the provider.
- The Arnett Caregiver Scale was used to assess provider's sensitivity, warm affect, disciplinary methods, and interaction with the child.
- The Child Care Observation System (C-COS) was used to assess the

range of social interactions between the child and provider, types of activities, and child's emotional state in the setting.

Results

Wave 1 findings suggest that children of welfare recipients entering the workforce are enrolled in low-quality child care when compared to the quality of centers and preschools in middle-class communities. An exception was found in two sites in California, where center-based programs exhibited fairly high quality. Most participating children were placed in home-based care rather than center-based care. Many single mothers who are required to work are placing their children in inadequate child care settings, which may affect early learning. Furthermore, there is a limited supply of licensed child care centers in their communities, restricting women's choice for center-based care and reducing the number of child care subsidies used.

In terms of children's early learning and development, the findings suggest that children of welfare families are lagging behind children in non-welfare families when comparing levels of language development. Moreover, disengaged parenting practices and high rates of depressive symptoms were found to limit children's development, though this may not be a function of welfare reform per se.

Findings from participating states revealed that welfare reform is moving women into the workforce, but reported wages are low. For instance, the median income reported ranged from $600 to $700 per month. Additionally, many women reported having difficulty in purchasing an adequate supply of food. In terms of economic or social support, many women reported feeling isolated. These findings suggest that while welfare rolls have dramatically decreased, there is cause for concern about whether getting off welfare improves the quality of life for women.

Wave 2 findings supported and extended these concerns (Fuller et al., 2002).

Public Use Files

No plans have been made for public use as yet. However, for more information see http://pace.berkeley.edu/pace_growingup.html on-line.

NOTES

The members of the NICHD Early Child Care Research Network wish to express their appreciation to the study coordinators at each site, the research assistants, and especially the families and child care providers who welcomed them to their homes and workplaces. Phyllis Gyamfi would like to thank Bruce Fuller, Sharon Lynn Kagan and the Graduate School of Education (PACE) at the University of California, Berkeley, for information on the Growing Up in Poverty Project. Jodie Roth and Natasha Cabrera would like to thank Carollee Howes and Ellen Peisner-Feinberg for their help in providing information on the Cost, Quality, and Outcomes Study. The authors are grateful to Lisa O'Connor and Christina Borbely at the Center for Children and Families for their editorial assistance.

1. The NICHD Early Child Care Research Network is primary author for this section of Chapter 8. The principal investigators are listed in the footnote to Part I of this chapter. The study is funded by the National Institute for Child Health and Human Development. For more information see http://www.nichd.nih.gov/od/secc/index.htm on-line.

2. Jodie Roth and Natasha Cabrera are primary authors of this section of Chapter 8. Principal investigators are Carollee Howes, Richard Clifford, Ellen Peisner-Feinberg, Mary Culkin, and Sharon Lynn Kagan. Funders include the Carnegie Corporation of New York and the William T. Grant Foundation. Most of the information presented here can be found in the CQO Study Team's technical report (1995) edited by Suzanne Helburn. More information is available from the department of Economics, Center for Research in Economic and Social Policy, University of Colorado at Denver. The CQO Study Team's (1999) follow-up report is available at http://www.fpg.unc.edu/~NCEDL/PAGES/cqes.htm on-line.

3. Natasha Cabrera is the primary author of this section of Chapter 8. Principal investigators are Abt Associates and the National Center for Children in Poverty at Columbia University. The funder is the Administration for Children and Families. For more information, see http://www.acf.dhhs.gov/programs/opre/childcar.htm on-line.

4. Phyllis Gyamfi is the primary author of this section of Chapter 8. Principal investigators are Bruce Fuller and Sharon Lynn Kagan. Funders include the Packard, Spencer, and Casey Foundations. The study is being carried out by UC Berkeley and Yale University, in collaboration with Mathematica Policy Research and MDRC. For more information, visit the Web site at http://pace.berkeley.edu/pace_growingup.html on-line.

CHAPTER 9

Welfare-to-Work Initiatives

CHRISTY BRADY-SMITH, MARTHA ZASLOW, TAMA LEVENTHAL,
GREG DUNCAN, AND KERRY RICHTER

Prior to the passage of the Personal Responsibility and Work Opportunity Reconciliation Law (PRWORA) of 1996, shifts in state-level policies initiated under the Family Support Act (FSA) of 1988 as well as in public opinion had created a context of widespread welfare reform.[1] Between 1993 and 1996, more than 40 states began implementing experimental, or "demonstration," welfare programs in an attempt to move recipients off welfare and into the job market (Child Trends, 1999; Corbett, 1995; Maynard, Boehnen, Corbett, Sandefur, & Mosley, 1998). Under the FSA of 1988, states received waivers from the federal government to launch a variety of new provisions to their welfare programs, including time limits on receipt of benefits, work requirements, "family caps" (no additional benefits for children born while the mother was on public assistance), and teenage parent residency and education requirements. Early evaluations of these programs revealed mixed results in terms of impacts on adult economic outcomes (see Chase-Lansdale & Brooks-Gunn, 1995; Gueron & Pauly, 1991; J. B. Wilson, Ellwood, & Brooks-Gunn, 1995; Wiseman, 1996; Zaslow, Moore, Morrison, & Coiro, 1995). Notably absent from these initial reports, however, was a serious examination of how welfare policy changes affected children and families (Zaslow, Tout, Smith, & Moore, 1998).

While many of the reforms initiated under the FSA of 1988 were embodied in the PRWORA of 1996, a new era of welfare reform was nationally implemented with the passage of this law. Aid to Families with Dependent Children (AFDC), the federal entitlement program for low-income families, was succeeded by Temporary Assistance to Needy Families (TANF), under which states receive block grants (pegged to state welfare expenditures in 1995) to administer welfare services. Under the new program, individuals are limited to 60 months of cash assistance (whether consecutive or not), and assistance is contingent upon participation in work-related activities after 24 months. Failure to comply with work requirements may result in sanctions. States have the option of implementing shorter time limits on total receipt and earlier onset of work requirements (over half of all states have done so). In addition, states can exempt up to 20% of their welfare caseloads from the lifetime limit due to hardship. Also relevant to young children are changes affecting child care, the Food Stamp Program, Supplemental Security Income (SSI) for children, benefits for legal immigrants, and the Child Support Enforcement program (see Greenberg et al., 2000, for a discussion of the key elements of the 1996 welfare law).

One of the most significant changes of welfare reform affecting families with young children is that mothers with young children are now expected to work (under AFDC and the FSA of 1988, mothers with children younger than 3 years of age were exempt from this requirement, although states could opt to extend the age downward to 1 year; J. R. Smith, Brooks-Gunn, & Jackson, 1997). Mothers with young children may have difficulty meeting such requirements because of constraints such as available child care (Ross & Kirby, 2000). These difficulties are likely to be exacerbated for mothers with very young children (from birth to age 3) for whom child care can be especially problematic (Brady-Smith, Brooks-Gunn, Waldfogel, & Fauth, 2001; Cherlin, 1995; Hofferth et al., 1991; Phillips et al., 1994).

If mothers of very young children have difficulty finding child care, and especially child care of high quality, this would suggest that maternal employment might have unfavorable implications for young children in the context of welfare reform. Yet there are also bases on which to predict favorable implications of maternal employment for young children, if employment is accompanied by increased family income and resources or increased social support received by the mother. Hoffman and Youngblade (1999) suggest that maternal employment is associated with more favorable maternal mental health, especially among low-income families. A series of studies show neutral to positive associations of employment and child outcomes among low-income families, although with some contradictory findings particularly for infants (summarized in Zaslow & Emig, 1997).

Recent work has started to examine employment that co-occurs with welfare receipt, and the transition to employment among mothers with a history of welfare receipt. On the one hand, this research suggests that there may be some benefits that accrue to mothers and their children from maternal participation in the labor force. For example, in a sample of low-income families, J. R. Smith, Brooks-Gunn, Klebanov, and Lee (2000) explored associations between combinations of maternal work and welfare receipt during the first 3 years of children's lives and maternal and child well-being. Their findings revealed that among families who combined welfare and work, children had cognitive and behavioral test scores similar to children from families where mothers worked consistently but did not receive welfare. Among these families, mothers were also similar in terms of mental health, social support, and coping skills. In contrast, among families who received welfare but mothers did not work, children had poorer cognitive and behavioral outcomes than children from families with mothers who worked consistently and did not receive welfare. Mothers from welfare-only families also provided less stimulating home environments, had poorer mental heath and lower social support, and used less effective coping strategies than mothers who worked consistently and did not receive welfare. Together, these findings suggest that maternal employment may have some benefits for mothers and their young children and that welfare receipt, in the context of employment, does not necessarily harm families and may even have some advantages (which most likely operate through increased family income).

On the other hand, further evidence raises the possibility that associations between maternal employment and child outcomes in families with a history of welfare receipt may be attributable to the characteristics of the families, rather than to the fact of employment. Zaslow, McGroder, Cave, and Mariner (1999) contrasted the developmental outcomes of children whose mothers, all with a history of welfare receipt, were and were not employed. Developmental outcomes in the areas of health, social and behavioral development, and cognitive development and academic achievement were consistently better among the children of mothers who had transitioned to employment. However, when an extensive set of maternal and family characteristics were taken into account, it was found that the differences in child outcomes were entirely attributable to the initial characteristics of the mothers and families rather than to the fact of employment. While this set of analyses was carried out among mothers who chose employment of their own volition, a critical question is whether a mandate to transition to employment has differing selection effects, and is associated with child outcomes in a different way (Zaslow & Emig, 1997; Zaslow et al., 1999; Zaslow, Tout, et al., 1998). Work in progress by McGroder and colleagues is examining selection factors and child outcomes in families in which the mother is fulfilling a welfare participation mandate.

Depending on the particular program, welfare reform may affect the income available to low-income families and/or the families' poverty level. Some policies (for example, the Minnesota Family Investment Program [MFIP] welfare waiver policy) explicitly aimed to reduce poverty, and included strong financial work incentives (Gennetian & Miller, 2000; Miller et al., 2000). Long-term welfare recipients with young children assigned to MFIP did indeed show increases in income and decreases in poverty (Gennetian & Miller, 2000). Other programs may aim simply to reduce welfare dependency and increase employment without providing financial incentives for working. While the long-term goal of such programs is to foster economic self-sufficiency, some programs have found increases in the proportion of program group families in poverty, using maternal report measures of income and benefits (for example, the Newark site of the Teenage Parent Demonstration [TPD]; Kisker, Rangarajan, & Boller, 1998; Maynard, Nicholson, & Rangarajan, 1993; and the Grand Rapids human capital development program in the National Evaluation of Welfare-to-Work Strategies—Child Outcomes Study [NEWWS—COS]; McGroder, Zaslow, Moore, & LeMenestrel, 2000). Given links between poverty and young children's development (Brooks-Gunn & Duncan, 1997; Duncan & Brooks-Gunn, 1997), the different patterns of impacts may have consequences for children's well-being.

The effects of welfare reform on young children also are likely to be mediated by parents' psychological well-being and parenting behavior (Brooks-Gunn, Smith, Berlin, & Lee, in press; McGroder et al., 2000; Zaslow et al, 1995). Based on models of family stress, if mothers face financial strain as a result of sanctioning or time limits, it may impact their emotional health. Changes in maternal mental health, in turn, may lead to changes in parenting behavior and subsequent child well-being. At the same time, increased financial well-being, sense of maternal competence, stimulation received from the job or social support on the job may improve maternal mental health and have positive implications for parenting and thus for children. Program impacts on maternal depressive symptoms and on parenting behavior have been reported in both a favorable and unfavorable direction in the context of differing welfare-to-work programs (for differing patterns of impacts, see findings for the observational study of mother-child interaction embedded in the New Chance Evaluation; Zaslow & Eldred, 1998; findings for the Newark and Chicago sites of the TPD; Kisker et al., 1998; Maynard et al., 1993; and results of the NEWWS—COS; McGroder et al., 2000). Program impacts on parenting behavior and maternal mental health were indeed found to mediate some of the impacts of the JOBS program on children in the NEWWS—COS (McGroder, Zaslow, Moore, Hair, & Ahluwalia, 2002).

Although not profiled in this chapter, the New Chance Demonstration[2] and the Teenage Parent Demonstration (TPD)[3] were enacted prior to the FSA of 1988. Both programs aimed to improve the economic self-sufficiency and parenting behaviors of teenage mothers likely to be dependent on government assistance. The New Chance Demonstration, a primarily voluntary program, offered comprehensive services to mothers and their children in order to help them make the transition to self-sufficiency. The TPD was a forerunner of future welfare programs requiring mandatory participation, offering support services, and imposing sanctions for noncompliance. Experimental evaluations found that New Chance had favorable impacts on parenting (Zaslow & Eldred, 1998), while TPD did not (Aber et al., 1995). However, nonexperimental analysis found that in the TPD evaluation, among parents with young children, increased economic self-sufficiency was associated with positive child outcomes and less harsh parenting overall (Aber et al., 1995; see Brooks-Gunn et al., in press, for a more detailed review of these findings).

A noteworthy aspect of the current wave of welfare reform is that the research community has focused greater attention on the evaluation of child and family outcomes than in the past. This chapter will provide profiles on a set of five current studies designed to address how children and families are faring in the wake of widespread welfare reforms. The first two initiatives focus on programs enacted under the FSA of 1988—the National Evaluation of Welfare-to-Work Strategies—Child Outcomes Study (NEWWS—COS; formerly called the JOBS Evaluation)[4] and the New Hope Child and Family Study.[5] The NEWWS—COS is an evaluation of selected, to-scale programs run by states under the FSA. New Hope, on the other hand, was a demonstration program. In many cases, these programs were precursors to the next wave of welfare reforms. Then, three new initiatives coinciding with the passage of the PRWORA of 1996 will be profiled—Welfare, Children and Families: A Three City Study,[6] the Project on State-Level Child Outcomes,[7] and Assessing the New Federalism (ANF): The National Survey of America's Families (NSAF).[8]

The Next Generation project, compiled by Manpower Demonstration Research Corporation (MDRC), has synthesized the impacts of different demonstration projects on the well-being of children (for more information, see their Web site at http://www.mdrc.org/NextGeneration/). Their synthesis includes evaluations from the NEWWS—COS, the New Hope evaluation, the Minnesota and Florida demonstrations of the Project on State-Level Outcomes, and the Self-Sufficiency Project conducted in Canada. All of these projects, except the Canadian demonstration, are reviewed in these profiles.

THE NATIONAL EVALUATION OF WELFARE-TO-WORK STRATEGIES—CHILD OUTCOMES STUDY (NEWWS-COS)

History

The Job Opportunities and Basic Skills (JOBS) Training Program was the programmatic implementation of the 1988 Family Support Act (FSA), the round of national welfare legislation that antedated the 1996 Personal Responsibility and Work Opportunity Reconciliation Act. The JOBS Program was designed to provide recipients of Aid to Families with Dependent Children with education, training, and employment, with the goal of avoiding long-term welfare dependency. While previous welfare-to-work programs primarily involved parents with older children, the JOBS Program also included parents with preschool-age children. Participation in the JOBS Program was mandatory for all AFDC recipients with a youngest child of 3 years or older (the age requirement could be younger at state option). The JOBS legislation required states to guarantee child care for participants if such care was necessary to attend JOBS activities. Medicaid and child care benefits were provided for a transitional period of 12 months after moving from AFDC to employment. The legislation also established new procedures for child support enforcement and establishment of paternity, and required states to offer a program (AFDC—Unemployed Parent) for two-parent families in which the principal wage earner was unemployed (Chase-Lansdale & Brooks-Gunn, 1995).

The National Evaluation of Welfare-to-Work Strategies (NEWWS; formerly called the JOBS Evaluation) was designed to examine the economic impacts of the JOBS Program on families in seven sites. The focus of this section is the NEWWS—Child Outcomes Study (COS), which was designed to examine the impacts of the JOBS Program on the well-being of children who were of preschool-age at the start of the evaluation, and is nested within three sites of the larger seven-site NEWWS Study. Using a random assignment design, the NEWWS Study examined the economic impacts of the program (examining such variables as receipt of welfare, employment, earnings, and total family income) in a sample of over 55,000 families in seven sites. The effects of various welfare-to-work strategies were being measured in each of the seven sites. In the three sites in which the NEWWS—COS is nested, families that had applied for or were receiving AFDC were randomly assigned to be in one of two program groups (the human capital development group or the labor force attachment group) or in a control group (free of the mandate to participate in the JOBS Program, yet eligible for all AFDC benefits). The program groups involved two distinct variants of the JOBS Program. The human capital development approach focused on providing basic education and training to enhance recipients' employability, while the labor force attachment approach focused on job search activities to facilitate a rapid transition to employment. For those assigned to the program groups, participation in these self-sufficiency activities was mandatory. Nonparticipation could result in sanctioning or a reduction in benefits.

The impact analysis of the seven-site NEWWS Study relied on data from both administrative records and from surveys, with the survey waves occurring 2 and, in some sites, 5 years after baseline (enrollment in the evaluation). During the first survey wave, some respondents completed tests of reading and math literacy. The NEWWS Study also encompassed a study of the program's implementation in the seven sites, and a cost/benefit assessment. The NEWWS Study was carried out by Manpower Demonstration Research Corporation.

The NEWWS—COS was carried out by Child Trends, under subcontract to MDRC, in three of the seven sites of the full NEWWS Study: Atlanta, Georgia; Grand Rapids, Michigan; and Riverside, California. Within these sites, families were included in the NEWWS—COS if they had a child between 3 and 5 years of age at baseline. The experimental design of the evaluation permitted an assessment of program impacts on children in families assigned to each of the experimental streams. Child outcomes were assessed 2 and 5 years after baseline through a combination of methods: direct assessments of cognitive development; mother and teacher reports of the child's social development, adjustment, and academic progress (with child reports as well for some measures at the Five-Year Follow-up); mother reports of the child's health; and interviewer ratings of the child's behavior. The assessment of child outcomes in multiple domains of development, and the reliance on multiple informants for the examination of child outcomes, are important features of the NEWWS—COS.

In one of the NEWWS—COS sites (Atlanta), a substudy was carried out with the aim of describing the families' circumstances and the children's development close to the time of the individuals' enrollment in the NEWWS Study. This special study, the NEWWS Descriptive Study, involved an in-home survey approximately 3 months after baseline. Because it was conducted so close to the start of the evaluation, the focus of the Descriptive Study was a detailed portrayal of the families and children rather than an examination of the impacts of the program.

Another substudy carried out only in the Atlanta site involved direct observations of mother-child interaction. This study, the NEWWS Observational Study, permitted a detailed examination of the question of whether participation in the JOBS human capital development program in the Atlanta site affected mother-child interaction and, further, whether the quality of mother-child interactions helped to shape any program impacts on children's development. The Observational Study was conducted 4–6 months and 4½ years post-baseline.

The Family Support Act called for an evaluation of the JOBS Program to determine the effectiveness of different ways of operating welfare-to-work programs. Reflecting a desire among legislators to get the most reliable estimates of program effects—estimates that would take into account normal welfare dynamics—the act specified an evaluation using a random assignment design (Smeeding, 1995; Zill, 1995). When considering its options for carrying out this mandate, the U.S. Department of Health and Human Services (DHHS) recognized the importance of the context in which JOBS would be implemented and decided to focus the NEWWS Study on innovative features of JOBS and to address new questions about the operation, effects, and cost-effectiveness of various types of welfare-to-work programs. Given that one of JOBS' innovations, relative to prior programs, was mandated participation by women with preschool-age children, DHHS requested a special study examining how parents of young children—as well as the children themselves—fared under the JOBS Program. The NEWWS—COS broke new ground in that this was the first time *national* welfare policy was evaluated from the perspective of implications for children.

Two bodies of research were critical in the evolution of the NEWWS—COS: evidence of the economic impacts of previous welfare-to-work programs; and evidence pointing to linkages between developmental outcomes for children and parental variables that were likely to be affected by participation in JOBS.

Previous research on welfare-to-work programs showed that these programs could be effective in terms of economic outcomes. For example, in the evaluation of the GAIN welfare-to-work program in California, families in the experimental group were earning more and receiving less in average AFDC payments 2 years after baseline, and these results were statistically significant (Friedlander, Riccio & Freedman, 1993). The average earnings impact for the 2-year period was $785, representing a 21% increase relative to the average earnings of control group members. When earnings gains were compared to welfare reductions and other losses in government assistance over a 5-year period, welfare recipients in five of the six studied California counties were, on average, better off financially as a consequence of GAIN (Riccio, Friedlander, & Freedman, 1994).

The finding that welfare-to-work programs can bring about significant increases in earnings is important from the point of view of children (although we note that earnings increases are not always accompanied by increases in total household income). A substantial body of research indicates that family economic variables (e.g., earnings, total household income, family socioeconomic status) are strong correlates of child outcomes. For example, Duncan, Brooks-Gunn, and Klebanov (1994; Duncan & Brooks-Gunn, 1997) present evidence of a linkage between family income and such important markers of children's development as IQ scores and behavior problems. These findings raised the possibility that if family income increases because of participation in a program such as JOBS, then outcomes for children might improve.

The JOBS Program, particularly in its human capital development stream, set as a further goal the enhancement of welfare recipients' basic education and job skills. A body of evidence also points to a connection between maternal educational attainment and children's developmental outcomes (e.g., Baydar & Brooks-Gunn, 1991; Desai, Chase-Lansdale, & Michael, 1989; Hauser & Mossell, 1985). Thus changes in maternal education resulting from JOBS participation might also serve as a basis for improved child outcomes.

It is important to note that, while JOBS directly targeted parental education, employment, welfare receipt, and earnings, it is also plausible that participation in JOBS might bring about changes in "noneconomic" variables within families that have been found to be linked with children's developmental status (Zaslow et al., 1995). For example, changes in maternal psychological well-being, the home environment, and participation in child care brought about by participation in JOBS could all potentially affect child outcomes. It is reasonable to hypothesize that JOBS would have positive impacts on earnings, income, and maternal education (with positive implications for child outcomes). It is plausible, however, that maternal psychological well-being, the home environment, and child care experiences, could be altered by JOBS participation or increased labor market participation in a positive or negative direction (Wilson et al., 1995).

Thus, for example, positive program impacts on maternal psychological well-being could be predicted on the grounds that employed mothers in general tend to show better mental health than mothers who are full-time caregivers (Hoffman & Youngblade, 1999; Repetti, Mathews, & Waldron, 1989; J. R. Smith, Brooks-Gunn, & Jackson, 1997; Warr & Parry, 1982). The involvement outside the home required by the JOBS mandate (through program participation and ultimately employment) could result in greater self-esteem and sense of control over events. Yet, at the same time, if participation in JOBS or employment involved substantial stress to mothers, then participation could have negative impacts on maternal psychological well-being (Jackson et al., 2000; Gyamfi, Brooks-Gunn, & Jackson, 2001). J. B. Wilson, Ellwood, and Brooks-Gunn (1995) identified such potential sources of stress as the need to make substantial changes in daily routines for both mothers and children, and to locate child care for young children under time pressure. Further, mothers could experience stress if they were being required to participate in out-of-home activities if they felt that children required maternal care.

Similarly one can make divergent predictions regarding changes in the home environment and in child care experiences. On the one hand, the home environment could improve if greater family income results in a move to a safer physical environment, if income is used to purchase books and toys, or if stimulation that mothers experience on the job comes to be manifested in more stimulating mother-child interactions (Klebanov et al., 1998). Yet, if mothers are substantially stressed by JOBS participation, research suggests that this could affect mother-child interactions negatively (Jackson et al., 2000; McLoyd, 1990). Child care of high quality could have positive implications for children's development, but unstable care or care of poor quality would have negative implications (Brooks-Gunn, Han, & Waldfogel, 2002; Hayes, Palmer, & Zaslow, 1990; NICHD ECCRN, 1997b).

Thus, the NEWWS—COS recognizes that welfare-to-work programs potentially carry both benefits and hazards for children (McGroder et al., 2000). This is particularly true for young children, for whom the quality of mother-child interaction and out-of-home care are especially important.

It is important to note that while existing research documents linkages with child outcomes of such measures as family economic status, maternal education, and maternal psychological well-being, this evidence is correlational in nature. That is, this evidence examines the associations between the maternal variables and measures of children's development when the mothers spontaneously determine their own "places" on these variables. For example, the mother chooses, within the constraints of her life circumstances, how much education to pursue. The associations between such maternal variables and child outcomes may be different when mothers are mandated to participate in educational or employment activities (Aber et al., 1995; Brady-Smith, Brooks-Gunn, Waldfogel, & Fauth, 2001; Zaslow et al., 1999; Zaslow, Tout, et al., 1998). The NEWWS—COS is an unusual opportunity to examine whether changes occur on measures of children's development when educational and employment activities are mandated (Zaslow et al., 1995).

In sum, there are multiple pathways by which maternal participation in the JOBS Program may affect children. The NEWWS—COS builds on the evidence showing that welfare-to-work programs can affect family earnings positively, and the evidence that links child outcomes to family income, maternal education, maternal psychological well-being, the quality of the home environment, and the quality of child care. It is, nevertheless, important to note that the pattern of associations with child outcomes may be different under circumstances of a mandatory program than when families make their own decisions regarding their employment, income, and educational level.

The underlying assumption of the Family Support Act was that the needs of poor families were best addressed through increasing parental education, job skills, and actual employment. At the same time, the Family Support Act saw a reciprocal obligation between the government and families. While it was the government's role to provide services to enhance employability, families receiving such assistance were obligated to take steps to improve their economic self-sufficiency. Failure to take such steps could result in a reduction in welfare benefits.

Current Status

Random assignment took place between September 1991 and January 1994. Information on the background characteristics and attitudes of sample members was collected just prior to random assignment. The in-home Descriptive Study survey was administered in Atlanta from March 1992 to December 1993. A report of the findings of the Descriptive Study was submitted to DHHS in May 1995 (Moore, Zaslow, Coiro, Miller, & Magenheim, 1995). The fielding of the 2-year survey was initiated in the fall of 1993 (Riverside) through the spring of 1994 (Atlanta and Grand Rapids), and was completed by the spring of 1996. The analysis file was made available in February 1997. The 2-year Child Outcomes Study report was released in June 2000 (McGroder et al., 2000). The fielding of the 5-year survey and the Children's School Progress Survey (CSPS) began in the fall of 1996 (Riverside) through the spring of 1997 (Atlanta and Grand Rapids), and was completed by the spring of 1999. The analysis files were made available in the summer of 1999. The 5-year Child Outcomes Study report was released as part of a larger NEWWS report in 2002 (Hamilton et al., 2001; McGroder et al., 2002).

The NEWWS Observational Study involves two waves of data collection carried out 4–6 months after baseline and approximately 4½ years after baseline. Both have been completed (see McGroder et al., 2000; Moore et al., 1995). Additional publications can be found on the Web sites of Manpower Demonstration Research Corporation (http://www.mdrc.org/) and Child Trends (http://www.childtrends.org/).

Goals

The goal of the project was to examine whether and how mothers' mandatory participation in a welfare-to-work program, with temporary grant reductions imposed for lack of compliance with the mandate, affected the well-being of children. More specifically, this project aimed to assess the impact of the two different JOBS welfare-to-work programs in each of three sites on young children, and to examine the mechanisms by which any such effects occurred.

Because the JOBS Program was the first time that mothers with preschool-age children were required to participate in activities to enhance economic self-sufficiency, it was considered particularly important to examine the possible occurrence of both favorable and unfavorable impacts for young children. Preschoolers were considered particularly likely to experience changes in their daily routines, extent and quality of contact with their mothers, and out-of-home care as a result of the JOBS Program. The study set as its criterion for a "policy-relevant difference" an impact on a child outcome with an effect size of at least one-third of a standard deviation. This was considered a sensitive criterion for the possibility of any favorable or unfavorable impacts on children.

Three domains of child development are included in the NEWWS—COS: cognitive development and academic achievement; physical health and safety; and social development, child adjustment, and problem behaviors. The inclusion of these three child outcome domains was considered necessary to provide a broad examination of possible child impacts.

Besides assessing differences in these key child outcome domains for families in each of the six programs (two programs in each of three sites), the project assessed the influence of intervening variables. The study asked how any discovered program impacts on child outcomes were mediated by changes in family economic status, maternal education, maternal psychological well-being, the home environment, and/or children's experiences of child care.

In addition to examining the impacts of the JOBS Program on all of the children in the study sample, the NEWWS—COS also examined program impacts for key baseline subgroups of children. For example, the study examined whether impacts occurred for children of mothers who had higher and lower educational attainment and literacy skills at baseline and whose mothers indicated a greater and lesser number of indications of psychological distress at baseline. The study also examined impacts on child outcomes for families with differing numbers of risk factors. That is, the study asked whether an accumulation of risk factors resulted in a different pattern of program impacts on children (see Brooks-Gunn, Klebanov, & Liaw, 1995; Liaw, Brooks-Gunn, 1994).

A further goal of the study was to carry out descriptive analyses focusing on the development of the children in the sample. Studies of children's development focus disproportionately on middle-class families. The NEWWS—COS is an important resource for examining the development of children in low-income families. Findings from the NEWWS Descriptive Study found that close to the start of the evaluation, children in the Child Outcomes Study in the Atlanta site were already at risk, particularly in measures of cognitive development. Yet the children in the sample also showed substantial heterogeneity. Variation in the development of the children in the Descriptive Study sample has been examined from multiple perspectives (e.g., Moore et al., 1995), and found to be predicted by characteristics of the children, maternal depressive symptomatology, parenting behavior, neighborhood characteristics, as well as by the accumulation of risk and protective factors in the children's families. The longitudinal nature of the NEWWS—COS makes it possible to extend these descriptive analyses, permitting an examination of factors associated with development over time extending into middle childhood.

Methodological work was also a goal of the NEWWS—COS. In preparing the surveys for the study it became apparent that existing measures of family processes and child outcomes had limitations, particularly when used with low-income samples. Accordingly, in developing the surveys for the NEWWS—COS, new measures were developed. For example, the new measure of cognitive stimulation had less of a focus on the possession and use of material possessions (e.g., books and toys) than earlier measures. Methodological analyses, being carried out as part of the NEWWS—COS and also through a grant from NICHD to improve survey measures of parenting (1R01 HD31056-01), are examining the characteristics and functioning of the new measures. For example, analyses contrast the internal consistency reliability of the existing and new measures of parenting, and compare the existing and new measures as predictors of child outcomes (Berlin, Brooks-Gunn, Spiker, & Zaslow, 1995; Sugland et al., 1995; Zaslow, Mariner, Moore, & Oldham, 1998).

Design and Methods

Sampling. Children participating in the NEWWS—COS were born between 1986 and 1990 and were 3–5; 5–7; and 8–10 years old at baseline, the Two-Year Follow-up, and the Five-Year Follow-up, respectively. The NEWWS Descriptive Study was carried out about 3 months after random assignment in a portion of the Atlanta sample only, when children were about 3 to 5 years of age. The NEWWS Observational Study involved two waves, the first occurring 4–6 months after random assignment, and the second 4½ years after random assignment. Children were restricted to the age range of 3–4 years at the first wave, and were approximately 7 to 9 years at the second wave.

As part of the NEWWS Evaluation, in which the NEWWS—COS is nested, JOBS-mandatory AFDC recipients in the three sites were randomly assigned to research groups when they attended a JOBS orientation, the first step in the path toward participation in JOBS. Within each site, individuals were randomly assigned to a group eligible for a labor force attachment approach to JOBS, a group eligible for a human capital development approach to JOBS, or a control group.

Families eligible for the NEWWS—COS sample were those in the three NEWWS Study research groups in the three sites who had at least one child between the ages of 3 and 5 years at baseline (i.e., at random assignment). One child in each selected family was designated as the focal child for the study. If there was more than one child in the family between the ages of 3 and 5, one child was selected at random to be the focal child.

All AFDC applicants and recipients whose youngest child was age 3 or over were required to participate in JOBS; some states required those with children age 1 or over to participate. Exemptions were granted to recipients who were ill or incapacitated, were caring for a household member who was ill or incapacitated, were under 16, were pregnant past the first trimester, or were living in areas where program services were unavailable. The total sample for the Two-Year Follow-up was 3,018 families: 1,422 from Atlanta; 950 from Riverside; and 646 from Grand Rapids. The sample at the Five-Year Follow-up was smaller (2,332 respondents).

Data collection. Spanish-only speakers were present in the Riverside and Grand Rapids samples only. All surveys and assessments were translated into Spanish, and bilingual interviewers completed the interviews with these families. Recipients who did not speak English or Spanish were excluded from the NEWWS—COS.

All sample members in the overall NEWWS Evaluation were single parents. For the Child Outcomes Study, the sample was restricted to single mothers only (excluding less than 10% of the sample who were single fathers). Marital status was captured in each subsequent survey wave, in order to track any changes that occurred after baseline.

Comparison groups. Since random assignment was used, individuals in the three groups (human capital development, labor force attachment, and control) did not differ systematically in their measured and unmeasured background characteristics. As a result, any differences in their subsequent job search, education, training, employment, or welfare experiences, as well as the well-being of their children, could be attributed with confidence to the effects of a particular welfare-to-work approach. Program effects were examined by testing for significant differences between groups on means or, for some measures, proportions. These analyses contrasted scores on child outcomes separately for the human capital development group and the control group, and for the labor force attachment group and the control group, by site. Subgroup impacts were examined by testing for significant differences on the child outcome measures within subgroups defined according to baseline variables. When significant program impacts were found, effect sizes were calculated.

As part of the overall NEWWS Evaluation, MDRC carried out an implementation, participation, cost, and impact analysis in all sites. Results for the three sites included in the NEWWS—COS are detailed in Hamilton, Brock, Farrell, Friedlander, and Harknett (1997).

Measures

As part of the overall NEWWS Evaluation, baseline information from the mothers in the study was collected by JOBS intake employees prior to random assignment. JOBS-eligible clients also took math and reading literacy tests at that time and completed a short survey (the Private Opinion Survey) with questions about attitudes toward welfare and employment as well as maternal psychological well-being.

The Descriptive Survey was conducted with 790 families in the Atlanta site on average 3 months after random assignment, generally in the families' homes. Mothers were interviewed, and children were given assessments of cognitive school readiness and receptive vocabulary. Mothers were asked to describe the child's health and social maturity. A range of further topics was also addressed, including maternal employment, child care use and history, maternal psychological well-being and physical health, parenting and the home environment, social support and neighborhood characteristics, contact with the child's father and with extended family. Mothers also completed a self-administered questionnaire (SAQ) with questions on some of these topics, and interviewers completed ratings concerning the home environment and behaviors of the mother and child.

The Two-Year Follow-up was conducted 2 years after random assignment. It consisted of a core interview with parents addressing questions of welfare dependence, family economic self-sufficiency, and JOBS participation, as well as a 20-minute interview specific to the Child Outcomes Study. Mothers reported on the children's behavior problems, positive social behaviors, academic progress and adjustment to school, and health. Again, children were assessed on cognitive school readiness and receptive vocabulary. In addition, questions were asked about each of the intervening mechanisms identified as potential pathways of influence on children (family economic status, maternal education, maternal psychological well-being, home environment, and child care). Interviewers again completed ratings, and mothers completed SAQs.

The Five-Year Follow-up was administered to parents 5 years after random assignment, usually in the families' homes, and consisted of a core mother interview which addressed questions of educational attainment, participation in educational and employment training activities, employment and job seeking behavior, and other questions about benefits central to the larger NEWWS Study. In addition, there were a 10-minute mother interview specific to the Child Outcomes Study, a child assessment, and parent and child self-administered questionnaires. Mothers and children completed sections of the Social Skills Rating System (SSRS), mothers rated the child's health, and the children were assessed with sections of the Woodcock-Johnson Tests of Achievement–Revised. As with the other survey waves, mothers responded to questions (in interview format and in SAQ format) concerning each of the possible "pathway" variables, and interviewers completed ratings.

The Children's School Progress Survey was a self-administered questionnaire mailed to the child's teachers. Data were collected about 5 years after baseline. Teachers were asked to describe the student's academic achievement and ability, behavior in school, days absent and tardy, need for and use of special resources and services in school, contact with the child's mother, and the school environment.

The NEWWS Observational Study involved further visits to respondents' homes approximately 4–6 months after baseline, and again 4½ years after baseline. This study was carried out only in the Atlanta site of the NEWWS—COS. During the observational study visits, mothers and children were videotaped engaging in a series of structured interaction tasks (e.g., reading a book together, playing a word guessing game, assembling blocks to match a model). Mothers were also given a brief interview and SAQ, and interviewers completed ratings. The videotapes of mother-child interaction were coded in two university research laboratories. A group led by Byron Egeland, Nancy Weinfield, and John Ogawa at the University of Minnesota, in collaboration with the full observational studies research team developed the protocol for assessing the affective quality of observed mother-child interaction. This group developed the coding system for assessing the affective quality of interaction and coded the tapes for these variables. A group led by Catherine Snow, Patton Tabors, and Jeanne De Temple at Harvard Graduate School of Education, in parallel, led the development of the observational protocol for assessing early interactions related to the emergence of literacy in the children. This group developed a system for coding the videotaped interactions from the point of view of literacy-related behaviors and has coded these behaviors (DeTemple & Tabors, 2000; Weinfield, Ogawa, & Egeland, 2002).

The measures of parenting and the home environment include items from the short form of the Home Observation for Measurement of the Environment (HOME—SF), as well as further items developed specifically for this study. The new measures seek to describe aspects of cognitive stimulation that do not require material possessions (e.g., toys and books) or expenditures (e.g., for trips to museums), extend the construct of discipline beyond the issue of physical punishment, and attempt to sharpen the construct of emotional support in the mother-child relationship. Methodological work within the Descriptive Study sample (funded through NICHD grant 1R01 HD31056–01) contrasts the HOME—SF scales with parenting scales that integrate the new items from the point of view of internal consistency reliability and prediction to child outcomes (Zaslow, Mariner, et al., 1998).

As part of the JOBS intake process prior to random assignment, information on ethnicity, earnings in the past 12 months, employment status, and public assistance status and history were collected. Ethnic groups included white non-Hispanic, Hispanic, black non-Hispanic, black Hispanic, Native American/Alaskan Native, Asian/Pacific Islander, and other ethnicities.

Disabled children were included in the study, although mothers who had a disabled child who required a great deal of care were exempt from the JOBS Program. In the Two-Year Follow-up, mothers were asked whether the focal child or any of their other children were currently getting help for any emotional, mental, or behavioral problem, and if any of their children had an illness or disability that demanded a lot of their attention and affected their job or school attendance. Measures were not altered to accommodate disabled children.

All child care information was provided by the mother. Information was collected on type of care, number of days/hours in care, the child's history of nonmaternal care, whether the mother missed work because of problems with child care arrangements, and child care subsidies received. A few maternal report measures of the quality of child care were included: the current group size/ratio and caregiver training (as well as maternal report measures of the cost of care and the use of subsidies).

As part of the larger NEWWS Evaluation, observations of program operations, interviews with program staff, and reviews of individuals' program case files were also conducted to assess the mothers' access to program activities and social services. These methods were also used to provide information on the nature, quality, and "dosage" of these activities and services.

Depending on how states responded to the 1996 welfare law, and the speed with which they responded, the law had the potential to affect the "treatment" received by the three research groups in each site involved in the NEWWS—COS. The state of Georgia, for example, responded to the 1996 welfare law by implementing welfare time limits throughout the state in late 1996. MDRC's position was that if research sample members were subject to welfare time limits, then they must be eligible to receive some type of welfare-to-work program services in order to enable them to find employment as quickly as possible and "stop the clock." As a result, the Atlanta NEWWS Study site was given permission to allow control group members to receive welfare-to-work program services in late 1996. As of that point, all Atlanta sample members had at least 3 years of follow-up; some had as much as 5 years of follow-up. In addition, at the same point in time, all sample members became subject to Atlanta's new Work First program, consisting of applicant job search and quick employment-focused activities. Using data from the 5-year client survey, researchers plan to assess the extent to which the treatment group differentials in Atlanta became blurred in the last 1 to 2 years of the 5-year follow-up period. Similarly, the state of Michigan implemented a Work First program during the latter part of the 5-year follow-up period. Thus all program group members and control group members who were not "protected," and were receiving welfare, were sent to a Work First program. Welfare reforms in the state of California had relatively little impact on the Riverside sample members at the 5-year follow-up.

Units of Analysis

Data analysis. The unit of analysis differs for different questions. Child impacts were assessed at the level of the individual child, with one child serving as the focal child in each family. The mother was the unit of analysis for such issues as maternal psychological well-being. The family was the unit of analysis for such issues as family income. Most results were presented separately for each of the programs, since the programs and populations being served in each site varied greatly.

As noted above, race and ethnicity were coded via respondent self-report at baseline. The primary analyses for the NEWWS—COS examined program impacts by group within site. However, subgroup impacts will be examined, where appropriate, by race/ethnicity. The study also will examine program impacts on family income and will assess whether changes in family income play a role in shaping program impacts on children.

Findings

A report on the impacts on families and children 2 years after baseline has been released (McGroder et al., 2000). The report on 5-year impacts has also been released. Based on the Summary Report for this study, the six JOBS programs (human capital development and labor force attachment programs in the three COS cities) examined had relatively few statistically significant impacts on children on average, but more impacts that would have been expected by chance. Overall, the researchers found favorable impacts related to cognitive development and academic achievement, unfavorable impacts on child health and safety, and mixed impacts with regard to behavioral and emotional adjustment (Zaslow, McGroder, Moore, & LeMenestrel, 2000).

When examined separately by site, child impacts tended to be more favorable in Atlanta, unfavorable in Riverside, and mixed in Grand Rapids. Yet the impacts found were relatively small, and only one was of sufficient magnitude (one-third of a standard deviation or more) to be considered "policy relevant."

Analyses also examined impacts by family risk in order to assess whether welfare-to-work programs had different effects on families with different levels of risk. Among children in higher-risk families, the impacts found tended to be favorable, though small, if the mother had been assigned to a human capital development program or to Atlanta's labor force attachment program. By contrast, findings indicated unfavorable impacts for children from higher-risk families in the other two labor force attachment programs, some of which reached the criterion for policy relevance.

Contrary to the initial research hypotheses, lower-risk families appeared to suffer unfavorable consequences if assigned to three particular programs: Grand Rapids's labor force attachment program, and both of Riverside's programs. Several of these impacts were of policy-relevant magnitude (one-third of which substantially exceeded the threshold for policy relevance), and nearly all of these were unfavorable.

Mediator analyses suggested that children can be affected by welfare reform programs through mechanisms that were direct targets of welfare reform (e.g., employment) as well as outcomes that were not directly targeted (e.g., parenting and maternal psychological well-being). The strongest mediation findings, however, highlighted the role played by the more proximal mechanisms to the child that were not direct targets of welfare reform, especially maternal psychological well-being and parenting. Findings also indicated that the impacts of some of the programs had opposing effects on aspects of family life (e.g., both favorable and unfavorable), which may explain the relatively small number and magnitude of significant impacts on child outcomes (Zaslow et al., 2000).

Limitations

The study is generalizable to young children in the AFDC population whose mothers were required to participate in the JOBS Program. However, the number of sites is limited, and the sample is not nationally representative. This is an issue of concern since the programs available, population characteristics, and program impacts vary greatly from site to site. Also, current welfare rules differ from those in 1996 in terms of time limits, sanctions, and the end to entitlement. The focus of the study is limited to children age 3 to 5 years at the outset of the mother's participation in JOBS.

While the study does contain direct assessments of the children's cognitive school readiness and achievement at multiple points in time, as well as teacher reports of their adaptation to school (and observational data for a subset of the human capital development and control groups), other information about the child is collected largely through mothers' self-report (e.g., ratings of the child's health and health care use) and has not been corroborated by other external sources. Information about child care is collected from mothers' reports without verification from providers. Similarly, measures of father involvement and child support are maternal report measures.

Public Use Files

Data from the Descriptive Study are available for secondary analysis from Sociometrics (http://www.socio.com AFDA Data Set Nos. 51–52). Originally, the videotapes and data from Wave 1 of the NEWWS Observational Study were available for secondary analysis at the Murray Center at Radcliffe College; use of the video archive required approval of a written proposal, with assurances of research use only and protection of confidentiality. This is no longer the case, however. There were concerns about subject privacy, and all tapes have now been destroyed.

MDRC and Child Trends report that the data files from the Two-Year and Five-Year Follow-ups are available for public use at http://aspe.hhs.gov/hsp/NEWWS/ on-line.

NEW HOPE CHILD AND FAMILY STUDY (CFS)

History

The long-term consequences of economic policies for children's development and healthy families have both theoretical and practical import. Policies for the poor in the United States have been, for the most part, concerned with the nonworking poor, primarily single parents. This portion of the chapter outlines the methodology and impacts of the New Hope Child and Family Study, a substudy attached to the New Hope Project Evaluation. New Hope was a random-assignment demonstration experiment designed to test the effectiveness of an employment-based antipoverty program. Unlike many welfare-to-work interventions, the New Hope Project's goal was reduction of poverty as well as work promotion; hence, it is of particular importance to public policy during the current period of rapid change in public assistance programs. New Hope provided job-search assistance, wage supplements that raise income above the poverty threshold, and subsidies for health insurance and child care.

The New Hope Child and Family Study (CFS) emerged from the research interests of the MacArthur Research Network on Successful Pathways Through Middle Childhood. The network includes experts in the fields of anthropology, developmental and cross-cultural psychology, economics, education, the history of childhood, pediatrics, social policy, sociology, and urban geography. Their work is designed to be of use to a broad audience, including not only academic researchers but also educators, practitioners, policy makers, parents, and children. Network members sought a project where they could examine the social, psychological, and material effects of a work-based intervention on children in low-income families.

A decision was made to link such a research project to an existing evaluation intervention. Network members reviewed several projects under evaluation by the Manpower Demonstration Research Corporation (MDRC) and chose the New Hope Project. MDRC researchers coordinated both the overall New Hope evaluation and the Child and Family Study. Aletha Huston led the Network team, which also included Greg Duncan, Robert Granger, Vonnie McLloyd, and Thomas Weisner.

The New Hope Project traces its roots to the Congress for a Working America (CFWA), a nonprofit organization founded in 1979 to develop and promote public policies that support full employment at living wages. During the 1980s, David Riemer—a lawyer and founding board member of CFWA (and later New Hope)—researched and wrote *The Prisoners of Welfare* (1988). The book examined the structural problems of both the welfare system and the labor market that cause people to be poor. Riemer proposed that the existing welfare system be eliminated and replaced with an alternative structure that provides various supports to people based on their employment experience (for further information on the origin and design of New Hope, see Brock, Doolittle, Fellerath, & Wiseman, 1997).

Current Status

Recruitment of the New Hope sample began in August 1994 and ended in December 1995. Members of the research sample completed an enrollment form and survey of opinions about employment prior to random assignment. All New Hope sample members with age-eligible children who were randomly assigned to either the program or control group were eligible for the 2- and 5-year surveys as well as the ethnographic study. An 8-year follow-up is currently being planned.

The 24-month survey interviews took place between December 1996 and January 1998 and could be administered either by telephone or in person. The 60-month survey interviews were completed in January 2001. In 1998 the research team began a 3-year ethnographic study of 44 families from the CFS. This sample includes members of both the program and control groups.

Goals

The New Hope Project offers an innovative and comprehensive approach to reduce poverty, reform welfare, and address the economic self-sufficiency of poor people who can work. New Hope consists of four components: job assistance, including referral to a wage-paying community service job when necessary; an earnings supplement to raise low-wage workers' earned income above the poverty line; subsidized health insurance; and subsidized child care. Certain principles underlie the program: that people who are willing to work full-time should have the opportunity to do so, that people who work full-time should not be poor, that people should have an incentive to increase their earnings, and that regular employment should be financially more rewarding than subsidized employment or other forms of public assistance.

New Hope's designers recognize that there are various theories about why approximately 11% of the U.S. population of working-age adults do not have income above the poverty level. Some focus on structural barriers such as too few jobs, seasonal economies, low wages, and the lack of affordable child care; others emphasize individual barriers such as the lack of job skills or personal motivation. New Hope addresses both kinds of barriers, the assumption being that if structural problems are first corrected, more people will work, and then the individual barriers of those who do not work can be addressed.

The New Hope Project is designed to provide information to policy makers on the implementation, effectiveness, and costs of the New Hope program. Is this a workable program model? Does it succeed in boosting employment, raising earned income, increasing economic security, reducing poverty, and lowering use of public assistance? Does the program affect family functioning and the lives of the children? Is the program a good investment for taxpayers and the program participants?

The primary analytic questions are the extent to which: (a) the likely increase in maternal labor supply alters family schedules to the benefit or detriment of children; (b) the higher incomes occasioned by the wage supplements translate into resources for children; (c) social-psychological changes in adults' stress or self-esteem are affected; and (d) how all of these changes in turn affect children's well-being, educational progress, and social development in early childhood through early adolescence.

The Child and Family Study is not primarily a program evaluation, but takes advantage of the following features of the New Hope Project to test a conceptual model specifying paths of potential influence: (a) the completely random-assignment allocation of families to treatment and control groups; (b) the exceptional quality of program implementation; (c) the high quality of the core design and data collection by MDRC; (d) a simultaneous and genuinely interactive analysis of data gathered in both structured interviews and ethnographic observations and a continuing collaboration of researchers with staff and community representatives; (e) an ongoing series of research collaborations among an interdisciplinary group of PIs as part of the MacArthur Foundation Network on Successful Pathways Through Middle Childhood;

and (f) the focus of the intervention on reducing poverty and offering employment-related benefits (health insurance and child care) as well as on requiring employment.

Theory of Change

New Hope's designers held a set of assumptions regarding how the program would change outcomes for individuals and families. The theory of change guiding the New Hope Project comes from a variety of sources: the aforementioned analysis by David Riemer and others regarding the labor market; correlational data from studies showing that certain outcomes, such as family income and well-being, tend to rise and fall together; evaluations of previous efforts to supplement income; and the experiences of practitioners. The model comprises six elements:

- *The New Hope offer.* When the New Hope offer was designed, there was no definitive evidence that such an intervention would change the work effort of low-income people. What did exist was some experience with design issues that allowed the designers to calibrate the size of the benefits and their schedule for being phased in and out. Of particular importance were the results from a previous large experiment showing that workers might decrease their work effort if their earnings were supplemented. This was one factor leading the designers to decide that participants would need to work full-time to qualify for New Hope's benefits.
- *Service and benefit use.* The New Hope offer was designed to make supports for work available at a level over and above what would occur without New Hope. Many social welfare programs have narrowly defined targeting or eligibility criteria. They serve only welfare recipients, for example, or focus on people who fit into a certain demographic group or family type. The New Hope project took the position that people's economic and personal circumstances are often in flux. They move onto and off of public assistance and in and out of poverty as they lose a job (or find one), have young children (or children grow older), experience a marital breakup (or get married), or become ill (or recover from illness). New Hope provided a flexible support structure that was intended to help people become and stay employed, even as their personal situation changed.
- *Employment and earnings.* With the increased use of New Hope's supports, work, earnings, and income were meant to rise and public assistance was intended to fall. When the program was designed, the assumption that service and benefit use would lead to improved economic outcomes was more a product of insightful analysis than prior empirical findings. However, other incentive-based interventions meant to encourage work

are being tested concurrently with New Hope, and the emerging news is encouraging. The Canadian government has tested a generous earnings supplement for long-term public assistance recipients, and the state of Minnesota's welfare reform program contains significant economic incentives for work. Findings from both evaluations indicate that the programs are raising employment, earnings, and incomes.

- *Adult well-being.* Increased employment, while perhaps stressful during some period of transition, was thought to improve adult well-being. Some of this improvement would occur because employment is socially desirable and unemployment and welfare are stigmatized. In addition, well-being would increase because of more income and less poverty.

- *Child contexts.* Changes in economic outcomes and adult well-being were likely to affect home environments and how parents and children spend time as individuals and together. For example, increased employment might decrease the time parents spend with children, and increased income might cause the parents to move to better housing or to purchase items such as books that support children's development. Also, changes might occur in the number or nature of the interactions between parents and children. Finally, employment, income, and the distinctiveness of the New Hope child care subsidy might all affect the nature and number of child care experiences.

- *Child outcomes.* Finally, New Hope's designers recognized that what happens to parents affects their children and vice versa. Two paths might lead to changes in child outcomes in the long term: participation in child care and the changes in home life. Existing evidence led project designers to presume that any changes at 24 months would be less dramatic than those which might occur over a longer period of time.

Design and Methods

The New Hope Project enrolled 1,362 low-income adults drawn from two inner-city areas in Milwaukee. Half of the enrollees were randomly assigned to a program group that could receive New Hope benefits and services; the other half were assigned to a control group that could not. New Hope broadly targeted poor people who could work. The program had only four eligibility requirements: that applicants live in one of the two targeted service areas, be age 18 or over, be willing and able to work at least 30 hours per week, and have a household income at or below 150% of the federally defined poverty level. New Hope enrolled individuals who were employed or unemployed, on welfare or not on welfare, married or unmarried, and living with or without children. Participation in the program was voluntary.

Random assignment of the New Hope sample began in August 1994 and ended in December 1995. About 55% of the sample (745 sample members) are included in the study of program effects on families and children. The subgroup, identified in this report as members of the Child and Family Study (CFS), was identified on the basis of having at least one child between ages 1 and 10 at baseline.

Members of the CFS sample were administered both a core and a parent questionnaire. If they had children between the ages of 6 and 12 at the 24-month survey and between the ages of 6 and 15 at the 60-month survey, then a survey was administered to the child as well. Surveys were also sent out to the teachers of age-eligible children (those over the age of 5). Additional background and demographic information was also collected on each participant.

All racial and ethnic groups are represented in the CFS subgroup except for Asians and Pacific Islanders (largely recent Hmong immigrants), who were excluded owing to concerns about the cultural appropriateness of the measures used to assess child and family outcomes. Interviews could be conducted in either English or Spanish, as all of the instruments had been formally translated into Spanish, but only 64 adults—and fewer children—were actually interviewed in Spanish at the 24-month interview. At the 60-month interview, 26 parents and no children were interviewed in Spanish.

The design provided for conducting all CFS interviews in person, including the core economic impact interview, unless the family had moved too far from Milwaukee. If there were children to be interviewed, a team of two interviewers went to the home, one interviewing the adult(s) and the other the child(ren). Otherwise a single interviewer administered the two adult instruments.

Measures

The parent interview, lasting 90 minutes to 2 hours, was composed of the "core," measuring economic and labor market variables, and the "child and family" section. Most of the questions and measures were drawn from other related surveys and from well-established measures in the child development literature, but often with modifications. The final set was selected through extensive pretesting with families living in poverty and with a small group of New Hope pilot families.

Core questionnaire. The core questionnaire comprised seven sections, or modules, and was administered only at 24 months. The first six sections were administered to all sample members; the last section, about participation in the New Hope Project itself, was administered only to those in the program group. This questionnaire required about 45 minutes to administer.

Much of the content of the core economic impact questionnaire was based on measures used in MDRC's evaluations of other interventions, many of which in turn had been borrowed or adapted from such government surveys as the Current Population Survey (CPS) and the Survey of Income and Program Participation (SIPP). Measures specifically related to the intervention received special emphasis. The questionnaire obtained retrospective data for the period since random assignment on participation in education and training programs, employment, use of child and dependent care, children's educational progress, and health insurance coverage. In addition, it obtained current information on job characteristics, household composition and income, and economic well-being and concerns.

Parent questionnaire. To qualify for the CFS sample, program participants had to have at least one child between ages 3 and 12 at the 2-year anniversary of sample enrollment. In these households, up to two children were selected as focal (that is, a subject of the study), and additional interviews were administered to the sample member and/or other family members. The key additional questionnaires for the CFS sample included a parent interview (with the New Hope sample member if he or she was the primary caregiver, otherwise with the other parent), which lasted about 45 minutes. The parent interview elicited some information about the family's life and about the primary caregiver's general attitudes toward parenting and other aspects of life. It also included modules for up to two focal children. All focal children were subjects of the parent interview, whether or not the children were old enough to be interviewed. For 24-month analysis, 580 families were included in the CFS study; in the 60-month analysis, 561 families were included.

The parent questionnaire included 13 sections; not every section was administered to every respondent, however. The questionnaire included alternate versions of some sections for children in two different age groups (ages 3–5 and 6–12 at the 24-month survey; ages 6–15 at the 60-month survey), as well as sections for a second focal child, and took 45 minutes to administer on average. The parent questionnaire asked about parent time use and included scales measuring feelings of mastery and hope, self-esteem, depressed emotions, and stress related to the parental role. In addition, it included child-specific questions about child care; children's health and health care; discipline; the parent's relationship with the child and the stress experienced in parenting this child; cognitively stimulating materials and activities available to the child; the parent's perceptions of the child's characteristics and qualities; and the child's television-watching habits, performance of chores, and involvement in recreational and educational activities. The parent interview concluded by obtaining the parent's permission to collect data from the child's school, information that would make it possible to locate the parent for follow-up surveys and interviewer observations made after leaving the household.

Child interview. Focal children who were at least age 6 were eligible to be interviewed themselves, so there could be up to two child interviews in each family. Two child questionnaires were developed: a 30-minute questionnaire for children age 6–8 and a 60-minute questionnaire for children age 9–12 at the 24-month interview and age 9–15 at the 60-month interview. Additional academic and cognitive assessments in the 60-month interviews took another 30 minutes for both groups of children. These were administered after a small rest period. Of the CFS cases, 78% had any usable child data at 24 months, and 71% had any usable child data at 60 months. There were 568 age-eligible children who completed the survey at 24 months and 840 children who completed the child or youth surveys at 60 months.

For children age 9 and older, the questionnaire included seven sections, tapping areas such as the child's regular activities, aspirations, social behavior, and feelings. It combined two formats: one in which the interviewer asked questions that the child answered orally and another in which the child recorded his or her answers to the interviewer's questions in an answer booklet. At the 24-month interview, this group consisted of 251 children. At 60 months, 543 children were interviewed, and 539 had usable data from the answer booklets.

The questionnaire for children age 6–8 was similar to the questionnaire for older children, but the section on activities was omitted and other sections were shortened or simplified. For instance, fewer response categories were used with the younger children, who were not yet capable of distinguishing fine gradations. Similarly, the younger children were not asked to fill in their own answers, but instead were encouraged to point to their answer on an answer card. This group consisted of 317 children at 24 months and 297 children at 60 months.

Teacher survey. New Hope sample members who completed the module of the 2-year survey about child and family impacts—the "parent interview"—and who had school-age children (5 and over) at the 2-year follow-up were asked for permission to obtain information from their children's teacher. Teachers were not told about the New Hope program. The purpose of the questionnaire was to obtain additional information about the school progress and social behavior of a subset of CFS children. For the 24-month data, questionnaires were mailed in three waves: in May 1997, October 1997, and May 1998. Reports from 462 parents indicated that 666 children were aged 5 or over and were attending school. Permission to contact teachers was granted for 566 of these children. Completed questionnaires were received for 424 of these children, an overall response rate of 75% of children with consent and 64% of the total sample of school-age children. For the 24-month analyses, 420 children had usable information from the teacher survey. A similar teacher survey in conjunction with the 60-month interviews was conducted between 2000 and 2002. Of the children in this study, 531 had at least one teacher respond to the teacher survey at 60 months.

Baseline data. Baseline characteristics were collected for all sample members using the Background Information Form (BIF) and the Private Opinion Survey (POS). The BIF was the primary source of data on baseline characteristics. In addition, the POS, which was voluntary, elicited applicants' attitudes and opinions on their work experience and related obstacles and aids to obtaining or retaining employment. Both the BIF and POS were completed prior to random assignment.

Administrative and tax records. AFDC and food stamp payment data (January 1995–December 2002) were obtained from the state of Wisconsin for eligible New Hope sample members and their spouses (spouse or partner declared at the time of random assignment). Unemployment insurance (UI) wage data were also obtained from the state of Wisconsin for the period between January 1994 and December 2002 for New Hope sample members and their spouses. Data from tax records were obtained for the purpose of estimating Earned Income Credit (EIC) benefits.

Findings

This section reviews the key findings of the 24-month Child and Family Study. At the time of publication, 60-month data were still being analyzed. Throughout the evaluation, children and families whose workers were or were not employed full-time at baseline are often examined separately because the economic and parenting impacts of the New Hope program were different for these two groups. Impacts were also measured separately for both boys and girls.

New Hope affected material well-being, psychological well-being, and time use. Employment and earnings impacts for the full CFS sample were substantial. CFS program group members earned $15,317 during the 2 years of follow-up compared with $13,859 for their counterparts in the control group. Most of the difference was concentrated among those not employed full-time at random assignment; differences in earnings impacts across the two employment subgroups were not statistically significant for the CFS. New Hope also increased the number of sample members whose earnings-related income exceeded the federal poverty standard. Compared to control group members, those eligible for program benefits reported reduced material hardship, mostly in the form of increased access to medical and dental care and reduced periods without health insurance. New Hope reduced sample members' stress and worries and increased their feelings of social support. The program also increased sample members' hopefulness about achieving their goals.

There were also changes in family dynamics and child activities. New Hope's child care subsidies made formal care programs more affordable and stimulated their use by program group families. More generally, children in New Hope families spent more time in formal, structured activities away from home than children in control group families. In contrast, there were few consistent program effects on patterns of children's time use and household responsibilities within the home. Among those working full-time at baseline, most measures of parenting quality were significantly more positive for program group members than for controls. Among this subgroup, New Hope significantly increased parent-reported warmth, cognitive stimulation, and parent-reported monitoring of children's activities. In addition, children in this subgroup reported significantly more positive relations with their parents. Both parents and children reported children's greater involvement in organized activities outside the home.

The study measured child outcomes in three major domains—education and aspirations, sense of competence and well-being, and social behavior—by comparing children in the program and control group families. Impacts on boys and girls were examined separately because researchers have found gender differences for the outcomes of interest and because there were some gender differences in the impacts of New Hope on child care experiences. Teachers reported higher levels of academic achievement and higher levels of positive social behaviors (social competence, compliance, and autonomy) for New Hope children than for control group children.

Program impacts were larger and more consistently positive for boys than for girls. According to teachers' reports, boys in program group families had higher achievement, better classroom behavior skills (working independently, following classroom rules, making transitions), more positive behavior, and fewer behavior and discipline problems than boys in control group families. Parents in program group families also reported higher levels of positive social behavior for their sons. These effects were large and reliable. Program group impacts occurred for children whose parents had been employed full-time at baseline and for those whose parents had not, but impacts on school performance, school progress, and classroom behavior were somewhat larger for the latter group.

Boys in New Hope families had higher aspirations and expectations for their future occupations and for advanced education than boys in control group families. The patterns of children's aspirations corresponded to those expressed by their parents. The patterns for girls were more mixed: New Hope girls were slightly less anxious and prone to worry than control group girls, but teachers reported that they displayed more behavior and discipline problems. The greater impacts on boys are understood in light of boys' greater risk of academic and behavior problems in the elementary years. Parents were concerned about boys' vulnerability to gangs and antisocial behavior, and they may have used the additional resources provided by New Hope to purchase extended day care and other activities that provided supervision and learning experiences.

The combination of circumstances brought about by New Hope led to improved school performance and social behavior, particularly for boys. An intervention that significantly reduces antisocial behavior and improves school performance for boys living in poor families could produce important long-term benefits. Many children in New Hope families are statistically at risk for delinquency and school failure as they approach adolescence. By definition, their families are poor; most are ethnic minorities, and most are headed by single mothers. If the experiences provided through New Hope can change young boys' trajectories toward better school performance, more competent social behavior, and fewer problems of poor behavior control, the odds of school completion and socially competent adolescent development will be increased.

Access to formal child care, extended day care in schools, and structured out-of-school activities appear to be important paths by which the New Hope impacts on children occurred. If that is correct, there are clear public policy implications. Public policy can readily increase availability of child care, after-school activities, and other opportunities for supervised, structured activities for children; these may, in turn, significantly alter developmental trajectories for children in low-income families.

Limitations

Three aspects of the New Hope Project affect its generalizability: the largely volunteer sample, the timing of the intervention relative to Wisconsin welfare reform, and the booming Milwaukee-area economy over the mid- to late-1990s.

New Hope was a voluntary program. Participants were recruited from two Milwaukee zip codes through a combination of outreach by project staff, referrals by other social service agencies, and other social networks. Researchers from the University of Wisconsin—Milwaukee interviewed a random sample of adults from the two target areas at the conclusion of program recruitment. A comparison of the characteristics of the New Hope Neighborhood Survey (NHNS) respondents interested in and eligible for New Hope services with actual program applicants in the research sample revealed few major differences (Brock et al., 1997).

Rapid welfare reform in the mid-1990s posed a changing counterfactual for the New Hope intervention. The state's reform effort, Wisconsin Works (W-2), began on September 1, 1997, and followed on the heels of two interim programs—Self-Sufficiency First and Pay for Performance—implemented by Wisconsin in the spring of 1996. Throughout the entire New Hope project period, neither the New Hope experimental nor the control group were exempted from nor ineligible for other welfare programs for which they met the requirements.

Given the timing of the New Hope program, a substantial majority of New Hope experimental and control families providing 24-month family and child-based interview data had done so before the implementation of W-2. Virtually all of the experimentals faced the W-2 counterfactual at the end of their 3-year New Hope eligibility and had accumulated 2 or more years of W-2 regime experience at the time of the 60-month interview. The controls have accumulated between 2 and 3 years of experience with the W-2 rules between baseline and the time of the 60-month interview. By the time of the 60-month interview, all families were subject to W-2 rules.

Between 1992 and 1997—the years that New Hope was piloted and formally evaluated in the 2-year evaluation—the Milwaukee area experienced a growing number of jobs and declining unemployment. Employment figures suggest that work was available for people who wanted it (Bos et al., 1999). The relative strength of the local economy affects the extent to which New Hope labor market findings can be generalized to other economic regions. However, this is less of a concern for the CFS's central family functioning and child outcome questions.

WELFARE, CHILDREN AND FAMILIES: A THREE CITY STUDY

History

The Three City Study attempts to evaluate the nation's experiment in poverty policy. The researchers are particularly concerned about the effect of welfare policy changes on children's well-being. Given state variation in welfare plans, the study focuses on three cities in different states—Boston, Massachusetts; Chicago, Illinois; and San Antonio, Texas.

Current Status

The first wave of the study was conducted from March to December 1999 in Boston, Chicago, and San Antonio. The second wave began September 2000, and the third wave began in March 2002. Numerous policy briefs have been released, and more are underway for release in the coming years. Broad dissemination to a wide audience is planned. See the Three City Study Web site (www.jhu.edu/~welfare) for postings of policy briefs, working papers, and publications.

Goals

The goal of the Three City Study is to examine the effects of different state welfare reforms (time limits, work requirements, family caps, sanctions, transitional nature of assistance) on children and their parents. Specifically, the study seeks to understand how adults respond to reform in terms of employment, schooling, training, residential mobility, and fertility. The effects of welfare reform on children's health and development as well as *why* and *how* the ensuing changes affect children will be explored by the researchers across states.

The study hopes to provide information on welfare reform to national, state, and local policy makers as well as to service providers. Several specific questions to be addressed include the following: How many times do mothers cycle in and out of the labor force? What hours do mothers work, and who cares for their children? How does welfare reform affect children's school performance, behavior problems, self-esteem, and health? Do adolescents avoid pregnancy?

Theory of Change

A central issue of the welfare debate with regard to children is whether they will be better or worse off as a result of welfare reform. The optimistic scenario is that leaving the welfare rolls for employment will make mothers economically self-sufficient, enhance their self-esteem and parenting skills, improve the quality of the home environment, and provide better role models for their children. All of these changes, in turn, could have benefits for children's cognitive, socioemotional, and physical development. A less optimistic scenario, on the other hand, is that mothers may confront serious challenges to combining employment and single-parenthood because of limited resources. Further, jobs for low-skilled workers are often difficult to find, pay low wages, lack health benefits, and require irregular hours. The result could be increased parental stress, lower quality parenting, inadequate child care, and greater economic hardship—areas that could have a strong negative effect on child and family well-being. Accordingly, the Three City Study plans to examine multiple dimensions of the impact of welfare reform on children and families.

Design and Methods

Longitudinal survey. Approximately 2,400 families with children were randomly sampled from selected low-income neighborhoods in Boston, Chicago, and San Antonio and were followed at 18-month intervals over 3 years (Wave 1 and Wave 2). In each city, neighborhoods were defined in terms of block groups, based on the 1990 census. The number of block groups selected varied by city. About 40% of the families interviewed were receiving public assistance at baseline. The other 60% of the sample were low-income families who were not receiving welfare. Households with a focal child in either infancy/preschool (age 0–4 years) or early adolescence (age 10–14 years) were eligible for participation. These age ranges were selected due to the vulnerability of these years to changes in the structure of the welfare system. In addition, by beginning with these two age ranges and following infants, young children, and adolescents for 3 years, the researchers will have both cross-sectional and longitudinal data that cover the span of young childhood through young adulthood. A second cohort of about 1,250 families with children will be interviewed in Wave 3. The rolling panel design permits pre- and post-comparisons of families that experience a program initiative between interviews, comparisons of the experiences of young families in earlier versus later cohorts of welfare reform as it evolves, and "cautious" comparisons across cities of the experiences of families subject to different state policies.

Embedded developmental study. The embedded developmental study consists of a more intensive developmental investigation than the longitudinal survey. This study includes a subset of approximately 700 families with preschool-age children (2–4 years) and is designed to explore how these families are functioning as well as the supportiveness and structure of children's environments. This age group was chosen because it is an important developmental period for subsequent intellectual, social, and physical growth. In addition, it is also a particularly challenging period for parents in terms of the provision of warmth, limit-setting, learning opportunities, and physical caregiving—all of which may become more challenging in the face of welfare reform. In addition to the measures collected in the longitudinal study, the embedded developmental study will include videotaping and coding of mother-child interactions, observations of child care settings, and interviews with fathers and child care providers.

Comparative ethnographies. For the comparative ethnographies study, geographic and demographic information was used to match families in low-income neighborhoods across the three focal cities. Using block groups selected for the survey, approximately 215 families were selected for the comparative ethnographic study. About 45 of these families include a child with a disability. These families will be followed throughout the 4-year length of the project. The purpose of the ethnographic study is to examine how the evolution of welfare reform influences neighborhood resources and affects the daily lives of families.

Measures

Longitudinal study. Intensive interviews with mothers and older children were conducted at each time point, as well as testing and assessment of children's social, emotional, and physical development. Interviews assessed the quality of family life, family functioning, parenting, type and quality of child care or school, and use of social services. Systematic social observations of neighborhoods were obtained. Information on the implementation of welfare reform at each site was ascertained by working with social service agencies and advocacy groups. Respondents were also asked extensively about their experiences with welfare reform.

Embedded developmental study. This component of the study collected additional data relevant to children's development. The study includes videotaping and coding of parent-child interactions during a puzzle task, observations of child care settings, and interviews with fathers and child care providers.

Comparative ethnographies. The ethnographies will be used to gain an in-depth perspective of how families and communities are coping with welfare reform that is not provided by the survey. In-depth life history interviews, diary studies, and participant observation with families were conducted in addition to intensive field research on the neighborhoods and on formal and informal social service organizations. Attempts will be made to link the ethnographies and surveys for measure development. Findings from the ethnographies will be used to structure the survey questions. The survey questions will be used to guide the direction of ethnographies.

Units of Analysis

Several levels of analysis will be conducted. Analyses will examine the association between changes in the welfare system and children's development, family well-being, parental employment, schooling, fertility, neighborhood resources, and social services. Exploratory analyses of state variation across the range of outcomes as a function of differential requirements will be investigated as well.

Findings

Preliminary focus group interviews indicate that time limits are being experienced differently in Boston than in Chicago. At the time of the focus groups, Boston had a 2-year time limit for parents with children over 13; Chicago had a 5-year limit. Boston recipients seemed to be experiencing greater distress about the short transition period to work; whereas Chicago recipients were worried about the imminent termination of benefits, but hopeful that they would make the transition within 5 years. A report on the findings from the initial 15 focus groups is available on-line (http://www.jhu.edu/~welfare). More than ten policy briefs have been released on topics such as welfare recipients' knowledge of welfare rules, characteristics of welfare leavers, sanctions, health policy, immigrant families, child care, marriage and cohabitation, and housing. The full reports are available on the Three City Study Web site.

The first report on children from Welfare, Children and Families: A Three City Study was released in 2002 (Chase-Lansdale, Coley, Lohman, & Pittman, 2002). The study included 1,885 low-income preschoolers and adolescents and their families from the first wave of the Three City Study. Compared to middle-class children from national samples, the children in the Three City Study did not score as well on cognitive, behavioral, and emotional indices. Within the Three City sample of preschoolers and adolescents, mothers' welfare status and sanctioning was related to child outcomes. Preschool children of mothers who were receiving welfare or had recently received welfare had the lowest cognitive scores. Preschool children of mothers who had recently left the welfare rolls had the highest levels of behavior problems. Adolescent children of mothers who were receiving welfare had lower scores on cognitive achievement and higher levels of behavioral and emotional problems compared to adolescent children of mothers who had left welfare or had never received welfare. Preschool and adolescent children in families that were sanctioned under welfare guidelines also demonstrated lower cognitive and behavioral functioning. Many of these associations could be explained by the differences that existed across welfare groups in terms of mothers' marital, educational, mental health, and physical health status and parenting practices. Although the study cannot offer causal linkages, it suggests that children in families that face sanctioning and children in the most disadvantaged families may require additional services and attention in order to improve their developmental trajectories.

Limitations

In the Three City Study, comparisons across states are problematic because of numerous uncontrollable factors, which the researchers acknowledge. Based on prior studies of low-income and welfare-dependent families, attrition could be a serious problem, which could yield a biased sample. The researchers report an 88% retention rate at Wave 2, so this may not be a serious problem. In addition, the ethnographies will provide very descriptive information on families and communities, but these findings tend to have limited generalizability. Provided the sample size designated for the ethnographic study is sufficiently large, this limitation could be mitigated. Validation of findings across types of data (qualitative and quantitative) also would enhance findings.

Public Use Files

A public use data set from Wave 1 of the survey is available through Sociometrics (www.socio.com/data_arc/cwp_o.htm). Check the project's Web site for updates.

PROJECT ON STATE-LEVEL CHILD OUTCOMES

History

The Project on State-Level Child Outcomes developed out of a growing interest among policy makers and researchers to assess how and to what extent welfare policies affect children—particularly in the areas of health, school achievement, and social and emotional development. Five states received funding from the Department of Health and Human Services to add child outcome measures to their existing welfare reform evaluations: Connecticut's Jobs First Program, Florida's Family Transition Program (FFTP), Indiana's Manpower Placement and Comprehensive Training Program (IMPACT), Iowa's Family Investment Program (IFIP), and Minnesota's Family Investment Program (MFIP). The participating states are diverse in their welfare policies and programs, recipient populations, geography, and political climate. Each state evaluation was run by a different principal investigator and research team. These teams, however, have worked together with the assistance of Child Trends and the NICHD Family and Child Well-Being Research Network in order to collect similar information on child outcomes and measures of family functioning that are not in the core interviews of the studies.

Current Status

The Child Well-Being Surveys were administered by each state at different times. Minnesota was the first to enter the field in August 1997, and Indiana was the last to enter in March 2000. Child impact reports from the Minnesota (MFIP) and Florida (FFTP) studies were made available in 2000 (Gennetian & Miller, 2000; Bloom et al., 2000). In 2002, the Iowa (IFIP) and Indiana (IMPACT) reports became available (Beecroft, Cahill, & Goodson, 2002; Fraker et al., 2002). As of the date of this publication, the Connecticut child impact report had not been released. See Table 9.1 for a schedule of each state's administration of the survey, sample size, and child impact report dates. The status of each state's evaluation can be assessed at the Web sites of Manpower Demonstration Research Corporation (MDRC; www.mdrc.org) for Connecticut, Florida, and Minnesota, Mathematica Policy Research (MPR; www.mathematica-mpr.com) for Iowa, and Abt Associates (www.abtassoc.com) for Indiana.

Goals

The primary goal of the Project on State-Level Child Outcomes is to measure the impact of welfare policies on the well-being of children and families. Due to the random assignment design employed in each state, differences between those who were (experimental group) and were not (control group) exposed to the state's welfare demonstration program can be attributed to the program rather than to individual characteristics or selection factors. Information regarding how different types of welfare policies affect children will also be available.

The characteristics of the welfare reform policies ("waivers") instituted by each state are key to the evaluations. Many of the waivers were precursors to the 1996 welfare reforms, which marked an end to the federal welfare entitlement program (AFDC) and the beginning of state block grants for welfare programs (TANF). With the passage of the 1996 PRWORA, states were given some flexibility to experiment with new welfare strategies within federal guidelines and requirements. For the most part, the states involved in this project did not make drastic changes to their waiver demonstrations (i.e., the programs being evaluated in this project). Thus the impact of these early welfare demonstrations can be likened to a comparison between AFDC and TANF, with the control groups representing AFDC and the waiver experimental groups representing quasi-TANF policies. State welfare policy changes that occurred over the course of these evaluations were tracked and will be discussed below.

The waivers adopted by each state fall into two general categories: personal responsibility and employment-related provisions (Child Trends, 1999).

Personal responsibility requirements and sanctions were instituted as incentives for welfare recipients to comply with mandatory employment-related activities. Policies dealing with personal responsibility include time limits for cash assistance, family caps (restriction in the amount of cash assistance for additional children in a family), stringent sanctions, and immunization and health screening requirements. For teenage recipients, school attendance, performance requirements, or residential requirements were included. Employment-related provisions include requirements to work or search for jobs, provisions of transitional child care and Medicaid, and increased earned income disregards.

The waivers enacted by Connecticut, Florida, Indiana, and Minnesota[9] included time limits on receipt of welfare cash benefits and requirements for employment. In Iowa, time limits were decided by the case manager on an individual case basis. In comparison to the provisions of AFDC, all states imposed stricter sanctions for noncompliance with program requirements. Connecticut and Indiana were the only states to impose family caps.

In order to "make work pay," all states, except Indiana, increased the earned income disregards normally allowed under AFDC so that families would be able to combine their earnings with welfare (Indiana did not increase its disregards until July 2000). States also attempted to create a quick attachment to the labor force by requiring most welfare recipients to find immediate employment, rather than engage in educational or training activities. These requirements were balanced with services, such as transitional child care benefits (extended to 24 months in Florida and Iowa; expansion of eligibility in Indiana; child care subsidies paid directly to the provider in Minnesota) and transitional Medicaid (extended to 24 months in Connecticut only; Child Trends, 1999).

Design and Methods

Design. Due to the design of each state's evaluation, the Project on State-Level Child Outcomes is the only research initiative reviewed in this chapter that is able to measure the impact of welfare reform on child well-being in five states. Welfare recipients were randomly assigned to the treatment or control group (see Table 9.1 for each state's period of random assignment). Members of the treatment group were exposed to their state's particular welfare reform provisions that had been approved via the waivers process. Although the timing of each state's welfare demonstration program preceded the implementation of the current TANF welfare regulations, most states anticipated the TANF regulations in many respects. For example, Iowa's treatment group was subject to the provisions of the Family Investment Program. The IFIP provisions are exactly the same as the current TANF provisions in every respect except for the 5-year time limits (time limits were set on a case-by-case basis under IFIP). Minnesota's FIP was also similar to the statewide welfare reforms enacted in 1998. The new program, however, has less generous financial incentives to work and requires all recipients to participate in employment-related activities after only 6 months of welfare receipt (versus 24 months under MFIP; Gennetian & Miller, 2000).

Method. The project investigators were guided by the following three priorities when selecting the method by which the suggested measures for each construct would be collected:

- Flexibility for the states to go beyond the measures of the common core of constructs, or to omit sections of the common core if justification was provided that their policies would most likely not affect a particular pathway variable
- Use of a common mode of data collection; specifically, a telephone survey for economic outcomes (and in-home follow-up of households who could not be reached by phone) and an in-home survey for parenting and child outcomes
- A focus on outcomes for children ages 5–12 at the time of follow-up (Child Trends, 1999)

In addition to telephone and in-home surveys, the state evaluators employed other methods of data collection, such as administrative records, to measure both child and family well-being. Although a set of questions in the states' child well-being surveys was asked of all children in the household, the focus was on children ages 5–12. This age range permits inclusion of children who were preschoolers when their mothers became subject to new welfare policies as well as children who were already of school age at that point in time (Child Trends, 1999).

Sample selection. As stated earlier, the sample of children and families used in the child well-being surveys was taken from ongoing samples in each state that were focused on adults who had been randomly assigned to either the demonstration program or control group when that state first implemented their demonstration program. Each state implemented their programs and performed random assignment at different times (see Table 9.1), with Iowa the first (October 1993) and Connecticut the last (January 1996) to randomly assign participants. For most states, the child well-being survey was introduced in the second or third wave of data collection.

The initial, adult-centered interview was conducted via telephone (or in-home follow-up of households without a telephone) or in the home. Prior to the adult interview, a "focal child" was randomly selected from all children between the ages of 5 and 12 reported to be living in the household at the time of random assignment. Minnesota, Connecticut, Florida, and Indiana selected children from single-female-headed families only. Iowa included single-female-headed families as well as single-male-headed families (5% of sample) and two-parent families (7% of sample). During the parent interview, the status of the focal child was determined. If the focal child was currently living in the household, the in-home child well-being survey was conducted. If the focal child was no longer living in the household, or was seen less than once a week by the primary caregiver, no child-focused interview was conducted for that household.[10]

Table 9.1 indicates the number of sites for each state's evaluation as well as the number of families interviewed in each state. The areas represented in the state evaluations range from one county (Florida), to statewide (Indiana). Households sampled in each state range from 1,475 to 2,539. No provisions were made for non-English surveys to be conducted.

Table 9.1. Timeline and State Characteristics in the Project on State–Level Child Outcomes

Demonstration Program	Random Assignment	Child Well-Being Survey Fielded	Sites	Sample Size	Date of Child Impact Report
Connecticut Jobs First Program	1/96–12/96	4/99–6/00	New Haven, Manchester	2,539	2/02
Florida Family Transition Program (FFTP)	5/94–10/96	8/98–7/99	Escambia county	1,877	12/00
Indiana Manpower Placement and Comprehensive Training Program (IMPACT)	5/95–4/96	3/00–11/00	Statewide	1,679	6/02
Iowa Family Investment Program (IFIP)	10/93–3/96	8/98–8/99	9 counties	1,475	6/02
Minnesota Family Investment Program (MFIP)	4/94–10/94	8/97–5/98	7 counties	1,929	9/00

Sources: Child Trends, 1999; LeMenestrel, Tout, McGroder, Zaslow, & Moore, 1999; and the state evaluation teams.

Measures

The measures used to examine the effect of state welfare policies on child well-being fall into one of the four areas specified in the conceptual framework: (a) variables that are direct targets of state welfare policies, (b) other adult variables likely to be affected by state policies, (c) child environment variables likely to be affected by target or other adult variables, and (d) child outcomes. Under each of these four broad areas are domains, such as employment or education. Under each domain are the measurable constructs that make up that particular domain. Figure 9.1 summarizes the constructs under each domain. States vary somewhat with regard to how each construct was measured.

Targets of state welfare policies. As the central aim of state and federal welfare reform is to move recipients off welfare and into jobs, the domains of income and employment were identified as areas that would be directly affected by policy reform. Another focus of welfare reform has been to discourage teenage childbearing and childbearing outside of marriage. Thus state welfare policies also target the domain of family formation and dissolution. Measures are included in each state's survey in order to assess the degree to which policy reforms affect the target areas of income, employment, and family formation and dissolution, and the various ways in which policies might affect these areas.

Other areas likely to be affected by state welfare policies. The Project on State-Level Child Outcomes identified five areas that may be influenced by welfare reform: mother's psychological well-being (depression), stability and turbulence, absent parent involvement, use of health and human services, and consumption expenditures. Each of these areas have direct or indirect implications for child well-being.

State evaluators administered the 20-item Depression Scale from the Center for Epidemiologic Studies (Radloff, 1977) in order to measure depressive symptoms in respondents. The surveys also examine four areas of stability and turbulence: changes in family structure and living arrangements, changes in residence, changes in schools and/or child care arrangements, and fluctuations in family income. Frequent changes in one or more of these four areas have been linked with poor child outcomes in numerous areas. Welfare changes have the potential to increase income through employment and income disregards or decrease income through sanctions or extra expenses related to employment, such as child care, insurance, and transportation.

Single-parent families and families in which one of the biological parents (generally the father) was not present were asked questions related to whether child support is provided, whether official paternity was established

Figure 9.1. Core constructs for the Project on State-Level Child Outcomes. "AC" indicates all children of the respondent. "FC" indicates the focal child (one child aged 5–12). *Source:* Child Trends, 1999.

TARGET OF WELFARE POLICIES	OTHER ADULT AREAS	CHILD'S ENVIRONMENT	CHILD OUTCOMES
Income • Total income • Sources of income • Stability of income • Financial strain/material hardship **Employment** • Any vs. none • Health benefits • Wages • Hours of employment • Stability of employment • Education/licenses • Job skills • Multiple jobs concurrently • Barriers to employment **Family Formation** • Nonmarital/marital birth • Child/family living arrangements • Marital status, whether married to child's biological father	**Psychological Well-Being** • Maternal depression **Stability and Turbulence** • Foster care • Stability in income • No. of moves of residence • Change in marital status or cohabitation • Reason child not living with family **Absent Parent Involvement** • Child support • Paternity establishment • Frequency of contact with child **Use of Health and Human Services** • Food stamps • Medicaid (awareness, use, eligibility) • Child care subsidy (awareness, use, eligibility) • Access to medical care **Consumption** • Percentage of income spent on child care and rent	**Child Care** • Type • Extent • Quality (group size, ratio, licensing, parent perception) • Stability • Child care history for last 2 years **Home Environment and Parenting Practices** • Child abuse/neglect (administrative data) • Domestic violence/abusive relationships • Family routines • Aggravation/stress in parenting • Emotional support and cognitive stimulation provided to child	**Education** • Engagement in school (FC) • School attendance (AC) • School performance (AC) • Suspended/expelled (AC) **Health and Safety** • Hunger/nutrition (FC) • Child health status (FC) • Regular source of care (FC) • Teenage childbearing (AC) • Accidents and injuries (AC) **Social and Emotional Adjustment** • Behavior problems (FC) • Arrests (AC) • Social competence (FC)

(with a court or legal agency), and the frequency with which the absent parent has had contact (in person or over the phone) with the child over the past year (Child Trends, 1999). These questions were designed to identify whether the state welfare policies regarding child support and paternity establishment impact noncustodial parental involvement.

A greater focus on the use of health and human services and case management is a cornerstone of some state welfare reforms. With this in mind, most surveys asked families whether they received services such as food stamps, Medicaid, and child care subsidies.

Aspects of the child's environment likely to be affected by target or other adult variables. Questions regarding the parent's use of child care and perceptions of the quality of the child care environment were included in order to examine the complex ways in which policy reform may affect child care use. Child care use increases substantially for welfare recipients facing mandatory work, job training, or education requirements (Moore et al., 1995). Furthermore, the quality of child care is related to children's cognitive and socioemotional development (NICHD ECCRN, 1996, 1998a, 1999a), with children from low-income families reaping the greatest benefit of higher quality care (Caughy, Di Pietro, & Strobino, 1994). The state evaluators will rely on parent-report to assess the quality of the child care environment in all states.

In order to assess the multiple dimensions of home life that may be affected by welfare reform, most states used a short form of the Home Observation for Measurement of the Environment (HOME-SF) to examine the quality of the home environment and parent-child interactions. The HOME-SF requires a visit to the home and includes both mother-reported and interviewer-reported questions. The Minnesota survey included only selected items from the HOME-SF. State administrative data were used to obtain information on the use of family and child services (foster care, adoption, family-centered services, family preservation, and group care) in Iowa.

Child outcomes. Child outcomes were assessed in the areas of education, health and safety, and social and emotional adjustment. Educational outcomes are measured in terms of the child's level of school engagement and school achievement. The research firms conducting the evaluations for each state (MDRC, MPR, and Abt Associates) tapped the domain of children's health and safety by asking questions about the adequacy of food available to families, health status of children, health insurance coverage, regular health care provider, rates of accidents and injuries, and teenage childbearing.

Two primary domains of children's social and emotional adjustment are explored in the child well-being state surveys: behavior problems and positive behaviors. Behavior problems, including internalizing (being depressed, withdrawn, or unhappy) and externalizing (acting out, being destructive, or cheating), and positive behaviors are rated by the primary caregiver.

Units of Analysis

The research teams for the states in the Project on State-Level Child Outcomes collected data on individual households, adults, and children. Connected with each individual is information related to the site and program status (whether or not the family is from the control or program group). Analyses may be grouped according to state, socioeconomic status, or racial groups. Evaluators have also proposed ways of synthesizing and integrating findings across the five state evaluations, some of which were included in the Next Generation project, a synthesis of five welfare and employment programs: FFTP, MFIP, NEWWS—COS, New Hope, and the Canadian Self-Sufficiency Project (Morris, Huston, Duncan, Crosby, & Bos, 2001).

Findings

The Minnesota Family Investment Program showed larger effects for long-term welfare recipients (i.e., more than 24 months) and their children than for recent recipients (i.e., new applicants or those who had received welfare for less than 24 months prior to random assignment) at the 3-year follow-up. Among long-term recipients, mothers in MFIP were more likely to marry, less likely to experience domestic abuse, and more likely to work and have higher incomes than mothers under AFDC. Children of long-term recipients in the MFIP program did better in school, were reported as having fewer behavioral problems, were more likely to be in formal child care, and more likely to have continuous health insurance coverage than children of long-term recipients under AFDC (Gennetian & Miller, 2000). For recent applicants, fewer effects of MFIP were seen. Among recent applicants, mothers in MFIP were slightly more likely to work, but did not have higher incomes than mothers under AFDC. Young children of recent applicants in MFIP were more likely than children of recent applicants under AFDC to have continuous health insurance, but did not differ in the areas of school progress or behavior problems. Adolescent children in MFIP, however, did less well on some measures of schooling than those under AFDC (Gennetian & Miller, 2000).

The researchers examined MFIP findings for long-term recipients separately for the "Full MFIP" and the "MFIP Incentives Only" group, compared to the control AFDC group, in order to determine whether mandating employment made a difference vis-à-vis child outcomes. Both the Full MFIP and the MFIP Incentives Only programs increased employment rates. The Full MFIP enhanced full-time employment (30 hours or more per week), and the

MFIP Incentives Only program enhanced part-time employment (Morris et al., 2001). The impact of the two MFIP programs on children, however, was similar. Adding an employment mandate made no significant difference in terms of parents' ratings of children's school achievement, behavior problems, or health. The only difference was found in parent reports of positive behavior—MFIP Incentives Only participants rated their children as displaying higher levels of positive behavior, whereas Full MFIP participants did not rate their children significantly different than control group AFDC parents (Morris et al., 2001).

In contrast to the findings for MFIP, the Florida Family Transition Program, Indiana's IMPACT program, and the Iowa Family Investment Program reported few (and mixed) impacts on child well-being. In the 4-year follow-up, parents in the FFTP group were less likely to have received welfare for more than 3 years, but were equally likely to be working and had about the same income as parents in the AFDC group. By the end of the study period, researchers found no differences between children of parents in the FFTP group and children of parents in the AFDC control group on measures of school achievement and behavior problems. Adolescent children in the FFTP group, however, were rated somewhat worse than their AFDC counterparts on some measures of school progress (Bloom et al., 2000). Reports of positive child behavior were lower for the FFTP group, but child health and use of child care was higher than the AFDC group (Morris et al., 2001).

The evaluation of IMPACT found very few effects on child outcomes when children were 5 to 12 years old (Beecroft et al., 2002). In fact, only one impact (in a negative direction) was found for social behavior and emotional well-being, and no impacts were found for child education or health outcomes. Children ages 10 to 12 in IMPACT families had higher arrest rates compared to those in the control group (2.2% vs. 0.5%). This one finding, however, may be an artifact of multiple significance tests rather than a real effect.

The IFIP also found few impacts on child outcomes. Families in IFIP used more formal child care and less informal care by relatives compared to families under state AFDC rules, possibly due to the extended child care subsidies available under IFIP. On the other hand, children ages 5 to 12 in IFIP families were more likely to have cared for themselves on a regular basis than their AFDC counterparts. Children in IFIP families were also rated lower on school engagement and were more likely to have been tardy for school compared to children in AFDC families (Fraker et al., 2002).

The contrasting findings for MFIP compared to the other state demonstrations may be understood by examining the welfare provisions offered in each state. The key differences between these programs lie in two areas: (a) the generosity of the earnings supplements and (b) the presence of time limits on welfare receipt. The FFTP earnings supplement was much less generous than that of MFIP, due mainly to Florida's low welfare benefit levels. The waivers implemented in Indiana and Iowa had no impact, or a negative impact, on household income. Furthermore, recipients in Florida were subject to a 2–3-year time limit (depending on the family's level of disadvantage) on welfare receipt in any 5-year period (Morris et al., 2001).

Generous earnings supplements that increase family income, with or without a mandate to participate in employment-related activities, appear to have had a positive effect on parent employment rates and child achievement. Time limits in Florida, on the other hand, do not appear to have had a strong negative effect on families, at least in the short-term. The results of these studies offer insight into the mechanisms through which welfare policy may impact children. The strength of the demonstration programs lies in the random assignment design, which allows researchers and policy makers to attribute group differences to program impacts. Although the welfare waiver policies examined in the Project on State-Level Child Outcomes differ somewhat from each state's current policy, the results currently available and forthcoming are able to inform the field of welfare policy in ways never before possible.

Public Use Files

Most state evaluators plan to make public use files available. More detailed information regarding each state's data files can be found on the Web sites of the evaluation firms.

ASSESSING THE NEW FEDERALISM (ANF): THE NATIONAL SURVEY OF AMERICA'S FAMILIES (NSAF)

History

Assessing the New Federalism began as a project dedicated to the investigation of the devolution of social policy from national to state control. ANF is a multiyear project focused on program changes and fiscal developments in the areas of health care, income security, job training, and social services. Child Trends, in collaboration with the Urban Institute, is studying the well-being of children and families in ANF. As part of this focus, the National Survey of America's Families was implemented to act as a baseline in assessing family well-being, as the responsibility for social programs moves from federal to state control. In order to track the changes occurring, the NSAF samples across states with a focus on low-income families. Changes from the initial baseline survey to the follow-up surveys are examined in order to identify the ways in which welfare reforms affect child and family well-being. The sample size and survey content make the NSAF one of the largest, most comprehensive surveys available on the well-being of children and adults in the United States. Two other major data collection strategies were included in ANF—a state database and in-depth case studies. The focus of this chapter will be NSAF.

Current Status

Between February and November 1997, project investigators randomly selected 44,461 households to participate in the first round of the NSAF telephone survey. Of these households, detailed information on 75,437 adults and 34,439 children (between the ages of 0 and 17) was collected. Respondents came primarily from 13 states that represent more than half of the U.S. population (Alabama, California, Colorado, Florida, Massachusetts, Michigan, Minnesota, Mississippi, New Jersey, New York, Texas, Washington, and Wisconsin). The initial results of the 1997 survey were made available in January 1999. Since the initial release of baseline findings, scores of policy briefs, discussion papers, and journal articles drawing on data from NSAF have been published and can be accessed at the ANF Web site (http://newfederalism.urban.org). The second round of the survey was fielded from January through November 1999. Results from the 1999 survey were released in October 2000. The third round of the survey was in the field in 2002. Weekly updates on current ANF projects can be obtained by joining their listserve (http://newfederalism.urban.org/nfdb/nfsurvey.cfm).

Goals

The goal of the Assessing the New Federalism project is to monitor, document and understand state policy reforms and changes in family well-being in the context of the devolution of responsibility for major social programs from the federal government to the states. The role of the NSAF is to measure both positive and negative changes in the quality of family life that may occur as a result of welfare reform. The survey should play an important role in preparing policy makers and program designers for an environment in which states play a greater role in the formation of policies to meet social needs (Urban Institute, 1999).

Although the intent in designing the survey was to rely on scales that had been used in the past by other national surveys and welfare evaluation programs, many of the measures were shortened due to the time constraints of a telephone interview. As such, a secondary goal of the project is to assess the psychometric properties of each measure, in order to judge the reliability and validity of the shortened measures and the feasibility of using the measures as indicators of family well-being.

Design and Methods

Sample design. The NSAF was conducted by Westat, a national survey research firm. The primary sampling method was a random selection of telephone numbers (main sample). A sample of households without telephones was also included (area sample). Households with low incomes were heavily oversampled. The sample is representative of noninstitutionalized, civilian children and adults under age 65 living in the United States and in the 13 states that were oversampled.

The total number of telephone contacts in the 1997 survey was 179,000 households. After screening, 42,973 households responded to a detailed 25- or 40-minute interview. Of the 37,000 nontelephone households screened for eligibility, 1,488 of those households received an extended interview (Kenney, Scheuren, & Wang, 1999). Thus the final number of interviewed households was 44,461 (telephone + nontelephone). Surveys were administered in English only.

Data collection. Two forms of interviews were conducted. The longer (40-minute) interviews consisted of questions about both children and their families and were administered to households with children under age 18. Information on up to two children (one under age 6, and one between the ages of 6 and 17) was obtained from the adult who knew the most about the care of the child. In 95% of all cases, the most knowledgeable adult was the biological, adoptive, or stepparent of the focus child(ren). About 28,000 long interviews were conducted. The shorter (25-minute) interviews consisted of questions relevant to adults only and were administered to households without children. About 20,000 short interviews were conducted (P. D. Brick, Kenney, et al., 1999; see also Kenney et al., 1999).

Overall response rates for children in the 1997 NSAF was 65% nationally. The long interview completion rate ranged by study area from 78% to 89%. For adults, the overall response rate was 62% nationally. The short interview completion rate ranged from 74% to 86% (J. M. Brick, Flores-Cervantes, & Cantor, 1999; Groves & Wissoker, 1999; for a comparison of response rates of other household surveys, see P. D. Brick, Kenney, et al., 1999).

Measures

The NSAF consists of questions related to a variety of policy-relevant areas of family and child well-being. These topics include economic security, health and health care, child well-being, family and adult environment, and other areas (see Table 9.2). Some questions pertain to a family's circumstances at

Table 9.2. National Survey of America's Families (NSAF): Survey Indicators

Indicator	Measures
Economic security	Family income
	Employment and earnings
	Welfare program
	Participation in child support
	Food security
	Housing and economic hardship
Health and health care	Health status/limitations
	Health care coverage
	Health care use and access
Child well-being	Child education
	School engagement
	Cognitive stimulation (reading and/or telling stories to children)
	Child care use
	Child social and positive development (participation in activities)
	Child behavior and emotional problems
Family and adult environment	Family structure
	Family stress and parent aggravation
	Parent/adult psychological well-being
	Participation in activities
Other areas	Social service use
	Household composition
	Attitudes on welfare, work, and raising children
	Demographics

Sources: Ehrle & Moore, 1999; Kenney, Scheuren, & Wang, 1999.

the time of the survey (February–November 1997, for Wave 1; January–November 1999, for Wave 2; January–November 2002, for Wave 3), while others cover the calendar year prior to the interview, or the 12 months prior to the interview.

Benchmark comparisons were made for child and family well-being measures that had been shortened or not used extensively in national surveys. The measures included the following: (a) children's school engagement, (b) parent psychological well-being, (c) children's behavioral and emotional problems, (d) parent aggravation, (e) cognitive stimulation (reading to children and taking children on outings), and (f) children's participation in activities (sports, clubs, and lessons), a subset of child social and positive development. Child care use will be used in future benchmark comparisons as the data become available.

Measures were examined for their psychometric properties (quality, internal reliability, construct validity) and were benchmarked against estimates from other national surveys using similar measures (Ehrle & Moore, 1999). Exact comparisons between the NSAF and other large national samples were not always possible, but a fair degree of confidence was attained by comparison across socioeconomic groups. Benchmark comparisons using socioeconomic subgroups revealed similar patterns between the NSAF and the comparison survey. Across the measures, missing data are minimal, the means fall within expected ranges, spread around the mean is sufficient, and standard errors suggest that estimates can be used with certainty (Ehrle & Moore, 1999).

Poverty and low-income status were based on the household size and income in relation to the poverty threshold for the interview year. Families and children were classified as "low-income" if the household income was less than 200% of the 1996 poverty line.

Findings

Scores of reports and publications based on data from the NSAF have been published and are continually updated on the Urban Institute's Web site. A review of all available reports is beyond the scope of this profile. In this section, we present "snapshot" findings from the NSAF 1997 and 1999 surveys.

1997 Snapshots of America's Families. Based on the initial 1997 survey, two broad findings are especially relevant. First, children living in households with low incomes were markedly different from those in higher income households on every indicator. Children from low-income households (43% of the 1997 NSAF sample) fared worse than their higher income counterparts in the areas of health care, parental employment, social engagement, and child development. Second, child well-being indicators differed greatly around the country. Nationally, 21% of children and 13% of adults lived in poverty, and 12% of children lacked any form of health insurance (Medicaid, state insurance program, or private). Dramatic variation was evident in the areas of poverty and health insurance. Approximately 11% of children in Wisconsin lived in poverty, while more than 34% of children in Mississippi lived in poverty in 1997. The lowest rates of uninsured children were found in Massachusetts, Michigan, Minnesota, and Wisconsin, with only 5% to 6% uninsured, compared to the highest rates of 19% and 21% in Mississippi and Texas, respectively. There was little variation across states in child behavioral and emotional problems—high levels were evident in about 10% of low-income children aged 6 to 11 in all states. Children in lower income families were more likely to have behavioral and emotional problems and were less likely to be highly engaged in school than children in higher income families (73% vs. 90%; Urban Institute, 1999).

Lower income families faced more challenges than higher income families in the areas of provision of food, affordable housing, and general living conditions. Nearly half of lower income families worried about or had difficulty providing food for their household, compared to one in seven higher income families. About 30% of lower income families, compared with 10% of higher income, could not pay bills related to housing at some point in the prior year (Urban Institute, 1999). Compared to the nation, families in Mississippi fared the worst in the area of employment. Families in Alabama, New York, and Texas fared the worst in the area of housing. Families in both California and Texas indicated the most difficulty in affording food (Urban Institute, 1999).

1999 Snapshots of America's Families. In some respects, child and family well-being improved from 1997 to 1999. The poverty rate for children and for adults declined during this time (from 21% to 18% for children and from 13% to 11% for adults). Employment rates for single parents increased (from 74% to 78%). Families experiencing food hardship declined (from 32% to 29%); this decline was experienced among low-income families as well (from 54% to 50%; Zedlewski, 2000).

Small changes in measures of children's well-being were found between 1997 and 1999. Where changes did occur, they were generally negative for children in higher income families and positive for children in lower income families. Overall, however, children in low-income families scored lower than children in higher income families on all child outcome measures (Moore, Hatcher, Vandivere, & Brown, 2000). Few changes were seen in children's home environment from 1997 to 1999 (Vandivere, Moore, & Zaslow, 2000).

Gains were not experienced in all areas or equally across socioeconomic and racial groups. The income gap between all black and white adults grew, even as the employment gap between low-income black and white adults shrank by almost 5% between 1997 and 1999 (Staveteig & Wigton, 2000). There was little growth in the proportion of adults who received health insurance coverage from their employers (from 71% to 72%; Zuckerman, Haley, & Holahan, 2000). And although uninsurance rates for children remained the same overall, they grew from 9% to 11% for children from families with incomes between 200% and 300% of the federal poverty threshold (Kenney, Dubay, & Haley, 2000). The gap in health insurance rates between whites and Hispanics also grew during this time (Staveteig & Wigton, 2000).

Other NSAF reports and findings. Researchers have used data from the NSAF to examine a broad range of topics relevant to child and family well-being. Topics focus primarily on health care, income security, job training, and social services, but also include child care use, child support, and special populations. In most reports, comparisons of findings are made for children of varying ages, families of various types (i.e., single- vs. two-parent families; low-income vs. higher income; poor vs. nonpoor, etc.), different racial groups, and by region or state. For access to these reports, see the Urban Institute's Web site (http://newfederalism.urban.org).

Public Use Files

The ANF project has released the state database online and has made the state case studies available. The Child Public Use File is also available online, and includes data on 33,703 sampled children under 18 years of age from the 1997 NSAF. Also included in the child file is related information on the adults who care for them and the family settings in which they live. Detailed information on the codes used and on each variable is available from the codebook (see Russell, Leonard, & Scheuren, 1999). Several other survey data files are also available for public use. All are documented in the 1997 NSAF methodology series (available on-line at http://newfederalism.urban .org/nsaf).

NOTES

Christy Brady-Smith and Tama Leventhal would like to thank Robert Granger, Lindsay Chase-Lansdale, Andy Cherlin, Lisa Gennetian, Barbara Goldman, Pamela Morris, Christine Ross, Erik Beecroft, Alan Weil, and Fritz Scheuren for their helpful suggestions on earlier drafts of this chapter. The writing of this chapter was supported by a Spencer Research Training grant awarded to the first author. Martha Zaslow would like to thank Kathryn Tout and Gayle Hamilton for their helpful comments and suggestions on this chapter, as well as her colleagues on the NEWWS—COS at Child Trends: Kristin Moore, Sharon McGroder, Suzanne LeMenestrel, Elizabeth Hair, Jennifer Brooks, Zakia Redd, Surjeet Ahluwalia, and Nancy Margie. The NEWWS—COS team is grateful to their Project Officer and colleagues at DHHS who have guided the NEWWS—COS in all its phases, including Audrey Mirsky-Ashby, Martha Moorehouse, Howard Rolston, and Alan Jaffe. Martha Zaslow also thanks her colleagues on the NEWWS Observational Study: Elizabeth Hair, Surjeet Ahluwalia, Byron Egeland, Nancy Weinfield, John Ogawa, Catherine Snow, Patton Tabors, Jeanne DeTemple, Robin Dion, and Jennifer Sargent. Greg Duncan would like to thank Christina Gibson, Lindsay Moore, and Jennifer Romich for editorial assistance. The authors are grateful to Magdalena

Hernandez and Sue-Hee Chung for editorial assistance. The authors are also thankful to the funders and principal investigators of the studies highlighted in this chapter, and have acknowledged them in Chapter 2.

1. Christy Brady-Smith and Tama Leventhal are the primary authors of this introductory section of Chapter 9.

2. For more information regarding the New Chance Demonstration, see Reichman & McLanahan, 1998; Quint, Bos, & Polit, 1997; Zaslow & Eldred, 1998. Executive summaries and a full listing of publications regarding this initiative are available at http://www.mdrc.org/PublicationsFull.htm on-line.

3. For more information regarding the Teenage Parent Demonstration Project, see Aber, Brooks-Gunn, & Maynard, 1995; Brooks-Gunn et al., in press; and Kisker, Maynard, Rangarajan, & Boller, 1998. Executive summaries and a full listing of publications regarding this initiative are available at http://aspe.os.dhhs.gov/hsp/isp/tpd/timeline.htm on-line.

4. Martha Zaslow, Kerry Richter, and Christy Brady-Smith are the primary authors of this section of Chapter 9. The NEWWS Child Outcomes Study was conducted by Child Trends, under subcontract to the Manpower Demonstration Research Corporation. The overall NEWWS Evaluation was conducted by MDRC, under contract with the U.S. Department of Health and Human Services, with support from the U.S. Department of Education. For a complete list of participating investigators and funders, see Chapter 2. For more information regarding this initiative, see http://www.mdrc.org/WelfareReform/NEWWS.htm or http://www.childtrends.org on-line.

5. Greg Duncan is the primary author of this section of Chapter 9. This study is part of a larger evaluation conducted by MDRC. Funders include the John D. and Catherine MacArthur Foundation, the W. T. Grant Foundation, the Annie E. Casey Foundation, and the National Institute of Child Health and Human Development (5-year follow-up). For more information regarding this initiative, see http://www.mdrc.org/WelfareReform/NewHope.htm or http://www.lafollette.wisc.edu/newhope/nh_info.htm on-line.

6. Christy Brady-Smith is the primary author of this section of Chapter 9. The Three City Study is a collaborative effort involving numerous investigators. For a complete list of participating investigators and funders, see the project summary in Chapter 2. A full description of the design of the Three City Study may be found in *Welfare, Children, and Families: A Three City Study. Overview and Design Report*, available at http://www.jhu.edu/~welfare on-line.

7. Christy Brady-Smith is the primary author of this section of Chapter 9. The Project on State-Level Child Outcomes is a public-private partnership. For a complete list of participating investigators and funders, see Chapter 2. For more information regarding this project and the state evaluations, see http://www.childtrends.org; http://www.mdrc.org; http://www.mathematica-mpr.com; or http://www.abtassoc.com on-line.

8. Christy Brady-Smith is the primary author of this section of Chapter 9. Assessing the New Federalism is under the direction of the Urban Institute and is funded through numerous sources (see Chapter 2 for a full listing of funders). Alan

Weil is the director of Assessing the New Federalism. The survey director is Fritz Scheuren, and the survey manager is Kevin Wang. For more information, write to: Assessing the New Federalism, Urban Institute, 2100 M Street, NW, Washington, DC 20037; or visit the Web site (http://www.urban.org).

9. The Minnesota sample also included an "MFIP Incentives only" group that was not subject to the mandatory employment services.

10. In Minnesota, a second child was selected to replace the missing focal child, but these children were not included in the impact analysis.

CHAPTER 10

Neighborhood-Based Initiatives

TAMA LEVENTHAL AND JEANNE BROOKS-GUNN

Concern over the rise of urban poverty and associated conditions in America's cities during the last quarter of a century is pervasive among scholars, policy makers, and the general public. Although concern has centered on poverty, the evolving dialogue has also included issues such as crime, single parenthood, welfare dependency, and race. The publication of W. J. Wilson's (1987) *The Truly Disadvantaged* focused attention on demographic shifts and the resultant influence on inner-city neighborhoods, which helped to reorient discussions of poverty and concomitant conditions from primarily the familial and individual levels to include the neighborhood level. Among social scientists and policy makers alike, this growing interest in neighborhood poverty was further fueled by the strikingly high number of children, particularly young children, living in poor urban neighborhoods (Congressional Research Service, 1992; Kahn & Kamerman, 1996).

The study of community influences is based largely on the ecological theory of neighborhood social organization (Sampson, 1992, 1997; Sampson & Groves, 1989; Shaw & McKay, 1942). This perspective suggests that structural features of neighborhoods are of prime importance in explaining deviant behavioral development because they prevent (or foster) the formation of neighborhood organization. Communities' formal and informal institutions, in turn, serve as regulatory and support mechanisms for residents' activities. The most important structural characteristics are viewed as concentration of poverty among residents, racial and ethnic segregation, and residential mobility.

Researchers have used Bronfenbrenner's (1979) ecological theory of human development to examine associations among neighborhood structural influences and child, youth, and family well-being at both the individual and community levels. This theory provides a framework for considering the types of mechanisms that link environmental influences, from distal to proximal sources, to developmental processes and outcomes (Aber, Gephart, Brooks-Gunn, Connell, & Spencer, 1997). An additional strength of Bronfenbrenner's theory (1979) is that reciprocal influences are acknowledged (e.g., parenting practices influence child outcomes, but child characteristics also influence parenting practices).

In terms of research, the recent publication of *Neighborhood Poverty* (Brooks-Gunn, Duncan, & Aber, 1997a, b)—the first systematic evaluation of neighborhood effects across young childhood and adolescence—is indicative of burgeoning interest in neighborhood contexts. Much of the current neighborhood research has focused on older children and adolescents as opposed to young children (for a review of these findings, see Leventhal & Brooks-Gunn, 2000). The research findings with respect to young children and neighborhood effects suggest that the presence of affluent neighbors or high-SES neighbors (rather than the presence of poor or low-SES neighbors) is associated with young children's IQ scores and verbal ability (Brooks-Gunn, Duncan, Klebanov, & Sealand, 1993; Chase-Lansdale, Gordon, Brooks-Gunn, & Klebanov, 1997; Duncan et al., 1994; Klebanov et al., 1997). Residing in an ethnically diverse neighborhood may be negatively associated with children's verbal ability, particularly for European American children, and neighborhood levels of male joblessness may be associated with children's socioemotional functioning, especially for school-age children (Chase-Lansdale et al., 1997). Several studies also point to the fact that neighborhood effects on young children's development may operate indirectly via parental behavior, quality of the home environment, and family functioning (Greenberg, Lengua, Coie, & Pinderhughes, 1999; Klebanov et al., 1997; Klebanov et al., 1994).

Paralleling the shift among scholars, interest in community-based initiatives is high (Connell & Kubisch, in press; Connell, Kubisch, Schorr, & Weiss, 1995; Kahn & Kamerman, 1996). For example, the family and community support movement attempts to integrate services for children and families in a community-based setting in addition to building social ties among community residents (Kagan, 1996; Kagan & Pritchard, 1996). Community development corporations (CDCs) and initiatives such as the Empowerment Zone and Enterprise Communities, on the other hand, have focused on housing, job creation, and civic infrastructure (Briggs & Mueller, 1997; Fuchs & Thompson, 1996; Sullivan, 1993; Vidal, 1992). Even more ambitious are comprehensive community initiatives (CCIs), which provide coordinated and integrated services to families in a neighborhood-based setting as well as economic and housing development (Brown & Richman, 1997; Kubisch, 1996). Noteworthy is the fact that children have not figured prominently in the design of many of these initiatives; family and community support services are perhaps the most child-oriented strategy (Berlin, Brooks-Gunn, & Aber, 2001; Leventhal, Brooks-Gunn, & Kamerman, 1997). Finally, many federal programs, such as welfare and other categorical programs (e.g., Head Start, WIC), have always been delivered at the local level, and recent legislation has given states more local autonomy over welfare and other programs serving poor children and families. Local concern may increase variation among communities in the quantity and quality of these programs, making community-level evaluations increasingly important (for a more detailed discussion of these issues, see Leventhal et al., 1997). In general, however, evaluation of the efficacy of these various strategies for delivering services to low-income families has been limited.

To date, the research field has been plagued by several methodological limitations in evaluating neighborhood effects on young children's development as well as in evaluating community-based programs in general. Some of the shortcomings of existing studies include the following:

- Absence of cluster-based or multilevel designs (i.e., neighborhood-based sampling frames)
- Absence of direct assessments of neighborhoods
- Lack of process-oriented measures
- Reliance on cross-sectional data
- Lack of data on community variation in quantity and quality of services and programs
- Nonexperimental designs

Also of primary concern is the fact that family residence in neighborhoods is not random and unmeasured characteristics of families may account for any observed neighborhood effects (i.e., selection or omitted variable bias; Duncan, Connell, & Klebanov, 1997; Tienda, 1991). While space does not permit a detailed discussion of each of these weaknesses, the essential point is that neighborhood- and community-based research designs are not common (for a detailed discussion of these issues, see Brooks-Gunn, Duncan, Leventhal, & Aber, 1997).

Several new initiatives have been launched that examine multiple levels of influence on development—individual, family and community. What differentiates these studies from their predecessors is the incorporation of neighborhoods (or communities) into the design phase of the study. These multilevel designs that study individual development within and across neighborhoods recently have emerged as a result of methodological advances in the field of social science. The advantage of such initiatives is that they permit a more accurate assessment of the role of neighborhoods in the lives of children and families. In addition, several experimental and quasi-experimental designs, which address problems of selection bias, have been employed as a result of collaboration among researchers and policy makers. These studies all move beyond census data to obtain richer information on neighborhood contexts (e.g., administrative data, community surveys, systematic social observation, and expert surveys). One of their primary goals is to understand the processes, such as parenting behavior, peers, and schools/child care, through which neighborhoods might influence child development.

This chapter describes two studies that belong to this new generation of neighborhood-based initiatives. First, a profile on the Project on Human Development in Chicago Neighborhoods (PHDCN) is presented. This study has been referred to as one of the most ambitious initiatives of this decade. The second study profiled, the Los Angeles Families and Neighborhood Study (L.A. FANS), is currently being fielded.

PROJECT ON HUMAN DEVELOPMENT IN CHICAGO NEIGHBORHOODS (PHDCN)

History

The Project on Human Development in Chicago Neighborhoods[1] was designed to better understand the influence of neighborhood, family, and school characteristics on children and youths' development. The theoretical foundations of the study draw heavily upon social disorganization theory and ecological models of human development, as outlined in the introduction. Of particular concern to the investigators are school achievement, mental health, antisocial and violent behavior, and substance abuse; PHDCN employs ecological and developmental perspectives to study these outcomes. Multiple contexts that influence human development are considered—families, schools and peer groups, and communities. Differences across communities are highlighted by this study (e.g., community outcomes examined include health [low birth weight, prenatal care], violence [crime, victimization], and care of children [foster care, abuse and neglect, available services]). Moreover, the dynamic interplay between the individual and these contexts is acknowledged, as is the evolving nature of both individuals and communities. Finally, the interaction of the various contexts, such as neighborhoods and schools, on development are considered, and neighborhoods also are viewed as a context for family functioning. Noteworthy is the fact that the neighborhood-based design allows the researchers to examine all of these issues.

Current Status

The planning phase of the PHDCN began in 1988. The project has two main components: an intensive study of Chicago's neighborhoods; and a longitudinal study of children, adolescents, and young adults. The first wave of data was collected primarily in 1995 and 1996, and data for Wave 2 were collected predominately in 1998 and 1999. Wave 3 data were collected in 2000–2001. The first Community Survey was conducted in 1995 and 1996, and a second Community Survey began in 2001 to coincide with the U.S. Census. Data collection has been completed.

Initial findings on community regulation from the first Community Survey (Sampson, 1997; Sampson, Morenoff, & Earls, 1999; Sampson, Raudenbush, & Earls, 1997) and Observational Study (Raudenbush & Sampson, 1999; Sampson & Raudenbush, 1999) have been published. Additional papers on measurement development related to exposure to violence are published (Kindlon, Wright, Raudenbush, & Earls, 1996; Selner-O'Hagan, Kindlon, Buka, Raudenbush, & Earls, 1998), and two methodological papers on the HOME inventory are in preparation (Kindlon, Brooks-Gunn, Brennan, Selner-O'Hagan, & Earls, 1999; Selner-O'Hagan, Leventhal, Brooks-Gunn, Bingenheimer, & Earls, 2001). In addition, the PHDCN has regular newsletters that are widely circulated, as well as technical reports (Barnes-McGuire & Reiss, 1993; Earls & Buka, 1997) and a profile (PHDCN, 1997) that are readily available. Up-to-date information on the study and its activities can be obtained from their Web site (http://phdcn.harvard.edu).

Goals

The primary purpose of the PHDCN is to study the origins and developmental pathways of social competence and antisocial behavior from birth through young adulthood within a variety of communities (PHDCN, 1997). It should be noted that a major focus is to elucidate the effects of community and neighborhood contexts on individual behavior using an innovative design and state-of-the-art methodologies (Earls & Buka, 1997). Consistent with these goals is the desire to provide important new information on crime prevention and intervention strategies to policy makers and community agencies and leaders. The study seeks to answer questions regarding the most effective approaches to the prevention of delinquency, criminal behavior, and substance abuse in terms of institutional base, target populations, and optimal age of participants.

Theory of Change

The study is attempting to identify family and neighborhood level processes that may account for the association between structural characteristics and child, youth, and family well-being at both the individual and community levels.

Design and Methods

The PHDCN is comprised of five components:

- The Longitudinal Study (with an embedded intensive study of infants), conducted in 1995–1996, 1998–1999, and 2000–2001
- The Community Survey, conducted in 1995–1996 and 2001–2002
- The Observational Study of Neighborhoods, conducted in 1995–1996 and in 2001–2002
- The Neighborhood Expert Survey, conducted in 1995–1996
- Administrative data available for 1990–2002.

Figure 10.1 provides a brief outline of the design of each of these components. A detailed description of the Longitudinal Study will be provided for comparison purposes with other chapters in this volume.

Longitudinal Study. The multilevel approach in this study led to a sophisticated neighborhood-based sampling frame. Neighborhoods were operationally defined as 343 clusters of city blocks from Chicago's 847 populated census tracts selected because of their geographic compactness and internal homogeneity with respect to socioeconomic and racial/ethnic mix, housing density, and family structure. Census data were used to define two stratification variables: SES (three levels) and racial/ethnic composition (seven levels). The neighborhood clusters (NCs) were cross-classified by these two variables, and a stratified probability sample of 80 NCs was drawn for the Longitudinal Study. The aim was to have an equal number of NCs in each of the 21 strata that varied by racial/ethnic mix and SES (however, several strata were empty or had an insufficient number of NCs; see Table 10.1 for an overview of the neighborhood-based sampling frame employed in the Longitudinal Study). The Longitudinal Study is comprised of seven overlapping age cohorts starting with the prenatal period and separated by 3-year intervals up to age 18: 00, 03, 06, 09, 12, 15, and 18. This accelerated longitudinal design allows the researchers to examine children and youth over a 5-year period, approximating what could be observed by tracking a single birth cohort for approximately 25 years. Table 10.2 reports the number of

---

THE LONGITUDINAL DESIGN

- Screen 32,000 households in 80 neighborhoods.

- Select 1,000 children in each of 7 age groups (0–1, 3, 6, 9, 12, 15, 18).

- Conduct baseline home-based interviews with parents and children in each cohort. Conducted over 30 months in 1995–2001.

- Conduct intensive study of early development in a subsample of 400 infants.

- Follow families over 5–7 years for repeated assessments of growth and development (3 waves of data collection).

THE COMMUNITY DESIGN

- Community survey in all 343 neighborhoods within the city limits ($N = 8,782$). Conducted in 1995–1996. Follow-up survey conducted in 2001–2002 to coincide with U.S. Census.

- Observational survey in 80 randomly selected neighborhoods (23,861 blocks recorded). Conducted in 1995–1996. Follow-up survey conducted in 2001–2002 to coincide with U.S. Census.

- Neighborhood experts survey of business leaders, law enforcement administrators, school administrators, political leaders, religious leaders, and community organization administrators ($N = 2,820$). Conducted in 1995–1996.

- Administrative records, including police and court records, public and parochial school records, and vital statistics.

Figure 10.1. Overview of Project on Human Development in Chicago Neighborhoods. *Source*: Adapted from Project on Human Development in Chicago Neighborhoods, 1997.

participants by age cohort from the first wave of the study conducted in 1995–1996 ($N = 6,234$) (Wave 2 conducted in 1998–1999 and Wave 3 fielded in 2000–2001).

The PHDCN has done extensive work on measurement development in terms of assessing individuals and families (see Earls & Buka, 1997). Detailed, home-based interviews are conducted with children older than 6 years

Table 10.1. Wave 1 of the Project on Human Development in Chicago Neighborhoods Sample by Neighborhood Composition

Racial/Ethnic Mix	Socioeconomic Status		
	Low	Medium	High
Over 75% African American			
Neighborhood clusters	9	4	4
Participants	643	295	292
75% European American			
Neighborhood clusters	—	4	8
Participants		339	527
75% Latino			
Neighborhood clusters	4	4	—
Participants	431	317	
Over 20% Latino and over 20% European American			
Neighborhood clusters	4	5	4
Participants	299	463	387
Over 20% Latino and over 20% African American			—
Neighborhood clusters	4	4	
Participants	369	420	
Over 20% African American and over 20% European American			
Neighborhood clusters	2	4	4
Participants	192	335	117
Other heterogeneous			
Neighborhood clusters	4	4	4
Participants	332	311	168
Total neighborhood clusters ($N = 80$)	27	29	24
Total sample ($N = 6,234$)	2,263	2,480	1,491

Source: Adapted from Project on Human Development in Chicago Neighborhoods, 1997.

of age, adolescents, and youth and all primary caregivers (except for participants 18 years of age or older) at each wave of data collection. The protocol
has been translated from English into Spanish and Polish. Since several cultures are assessed in PHDCN, measures are intended to be sensitive to this
variation. Although an effort is made to be consistent in measures used across
cohorts, some items are adapted or added to tap relevant constructs for a

Table 10.2. Number of Participants Assessed in Wave 1
of the Project on Human Development in Chicago
Neighborhoods by Age Cohort

Cohort	Number of Participants
00	1,270
03	1,002
06	988
09	832
12	810
15	702
18	631
Total	6,235

particular age cohort. Some common information obtained on children and youth at each wave includes: exposure to violence, verbal IQ, reading achievement, behavior problems, efficacy and competence, provision of social relations, health, parent-child conflict, and temperament. Trained interviewers also conducted diagnostic interviews for depression, anxiety, and posttraumatic stress disorder in 1998–1999 and 2000–2001. An intensive study of 413 infants in the age 00 cohort was conducted in 1995–1996, which focused on cognition, physical and emotional health status, temperament (inhibition/disinhibition and distress to limits), and home/caretaker characteristics (including videotaped interactions). For the entire age 00 cohort, who were approximately 5 years old at Wave 3 (conducted in 2000–2001), information on emotional competence, attention, and self-regulation was obtained via behavioral observations. For older children and youth, information on substance abuse, offending, peers, and employment was ascertained at each interview.

The primary caregiver, typically the mother, was interviewed at each assessment. Information about the father was collected as well. Demographic information including household composition, racial/ethnic background, household income (all sources), and employment status was obtained from her interview. Ethnicity and race were coded to be consistent with the 1990 Census. Additional measures collected on families at each assessment were: family environment, parental conflict, physical and mental health histories, provision of social relations, acculturation, and the home environment. The PHDCN revised the HOME inventory developed by Caldwell and Bradley (1984) to be more comparable across the ages by adding items to each age version of the HOME inventory from the other age versions. In Wave 2, conducted in 1998–1999, the research team also expanded the response scale of the HOME inventory from a simple yes/no format to a frequency count. For participants 18 years of age or older, all information was collected during interviews with the youths (as opposed to the primary caregiver).

The study incorporated items addressing the 1996 welfare legislation. Questions were added to Waves 2 and 3 that assessed knowledge of time limits and work requirements. In Wave 1, no data were collected on quality of child care and school, although information on type of child care received and type of school attended was collected. In Waves 2 and 3, quality of child care was evaluated via maternal report using the Emlen (1997) scales. In conjunction with Wave 2 in 1998–1999, assessments of the quality of child care that children in the 00 and 03 cohorts attended were conducted (approximately 200 centers) using a structured observation (ECERS-R; Harms et al., 1998). Data on medical, educational, and psychosocial service use also were obtained in Wave 2, conducted in 1998–1999, and again in Wave 3, fielded in 2000–2001.

Given the framework of the study (i.e., nested, longitudinal), multilevel analyses, including hierarchical linear modeling and growth curve modeling, will be used to examine both individual, family, and community outcomes related to social competence and crime and delinquency, as specified earlier. Two levels of interest for this component of the study are outcomes between participants within neighborhoods and outcomes of individuals over time (Raudenbush, 1997). A focus of the Longitudinal Study will be to investigate the relation of family and community influences on individual outcomes over time. Policy-relevant factors such as race, ethnicity, acculturation, and income have figured prominently in the design of the study and will be included in analyses at both the individual and community levels.

Community Design (Community Survey, Observational Study, Administrative Data, and Expert Survey). As part of the community design, PHDCN has done extensive work on the development of measures of neighborhood contexts including the Community Survey, the Observational Study, the gathering of Administrative Data, and the Expert Survey. The Community Survey used the same sampling frame as the Longitudinal Study; however, data were collected on all 343 NCs that comprise Chicago. In addition, a separate sample from the Longitudinal Study was obtained. Approximately 5,000 individuals were interviewed in 1995–1996 with an average of 20 to 50 individuals per NC (average of 50 interviews conducted in 80 target NCs). Participants rated their neighborhoods on a number of dimensions including social and physical disorder, social cohesion, informal social control, danger, and availability of resources (Sampson, 1997; Sampson et al., 1997). A second Community Survey was conducted in 2001–2002 with a new cross-sectional sample.

For the Observational Study, data were collected via video-taped observations of the 80 selected NCs in conjunction with the Longitudinal Study. Subsequently, trained observers coded the data using a structured format (Raudenbush & Sampson, 1999; Sampson & Raudenbush, 1999). Approximately 25,000 street- or face-blocks (two sides of the street) were observed. This component of the study focuses on evaluating the physical and social conditions of neighborhoods.

In addition to census data, which describe the demographic characteristics of neighborhoods, administrative data from local agencies including crime reports from police departments, health outcomes from vital statistics records, information on schools from the educational department, and data on child care supply and demand from the Census Bureau are also being obtained for the study period. The unit of analysis is the 343 NCs. The administrative data will be used in conjunction with all other components of the study.

The Expert Survey conducted in 1995–1996 entailed approximately 3,000 interviews with "experts" in the 80 target NCs. Experts included business, political, and religious leaders, school administrators, law enforcement administrators, community organizers, and other community leaders. Information on the social and political structure of neighborhoods was ascertained.

The community components of PHDCN will chart neighborhood change over time. Using multilevel techniques, the researchers will focus on examining neighborhood outcomes related to crime and violence (see Sampson et al., 1997; Sampson, 1997). Analyses also will examine whether the neighborhood dimensions under investigation differ across the various components of the community study, and if so, how they diverge.

Findings

Currently, results from pilot work, the Community Survey, and the Observational Study are available. A technical report documents the extensive measurement development conducted to date (Earls & Buka, 1997). Several articles based on pilot studies have appeared on the development and psychometrics of an instrument assessing individuals' exposure to violence, the My Exposure to Violence scale (Kindlon et al., 1996; Selner-O'Hagan et al., 1998). Building on the work of previous research in this area, the new scale measures both the amount of violence to which a person has been exposed as well as the extremity of the event.

Another set of methodological analyses on the HOME inventory is underway. Focusing on the age 00 cohort, the researchers have begun to explore the psychometric properties of the HOME scale for infants across heterogeneous cultural and/or socioeconomic groups (Kindlon et al., 1999).

Preliminary analyses suggest that the internal consistency of the HOME inventory did not differ across SES, but did so across African Americans, European Americans, and Latinos. In addition, for children in the age 03 to 15 cohorts, researchers are developing a psychometrically valid and reliable assessment of the home environment that produces similar scales across ages as well as scales unique to specific developmental stages (e.g., early school learning, adolescent problem behavior; Selner-O'Hagan et al., 2001).

Initial results from the Community Survey have investigated the role of neighborhood "collective efficacy" (Sampson et al., 1997). This term was originally conceived by Bandura (1986) and recently employed by PHDCN to describe the extent of social connections in the neighborhood and the degree to which residents monitor the behavior of others in accordance with socially accepted practices (Sampson et al., 1997). Essentially, collective efficacy is a combined measure of informal social control and social cohesion. The measure is comprised of 10 items with informal social control assessed by items tapping the likelihood that neighbors could be counted on to intervene in various situations, such as children skipping school and hanging out on a street corner, children spray painting graffiti on a local building, children disrespecting an adult, a fight in front of their house, and the threat of the local fire station being closed down by budget cuts. Social cohesion was evaluated by items assessing how strongly residents agreed that people are willing to help neighbors, the neighborhood is close-knit, residents share values, people in the neighborhood could be trusted, and people in the neighborhood do not get along. All of these items were rated on a Likert-type scale.

In PHDCN, collective efficacy was associated with neighborhood structural factors (concentrated disadvantage, residential instability, and immigrant concentration) and rates of community violence (perceived violence, violent victimization, and homicide rates). In addition, collective efficacy mediated a substantial part of the association between neighborhood structural factors and neighborhood violence (Sampson et al., 1997). In related work, Sampson (1997) found that a measure of informal social control of children, similar to collective efficacy, was associated with neighborhood rates of adolescent delinquency. In fact, informal social control of children accounted for about 50% of the effect of neighborhood structural characteristics (residential stability) on adolescent delinquency.

Initial studies from the Systematic Social Observation have also examined links between disorder (physical and social) and collective efficacy (Raudenbush & Sampson, 1999). Social disorder entails observations of public activities, such as fighting, gang activity, loitering, drinking, drug use, and prostitution; and physical disorder entails observations of items, such as graffiti, garbage, vacant housing, and abandoned cars. The findings suggest that even after accounting for neighborhood SES-demographic composition and prior crime rates, physical and social disorder, as measured via Systematic Social Observation, were associated with community levels of collective efficacy assessed in the Community Survey.

Limitations

The sophisticated design employed and the extensive methodological work undertaken in the PHDCN leave few limitations. Perhaps the greatest limitation to the generalizability of this study is that it is being conducted in a single city, Chicago. However, work is underway to conduct a comparative community survey in Stockholm, Sweden.

Public Use Files

To date, data from the Community Survey are available to the public through the Inter-University Consortium for Political and Social Research (http://www.icpsr.umich.edu), but other files are not yet available to the public. Data collection is complete. The researchers hope to make remaining data files available to the public within a reasonable time frame.

LOS ANGELES FAMILY AND NEIGHBORHOOD STUDY (L.A. FANS)

History

Another new neighborhood-based study is the Los Angeles Family and Neighborhood Study,[2] which is being initiated in the county of Los Angeles. In the wake of recent policy changes, particularly welfare reform, Los Angeles is an important "test case" in which to explore these changes because of the large immigrant population and because Los Angeles, like other urban areas across the country, is marked by growing economic and social inequality. Most studies examining the impact of welfare reform are focusing on maternal, child, and family outcomes (see Chapter 9). However, this new set of policies is also likely to have widespread effects on the communities in which families reside, particularly low-income families; these changes, in turn, will have implications for child and family well-being.

Current Status

Data collection began in 2000 and continued through 2002. There are plans for a second wave of data collection in 2003–2004.

Goals

The overarching goal of this study is to examine neighborhood and family origins of children's successes and failures across a wide range of outcomes, particularly in light of welfare reform. Three specific issues will be considered:

- *Effects of neighborhoods on children and families.* How does community variation in resources affect child outcomes in several areas including cognition, schooling, behavioral and emotional development, health, criminal involvement, substance use, and teenage child-bearing?
- *Effects of welfare reform at the neighborhood level.* What are the trajectories of neighborhoods as a result of welfare reform (i.e., decline vs. gentrification) and further, what are the consequences of such changes for children and families?
- *Residential mobility and neighborhood change.* How are neighborhood migration patterns (i.e., movement of individuals into and out of neighborhoods) associated with neighborhood trajectories over time?

Theory of Change

The researchers consider neighborhoods a primary context in children's lives, and larger policy issues, such as welfare reform, are anticipated to have a substantial impact on neighborhoods and, consequently, on children and families. In all likelihood, there will be an interactive effect between the availability of community resources and policy changes such that some communities will benefit, while others will be harmed.

Design and Methods

L.A. FANS is comprised of three components: a longitudinal household survey, a longitudinal survey of children and their primary caregivers, and a neighborhood expert survey. Since this volume focuses on young children, we highlight the child component of the study.

Longitudinal Survey of Households and Children and Families. The researchers are employing a longitudinal study of a representative stratified cluster sample of households and neighborhoods (defined as census tracts) in Los Angeles county. Neighborhoods were stratified by income (very poor, poor, and nonpoor) using 1997 estimates from Los Angeles County data, and then 65 neighborhoods were randomly selected to yield a representative stratified sample of 20 very poor neighborhoods (tracts in lowest 10% of distribution), 20 poor neighborhoods (tracts in 10% to 40% of distribution), and 25 nonpoor neighborhoods (tracts in top 60% of distribution). Forty households were randomly selected per neighborhood, and households with children under 18 years of age were oversampled to comprise seventy percent of the sample. In each household, one randomly selected adult was interviewed ($N = 2,700$) and one target child was randomly designated per household, but up to two children per household and their primary caregiver were assessed ($N = 3,200$). If the randomly selected adult was not the child's primary caregiver, additional information was obtained from the primary caregiver. The randomly selected adult and the randomly selected child will be followed throughout the longitudinal study. Approximately 500 additional households (1,000 children) will be added over the course of the study; these families will be evenly distributed across the 40 very poor and poor neighborhoods. Children in the sample come from diverse backgrounds across SES groups. The purpose of this additional sample is to capture changes in neighborhood migration (i.e., moves into and out of neighborhoods).

Two waves of data on families will be collected over 4 years beginning in 2000, and additional funding is being sought to extend the study for additional waves of data collection. Two unique criteria of the design are that children and families will be followed even if they move out of a target neighborhood, and a new sample of new entrants into neighborhoods will be obtained in each wave of the study. Thus L.A. FANS is the only neighborhood-based initiative examining migration by adding families who depart and enter neighborhoods.

All surveys are administered in the home. A household survey obtained detailed sociodemographic information on households. The adult survey gathered data on welfare use and use of other social programs, neighborhood conditions, and social ties. Additional information was collected from adults who are the primary caregivers for children, including self-efficacy, depression, social support, and reading comprehension. Data on families gathered are family dynamics, parent-child relations, family routines, and quality of the home environment. Primary caregivers also reported on children's behavior and disciplinary problems, contact with fathers and/or absent parent, schooling/child care, health status, receipt of services, and friends. Cognitive assessments were administered to children age 3 and older and children age 9 and older were interviewed as well. The child survey collected information on school achievement, school environment, peer group, social interactions, employment, violence, problem behaviors, and social relations with adults. A majority of the measures were drawn from national studies. The protocol was administered in English and Spanish.

The study seeks to examine neighborhood change over time as well as changes in child and family well-being. Multilevel modeling will be employed, given the neighborhood-based design of the study. Because L.A. FANS is employing a panel design of children and families coupled with an annually representative sample of each sampled neighborhood, the researchers will also examine neighborhood selection processes (i.e., following who moves into and out of neighborhoods).

Neighborhood Expert Survey. The neighborhood expert survey is composed of interviews with public school and secondary school principals, key informants (approximately 8 per neighborhood), and family- and child-related services providers (approximately 10 per neighborhood) in the 65 target neighborhoods. School principals completed a survey on school characteristics and quality. Key informants include school officials, teachers, librarians, and local business and religious leaders. Key informants reported on their area of expertise (e.g., police officers asked about safety, crime, and gang activity and business owners asked about business climate and sales). The service providers were asked about the operation and history of their programs and organizations, especially in the context of welfare reform. Additional questions were asked about other local service providers. All neighborhood experts were asked about their neighborhoods including safety, problems, social organization, ethnic relations, major changes, and resources. Observational information on neighborhoods, such as physical and social conditions, also was obtained. Analyses will focus on variation in neighborhood trajectories in the wake of welfare reform.

Findings

Data will be collected through 2004.

Limitations

The most significant shortcoming of this study is that it is being conducted in a single city—Los Angeles—limiting generalizability to other cities or regions in the country.

Public Use Files

Early Release public use data and documentation are available at http://www.lasurvey.rand.org on-line.

NOTES

We would like to thank the United States Department of Housing and Urban Development (HUD), the National Institute of Child Health and Human Development, the National Science Foundation, and the Russell Sage Foundation for their support. We are also grateful to the NICHD Research Network on Child and Family Well-Being. We would also like to acknowledge Tony Earls (PHDCN), Alicia Schoua-Glusberg (PHDCN), Mary Beth O'Hagan (PHDCN), and Anne Pebley (L.A. FANS) for assistance with the profiles for their respective studies.

1. The Project on Human Development in Chicago Neighborhood is an interdisciplinary collaboration under the direction of Felton Earls, Harvard Medical School. The primary funders of PHDCN are John D. and Catherine T. MacArthur Foundation and the National Institute of Justice. Additional funding was provided by the National Institute of Mental Health, the U.S. Department of Education, and the Administration for Children, Youth, and Families. For more information regarding this initiative, see http://phdcn.harvard.edu on-line.

2. The principal investigator is Anne R. Pebley (RAND Corporation and UCLA), and the primary funders of this study are the National Institute of Child Health and Human Development, the Office of the Assistant Secretary for Planning and Evaluation (ASPE), and Los Angeles County. For more information regarding this initiative, see http://www.lasurvey.rand.org on-line.

CHAPTER 11

Initiatives on Children with Special Needs

KATHLEEN HEBBELER AND DONNA SPIKER

Not all children develop typically. Each year, between 120,000 and 160,000 children are born with major birth defects according to the Centers for Disease Control (Edmonds, 1999). Nearly 200,000 children under age 3 receive early intervention services because of a developmental delay, diagnosed condition, or a serious risk condition (U.S. Department of Education, 1998). Nearly 560,000 children aged 3–5 are receiving special education services (U.S. Department of Education, 1998). Four million school-age children have serious functional limitations (Hogan, Msall, Rogers, & Avery, 1997). Eleven percent of all children between 6 and 17 years old receive special education or related services (U.S. Department of Education, 1998).

Any beginning student of child development is familiar with the concepts of delay, disability, and atypical development. Yet these same concepts have only recently begun to be incorporated into the designs of major national studies. The new wave of studies on young children described in this report differ from studies conducted 10 or 20 years ago in that funders and researchers have recognized the importance of including children with disabilities in the study. In the past, large-scale studies often excluded all or some children with disabilities or made no effort to accommodate them (Vanderwood, McGrew, & Ysseldyke, 1998; McGrew, Thurlow, & Spiegel, 1993).

Exclusion of children with disabilities from national studies had two serious consequences. One was that the findings from the study did not generalize to the entire population of children in the age or program group that was the target of the research, although this was sometimes not acknowledged. The second consequence was that the knowledge base about children with disabilities did not benefit from what was learned. Fortunately, exclusion of children with disabilities from large-scale studies has increasingly come to be seen as unacceptable on both scientific and equity grounds.

Exclusion was not simply a matter of oversight or discrimination. Including children with disabilities in large studies is a conceptually complex and expensive endeavor if done to the fullest extent possible. Full inclusion in major research efforts involves far more than a change in the criteria for sample selection. The decision to include children with disabilities raises the need for numerous additional considerations related to the design, data collection, and analysis.

The first half of this chapter discusses general considerations related to including children with disabilities in large-scale studies, using examples from the National Evaluation of Early Head Start (EHS) and the Birth and Kindergarten Cohorts of the Early Childhood Longitudinal Study (ECLS-B and ECLS-K). A strength of these studies for understanding the development of children with disabilities is that they will allow for comparisons between children with disabilities and typically developing children as well as comparisons of the families of these groups of children. Some shortcomings also exist and will be discussed.

The second half of the chapter presents an overview of the National Early Intervention Longitudinal Study (NEILS),[1] an ongoing study focusing exclusively on infants and toddlers with disabilities. The strength of a study focusing exclusively on children with disabilities is that it allows for an in-depth examination of the myriad issues unique to this population. Drawbacks are that such studies are costly, provide no comparable findings for the general population for much of the data, and are not part of an ongoing national information system (Vanderwood et al., 1998).

INCLUSION AND STUDIES OF THE GENERAL POPULATION

Inclusion of children with disabilities in large-scale studies can occur to varying degrees. At the most minimal level of inclusion, children with disabilities are included in the sample to the extent they are members of the population being studied but no modifications are made to the measurement techniques. If the study includes direct assessment of children, as many studies do, some children with disabilities will not be able to participate in the assessments and others will be tested but their results will be invalid. For questions asked of families, lack of modification means that some questions might be inappropriate, important information will not be collected, or both. Findings from such a study would address children with disabilities to a limited extent only, because in many essential areas, such as child functioning, the study will have missing data for these children. This type of study contributes to what is known about children with disabilities in areas such as demographic characteristics or family functioning, but makes only a limited contribution in the area of child outcomes, which is typically an important focus of the research.

Resources will almost certainly be a major determinant of how extensively children with disabilities can be included in a study. In that dream world of unlimited resources, every child with a disability could participate meaningfully in every aspect of the data collection. Similarly, all data collected from families could explore the commonalities as well as special circumstances associated with parenting a child with a disability. When resources are limited, however, decisions will need to be made in several interrelated design areas: research questions, sampling, and instrumentation. These decisions will determine the data available for analysis and, consequently, what can be learned from the study about children with disabilities. We begin by describing in general how children with disabilities have been included in three national studies and then use examples from these studies to discuss inclusion in more detail.

Early Childhood Longitudinal Study—Birth Cohort (ECLS-B)

The ECLS-B focuses on the relation of early health and development and experiences in the first few years of life to children's developmental status at school entry (see Chapter 12). The study is planning to follow a sample of 12,000 babies born in the year 2001 from birth through first grade. Children who are born with disabilities or who develop disabilities in the early years of life will be included and maintained in the sample. The sample for ECLS-B will also include an oversample of 3,000 very low and low-birth-weight babies. This oversample can be expected to increase the number of children with disabilities in the study since a disproportionate number of these babies are likely to be diagnosed later as having a disability. Estimates of the prevalence and incidence of disabilities in early childhood vary so it is difficult to predict the exact number of children in the ECLS-B sample who will be diagnosed as having a disability over the course of the study, but 3% to 10% of the sample ($n = 360$ to $1,200$) would be a reasonable estimate.

The National Evaluation of Early Head Start

The National Evaluation of Early Head Start (EHS), a program for birth to 3-year-olds and their families, includes a sample of approximately 3,000 families living in 17 diverse communities across the country (see Chapter 3). The evaluation is measuring a broad range of outcomes, collecting data on families' experiences with programs, and linking outcomes to experiences. The evaluation includes an implementation study to look at program implementation; an impact evaluation to examine the effects of EHS on children and families; local research studies designed by local researchers; and policy studies in topic areas such as welfare reform, fatherhood, and children with disabilities. To examine the impact of EHS, families were randomly assigned to the program group or the comparison group.

Early Head Start, like the Head Start Program, has a mandate that at least 10% of the children served be children with disabilities. The random assignment feature of the study design meant that children with disabilities could not be explicitly invited or recruited for program participation during study recruitment. It is possible that 10% of the sample will not be children with disabilities. Again, it is difficult to estimate how many of the EHS sample will be identified as having a disability in the first 36 months of life, but 10% of the EHS and the comparsion groups would be about 300 children who will be diagnosed with a disability over the course of the study. Ten percent would be an upper end estimate; 5% or less would be more likely. A group of researchers with expertise in disability research has been assisting the EHS evaluation with the design, data collection, and analysis issues related to disability

Early Childhood Longitudinal Study—Kindergarten Cohort (ECLS-K)

The ECLS-K is designed to provide descriptive data on children's status at entry to school and through the early years of elementary school (see Chapter 12). The study will also provide answers to a range of questions about the association between success in school and family, school, community and individual factors. The study is following a nationally representative sample of approximately 22,000 children who entered kindergarten in 1998–99. These children will be followed through fifth grade.

Kindergarten children with disabilities who were selected for the study will be retained in the sample, as will children who are identified over the course of the longitudinal study as having a disability. The first 6 years of school are the years over which increasing numbers of children are identified as needing special education especially for learning disabilities (U.S. Department of Education, 1998). Between 3,000 and 3,200 of the children in the ECLS-K sample are estimated to be identified as needing special education over the course of the study. One component of the design phase of ECLS-K involved the development of research questions for disability issues, an extensive review of all instrumentation from a disability perspective, and the development of an additional instrument for any sample child's special education provider (Hebbeler, Blackorby, McKenna, Gerlach-Downie, & Clayton, 1997).

Design and Methods

The following sections address design and analysis issues for large-scale studies that include children with disabilities and will draw extensively on examples from the three studies just described.

Research questions. A typical approach to examining variation for subgroups in the general population is to generate a series of secondary questions related to the primary research question. For example, the question "Did program participants show improved outcomes?" would have the following related questions: Were there differences by gender? by race/ethnicity? by language spoken in the home? by family structure? "Disability status" is certainly a characteristic that can and should join this list of variables. Researchers and practitioners concerned with childhood disability will want to see the principal study questions addressed for children with disabilities in comparison to the rest of the population. The study's research questions should include descriptive questions that address the ways in which children with disabilities and their families resemble or differ from the general population. They should also include explanatory questions that examine whether factors related in the general population (for example, poverty and school achievement) are also related for children with disabilities.

A full exploration of key areas of interest for children with disabilities, however, requires going beyond adding disability status as an independent variable to a list of other such variables. There are unique issues associated with disability that large-scale studies are especially well positioned to elucidate. Among these are age at onset of the disability, the identification process, and special services being received or received in the past because of the disability. These issues require the development of an additional set of research questions for children with disabilities.

For example, additional research questions for children with disabilities were formulated for the ECLS-K:

- How many and which children with disabilities receive special services prior to kindergarten? During kindergarten? Grade 1? (and so forth)
- What are the ages/grade levels at which children with different disabilities are identified as having a disability?
- At what ages/grade levels do they begin to receive special services?
- To what extent have children with disabilities participated in early intervention, preschool special education, and other special services prior to kindergarten?
- How much time do special education students spend in general education classrooms?

- What types of supports are provided to general education teachers who have special education students in their classrooms?
- To what extent do children with disabilities participate in typical recreational activities in their communities?

Similarly, a set of research questions unique to children with disabilities and their families has been developed for the evaluation of Early Head Start. These questions address identification, services, and coordination between Early Head Start and the local early intervention program that could be serving this same population.

Articulating the specific research issues the study will address is an extremely important part of the design process because the research questions drive the development of the instrumentation and the selection of measures. For example, the issue of inclusion of children with disabilities in community recreation in the ECLS-K sample (see research question above) is of considerable policy and philosophical significance because it reflects the move to integrate people with disabilities of all ages in the typical life of their community. Early drafts of the ECLS-K parent interview did not include questions about children's recreational activities. These items were added because of the research question about participation of children with disabilities in recreational activities listed above. These items are especially interesting examples because, to many people, survey items about participation in music lessons or soccer seem to have little to do with disability, and yet they are very germane to the issue of community integration for a 5-year-old.

A specific set of research questions articulating key disability concerns also can serve as a check throughout the design process to insure that the items or measures providing data for these questions are retained in the final version of the instrumentation. Justification for any given item can become especially important when early drafts of interviews or surveys turn out to be too lengthy, as often happens, and hard decisions have to be made about which items to delete.

Sampling. A large-scale study that does not specifically exclude children with disabilities is likely to have some of these children in the sample. Estimates of the prevalence of disability for a given age group vary widely depending on the age group and how disability is defined, as will be discussed in more detail later in this chapter. However, measures indicate that between 1% and 15% of children have a disability. Different disabilities are diagnosed at different ages throughout childhood; thus the percentage of children with disabilities in the population increases for each age group through the first decade or so of life. A small percentage of disabilities are identified at birth; others emerge over the first year of life. Between 2 and 5 years of age children typically become proficient communicators; those who do not are recognized as having a disability. Between 5 and 10, children are expected to master classroom subjects such as reading and mathematics as well as the behavioral expectations of the school setting. Those who have severe difficulties in one or more of these areas will also be identified as children with a disability.

One of the consequences of the phenomenon of disability prevalence increasing with age is that studies with representative samples of very young children will include a small number of children with identified disabilities even with a very large sample. The prevalence of disability among infants is very low compared to that for 10-year-olds. Inclusion of infants with disabilities in cross-sectional studies is important to generate nationally representative estimates. The study will be limited, however, with regard to what can be learned about young children with disabilities as a subpopulation because of the small sample size. In a longitudinal study, there will be more children who will be diagnosed as having a disability over the course of their childhood if the study follows them long enough. The ECLS-B will have more children with disabilities in the sample each year as the sample ages.

When researchers are interested in a particular population in a national study, the study design will involve oversampling when the sample size for this particular population will not be sufficient through regular sampling procedures. For instance, both the ECLS-B and ECLS-K have oversamples of certain populations. A major decision related to study design and children with disabilities is whether to oversample children with disabilities in general and some disability groups in particular.

In some studies, there is no option to oversample children with disabilities because there is no way to identify them through the sample selection procedures. In ECLS-B, for example, children are being selected for the study based on birth certificate data. Birth certificates are inconsistent with regard to reporting of disabilities and even if the data were perfect, the oversample would still consist only of disabilities identifiable at birth which would not be a representative sample of disabilities present in young children. ECLS-B is oversampling very low and low birth weight children, however. Since these children have a higher probability of developing a disability, the total number of children with disabilities in the sample should increase over time, and children with disabilities should be overrepresented to some degree.

The evaluation of Early Head Start also could not oversample children with disabilities because children were randomly assigned to program and comparison groups based on regular recruitment procedures. The Early Head Start programs could not have actively recruited families of children with disabilities or encouraged referrals from other programs or agencies knowing the families would have had to agree to take either the program or comparison group depending on their assignment.

Increasing sample size is especially important for some disability groups. Because there is more variability within the population of children with disabilities than in the general population, adequate sample sizes of children with different kinds of disabilities are desirable. "Children with disabilities" is not simply a subgroup of the general population; it is a subgroup made up of many other subgroups. These subgroups include children who are blind or deaf, or have orthopedic impairments or mental retardation. The heterogeneity within the population of children with disabilities poses substantial challenges for sampling and also for analysis. Research on the effectiveness of an intervention with children with disabilities has typically focused on a particular group of children with disabilities with similar characteristics, for example, children with Down Syndrome (Spiker & Hopmann, 1997), children with communication disorders (McLean & Cripe, 1997), or children with motor disabilities (Harris, 1997), because children with different disabilities differ significantly in their functional skills and limitations.

The variability within the population of children with disabilities is further complicated by the wide variation in incidence. Among 6-year-olds receiving special education, only 0.6% have a visual impairment compared to 67% with a communication disorder, 7.1% with mental retardation, or 1.3% with a hearing impairment (U.S. Department of Education, 1998). Analyses conducted as part of the design process for the ECLS-K showed that among the more than 3,000 children with disabilities projected to be in the sample (which is a very large number of children with disabilities), only 11 are projected to be children with visual impairments. Only 33 are projected to be children with hearing or orthopedic impairments whereas nearly 1,200 are expected to be children with communication disorders (Hebbeler et al., 1997). Even with a national sample of 22,000 five-year-olds that includes children with disabilities, the ECLS-K will be able to say very little about children with low-incidence disabilities such as blindness, deafness, autism, or orthopedic impairments.

In theory, the remedy to this problem is to oversample children with low-incidence disabilities. In reality, this can be very difficult (i.e., costly) to do with a sample that is drawing a single-age-year cohort because there are so few of these children and they are dispersed over many schools and school districts. There are less than 2,000 six-year-olds with visual impairments in the entire country.

The U.S. Department of Education explored the feasibility of oversampling four low-incidence groups for the ECLS-K but decided that the cost was too prohibitive relative to what would be learned. Subsequently, the department decided to fund a longitudinal study focusing solely on children with disabilities with a sample drawn from 6- through 12-year-olds (SRI International, 1999). Drawing from several age cohorts provides a way to get a sufficient number of even low-incidence disabilities clustered in a feasible number of school districts.

Measures

Large-scale studies typically include measures such as written surveys or phone interviews developed specifically for the study and other standardized measures such as the Bayley Scales of Infant Development or the Peabody Picture Vocabulary Test. Often, the surveys or interviews developed for the study include items or sets of items used in other studies. Challenges related to children with disabilities and instrumentation include the specific survey or interview items that will allow children with disabilities to be identified in the sample and described in subsequent analyses as well as the accommodations to the standardized measures that will allow children with disabilities to participate in the assessments.

Identifying and describing children with disabilities. A researcher interested in gender differences would not have a great deal of difficulty identifying the girls and boys in the sample since gender is a variable included in all major studies and can be reliably reported. And while race/ethnicity is considerably more complicated than gender as an independent variable or for identifying groups of children for special analyses, the researcher interested in race or ethnic issues can find much of the information needed to identify a given population in a few key survey items. The issue is far more complex for identifying children with disabilities in a large national sample. There is no single or even small set of marker variables that will effectively identify all children with disabilities. Approaches to identifying children with disabilities include using receipt of services or use of special equipment to indicate the presence of a disability, use of terminology that conveys the etiology of the disability or the resulting deficit, use of functional characteristics, and, lastly, perception of disability by others. These approaches are not mutually exclusive. Because each may identify slightly different sets of children, the more approaches a study uses, the more broadly the net will be cast for identifying who in the sample has a disability. Each of the approaches to identifying and describing disability will be described in turn.

Receipt of special services or use of special equipment is one way to identify children with disabilities in the sample. Those children receiving early intervention services (for children birth through age 3) or children receiving special education (for children age 3 through secondary school) are considered to be children with disabilities. In this approach, a program's definition or eligibility criteria define disability. ECLS-K, for example, will use school records to identify children receiving special education or related services. A shortcoming with this approach is that not all children with disabilities receive or are eligible for certain services such as special education or Supplemental Security Income (General Accounting Office, 1998). If the child's disability does not interfere with the child's ability to perform in the school, then the child is not eligible for special education. Also, if parents are being used as the primary source of information about receipt of special services, as they are in ECLS-B and EHS, parents sometimes do not realize that their child's services are special services. The parent knows the program as the "Peanut Butter and Jelly Preschool," not as an early intervention program for children with disabilities. Similarly, for older children, the parent might know the child goes to the speech therapist but might not think of this service as part of special education.

A second approach to identifying and describing disability is based on category labels or medical diagnoses. Children who have been given one of these labels by a medical or educational professional are considered to have a disability. This approach works best when the study has access to the program or professional that uses the label. For example, schools can provide the categorical description of why the child is receiving special education.

The federal legislation addressing special education, the Individuals with Disabilities Education Act (IDEA), identifies categories of students who are eligible to receive special education and related services in schools. Examples of these categories include learning disabilities, hearing impairments, health impairments, autism, and mental retardation. The IDEA categories or slight variations on them are used across the country because state and federal laws contain categories of disability and because states are required to report to the federal government on how many children in each category are being served. For research on school-age children with disabilities, this means that their special education records are likely to contain one or more of these categories as a descriptor of the child's disability. The ECLS-K will be collecting these categorical descriptors for sample members receiving special education.

The categorical approach to describing disability has several weaknesses. The categories do not work very well as descriptors of children because extreme variation exists within these categories due to differences in severity and because disability often has multiple dimensions. Consider children with cerebral palsy, which is a medical diagnosis and an example of classifying children with disabilities by etiology. Children with this diagnosis might have mild to severe motoric impairments as well as mild to severe communication disorders. The only things these disparate groups of children would have in common would be the etiology of their impairments, which is why etiology is of limited usefulness as a descriptor.

Another shortcoming of the categorical approach to disability is that it is ill-suited to survey methodology, especially interviews with parents. Parents need to be able to report reliably the label or labels which the medical or education profession has applied to their young child, which they might or might not be able to do reliably.

An alternative suggested by various authors is a multidimensional approach that looks at the functional characteristics of the child (Bailey, Simmeonsson, Buysse, & Smith, 1993; Hogan et al., 1997). The particular dimensions proposed differ across systems. The Bailey, Simmeonsson, Buysse, and Smith (1993) system, for example, looks at audition, behavior/social skills, limbs, intentional communication, tonicity, physical health, eyes, and structural status. The Hogan, Msall, Rogers, and Avery (1997) approach identifies self-care, mobility, communication, and learning ability as critical dimensions.

Both the ECLS-K and the EHS evaluation are collecting data on multiple functional dimensions. ECLS-K asks parents how their child compares to other children with regard to paying attention; learning, thinking and solving problems; activity level; use of limbs; pronunciation of words and communication; hearing; and vision. If the parent indicates a possible problem in an area then a series of follow-up questions is asked to see if the child has ever been evaluated by a professional for this problem, if a diagnosis was made, and if so, when. These items will provide comprehensive data on the general population of 5-year-olds and allow multidimensional descriptions of the nature of atypical development for children with disabilities.

The last approach involves looking at whether anyone in the child's environment considers the child to have a disability. This approach is well-grounded in disability rights and policy. The Americans with Disabilities Act (ADA) defines disability as any one of the following:

- A physical or mental impairment that substantially limits one or more major life activities of such individual
- A record of such impairment
- Being regarded as having such an impairment

The first part of the definition refers to the functional approach just described. The latter part of the definition refers to society's perception of the person as having a disability. The National Health Interview Survey (NHIS) is conducted annually to monitor the health, health care needs, and health care services of the nation. In 1994, NHIS contained a Disability Supplement with special questions about disability; two of these questions were as follows:

- Do you consider yourself (or anyone in your family) to have a disability?

- Would other people consider you (or anyone else in the family) to have a disability?

These items provide information about how the individual is perceived within the context of his or her family and by society at large which could be a salient aspect of disability for young children and their families.

The variety of approaches described demonstrate that identifying the children with disabilities in a large-scale national study is not a simple task nor is describing the nature of their disability. Some approaches will be better suited to some research issues than others. Studies of the cost of disability and disability services might be best served by defining disability in terms of the services received or the special equipment needed. Studies focusing on describing and explaining child growth and development will need a method for describing subcategories of children with disabilities. The functional approach provides the richest descriptive data about children with disabilities. Researchers interested in children with a particular diagnosis, such as children with autism, will want to be able to identify these children in the database. In sum, studies designed to meet multiple needs will best meet those needs with multiple approaches to the identification of disability.

Accommodations and alternate assessments. The use of standardized instruments, especially child assessments, is commonplace in large-scale studies. The benefits are numerous. The instrument has been well-researched, can be reliably administered, and provides data that can be compared across other studies. The set of strict rules for how the assessment is to be administered and scored allows for reliable administration. These same rules, however, often mean that the scores obtained by children with disabilities are not a reflection of their true skill level—if the assessment can be given at all.

The solution is to administer the assessment with accommodations or, for those few children with disabilities who will not be able to participate even with an accommodated assessment, to administer an alternate assessment. Research on accommodations for children with disability is in its very early stages (McDonnell, McLaughlin, & Morison, 1997). It has been driven by statewide testing programs for school-age children and, more recently, by federal requirements to include children with disabilities in these assessments. Much remains to be learned about the application of accommodations in general but especially to the assessment of young children.

An accommodation to the test procedures is intended to remove the distortions or biases caused by the child's disability. For a child with a disability, the test format, administration, or response procedures may interfere with the child's demonstration of true competencies. Accommodations are designed to improve the validity of scores for children with disabilities, not to give the child an advantage (ERIC/OSEP Special Project at ERIC Clearinghouse on Disabilities and Gifted Education, 1998). Examples of accommodations include varying how the assessment is presented (e.g., large print or magnification), how the child responds (e.g., signs the response), the setting (e.g., a specifically designed location), and scheduling (e.g., extended time). Critical issues related to using accommodations are which child gets which accommodation, who decides, and on what basis (Hollenbeck, Tindal, & Almond, 1998).

A common yet solvable problem in studies involving the assessment of young children is the use of a limited set of items from a larger battery. Sometimes studies assessing large numbers of children at the same age administer and train assessors on only age-appropriate items from a bigger battery. This is done on the assumption that these are the only items that will need to be presented because all the children are the same age. This can be an extremely efficient method for collecting data with typically developing children. For a child with a developmental delay, it could well mean a very low score at each measurement time point because the child is never being tested at an appropriate level. Modifying the testing procedures to allow administration of items at significantly lower age levels will provide the child with delayed development an opportunity to show competencies as well as growth over time.

Although little research on the effect of various accommodations with standardized tests for school-age children exists, there is even far less on assessments involving young children. Much more research is needed to identify appropriate accommodations and corresponding decision rules for their use with the standardized assessments commonly used in studies of young children. Those charged with designing and implementing large-scale studies need to, first, make every effort to select instrumentation that allows the broadest range of children to be assessed, thus bypassing the need for accommodations, and second, when accommodations are required, design and research these alternatives for the selected assessments.

During the design of the ECLS-K, a set of possible accommodations to the child assessment was developed with extensive input from a variety of disability experts. A special instrument asking about the child's limitations was developed for completion by the child's teacher. The information provided by the teacher served as the basis for identifying the appropriate accommodations for the child in the testing situation.

The EHS evaluation also includes accommodations for children with disabilities. The data collection included videotaped tasks of mother-child interaction. These tasks were differentially modified for children with visual impairments, hearing impairments, and physical impairments, with the intent of providing the mother and child with comparable task demands to those experienced by typically developing children.

For a small percentage of children with disabilities, no accommodations exist that will allow the child to be included in an assessment (Ysseldyke & Olsen, 1999). These are usually children with severe cognitive deficits and multiple impairments. For these children, an alternate assessment is needed to allow outcomes to be measured at a single time point and especially over time. The data will not be comparable to that of other children but a score on an alternate assessment is preferable to no measure of child development. For the ECLS-K, a special education teacher completed an alternate assessment for children who were unable to participate in the regular assessment because of the severity of their disabilities.

Analysis

If the issues around sampling, identification, and measurement of disability and around assessment have been well conceptualized and addressed in the design phase of the study, then the data analysis is relatively straightforward. The primary analytic challenge of identifying the children with disabilities in the sample should be based on specific items that were included in the instrumentation for this purpose. Similarly, describing children with disabilities or analyzing data for subgroups should be possible because the necessary variables have been included in the data collected. If children with disabilities in general or children with particular low-incidence disabilities or functional limitations have been oversampled, then a sufficient sample size to support analyses for these groups will be available.

The problem of missing data in the database for children with disabilities, especially assessment data, poses an analytic challenge. If children could not take part in the assessment and if there is no alternate assessment, then some segment of children with disabilities in the study will be missing data on one or more measures. When this situation occurs, researchers must describe and report the size and nature of the population for whom data could not be collected. Such a recommendation sounds so obvious as to be hardly worth writing, and yet, how often are data reported in the form "X% of the 5-year-olds could identify Y letters of the alphabet," while not noting that some percentage of the sample could not be administered the task?

For the unfortunate major study that has included children with disabilities in the sample but has not intentionally addressed how to adjust the study design to incorporate an appropriate set of measures and data items related to disability, the task at the analysis phase will be daunting. The researcher at that point can only make the best of whatever data are available.

The Next Generation of Studies of the General Population

Significant progress has been made toward including children with disabilities in the samples of important national studies of young children. More research needs to be done on the specifics of how to move beyond sample inclusion to complete inclusion in all aspects of the design. Vanderwood et al. (1998) have offered several recommendations for future studies:

- Develop inclusive sampling frames.
- Increase partial participation, for example, in data components that do not require a direct response from the child.
- Include children with disabilities during instrument development to identify items, tasks, and procedures that may need to be eliminated or modified to allow more children to participate (this recommendation could be expanded to the inclusion of families of children with disabilities as well).
- Develop a more uniform standard disability variable system.
- Include additional variables that better describe those individuals included in or excluded from national studies.

Many challenges and barriers exist when including children with disabilities in major national studies. However, innovations are evident in the three studies discussed above, the ECLS-B, the EHS evaluation, and the ECLS-K. They can be the foundation for even more progress by the next generation of large-scale national studies.

The next section describes a major national study that is following a sample of children who were identified as having a disability prior to age 3. The National Early Intervention Longitudinal Study and other studies of children with disabilities are an important complement to studies of the general population in that they allow disability issues to be explored in depth. They also may be the laboratory for the methodological advances necessary to solve some of the current dilemmas faced by studies of the general population.

NATIONAL EARLY INTERVENTION LONGITUDINAL STUDY (NEILS)

History

Before 1986, early intervention services for infants and toddlers were provided only in some states and only to some children with disabilities or developmental delays and their families in those states. The passage of Part H, now Part C, of the Individuals with Disabilities Education Act (IDEA), made the provision of early intervention services a national policy. In the decade that followed the passage of the law, states built or adapted early intervention systems in accordance with their understanding of the law's vision. According to data reported to the U.S. Department of Education, the number of infants and toddlers served in early intervention programs has grown steadily as the state's early intervention systems have developed (U.S. Department of Education, 1998). State evaluations and personal testimony have attested to some of the benefits and challenges associated with implementing this far-reaching legislation. However, much remains to be learned about Part C and the children and families who receive early intervention services under its auspices.

In January 1996, the Office of Special Education Programs (OSEP) funded SRI International, in conjunction with the Frank Porter Graham Child Development Center (FPGCDC) of the University of North Carolina at Chapel Hill, the Research Triangle Institute (RTI), and the American Institutes for Research (AIR), to conduct a longitudinal study of a nationally representative sample of children and families who are participating in early intervention services through Part C of IDEA. The first year of the National Early Intervention Longitudinal Study involved a design phase in which the overall study design, the sampling plan, and the instrumentation were developed. A national panel of advisors reviewed a preliminary design report and provided feedback.

The design of the NEILS is based on a conceptual framework that identified three key focal areas and their interrelationships as central to the study:

- The characteristics of children and families served in early intervention
- Early intervention services and service delivery
- The outcomes experienced by children and families who are served

NEILS is following a nationally representative sample of children from birth to 3 years of age and their families through and after their early intervention experiences. Current plans call for children and families to be followed from their entrance into early intervention until children are 5 years of age.

The context of Part C. Unprecedented legislative and societal initiatives on behalf of individuals with disabilities characterize the past several decades. The Americans with Disabilities Act has defined broad principles of equality of opportunity, economic self-sufficiency, full participation, and independence to ensure the full citizenship of children and adults with disabilities. Public Law 94-142, in a similar manner, reaffirmed society's commitment that all students with disabilities have the right to a free and appropriate public education. A particularly ambitious legislative initiative was embodied in the Infants and Toddlers with Disabilities Program (Part H, now Part C) of P.L. 99-457, which articulated an agenda that would provide early intervention and family support services to prevent or reduce the potential impact of disabilities for infants and young children and their families (Safer & Hamilton, 1993). Taken together, these national mandates define a comprehensive approach to promote the development and quality of life of infants, children, youth, and adults with disabilities through individualized programs of services to reduce or prevent the impacts of impairment or disabilities.

Part C provided federal funds to assist states in planning and implementing a system of early intervention services. The four purposes of this federal program are:

- To develop and implement a statewide, comprehensive, coordinated, multidisciplinary, interagency early intervention program
- To facilitate the coordination of payment for these services from federal, state, local, and private sources
- To expand and enhance the quality of early intervention services
- To identify, evaluate, and meet the needs of historically underrepresented populations, particularly minority, low-income, inner-city, and rural populations

Part C is a unique federal program in many ways. The program's primary intent was to fund the coordination of federal, state, and local programs serving infants and toddlers, rather than to provide actual services (Florian, 1995; Harbin et al., 1998). The law has a strong family orientation that encompasses the resources, priorities, and concerns of the families of eligible children as they relate to the needs of the child. The law allowed states some discretion in who they would define as the eligible Part C population. The federal law defines the eligible population as any child under 3 years of age who (a) is experiencing developmental delay (criteria to be determined by the states), or (b) has a diagnosed condition with a high probability of resulting in a developmental delay, or (c) is at risk for experiencing developmental delay if early intervention services are not provided. The third category of children is served at the state's discretion and only a few states (less than 10) have ever opted to include them in their eligible population for early intervention.

Implementation of Part C. What is known about how Part C is being implemented and its intended beneficiaries across the nation? Data from the Office of Special Education indicate that more children are being served in early intervention each year (U.S. Department of Education, 1998). These same data show wide variation across states in the percentage of the population being served. Some states are serving more than 5% of their birth-to-age-three population in early intervention. Others are serving less than 1%.

Given the latitude Part C allows states, one could expect to find substantial and potentially important variation in the way in which early intervention programs have been implemented at the state and local level. In fact, variability among states in terms of their implementation of P.L. 99-457, has been reported (Bailey, Aytch, Odom, Symons, & Wolery, 1999; Gallagher, Harbin, Eckland, & Clifford, 1994; Hebbeler, 1997). Some of the potentially significant ways in which states and localities differ include the following:

- The wide diversity of family circumstances, resources, priorities, and plans for their children
- The diverse backgrounds, traditions, and approaches of the variety of professions that are involved in providing early intervention services
- The history of early intervention service provision, including which agencies and how many agencies have provided services to this population
- The different levels and stages of agency readiness, willingness, and financial capacity to implement the Part C program

What is not known, however, is how these variations may be related to the type and quantity of services provided, the quality of service delivery, and the outcomes experienced by children and families.

The Early Childhood Research Institute on Service Utilization studied early intervention service provision in nine communities in three states. Their findings indicate that the median amount of scheduled early intervention services was 1.8 hours per week, but that 1.3 hours were actually provided. Approximately one-third of the families studied received all of the services they were scheduled to receive. Infants were primarily served in their homes and in center-based programs, whereas toddlers were served in centers and in other community-based settings. Children of families in which mothers had more education and higher annual incomes were more likely to be served in integrated settings and to have received a higher proportion of therapeutic services (Harbin et al., 1998). These findings begin to paint a descriptive picture of the provision of early intervention services. However, they are based on 157 families and may not generalize beyond the nine communities in which these families reside.

In sum, little is known nationally about the provision of early intervention services and outcomes for children and families. States vary in how they have structured and implemented their early intervention systems (Hebbeler,

Spiker, Wagner, Cameto, & McKenna, 1999). Far more information is needed to understand what that variation means for children and families participating in the program. Much remains to be learned about both the process of delivering early intervention services and the associated outcomes. Information is needed on who is participating in the program, the services they are receiving, where those services are being provided and by whom, the cost of services, and the outcomes children and families are experiencing. These questions have been answered for early intervention in controlled research settings, in specific states, or for small samples, but they have not been answered for early intervention as it is being implemented today across the country.

Goals

NEILS is addressing four key study questions:

- Who are the children and families served in early intervention?
- What early intervention services do participating children and families receive and what are the costs of these services?
- What outcomes do participating children and families experience?
- How do outcomes relate to variations in child and family characteristics and services received?

Theory of Change

The overall goals of the Part C legislation are to optimize and improve the development of young children with disabilities and to support families' ability to promote the child's development through the provision of early intervention services. It is hypothesized that the child's development will be optimized over what it would have been without such services for children and families.

The study's approach to answering these questions is guided by a conceptual framework consisting of several related components (see Figure 11.1). This framework reflects a transactional/ecological perspective, which holds that development in young children with disabilities is influenced by many interrelated factors, including those that are biological (e.g., genetic disorders), social (e.g., family members' interactions with the child), environmental (e.g., the toys available in the home), and cultural (e.g., the family's traditions and beliefs about child rearing). Similarly, family systems theory views the family as a system that is influenced by many factors, including its composition, resources and supports available, the community in which it lives, and the family's beliefs and expectations. A critical feature of a transactional model

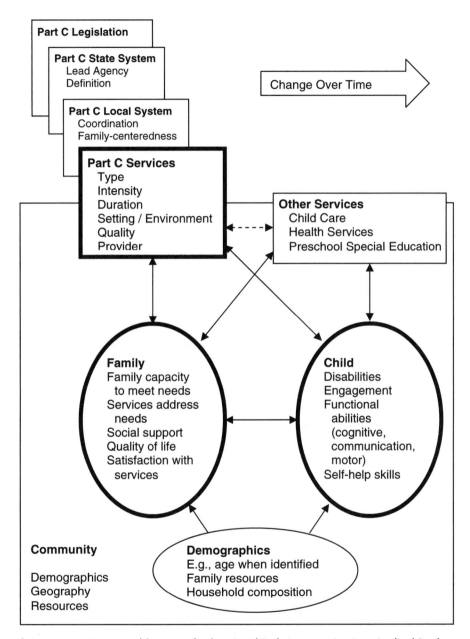

Figure 11.1. Conceptual framework of National Early Intervention Longitudinal Study.

is the assumption that influences between the child and family are recipro-cal. The family exerts significant influence over the child's development, but the child also influences the family through a need for care, the child's temperament, and so on. Components of the framework are described below.

Children and families. Describing the children and families in early inter-vention programs is one of the primary goals of the study. Understanding who they are is critical to understanding what happens to them during and after their early intervention experiences. The nature of children's abilities and disabilities will be a particularly important construct for nearly all of the NEILS analyses. The International Classification of Impairments, Dis-abilities, and Handicaps system (ICIDH; World Health Organization, 1980) provides the framework for this description. Critical family variables include size, structure (parents married, divorced, never married, and so on), whether there is another child with a disability in the household, parental ages, race/ethnicity, languages spoken in the home, income level, receipt of public as-sistance, and the employment and education level of parents.

Children and families are intended to benefit from their participation in early intervention. Thus, documenting the outcomes experienced by children and families is another important goal of the study. Child outcomes mea-sured in the study include the following:

- Developmental accomplishments in the domains of functional mobil-ity; independence in feeding, dressing, and toileting; expressive and receptive communication; and object and social play
- Functioning with regard to vision and hearing and the use of hands, arms, legs, and feet—descriptive characteristics of both the child and child outcomes
- Child engagement—how children interact with their environment, including distractibility, independence, activity level, and persistence
- Child behavior—behavioral aspects of infancy and toddlerhood, in-cluding playing with other children, aggressiveness, temper tantrums, and difficulties related to sleep
- Need for continued early intervention service
- Progress toward outcomes specified in the Individualized Family Ser-vice Plan (IFSP)
- The extent to which parents report that early intervention makes a difference in the child's life
- Parental reports of the child's quality of life
- Need for special education
- Academic achievement in early elementary school

NEILS examines two broad types of family outcomes (see Bailey et al., 1998). The first type of outcome refers to the family's perception of the early intervention experience:

- The services the child and family receive (e.g., service quantity and quality, degree of individualization, focus on the child's strengths vs. difficulties)
- Early intervention professionals who work with the child and family (e.g., the number of professionals and the communication among them, respect accorded the family, cultural competence)

The second type of family outcome refers to the perceived impact of the services on the family:

- The extent to which early intervention makes a difference in the family's life
- The extent to which early intervention enables the family to help their child grow, learn, and develop
- The family's ability to work with professionals and advocate for services
- The family's support system
- The family's view of the future
- The family's quality of life

Early intervention services. The framework depicts the services delivered to the child and family as one of the factors influencing outcomes for both children and families. Children and families are also hypothesized to exert influence on the nature of services they receive. Presumably, families and children with more intense needs would receive different kinds or amounts of service than those with fewer needs. The following dimensions of services are being measured in the study:

- Type of service (e.g., speech/language therapy)
- Location of service (e.g., home, center)
- Provider of the service (e.g., nurse, physical therapist)
- Quantity of service (e.g., minutes received in the past 6 months)
- Duration of service (e.g., number of months over which service was provided)

Other services. In addition to early intervention, the family receives other services that also are hypothesized to influence child and family outcomes. Health care and child care services are examples of such services that are being measured in NEILS.

Contextual factors. The family's services and the local service system are shown as occurring in the context of multiple levels of implementation, including features of the federal law and regulations, the state-level translation of the law, and other state contextual factors.

The interactions between early intervention and other services and the child and family are embedded in and influenced by community-level factors, such as demographics (e.g., urbanicity), geography, and resources. For example, communities with high unemployment may have many families with limited financial resources who are experiencing high stress levels, which may result in less-than-optimum child development. These same communities may have few resources for services and thus may provide more limited or lower quality early intervention services than communities with greater resources. This, too, would be hypothesized to produce less-than-optimum child development. Thus community factors are seen as potentially affecting the child through the family and through the services provided.

Change over time. One final feature of the framework is its longitudinal nature. The study design recognizes that all the components change over time. Children's outcomes will change as they develop; multiple dimensions of family status also can change as children age and as families have more experience with early intervention. The nature of the early intervention services provided also is likely to change as children move from infancy through toddlerhood. Longer term outcomes for children and families also are of interest. In addition to looking at the status of early intervention recipients over the course of program participation, the study will examine later outcomes for children and families, especially at the end of the preschool years and in early elementary school.

Design and Methods

Sampling. A nationally representative sample of 3,338 children and their families from 94 counties in 20 states has been enrolled in NEILS. The children and their families were recruited as they entered early intervention for the first time. Families were recruited for the study if the child was between birth through age 31 months. Part C continues until the child is 3 years of age, but NEILS enrollment excluded children who entered early intervention after 31 months of age because these children would receive few services before they would transition out of the program. The design calls for longitudinal follow-up until the children turn 3 years of age (when early intervention services end), with additional assessment at age 5. The sample size was determined to be sufficient to draw meaningful conclusions through the children's fifth birthdays. The NEILS sample design is described briefly below. For more detailed information, see Hebbeler and Wagner (1998).

State sample. The state sample was selected to maximize variations among states on important dimensions that influence early intervention. A sample of 20 states was considered adequate to represent the variations desired. An examination of the state-reported counts of children served on December 1, 1995, showed that the nine states serving the largest numbers of children under Part C accounted for approximately 60% of the participants in Part C nationally (U.S. Department of Education, 1997). These states were selected for the NEILS sample with certainty. To select the remaining states, the country was divided into three regions, and an additional 11 states were selected randomly from these regions with probability proportional to the size of the states' birth-to-age-3 population. All states selected agreed to participate in the study.

A target number of children to recruit for NEILS was assigned to each state by allocating the total sample to each region and then to each sampled state proportionate to the number of children served in Part C. The sample size for two less-populated states was increased further to ensure that a reasonable number of children were representing each state. The identified target sample sizes for individual states ranged from 46 to 389.

County sample. The concept of "local community" for Part C services has many meanings because of the tremendous within-state variation in how early intervention services are organized and delivered. States are divided into local jurisdictions for the provision of services, but the nature and size of the jurisdictions differ from state to state. Because a uniform sampling unit was required across all states, the county was identified as the geographic unit for sampling. The county was identified as the local sampling unit because county boundaries are clear and many public agencies are organized around county lines.

Three to five counties initially were selected randomly for each state, the probability of selection being proportional to the size of the birth-to-age-3 population in the county, with the additional criterion that at least 10 new children were projected to be served in early intervention in a year in the county. This latter provision was necessary for efficiency and cost-effectiveness in sample recruitment efforts.

A total of 83 counties initially were selected within the 20 states. Three of the originally selected counties declined to participate in the study and were replaced with previously identified alternates within the state. Eleven other counties were added late in the recruitment period when it became clear that some counties were recruiting families at a slower rate than predicted and that the total expected sample size might not be achieved.

Representing both urban and nonurban areas adequately was of particular analytic interest to the study. Using census counts of children residing in rural and nonrural areas and U.S. Department of Education data on children served in Part C, it was estimated that the sample would include 400 children from rural counties.

Each state's target sample was allocated to the counties to approximate the ideal of giving each child in Part C an equal probability of being selected. The size of the sample allocated to individual counties ranged from 4 to 134.

Child sample. To recruit the sample of children, all "points of entry" in the sampled counties were contacted and asked to recruit families for the study. A point of entry (POE) is any program or agency by which a family could enter into the early intervention system in a county. Some counties have a single point of entry, whereas others have multiple locations where families can enter early intervention. Some counties with multiple points of entry are divided into smaller geographic units, with each unit having a single POE. Other counties have multiple entry points that cover the same geographic area but serve different types of children. A total of 193 POEs recruited children for the study.

The recruitment period for the study was September 1997 through November 1998. POEs in the sampled counties recruited for as long as necessary to reach their target numbers. The recruitment period for counties ranged from 2 to 15 months.

POEs were asked to provide a small amount of information on all families enrolling in early intervention during the site's recruitment period so that the study could describe briefly the full population of children and families that enrolled in early intervention, regardless of whether they agreed to participate in NEILS. However, a lower-than-expected number of enrollment forms at some sites suggested that these sites may not have reported data on all enrolling families as they were instructed. Alternatively, shortfalls in enrollment may have resulted because projections were derived from state-reported enrollment data, which are known to be variable in definition and accuracy across states. In either case, NEILS data may not generalize to the entire population of children and families receiving early intervention, although the size of any discrepancy is unknown.

Programs were asked to invite into the study only families who had never received early intervention services for the target child. Among these families, only families who lived in the sample counties, whose child was less than 31 months of age, and who had either an English- or Spanish-speaking adult in the household were eligible for the study. If a family had more than one child eligible for early intervention (e.g., twins or triplets), only one child was eligible for the study. Overall, 85% of the families who were reported by points of entry as enrolling in early intervention during the recruitment period at their site were eligible for the study by these criteria. Seventy-one percent of the families invited to be in the study agreed to participate.

Data collection. Data were gathered for the study at enrollment from repeated family telephone interviews continuing through children's third birthdays, from early intervention professionals who are knowledgeable about services provided to individual children and families, and through mailed surveys of other early intervention professionals serving NEILS families and directors of programs or agencies that employ them. Additional data collected from program directors will support an examination of expenditures on early intervention. Additional data collection is occurring when children are age 5.

Enrollment data. Enrolling programs completed a one-page form on all families who entered early intervention for the first time. The form requested information on the child's date of birth, race/ethnicity, gender, whether there was a phone in the home, whether the child was in foster care, whether the family received public assistance, the nature of the condition or delay for which the child was eligible for early intervention, and the dates of referral and signing of the Individualized Family Service Plan (IFSP).

These data address important questions about the children and families enrolling in early intervention, such as the average age at which children with different apparent disabilities, delays, or risk factors are enrolled in early intervention, and some of the demographic characteristics of their families.

Additional information was collected from families who agreed to participate in the study, including the name and location information of the adult best able to answer questions about the child, and the name and location information of an early intervention professional best able to provide information about services provided to the child and family.

Family interviews. Each family was interviewed by telephone shortly after agreeing to be in the study, at anniversaries of enrollment until the child was 32 months of age, and at the child's third birthday. Interviews are conducted regardless of whether the child and family remain in early intervention. Follow-up interviews are also conducted when the child reaches age 5. Topics addressed in the family interview include demographic information, child's development and behavior, the child's vision, hearing, and mobility, early intervention services provided and parent's perception of those services, and the child's participation in child care and preschool. Interviews are conducted with the family member identified as most knowledgeable about the child and the child's early intervention services. Families without telephones are sent a postcard with the toll-free telephone number for the study and are encouraged to call and arrange an interview at a time and phone number that is convenient for them.[2] Computer-assisted telephone interviewing (CATI) guides the questioning sequence. Enrollment interviews lasted an average of 38 minutes. Interim interviews are marginally shorter, and interviews at third birthdays are slightly longer.

Families who are not reached by telephone for an interview within a specified time period are sent a 12-page mail questionnaire that contains key questions from the telephone interview.

Service records. When a family enrolled in the study, the recruitment staff person at the enrolling program identified the early intervention professional who is the most knowledgeable about the services the family receives. At the end of each 6-month period after the first IFSP is completed, this identified professional is mailed a "Service Record," which collects information on the early intervention services for the child and family in the preceding 6 months. Information collected includes the type, location, and amount of serves provided each week, the kind of professional providing services, extent of child's delay or disability, and the child's progress. If a child changes programs during a 6-month period, a provider from each program that served the child and family during the time period is sent a Service Record.

When the child reached his or her third birthday, a special version of the Service Record asked for the same information about services as the regular form but also what services the child and family expected to need on leaving early intervention and whether the child would be receiving special education and related services through the local school system.

Service provider surveys. The first Service Record sent to the early intervention professional most knowledgeable about services provided to a child and family included a form for the respondent to provide the names of all the other early intervention professionals who worked with the child or family during their first 6 months in early intervention. Each of these individuals was sent a Service Provider Survey. Service providers report on their background, training, and experience; the number and kind of clients they serve; the types and setting of their services; and perceptions of the services in the area.

Program director surveys. The Program Director Survey is mailed to the director of each of the programs that employ an early intervention professional who served a NEILS family in their first 6 months in early intervention, as reported by the professional who completed the first Service Record for each child and family. Program Director surveys include similar information to the Service Provider survey, as well as questions about the number and types of employed and contracted personnel in their program.

Current Status

Children and families entered the NEILS sample over a 14.5-month period in 1997–1998, and much of the data collection is tied to when they enter the study. Thus each stage of data collection extends over more than a year.

Family enrollment interviews were conducted from November 1997 through February 1999. Interviews with families of children turning 3 years of age extended from June 1998 through February 2002. Family interviews for children turning 5 years old are being conducted annually in the fall from 2000 through 2004.

Mailing of Service Records began in March 1998. Data collection for Service Records covering the first 6 months of early intervention participation were completed in 1999. Service Records were sent as long as children remained in early intervention.

The Service Provider and Program Director Survey administration was conducted from October 1998 through spring 2000.

Units of Analysis

Findings from NEILS will be reported as the various data collection components and waves are completed, with the first findings regarding characteristics of children and families who enroll in early intervention available in the first NEILS Data Report (Hebbeler et al., 2001). Findings will be disseminated in a variety of formats including presentations, technical reports, journal articles, and the NEILS Web site (http://www.sri.com/neils).

The analytic strategies will focus on children and families as the units of analysis. Child variables such as type of disability, functional characteristics, and gender will be analyzed within the context of family variables such as ethnicity and poverty. These data will then be nested within community variables such as urbanicity and poverty of a community. State variables related to the administration of the Part C system (e.g., designated lead agency, service delivery models, service delivery agencies) will also be used to examine the influence of system variations on child and family outcomes and service provision.

Because Part C is a legally mandated national program, there is no control group for comparison purposes. The analytic approach will be to examine variations in the associations among key constructs in order to generate hypotheses for explanatory verification.

Limitations

The limitations of NEILS relate to the sample and the data collection strategies. Demonstrating that the sample enrolled and retained for follow-up is nationally representative of all children and their families receiving early intervention services will be difficult because the characteristics of the population in early intervention are unknown. For instance, we can compare the family background characteristics of the NEILS sample to national census data, but the population of children and families receiving early intervention services may not be representative of the general population.

Since NEILS is relying exclusively on parent interviews and provider and director written surveys, some types of information may be somewhat limited or unavailable. For instance, the parent interviews provide limited information about such issues as the quality of the home environment, parent-child interactions, or child care arrangements. Additionally, the data about child functioning is based on parent report and service provider ratings (and later on teacher ratings) without direct assessment of the children.

Public Use Files

The NEILS database will be made available publicly at the completion of various data collection phases of the study.

CONCLUSION

In conclusion, a decade from now what is known about the development of young children with disabilities, their families, and their services will have increased substantially because of studies such as those described in this chapter. Hopefully, not only will we know more about children with disabilities, but we will also know more about how to design large-scale studies that include children with disabilities in the sample, ask and answer meaningful research questions about childhood disability, describe disability in adequate and comparable terms across studies, and collect valid data on child development and school achievement for all children including those who are developing atypically. Much work remains to be done to achieve these goals.

NOTES

We would like to acknowledge and thank the families of children with special needs who have so graciously agreed to be part of NEILS. We also would like to thank the service providers and directors of early intervention programs around the country who recruited the families for the study and found time in their busy schedules to complete NEILS data forms.

1. The principal investigators of NEILS are Kathleen Hebbeler, Donna Spiker, Sangeeta Mallik (SRI International); Susan Kinsey (RTI); Don Bailey, Robin McWilliam, Rune Simeonsson, Anita Scarborough (FPGCDI); Jay Chambers, JoAnne Lieberman (AIR). NEILS is funded by the Office of Special Education Programs (OSEP), cooperative agreement #H159E50001 (U.S. Department of Education), and conducted by SRI International; Frank Porter Graham Child Development Institute (FPGCDI) (UNC-Chapel Hill); Research Triangle Institute (RTI); and American Institutes for Research (AIR). For more information see http://www.sri.com/neils on-line.

2. If the adult respondent for the enrolled child is deaf, the telephone interview is conducted through a sign language interpreter whose services are arranged for by the early intervention program that serves the family and paid for by NEILS.

CHAPTER 12

Four New National Longitudinal Surveys on Children

ALLISON SIDLE FULIGNI, LISA MCCABE,
SARA MCLANAHAN, AND JODIE ROTH

National data sets have been used by policy makers and social scientists for decades. The United States Population Census is the most familiar source for data on the national population, although other surveys draw random samples of the population which provide data that can be generalized to the national population. Oversampling of certain groups provides estimates for those subpopulations. Policy makers must know the status of the population for whom they are writing legislation, and can use nationally representative longitudinal studies to track the impacts of policies and policy change on the population. Social scientists also use nationally representative data sets to assess trends in human behaviors, and interactions between person-level characteristics, relationships, life events, and characteristics of the settings in which people live (family, neighborhood, community, and government).

Attention to young children in large national data sets is a relatively new phenomenon. Until recently, most of the child-focused archived data sets were the classic early longitudinal studies, which were initiated in the 1920s and 1930s (e.g., the Terman Study, the Fels Study, the Harvard Medical School Study of Adult Development). But as children have become a larger proportion of the poor population in this country, as the immigrant population includes many more children and adolescents, as family structure is becoming less traditional, and as new research on early development documents the importance of the early years for later developmental outcomes, the addition of young children to national data sets has become an important endeavor (Brooks-Gunn, Berlin, Leventhal & Fuligni, 2000; Brooks-Gunn et al., 1991). In the 1960s, a number of large-scale, often nationally representative, studies were begun by economists and sociologists who were interested in (a) labor market experiences (the National Longitudinal Studies [NLS]; Wolpin, 1987); (b) income and work (the Panel Study of Income Dynamics [PSID]; Duncan & Morgan, 1985); or (c) educational achievement and attainment (High School and Beyond and the Class of 1972 studies; Coleman, Hoffer, & Kilgore, 1981). These were long-term longitudinal studies of individuals and families, typically starting with adolescents or adults. Almost nothing was collected on children in the first decade of life (Chase-Lansdale, Mott, Brooks-Gunn, & Phillips, 1991). A major breakthrough occurred when the National Longitudinal Study of Youth (NLSY) added a child supplement. Here, for perhaps the first time in the United States, was a sample of children who were being assessed through the childhood years, as women in the NLSY who became mothers were followed in conjunction with their offspring (Chase-Lansdale et al., 1991). While limited in the amount of information collected on developmental processes, this data set provided the first glimpse into the lives of young children on a large scale (Baydar & Brooks-Gunn, 1991). These data have been used to study effects of income, child care, maternal education, parental work status, receipt of child support, welfare receipt, family structure, birth of siblings, and neighborhood residence upon children's math and reading achievement as well as on their behavior problems (as reported by their mothers).

Since the addition of a child supplement to the NLSY, we have seen in the past decade the addition of child portions or child supplements to several ongoing national longitudinal studies, and even the creation of a few large-scale longitudinal studies with national samples that focus specifically on early childhood.

In this chapter, we provide detailed profiles of four major, current, national longitudinal studies focusing on young children. The Early Childhood Longitudinal Studies (ECLS), follow two large cohorts of children—one from birth (ECLS-B)[1] and one from kindergarten entry (ECLS-K)[2]—and track their experiences and development in several different contexts. The Fragile Families and Child Wellbeing Study[3] follows a sample of married and unwed couples from the birth of their child through the child's fourth birthday, and focuses on new births to unwed parents, examining effects of welfare and child support laws on these "fragile families." The Child Development Supplement of the Panel Study of Income Dynamics (PSID-CDS)[4] adds detailed information on children's multiple environments to the ongoing longitudinal data on economic and demographic information which has been collected since 1968. Each of these studies provides rich data on children's social, emotional, cognitive, and health status; the multiple settings (school, child care, and home) in which they develop; and community-level information such as social and educational services, expenditures, and policies.

EARLY CHILDHOOD LONGITUDINAL
STUDY—BIRTH COHORT (ECLS-B)

History

The Early Childhood Longitudinal Study—Birth Cohort is part of the U.S. Department of Education, National Center for Education Statistics (NCES) longitudinal studies program that also includes the Early Childhood Longitudinal Study—Kindergarten Cohort (to be discussed in the following section). Research on early brain development demonstrating the critical importance of the early years for later child outcomes encouraged NCES to include a study that follows children from birth in the longitudinal studies program. Additionally, the lack of longitudinal research looking at multiple domains (e.g., health care, child characteristics, nonparental care) across a nationally representative birth cohort lead to the development of the ambitious ECLS-B project.

Along with NCES, collaborators for the ECLS-B include the National Center for Health Statistics, the National Institutes of Health (NIH; with funding from the National Institute of Child Health and Human Development, Office of the Director, the National Institute of Mental Health, the National Institute of Nursing Research, the National Institute on Aging and the Office of Behavioral Social Sciences Research), the U.S. Department of Agriculture, the Administration on Children, Youth, and Families, the Office of Special Education Programs, the Division of Nutrition and Physical Activity/Centers for Disease Control and Prevention, the Administration for Children and Families, and the Office of Minority Health.

Current Status

Field testing for ECLS-B began in the latter half of 1999. The full-scale study, including approximately 13,500 children born in 2001, recruited participants and collected initial data from birth certificates. The first home visits, conducted when the children were 9 months old, began in late 2001. Data collection will continue until the children reach first grade.

Goals

ECLS-B aims to provide both descriptive and analytic data to an audience that includes researchers as well as practitioners who work with families. Specifically, the ECLS-B gathers descriptive information about children's health status; experiences in a variety of contexts including home, nonparental child care, and formal school; and children's development and growth through first grade. Analytic data will focus on three main areas of interest: (a) children's growth and development in critical domains (e.g., physical, cognitive, social, emotional, and language development); (b) transitions to nonparental care, early childhood education programs, and kindergarten; and (c) school readiness. More information about specific research questions of interest can be obtained from the ECLS-B Web site (http://nces.ed.gov/ecls/Birth/agency.asp).

Theory of Change

The ECLS-B study operates based on the premise that preparation for entry into formal school settings begins at or before birth and continues throughout early childhood. The designers also place an emphasis on investigating the whole child using a multifactor model that includes multiple ecological contexts. In this way, interactions among child and family characteristics, health status and care, nonparental care, and community characteristics can be explored, especially as they relate to school readiness.

Design and Methods

The nationally representative ECLS-B sample was identified through birth certificates and includes approximately 13,500 children born in the year 2001. Six groups of children were oversampled: Asians, Pacific Islanders, and Native American Indians, moderately low birth-weight infants (1,500–2,500 grams), very low birth-weight babies (less than 1,500 grams), and twins.

This longitudinal study will follow children from birth through the end of first grade, with data collection at 9, 18, 30, and 48 months, kindergarten, and first grade. Data collection consists of both child assessments and a primary caregiver interview at each time point. In addition, at 9 months and two other times yet to be determined, residential and nonresidential fathers will be asked to fill out a questionnaire.

Information will also be gathered from the child's nonparental caregivers and teachers. At 18 and either 30 or 48 months, early childhood program caregivers and teachers will be interviewed by phone, and quality of care will be observed on a subsample of 1,200 children. In kindergarten and first grade, school administrators and teachers will be contacted for information about the child and the school environment.

Measures

Because this study intends to focus on the whole child, measures from a variety of domains are included. Information such as date of birth is gathered from birth certificates. During home visits, children are assessed for physical growth, cognitive development, psychomotor and perceptual development, language development, behavioral development, emotional regulation, and socioemotional development. Mother-child interaction is also measured. In addition, parent (or primary caregiver) interviews are designed to collect data on pregnancy, parenting behaviors and attitudes, child care, child and family health, neighborhood and home environment, welfare use, and demographic characteristics of the family. The father questionnaires focus on the father's experiences with the child, knowledge and attitudes about parenting, and his relationship with his spouse/partner.

Child care providers and preschool teachers will provide information about their own background, experience, and teaching practices, as well as data about the individual child's development and learning environment. From school administrators and teachers, information about physical and organizational characteristics of the school, education philosophies, and programs will be gathered in addition to data about the child's cognitive and social development.

Unit of Analysis

Data at the individual, family, community, and school levels will be collected. Planned analyses will focus on exploring the relations among child characteristics, family characteristics, the child's early experiences in home and nonparental care, and the child's readiness for and transition to school.

Findings

As data collection is in preliminary stages, no results are yet available.

Limitations

As with any longitudinal study, the biggest limitation of ECLS-B is the potential problem of attrition. Given the length of the proposed study, it is likely that some families will decline or be unable to participate in the full investigation, resulting in a biased sample.

Earlier in the history of this study, a decision regarding whether to gather information from nonresidential fathers had not yet been made. Since the designers of ECLS-B decided to include nonresidential fathers in the study, information about a key facet of children's early development will be collected, averting a potential limitation in the data.

Finally, the inclusion of twins in the sample poses unique problems with regard to the use of some child assessment measures. For example, the NCAST Teaching Task is designed to be implemented with a caregiver and one child. Such a measure may not as accurately assess the quality of typical parent-child interaction for families in which the parent regularly interacts with twins. The ECLS-B designers, however, have spent time addressing this issue and plan to adapt and field test this measure for use with triadic interactions (mother, twin, twin).

Public Use Files

The first set of data files, including the 9-month parent interview, child assessment data, and the father questionnaire, are scheduled to be released by NCES in the spring of 2003 or 2004. Data will continue to be made available to the public throughout the course of the investigation, approximately one year after the end of data collection.

EARLY CHILDHOOD LONGITUDINAL STUDY—KINDERGARTEN COHORT (ECLS-K)

History

The Early Childhood Longitudinal Study—Kindergarten Cohort was conceived out of the recognition of the lack of systematic information available about young children's experiences as they enter formal schooling and progress through the elementary grades. ECLS-K was designed to provide nationally representative information about children entering kindergarten, as well as representative information about their teachers and kindergarten programs.

The primary funding for ECLS-K comes from the U.S. Department of Education, National Center for Education Statistics. Additionally, financial and technical support are provided by the Administration on Children, Youth, and Families (ACYF), U.S. Department of Education, and the U.S. Department of Agriculture.

Current Status

An extensive design phase and large-scale field test were conducted in the 1996–1997 school year by the National Opinion Research Center. The contract for the actual ECLS-K data collection was awarded to Westat,[5] and data collection for the base year of the study began with kindergartners in the fall of 1998 ($N = 22,000$). Follow-up data were collected in the spring of 1999 and the children will be followed through the spring of 2004 (the end of fifth grade). Three reports have been released. *America's Kindergartners* (West, Denton, & Germino Hauksen, 2000) and *The Kindergarten Year* (West, Denton, & Reaney, 2001) report on children's knowledge and skills at the beginning and end of kindergarten, for all children, and with respect to individual differences in children according to age at school entry, race/ethnicity, health, educational experiences at home, and child care histories. *Children's Reading and Mathematics Achievement in Kindergarten and First Grade* (Denton & West, 2002) provides a follow-up report with first-grade data (see http://nces.ed.gov/pubsearch/index.asp).

Goals

ECLS-K will provide information on a nationally representative sample of young children including their status upon kindergarten entry, their initial transition to school, and their adaptation through fifth grade. In addition to this descriptive information on the nation's children, ECLS-K is designed to enable comparisons of the school success of groups of children based on numerous family, community, school, and individual variables.

The study has three major areas of focus: children's transition to school; their schooling and performance in the early grades; and interactions between school, family, and community. Within these contexts, the four key issues addressed by the study are: (a) school readiness; (b) children's transitions to kindergarten, first grade, and beyond; (c) the relationship between children's kindergarten experience and their elementary school performance; and (d) children's cognitive growth and progress through elementary school. The primary research questions guiding the ECLS-K are as follows:

- What is the status of children's development (as defined by cognitive, socioemotional development, behavior, and physical status measures) at entry to kindergarten?
- How do variations in children's developmental status (as defined by ECLS-K cognitive, socioemotional, and physical measures) at kindergarten entry affect later success in school?

- How are variations in children's developmental status at kindergarten entry related to the family's social, demographic, and contextual variables at the time of kindergarten entry?
- How do family sociodemographic and contextual variables influence later success in school within and across outcome domains and within gender and race/ethnicity subgroups?
- Over and above the effects of sociodemographic variables, what are the effects of family processes and parenting practices (home environment, activities, and cognitive stimulation) on children's readiness, developmental status, and socioemotional adjustment?
- How do critical family processes and parenting practices influence later success in school?
- What are schools' criteria for kindergarten entry?
- What are parents' and teachers' definitions of readiness—that is, what beliefs and standards do they have for children's behavior and academic performance at entry into kindergarten?
- How do instructional practices, content coverage, time on task, and methods of providing feedback differ across classrooms or schools in kindergarten, first, and second grade?
- How do teachers and schools deal with the diversity of children's skills?
- How do children's opportunities to learn differ across classrooms and schools, and what are the consequences of those differences for children's development?
- How does the length and schedule of the school year affect children's progress, especially cognitive gains?
- What are the varieties of service delivery models in place for special education?
- How do schools teach children who have little or no proficiency in English?
- How and when do schools provide services to children identified as gifted and talented?
- What kinds of programs do schools provide to children who are falling behind academically?
- How do neighborhood or community differences influence children's development?
- How do basic demographic and organizational differences between schools influence children's academic and social development in the early elementary school years?
- Do the school or administrative climate, teacher's opportunities for staff development, or school goals for teachers' progress in the classroom influence children's development in the first three grades of school?
- Do teachers' age, gender, or race/ethnicity influence children's outcomes, on average or in interaction with children's social backgrounds?

- What are the effects for children's academic development of teachers' educational background or experience?
- How do class size, child/teacher ratio, use of aides or volunteers, and use of team teaching influence children's progress through school?
- How does the physical space in the classroom influence child outcomes (including the orientation of desks, the availability of learning centers, and so on)?
- Are differences in classroom materials and supplies related to differences in children's outcomes?
- What are the child care arrangements for children in the early grades?
- How do child care arrangements differ by family sociodemographic factors, SES, and race/ethnicity?
- How does parental involvement in children's education affect school performance over the course of the early grades?
- What affects the extent of parental involvement?
- What kinds of extra services or programs do schools provide to families, children, or community members?[6]

Theory of Change

The conceptual model that guides the ECLS-K design proposes that children's transition and adaptation to schooling is affected by multiple interactions between the child, family, school, and community. Child characteristics (including health status, temperament, and developmental level), family characteristics (including demographic and socioeconomic variables, home and housing environments, family functioning, and family composition), parent-child interactions, and community structure (such as population density, crime rates, and social support availability) all affect child performance in kindergarten and the subsequent elementary grades. In addition, characteristics of early child care (child care type, quality, stability, and so on) and the elementary school itself (location, size, classroom characteristics, student body characteristics, and so on) are also hypothesized to contribute directly to kindergarten and elementary school outcomes. The child outcomes of interest are not limited to cognitive achievement, but also include such indicators of adaptation as attendance, peer relationships, attitudes about schooling, socioemotional development, and special education assignment.

Design and Methods

Research design. ECLS-K is a longitudinal study that began with a nationally representative random sample of approximately 22,000 kindergarten students. The study will obtain data from these children, their families, schools, and communities through the children's fifth-grade year in school. All children entering the sample in Wave 1 of data collection entered kindergarten in the fall of 1998; their years of birth are approximately 1992–1994. During the base year of the study, data were collected once early in the school year and once toward the end of the year (spring 1999). Children were reassessed in the spring of the following year. Additional follow-up assessments are planned for spring of third and fifth grades.

Sampling procedures. In order to obtain a sample of kindergartners representative of all kindergarten students in all U.S. public and private kindergarten programs, a sampling procedure was designed using clusters of schools and school districts. First, a sample of about 100 Primary Sampling Units (PSUs) nationwide was selected. Within these PSUs, counties or school districts were selected. Ultimately, a sample of 1,000 schools within the PSUs was selected, and from these schools the sample children were drawn, at a rate of approximately 23 children per school. As the study progresses longitudinally, sample children will be followed if they change schools, so the number of sites is expected to increase with each wave of data collection.

In order to enable powerful data analysis among ethnic subgroups, it was necessary to oversample children of Asian or Pacific Island and possibly Hispanic ethnicities at rates higher than their distribution in the population. The goals of this sampling procedure were to create a sample of kindergarten programs and teachers that is representative of the experiences of children nationally, and to create a sample of kindergarten students that represents the national population and enables comparisons of policy-relevant groups. At the time of the first-grade follow-up, the analytic sample included 50% male children; 62% white, 17% black, 13% Hispanic, 3% Asian, 5% "other" race/ethnicity; and 19% poor children (Denton & West, 2002).

Data collection. Data collection is conducted by a team of extensively trained child assessors and field interviewers. Assessments of children are conducted individually during schooltime. Parents are contacted by telephone ahead of the scheduled assessment date to ensure that they understand the study and to answer any questions parents may have. In many cases, the parent interview is conducted during this phone call; in others, an appointment is set up to complete the telephone interview. When phone interviews are unsuccessful or incomplete, in-person follow-ups are conducted to complete the parent interviews. School-level information is supplied by school administrators via a self-administered questionnaire. Data from teachers (via self-administered questionnaires and assessment forms) were collected in the late fall of the base year in order to allow sufficient time for teachers to know individual students. Spring data collection from teachers coincided with student data collection.

Characteristics of sample families. All family structures were included in the sample. The parent or guardian selected to respond to the parent interview was the individual who knew the most about the target child's care and education. Family language use is accommodated by various data collection procedures. The parent interview was translated into Spanish, Chinese, Hmong, and Lakota for the first year of data collection. The child mathematics assessment was translated into Spanish, and a published Spanish language and literacy measure (the preLAS, CTB McGraw-Hill) was used to measure literacy in Spanish-speaking children. Children's English language proficiency is assessed and monitored. Once the child's English proficiency passes a certain cut-off point, it is not assessed again.

Measures

The ECLS-K child data set is designed to provide information on children's physical, socioemotional, and cognitive development, and their academic achievement through their early schooling years. This information is obtained through direct child assessments, as well as through parent and teacher reports. In addition, data collected from parents, teachers, school administrators, and other sources provide information on the multiple settings that may influence children's transitions. Child assessments include widely used standardized measures of children's general knowledge, language and literacy, and quantitative abilities, as well as reading, mathematics, and general knowledge assessments designed specifically for ECLS-K. Physical domains such as children's height, weight, and fine and gross motor development are also assessed directly. Parent interviews cover topics such as family contexts, structure, and processes; parenting styles and practices; psychological well-being and health; ratings of child health, well-being, and social skills; perceptions of neighborhood safety; parent involvement in schooling; and parent perceptions of school policies, practices, and services. Teachers are interviewed about their own background and experience, classroom and school characteristics and resources, perceptions of parent involvement and school practices, and ratings of target children's social skills. In addition, school records provide data on school characteristics and children's attendance and special service receipt. Census data and other school administrative data are consulted for neighborhood- and school-level characteristics.

Ethnicity. Parents report their own and the child's ethnicity and race, using the new ethnicity/race measure from Office of Management and Budget.

Poverty. Parents report several family characteristics that relate to family economic status. These include: family income, parents' education and occupations, history of financial hardship (nonpayment of bills, inadequate food), and receipt of public assistance (including AFDC, WIC, food stamps, federal school lunch and breakfast programs).

Cultural relevance. To the extent that children's cultures are expected to influence their transition to schooling, ECLS-K is designed to measure variation in the cultural settings in which children live. This is accomplished by recording racial and ethnic backgrounds of parents and children, family immigration status, religious preferences, and parenting practices.

In terms of the child and parent instruments themselves, the issue of cultural relevance has not been a primary factor in design. Instead, great care has been taken to create child assessments that are developmentally appropriate and meaningful and to address the issue of language use in collecting data from children and parents. For children, limited English proficient (LEP) status is a meaningful variable that will be measured at baseline and tracked in subsequent years. The math direct assessment has been translated into Spanish. When children become sufficiently proficient in English, they will be assessed using the standard ECLS-K battery. Efforts are also being made to accommodate non-English speaking parents. The parent instrument is available in Spanish, Chinese, Hmong, and Lakota, and translation services (by ECLS-K interviewers or hired translators) will be used for parents with other language needs.

Children with disabilities. Children are not excluded from ECLS-K due to special needs or disabilities. For the core data set, disabled children will provide as much data as possible. Children are identified who require accommodations, defined broadly for operational purposes to include glasses, shyness, need for medication, as well as more severe limitations. When possible, accommodations are made in order to collect data from disabled children, such as conducting the assessments in multiple sessions; providing special lighting, acoustics, or furniture; or providing other devices of assistance. The direct battery accommodates all but the most severely disabled children, those with Individualized Education Program (IEP) requirements, the blind, and the deaf. If an individual child's disability precludes him or her taking the assessment, this fact will be recorded, and all other data will still be collected. Thus teacher, parent, school, and records data will be collected on all children. In the spring, a subset of the Adaptive Behavior Scale, Pro-ED, is conducted with special education providers for children who have been excluded due to disability.

Home environment. Extensive parent interviews provide information on the family setting (see above for specific topics covered). These interviews will be generally conducted by phone, so no additional observer coding will be possible.

Role of fathers. There is no survey of the fathers in the current study design. Fathers are interviewed only if they are the primary caregiver to the target child.

Child care environment. According to the ECLS-K model, child care history in the preschool years is considered to have an influence on children's transition to schooling. ECLS-K collects data on both the child's current child care arrangements and arrangements prior to kindergarten entry. All child care data is provided by the parent. Information is collected on current child care arrangements (type, location, time in care, adult/child numbers and ratios), summer camp or summer school attendance, and child care history (including the above characteristics, as well as the child's age when entering care, and types of Head Start programs attended). Child care cost information is collected for the year prior to kindergarten and the first-grade spring follow-up. There are no measures of child care quality beyond assessments related to the numbers of children and adults present.

Health care. Children's current and past health status is addressed in the parent interview. In particular, parents describe children's health concerns, routine health care, and insurance coverage.

Social services. Family receipt of social services is not covered extensively in the ECLS-K instruments. Public assistance received by the family and child participation in school meal programs is recorded, as well as parents' perceptions of the availability of social, material, and emotional support.

Implications of the 1996 welfare bill. The changes in the nation's welfare system do not have direct implications for carrying out this study. However, many economists and other experts believe that families with young children will be most affected by these changes, and the ECLS-K may be able to provide information on families' experiences dealing with the new program requirements.

Units of Analysis

ECLS-K will collect information from multiple sources at multiple levels of hypothesized influence on child functioning. Data are collected on individual children, families, their classrooms and teachers, schools, and communities. The measures were created to enable specific analyses addressing each primary research question. Therefore, data will be analyzed by research question.

　　Although data collection will take place from 1,000 or more different sites, site-level analyses are not central to the purposes of the study. However, such analyses will be possible. School-level data will be most useful for the kindergarten year, as weights will be meaningful, and there are enough children in some classes to provide for classroom-level analyses.

The great attention paid to sampling procedures will enable data analysis that looks at subgroups of the population. Data will be analyzed with attention to ethnic groups and disabled students in particular. Data analysis according to other policy-relevant variables (such as income or poverty status) will also be possible.

Findings

The most recent ECLS-K report looks at children's learning and development longitudinally, across kindergarten and first grade (Denton & West, 2002). It provides data to address the question of "what children know" in kindergarten and first grade. Specific skills are tracked over time. For example, at the beginning of kindergarten, 31% of children understood the letter-sound relationship at the beginning of words, and 18% of children understood the letter-sound relationship at the end of words. By the end of the kindergarten year, 74% of children understood the letter-sound relationship at the beginning of words, and 31% of children understood the letter-sound relationship at the end of words. By the end of first grade, almost all children had mastered the letter-sound relationship at both the beginning and end of words (98% and 94%, respectively). In addition, by the spring of first grade, 76% of children could add and subtract basic whole units; 27% of children could multiply and divide simple whole units.

The 2002 ECLS-K report also examined individual differences in children's skills. The report revealed differences in children's achievements in reading and math according to their family's poverty status, race/ethnicity, and school type. For example, children in families with incomes below the federal poverty line consistently scored approximately ½ of a standard deviation, or five to seven points, below the national average. White children generally scored near the national average on achievement tests. Black children generally entered kindergarten with test scores three to four points below the national average, and this discrepancy remained through the end of first grade. Hispanic children entered kindergarten with reading scores about four points below the national average, but by the spring of first grade came within one point of the national average reading score. Hispanic children's math scores were consistently within two to three points of the national average. Asian children consistently received reading scores three to four points above the national average. Asian children's math scores were above the national average during kindergarten, but within two points of the national average by the end of first grade. Children who attended private schools typically received higher test scores both at kindergarten entry and through the end of first grade.

Looking longitudinally, the ECLS-K data demonstrate the benefits for first graders of good health, positive approaches to learning, and specific scholastic achievements at kindergarten entry. For example, children who were read to at least three times per week prior to entering kindergarten and who could recognize numbers and relative size at kindergarten entry had higher reading scores than their peers. Kindergarten and first-grade children who were read to at least three times per week were about twice as likely to score in the top 25% in reading as those who were read to less than three times per week.

Limitations

Because of the lack of sophisticated standardized achievement measures for children as young as those studied in ECLS-K, scales had to be designed specifically for this study. This is an area of possible limitation, since it is not known how these scales function or how valid they are. However, a great deal of effort and pilot testing was done to create measures. ECLS-K achievement scale scores were designed to be both norm and criterion referenced. The tests are adaptive, such that children will complete assessments that are tailored to their own ability level. This procedure minimizes the chance of obtaining floor or ceiling effects among children who are performing at the outer ranges of typical children in their grades. It also enhances the ability to measure and follow cognitive change throughout the study.

A second area of possible limitation is in the generalizability of findings. Great care has been taken to ensure a nationally representative sample of children in the base year, as well as to sample sufficient numbers of children in particular groups to allow comparisons across subgroups. However, after the first year the ECLS-K study will be a cohort study. As subtle changes occur in the population, these changes will not be accommodated for in the ECLS-K sample—the sample will continue to reflect (except for attrition) the population as it existed when the sample children entered kindergarten. Similarly, the base-year data will provide school-level data that are representative of the nation's kindergarten programs, both public and private. However, as the children are followed longitudinally, moves and school changes will occur and school-level data will no longer be assured of being nationally representative.

Both of these issues (validity of newly created scales and sampling issues) are unavoidable, and have been addressed extensively by the study's planners.

Public Use Files

Public use files have been made available by the National Center for Education Statistics (see http://nces.ed.gov).

FRAGILE FAMILIES AND CHILD WELLBEING STUDY

Nearly one-third of all children born in the United States today are born to unmarried parents. The proportions are even higher among poor and minority populations, 40% among Hispanics, and 70% among African Americans (Ventura et al., 1995). In some instances, the parents of these children are living together in a marriage-like relationship. In others, they have a close relationship, but the father lives in a separate household. In still other cases, the father has virtually no contact with either the mother or child. In this study the new parents and their children are called "Fragile Families," because of the multiple risk factors associated with nonmarital childbearing, and to signify the vulnerability of their relationships. A major goal is to learn more about the nature of the relationships in these families, including determining the extent to which the parents see themselves as families in the traditional sense of the word and understanding the forces that pull them together and push them apart.

History

The proportion of children born to unmarried parents has increased dramatically during the past 40 years, yet very little is known about the resources of and relationships in these families, and the ways in which government policies affect their lives. As a consequence, public perceptions are often shaped by unsubstantiated myths about unmarried couples, and policy makers and community leaders are often forced to rely on anecdotal evidence in designing policies and programs. Without adequate information, such programs may not be as effective as intended, and in some cases they may even unintentionally undermine the stability of these fragile families.

The research on Fragile Families is an extension of previous research on the effects of father absence on children's well-being (McLanahan & Sandefur, 1994), the child support system (Garfinkel, 1992; Garfinkel & McLanahan, 1986; Garfinkel, McLanahan, & Robins, 1992, 1994), and on nonresident fathers (Garfinkel, McLanahan, Meyer, & Seltzer, 1998).

Nearly all of the extant work is based on formerly married parents and their children. The lack of information on unwed parents is due to several factors. Many data sets do not distinguish between children born inside and outside marriage; many data sets do not contain enough cases of children born outside marriage to sustain analyses; and finally, the data on unwed fathers are very inadequate, especially if the father never lived with the child (e.g., fathers' capabilities, parent relationships, and potential effects of policy changes on children's well-being). For example, in the National Study of Families and Households (NSFH), about 3.8 million nonresident fathers were not represented (Garfinkel et al., 1998). Garfinkel and his colleagues estimate that about a third of the "missing fathers" were not in the survey frame, including fathers in prison, fathers in the military, and fathers who are part of the census undercount (i.e., homeless men and other individuals who are loosely attached to households). The other two-thirds of the "missing fathers" are in the survey, but do not acknowledge their status. The problem is particularly serious for low-income fathers and for men who father children outside marriage (also see Rendall, Clarke, Peters, Ranjit, & Verropoulou, 1997).

Quite a bit is known about the women who give birth outside of marriage (Moore, 1995), but very little about the characteristics and capabilities of unwed fathers. Policy makers are particularly interested in two aspects of fathers' capabilities—their earnings capacity and their propensity for violence. These two factors are fundamental to the success or failure of the new welfare and child support laws, which envision a greater role for nonresident fathers in supporting mothers and children.

Current Status

Baseline questionnaires were administered to over 4,700 new mothers and the fathers of their babies in 20 cities across the U.S. The data were collected in three waves, from the spring of 1998 to the fall of 2000. Response rates for the fathers were excellent: interviews were completed with over 90% of the married fathers and 75% of the unwed fathers, the group that is by far the most difficult to recruit. One-year follow-up interviews were completed for the first wave of cities in the fall of 1999 and were continued in the later cities. The two pilot cities have begun 30-month follow-up data collection. Further waves of follow-up data collection will continue until the babies are 4 years old, and a developmental assessment will be done at that time.

Goals

Most people believe that children would be better off if their parents lived together and their fathers were more involved in their upbringing. Indeed, public policy is now attempting to enlarge the role of unwed fathers both by cutting public cash support for single mothers and by strengthening paternity establishment and child support enforcement. Yet the scientific basis for these policies is weak. We know very little about the men who father children outside marriage, and we know even less about the nature of their relationships with their children and their children's mother. To make informed policy decisions, we need to better understand the family circumstances of one of three births occurring in the new century.

The Fragile Families and Child Wellbeing Study follows a new birth cohort of over 4,700 children in an effort to learn more about the fastest growing group of families in the United States today—unmarried parents and their children—and addresses four major questions:

- What are the conditions and capabilities of new unmarried parents, especially fathers? How many of these men hold steady jobs? How many want to be involved in raising their children?
- What is the nature of the relationship between unmarried parents? How many of these couples are involved in stable relationships? What proportion expect to marry? What proportion are exposed to high levels of conflict or domestic violence?
- What factors push new unmarried parents together? What factors pull them apart? In particular, how do public policies affect parents' behaviors and living arrangements?
- What are the long-term consequences for parents, children, and society of new welfare regulations, stronger paternity establishment, and stricter child support enforcement, and changes in health care and child care financing and delivery?

The study design has multiple benefits. First, by gathering data at birth and tracking child development throughout infancy and early childhood, distinctions can be made between differences that are present at birth (or shortly thereafter) and those that evolve over time. Second, by following fathers as well as mothers, more can be learned about fathers, and the parents' relationship can be studied from two points of view. Third, by following children as well as parents, connections can be made between changes in parents' behavior and/or family environment and fluctuations in child health and development outcomes.

Theory of Change

An emerging literature on married fathers is beginning to identify the numerous ways in which fathers can be involved in child rearing: providing economic support, nurturing, and caregiving; engaging in leisure and play activities; providing the child's mother with financial, emotional, or practical support; providing moral guidance and community (Marsiglio & Day, 1997). This new conceptualization is very useful in identifying multiple domains of fathers' involvement, and can easily be extended to research on unmarried fathers. In fact, the few ethnographic studies that have looked at unwed fathers report that many of these men are describing their roles in terms similar to those used by married fathers (Furstenberg & Harris, 1992; Waller, 1997).

Despite the new images of fatherhood, being the breadwinner continues to be central to the meaning of fatherhood for most men and women, and a father's ability to fulfill a breadwinner role continues to be a strong predictor of his relationship with his child. Fathers who are unable to live up to the breadwinner ideal are less likely to find the father role rewarding and more likely to withdraw from their children in order to save face. Alternatively, the mothers who serve as gatekeepers to the children may push the fathers out (Marsiglio & Day, 1997), given the uncertainty about the father's role (Tanfer & Mott, 1997). Parents' prior expectations about the father's rights and responsibilities, and the level of agreement among individual couples about these issues, may be good predictors of whether or not a couple will be able to cooperate and, ultimately, of whether a father will remain involved with his child. If the parents disagree, or if they agree, but the father cannot live up to their expectations, his connection to the child is likely to decline over time.

A central question is whether strengthening relationships in fragile families will benefit the parents and children in these families. Obviously, when relationships depend on parents' individual decisions about whether they live together and cooperate in raising their child, one would expect there to be a correlation between family formation and parents' welfare. An unresolved question, however, is whether parents will be better or worse off when fathers are forced to pay child support and when mothers are forced to depend on fathers for support (Garfinkel et al., 1998).

For most mothers, stronger child support enforcement should increase family income and therefore increase economic welfare. However, for mothers dependent on welfare—that is, most unwed mothers—stronger child support enforcement may lead to a reduction in total income. The few studies that have attempted to identify the effects of child support enforcement on parents' relationships have found some evidence that stronger enforcement will lead to higher conflict (Seltzer, 1994), especially among never-married parents. Furthermore, given what we know about the incidence of domestic violence among welfare mothers, it seems likely that some mothers will be worse off under the new laws. The question is, How many, and which ones?

Men may also be affected by changes in child support policies. Stronger enforcement will reduce the incomes of nonresident fathers and may drive some of them to underground labor markets. Stronger enforcement may also impoverish fathers and their new families, although Meyer finds very little evidence for this (Meyer, 1998). Stronger enforcement could also have positive effects on fathers. Social control theory and the idea of attachment to social institutions are commonly used by sociologists to explain crime and deviant behavior. Deviance is said to result when an individual's bonds to society are weak or broken (Durkheim, 1897). Social ties are said to create informal social controls that result in less deviance and antisocial behavior (Hirschi, 1969; Kornhauser, 1978). One form of social ties is attachment to the family. Studies have shown that attachment to the family of origin reduces delinquency during adolescence (Sampson & Laub, 1993) whereas marriage increases social mobility and overall well-being in adulthood (for a review, see Waite, 1995).

The theory of social control could also be applied to fatherhood. If a child's attachment to his or her parent affects behavior, it seems equally plausible that a father's bond to his child would also have important effects. This involvement with one's child and commitment to family responsibilities may increase social stability and mobility. There is some empirical evidence that nonresident fathers who are involved with their children have higher earnings than fathers who are not involved (Lerman & Sorensen, 1997). These results, however, are very preliminary and do not take account of unobserved differences between fathers who stay involved and those who do not. Thus we cannot tell whether father involvement is a cause or a consequence of higher earnings.

By following children born to unmarried parents from birth and by collecting information on initial health status and parental commitment and relationships as well as changes in family relationships and economic circumstances, the Fragile Families study will give us insight into the mechanisms at play.

Design and Methods

Data for the Fragile Families and Child Wellbeing study are being collected in 20 U.S. cities, stratified by labor market conditions, welfare policies, and child support policies. The sample is representative of nonmarital births in each city and is nationally representative of nonmarital births to parents residing in cities with populations over 200,000. A comparison group of married parents is also being followed. The total sample size is approximately 4,700 families, including 3,600 unwed couples and 1,100 married couples.

New mothers are interviewed at the hospital within 48 hours after they have given birth. Fathers are also interviewed whenever possible at the hospital, or as soon as possible following birth. Follow-up interviews with both parents are conducted when the child is 12 months, 30 months, and 48 months of age. Data on child health and development are collected each year from the mother; in addition, in-home assessments of child well-being will be carried out at the 30- and 48-month interviews.

Sampling from births at hospitals is an excellent method of obtaining a representative sample of children born outside marriage and their unwed mothers and a nearly representative sample of unwed fathers. Such a sample is ideal for addressing questions regarding the capabilities of the parents and the well-being of the children. Though the sample of fathers is only nearly representative, the mother sample allows for an assessment of the severity of the problem and at least partial correction. In order to ascertain the extent to which the interviewed and not interviewed fathers differ, all the mothers are asked a series of questions about the fathers. Two particular foci are the father's earnings and domestic violence.

There were two reasons for sampling from hospitals rather than from birth records: higher response rates and lower costs. Levine and Bryant (1997) note that the 1988 NCSS, which sampled from birth records, was able to locate and complete interviews with only 80% of the mothers. Presumably, the response rate was even lower for nonmarital births.

The 16 cities in the nationally representative sample were chosen on a random stratified basis from all cities with populations over 200,000. (In addition to these 16 cities in the nationally representative sample, the Fragile Families study is being conducted in 4 other cities with funding from foundations with interests in those particular cities.) Prior to random selection, cities were stratified into nine cells. Cities were ranked in terms of the strength of their labor markets, the strictness of child support enforcement, and the stinginess of their welfare grants. Cities in the top or bottom third of all three distributions formed eight of the nine cells. Cities that fell in the middle on one or more dimensions formed the ninth cell. One city was selected randomly from each of the eight extreme cells, and eight cities were selected randomly from the remaining cell. The sample size in each of the extreme cells is 325 births (250 nonmarital and 75 marital births); the sample size in the nonextreme cell is 100 births (75 nonmarital and 25 marital births).

There are three reasons for concentrating observations in cities with more extreme environments. First, city environments vary dramatically in a number of ways that are likely to affect individual behavior and family relationships. The effects of environmental influences such as labor markets, child support and welfare policies, sex ratios, and race/ethnic composition are not well understood and could easily interact with one another and with individual-level variables in our models. The generosity of welfare, for example, might have a weak effect on marriage in the context of a strong labor market and strong child support enforcement, but a strong effect in the face of a weak labor market and lax child support enforcement. Second, concentrating observations allows us to more accurately describe the environment in each city. Third, the most efficient design for detecting the effects of differences in child support, welfare, and labor market regimes is to concentrate observations in cities with extreme values (i.e., those with the highest and lowest welfare benefit levels and the strongest and weakest child support and labor market regimes).[7] By maximizing the variance in these explanatory variables, the variance of their estimated coefficients is maximized.

Eligible participants for the study are limited to English- or Spanish-speaking mothers, as well as the fathers named by the mothers. For participants who speak only Spanish, consent is obtained and the questionnaires are administered in Spanish. Some hospitals prohibited the interviewing of parents less than 18 years old. In these hospitals, mothers were not interviewed if either they or their baby's father were under 18. The procedure for recruiting subjects for the study involved a field manager checking hospital rosters for all births occurring on a given day, and determining from the rosters which births were from the eligible populations defined above. Eligible mothers were then approached to determine if they would be willing to be interviewed for the study. Mothers who consented to be interviewed received incentive payments as compensation for their time. Fathers were interviewed immediately if they were present at the hospital; otherwise, they were contacted using the information provided by the mothers. The procedure regarding consent and payment for the fathers was similar to that for the mothers.

Since the main purpose of this study is to gather information on families of all types, especially those less frequently studied, data on many variations of family structures will inevitably be included. These structures include fathers, single mothers living alone, single mothers living with grandparents and/or boyfriends, and also unwed couples living together with their child.

Measures

The baseline and one-year questionnaires cover a broad range of topics—within the domains of economics, sociology, psychology, and social work—in order to help us learn about the many different factors that may affect the relationships of unwed parents and the well-being of their children. The baseline questionnaires for mothers and fathers include sections on (a) prenatal care, (b) mother-father relationships, (c) expectations about fathers' rights and responsibilities, (d) attitudes toward marriage, (e) parents' health, (f) social support and extended kin, (g) knowledge about local policies and community resources, and (h) education, employment, and income. Follow-up interviews will gather additional information on access to and use of health care and child care services, experiences with local welfare and child support agencies, and parental conflict and domestic violence.

Data on child health and social and emotional development will be collected from the parents during each of the follow-up interviews, and in-home assessments of child well-being will be carried out at 48 months. Child well-being measures overlap with those used in other studies, including the Infant Health and Development Program, the Early Head Start Evaluation, the ECLS—Birth Cohort Study, the Panel Study of Income Dynamics—Child Development Supplement, and the National Health Interview Survey.

Units of Analysis

The Fragile Families data will allow researchers to address a number of descriptive and analytical questions relevant to child care, health care, welfare, child support, and housing policies. One set of analyses will describe the capacities and well-being of parents and children, the relationships among family members (fathers and mothers, parents and children, nuclear family members and extended kin), and the role of government, community programs, labor markets, and other environmental influences. The data can be used to describe capabilities, relationships, and well-being at a single point in time (e.g., when the child is born, when the child is 30 months old, and so on), or they can be used to describe the cumulative experiences of families and family members over a period of time (e.g., the first 12, the first 30, the first 48 months of a child's life).

Another type of analysis will assess the stability and change in parents' capabilities and relationships. The new data can also be used to describe patterns of family process and adaptation across the different racial and ethnic groups and across cities with different policy and labor market regimes. In addition, the samples in some of the cities are large enough to be analyzed separately and thus become akin to case studies.

Findings

Reports evaluating the baseline data from Austin and Oakland were posted in April 1999. Data reports from Baltimore, Philadelphia, Detroit, Newark, and Richmond were made available in August and September 2000. These city reports are available at the study's Web site (http://crcw.princeton.edu). From the initial exploration of the Fragile Families data in these seven cities, three findings stand out. First, parents in fragile families are initially highly committed to each other and to their children. Almost half of unmarried parents live together, and over 30% of the remainder are romantically involved. More than two-thirds expect to marry. Eight out of 10 unmarried fathers provided support during the pregnancy, and more than 8 out of 10 unwed mothers plan to put the father's name on the child's birth certificate. The overwhelming majority of unmarried mothers want the father to be involved in raising their child. The challenge for policy makers and community leaders is to nourish rather than undermine these commitments.

Second, most unmarried parents in these seven cities are poorly equipped to support their families. Most fathers have an income of less than $20,000 a year and most mothers earn less than $5,000 a year. The human capital of both parents is low. Over a third of both mothers and fathers lack a high school degree. Less than a third have more than a high school degree. In Oakland, 14% of fathers and nearly one out of five mothers did not work in the previous year. Increases in human capital, employment, and earnings are likely to play critical roles in the success or failure of parents in maintaining stable families.

Finally, the majority of unmarried mothers in the seven cities are healthy and bear healthy children. However, 1 in 5 of these mothers do not receive prenatal care in the first trimester, and more than 1 in 10 give birth to below-normal-weight babies. Furthermore, about 1 out of 4 mothers drink alcohol, use drugs, or smoke cigarettes during their pregnancies. Improving the health care of all mothers during pregnancy should be an important objective of local policy makers.

Limitations

One limitation of the design is that it will not be representative of births from smaller cities, suburbs, and rural areas. A future study, perhaps in conjunction with the NCES birth cohort or as an extension of the Fragile Families study, should examine these groups. Another limitation is sample size within the large cities. A larger sample within each of the cities with extreme child support, welfare, and labor market regimes would increase the power to detect differences within and across these cities. While such an increase in power would be desirable, rather than increasing sample size now, a superior alternative would be to draw a second birth cohort sample in these same cities 5 years from now. This strategy would increase sample size and would open up the possibility of examining within-city changes over time.

Public Use Files

Baseline data are available to registered users. For more information on what is available and how to register, see http://crcw.princeton.edu/fragilefamilies/data.html on-line.

PANEL STUDY OF INCOME DYNAMICS—
CHILD DEVELOPMENT SUPPLEMENT (PSID-CDS)

History

The Panel Study of Income Dynamics (PSID)—a nationally representative longitudinal study of U.S. individuals and the families in which they live— began in 1968 with 5,000 families (M. Hill, 1992). These families, as well as their children who leave home to start their own households, are interviewed yearly. In 1997, its 30th year of data collection, approximately 7,000 families, with over 19,000 individuals, participated. The interview content is broad, with a focus on dynamic aspects of economic and demographic behavior. More specifically, the PSID collects information on family economics, such as income, occupation, wealth, expenditures on food and housing, and income transfers; and family structure, including marriages, divorces, births, and deaths.

The Child Development Supplement (CDS) to the PSID addresses the need to better understand the influence of cognitive, social, emotional, and physical well-being factors on children's ability to become productive, self-sufficient adults. It adds detailed information on the many settings in which children live and learn to the rich economic data collected as part of the PSID. Together with the PSID, the CDS provides researchers with high-quality annual measurements of economic and demographic conditions at both the family and neighborhood levels, beginning at birth, as well as teacher and school or child care characteristics at the time of the interview, for a representative sample of children and adolescents.

Questions about how changes in families, neighborhoods, and schools during the past decades affect children's lives and their ability to become productive, self-sufficient adults led to the development of the PSID-CDS. In the past 20 years, the American family has experienced great demographic and economic changes that can work to both the detriment and advantage of today's children. For example, the increase in single-parent families, maternal employment outside the home, and childhood poverty along with the declining labor-market prospects for less-skilled, particularly male, workers can decrease the resources available to children. At the same time, the higher schooling levels of parents and smaller family size can be a benefit. As a result of these changes, children spend more time out of the home, in schools or day care. The CDS collects information on the many settings in which children live and learn. The measures of the CDS were designed to provide data on how these trends affect children's cognitive, social, emotional, and physical well-being (Hofferth, Davis-Kean, Davis, & Finkelstein, 1997).

The CDS is rooted in a resource theory of child development: The financial, time, human capital, social, and psychological resources provided to children by their familial and extrafamilial environments are crucial to child development. Families and communities "invest" in their children through these resources. "Resources" are viewed very broadly, as per Haveman and Wolfe (1994). They can be defined as consisting of the purchased resources, time, interpersonal connections, and institutions that can be used to promote the development of children. "Investments" are resources spent on promoting children's development, now and in the future, including time and money spent to enhance future health or abilities. As described by Bronfenbrenner (1979), these resources come from the various contexts in which children live, including the family, school, neighborhood/community, and larger societal systems (e.g., government policies, media influences). However, the availability of resources is always constrained by cost and quality of the resources.

An emerging literature focuses on the interplay of family resources, such as income, time spent with child, human capital, and psychological resources, and how they might influence children (Haveman & Wolfe, 1994; Hofferth et al., 1997). Little is known about parental trade-off of time and income and how it influences children (C. R. Hill & Stafford, 1985; Lazar & Michael, 1988). For example, does the additional income from two working parents offset the reduction in the amount of time spent with the children? Similarly, the quality of resources is important. Mothers who are tired, unsatisfied, and/ or stressed by juggling work and parenthood may provide fewer stimulating experiences for their children (J. B. Wilson et al., 1995). Resources from the other contexts of children's lives, such as day care or school, also need to be considered. For instance, high quality day care may compensate for the reduction in quality time with parents.

Current Status

Data collection for the 1997 CDS is complete. The data have been entered and cleaned, and data analysis is underway. Results are beginning to be published and disseminated publicly. The first public dissemination occurred in November 1998, with a press release of a report documenting changes in how children actually spent their time in 1997 compared with how children spent their time in 1981 (Hofferth, 1998). Researchers have recently published papers about other aspects of children's time use (Hofferth & Sandberg, 2001; Sandberg & Hofferth, 2000; Yeung, Sandberg, Davis-Kean, & Hofferth, 2001). Additionally, plans are under way for a follow-up in 2003.

Goals

The objective of the CDS is to provide researchers with a comprehensive, longitudinal database of average children and their families uniquely appropriate for dozens of innovative studies of child development. As stated in the study's original grant application to the National Institute of Child Health and Human Development, the CDS addresses an important gap in data by supplementing the PSID—a high-quality, representative national sample with over 3 decades of information of participating families—with (a) cognitive, socioemotional, and health measures of child development from a nationally representative sample of children; (b) measures of family, school, and community resources and expenditures on children from parents, teachers, and school administrators; and (c) Census Bureau data on neighborhoods (Hofferth et al., 1997). These data will support studies of the way in which time, money, and social capital at the family, school, and neighborhood levels are linked to children's and adolescents' cognitive and behavioral development as they become self-sufficient adults. These data will also shed light on how parental psychological resources and sibling characteristics influence child and adolescent development (Hofferth, 1998).

With these data, researchers can approach studies in several ways:

- Relate a rich history of family and neighborhood demographic and economic experiences to child outcomes
- Describe time use in 1996 and changes between the early 1980s and 1996, such as the amount and nature of time parents and other caretakers spend with children, the amount of time young adolescents spend in unsupervised activities, how time is used in classrooms, and how U.S. children's time use compares with that of children in other countries
- Model time inputs to understand time investments
- Investigate race/ethnic differences in time use and outcomes
- Use sibling differences to control for unmeasured heterogeneity in examining child outcomes (Hofferth et al., 1997)

Theory of Change

Resource theory predicts that changes in the availability and quality of resources will affect child development outcomes. One of the goals of this study is to investigate how economic and demographic changes over the past decades have impacted the availability and quality of resources.

Design and Methods

Information was collected from families participating in the PSID with children under age 13. Interviews were conducted between March 1997 and early December 1997, with a 2-month break during July and August. The final sample consists of 3,563 noninstitutionalized children in 2,394 households. Children in the sample were born between 1985 and 1997. Although data has been collected only once, a further follow-up is anticipated, scheduled for 2003.

The PSID started with 5,000 U.S. households drawn from a nationally representative sampling frame in 1968, oversampling low-income families. Individuals from the household, regardless of where they are currently living, are interviewed yearly. About half of the original sample is still being followed. A representative sample of 440 immigrants to the United States since 1968 was added in 1997.

All families participating in the PSID with children under the age of 13 were asked to take part in the CDS. The response rate was 88%. In families with more than two eligible children, two were selected at random to participate.

Trained interviewers contacted eligible families by phone to explain the study and obtain permission. Families who declined to participate were sent a persuasion letter. When the family gave permission, an appointment was made for a trained interviewer to visit the family at home to conduct face-to-face interviews with each participating child over age 3 and the primary caregiver, typically the mother. In the home, the interviewer first explained and obtained signed consent forms before administering standardized achievement tests to children aged 3 to 12, interviewing the primary caregiver about each child in the study, and interviewing each child in the study. The respondents also completed self-administered questionnaires and a time diary. The primary caregiver completed a questionnaire about herself and the household. Depending on the child's age either the child or the primary caregiver (or the child and primary caregiver together) recorded the child's activities in a 24-hour diary for one randomly assigned weekday and one randomly assigned weekend day. A time diary was completed for each child in the study. If there was another caregiver (such as a father, step-father, grandparent) living in the home, he completed a self-administered questionnaire about each child in the study and one about himself and the household.

If the child's father did not reside in the home, the interviewer asked the primary caregiver for permission and information on how to contact him. Via a telephone interview, the nonresidential father completed a questionnaire about each child in the study and one about himself and the household. The interviewer also asked for permission and contact information for each study child's teacher and school or child care. Each study child's preschool/day care, elementary, or middle school teacher, or home-based child care provider received a questionnaire and time diary in the mail along with a copy of the parent's consent form. If the child was home schooled, then the person who taught the child completed the teacher questionnaire and time diary. A self-administered questionnaire about the school environment was also mailed to the school or child care administrator. The administrator completed only one questionnaire, regardless of how many children in the study attended the school.

A Spanish language version of the assessment was used for Spanish-speaking children. All other data collection materials were in English.

Measures

Child. All respondents provided information on the child, often answering the same questions. Subtests of the Woodcock-Johnson Tests of Achievement (Woodcock & Johnson, 1989, 1990) were used to assess verbal and math skills for children aged 3 and older, including letter-word identification (ages 3–12), passage comprehension (ages 6–12), calculation (ages 6–12), and applied problems (ages 3–12). Additional math skills were assessed using the forward and backward digits subtests of the Wechsler Intelligence Scale for Children—Revised (Wechsler, 1974) for children aged 3 to 12. Children older than 8 also responded to questions about their perceptions of their math, reading, and general abilities (task perception/self-concept).

The primary caregiver reported on the child's ethnicity; physical health and access to health care; child's temperament; history of child care arrangements (including type, length, and cost); school enrollment; food security; home environment (assessed using an adaptation of the HOME); and relationship and contact with absent father or mother. All parent figures (primary caregiver, other caregiver, and absent father) provided information on the family structure, closeness, and activities; levels of monitoring; involvement with child's schooling; and children's socioemotional well-being using the Behavior Problem Index (BPI; Achenbach, 1978) and Positive Behavior Scale (Quint et al., 1997) for children 3 and older. The teacher also rated the child's socioemotional well-being using the BPI; parent's involvement in school; child's skills and abilities, including special services and needs; structure of child's learning activities; composition of child's classroom; and the adequacy of supplies.

Time diary information on the child's day was collected from the primary caregiver (or the child if old enough) and the teacher or day care provider. For a 24-hour period, every activity the child did was recorded, along with its duration, where the child was, who was doing the activity with the child, who else was there (but not directly involved in the activity), and what else the child was doing. Specifics about television programs and video or computer games also were recorded. While at school, the teacher (or the child if in middle school) recorded all activities, with specific information about duration, child's location, who was with the child, how the class was structured, what instructional format and materials were used, and the child's behavior.

Parents. All parent figures (primary caregiver, other caregiver, and absent father) also provided information about themselves and their family life. They answered questions about their work schedules; daily activities; family conflict; attitudes toward child rearing and parenting; division of household tasks; mental health (measured by the Rosenberg self-esteem scale); Pearlin self-efficacy scale (Pearlin, Menaghan, Lieberman, & Mullan, 1981); the CDI depression inventory (Kovacs, 1982); and alcohol consumption. Absent fathers provided details on income, and the primary caregiver reported on her levels of social support and economic strain. The primary caregiver also completed the passage comprehension subtest of the Woodcock-Johnson. There are no direct questions about the household income in the CDS because of the extensive economic data available from the PSID core questionnaire. However, there are questions about use of government programs, such as WIC and food stamps, food security, and economic strain.

Teachers. The teachers (including child care providers) provided demographic information about themselves and about their preparation and philosophy toward teaching. In the time diary, they also reported their commuting time, what they did at school before and after the official school day, and any school-related activities completed at home.

School. The administrator (including child care administrators) provided information on the length of the school year, student body (ethnicity, poverty), retention rate, transfer rate, composition of teaching staff, expenditures, safety, and teacher morale.

Other. The primary caregiver reported on the safety and closeness of the neighborhood.

Findings

Data are being analyzed by research issue. The scope and size of the data set, as well as its link to the PSID, allow for an almost endless possibility of research questions. The data are available to the public, and can be used to answer a wide range of questions about children's environments. The first stage of data analysis has focused on providing a snapshot of children in 1997—what they do and how they are doing.

At this time, there are several completed reports of the time diary data. One compares how children aged 3 to 11 spent their time in 1997 and 1981

(Hofferth & Sandberg, 2000). For more information, see http://www.isr
.umich.edu/src/child-development/home.html on-line. Major findings are
summarized below.

Between 1981 and 1997, the following differences in time use were
found:

- In 1981, children spent on average 4 weekday hours in "school" (includes school or preschool, time spent at the babysitter's home, and
  time spent traveling to and from school). In 1997, children spent
  almost 6 hours.
- Between 1981 and 1997, free time decreased from 40% to 25% of a
  child's day.
- Children did about twice as much household work in 1997 than they
  did in 1981.
- Children spent more time studying on weekdays in 1997 than in 1981,
  but the same amount of time reading for pleasure as in 1981.
- In 1997 and 1981, boys spent more time in organized sports than girls.
  For both boys and girls, the amount of time spent in organized sports
  on weekdays and weekends increased. However, very little time was
  spent in other leisure activities in 1997.
- Surprisingly, the amount of time spent watching television on weekdays declined slightly from 2 hours in 1981 to 1½ hours in 1997. But
  on the weekend, boys watched less television in 1997 and girls watched
  more than in 1981.

Differences in time use by parent demographic characteristics are as follows:

- Children in traditional families (male breadwinner and female home-
  maker) spent more time in free play than children with either two
  working parents or a single working parent.
- Children in traditional families did more household work than children in other types of families.
- Children in families with a more educated head of household or older
  parents spent more time reading for pleasure. Children in single-parent
  families spent less time.
- Girls spent less time playing sports than boys, and this gap grows as
  the children age. White children (holding other factors equal) spent
  more time in sports than black and Hispanic children.
- Children in traditional families watched more TV than children in two-
  income families. Children of less-educated parents watched more TV
  than children of better educated parents.

The second published paper reports on children's well-being, focusing on their relationships, health, and behavior (Hofferth, 1998). Major findings are listed below.

HOW WELL ARE CHILDREN DOING?

- Most parents believed their children are easy to get along with and great kids. Ninety percent of the children were characterized by 10 or more positive characteristics.
- Parents rated 65% of the children as extremely or very close to their parents. Sixty-six percent of parents reported very warm behaviors with their child, such as hugging or spending time together. However, the closeness and warmth declines as children grow up.
- Parents were involved in their children's schooling. About half participated in five or more different activities in the child's school over the school year. And almost 75% reported having regular conversations with their child about school activities and experiences. Seventy-one percent expected their children to obtain at least a college degree.
- Children had about 51 hours a week of discretionary time. Of that time, children spent very little time reading (1.3 hours) and studying (1.7 hours), and more time watching TV (12.0 hours). The amount of time they spent watching TV increased with age while the amount of time they spent reading for pleasure remained the same.
- Only 1 in 8 children used the computer. The amount of time spent on the computer increases as children age.
- Parents reported that 84% of the children were in excellent or very good health.
- Approximately 26% of the infants and 43% of the school-age children did not have a routine medical checkup. Only 82% of the children had health insurance coverage for all 12 months in the previous year.

WHAT MATTERS MOST FOR CHILDREN'S ACHIEVEMENT AND ADJUSTMENT?

- Not surprisingly, children's achievement was related to the head of the household's education and the mother's verbal skills.
- Having more siblings under 18 was associated with lower scores on verbal tests.
- Children from traditional families scored higher on the verbal tests.

- Children from families headed by a single parent had more behavior problems, as measured by the Behavior Problem Index (Achenbach, 1978).
- Family income in 1997 had a small effect on children's achievement test scores.
- Children who changed schools two or more times in the past year exhibited more school problems.

The report concluded that although parents may be spending less time with their children than in the past, it is how that time is spent and the quality of the relationship that matters.

Limitations

The study is based on a nationally representative sample of children and parents, with an over-sampling of minorities. Information obtained from teachers should not be used to represent all American students and their teachers. There was a lower response rate for the teachers. Thus the information on the school day cannot be considered representative of the nation's schools.

Public Use Files

Information about the study, including all measures, is available at http://www.umich.edu/~psid/ on-line. The Child Development Supplement home page is located at http://www.isr.umich.edu/src/child-development/home.html on-line. All data from the CDS are available to the public at this Web site, including questionnaires and documentation.

NOTES

Allison S. Fuligni and Lisa McCabe are grateful for support from the Administration on Children, Youth, and Families; National Institute for Mental Health; and the MacArthur Network on the Family and the Economy. For assistance with verification of study details, Fuligni and McCabe would like to thank Karen Tourangeau and Gary Resnick at Westat. Sara McLanahan would like to acknowledge the work of Kate Jamieson for Fragile Families, and Jodie Roth would like to thank Sandra Hofferth. All of the authors would like to acknowledge the support of NICHD Research Network, OERI, and ASPE. The authors are grateful to Phyllis Gyamfi, Christy Brady-Smith, Lisa O'Connor, Christina Borbely, Erin O'Connor, and David Megathlin for their editorial assistance.

1. Lisa McCabe is the primary author of this section of Chapter 12. The ECLS-B initiative is being conducted by the U.S. Department of Education, National

Center for Education Statistics, National Center for Health Statistics, and National Institutes of Health. Funders include the National Institute of Child Health and Human Development. For a complete list of collaborators and funders, see Chapter 2. For more information on this initiative see http://nces.ed.gov/ecls/Birth/agency.asp on-line.

2. Allison S. Fuligni is the primary author of this section of Chapter 12. The ECLS-K initiative is being conducted by and primarily funded by the US Department of Education, National Center for Education Statistics. Additional funders include Administration of Children, Youth, and Families, U.S. Department of Education, and the U.S. Department of Agriculture. For a complete list of funders see Chapter 2. For more information on ECLS-K, see http://www.nces.ed.gov/ecls on-line.

3. Sara McLanahan is the primary author of this section of Chapter 12. The principal investigators are Irwin Garfinkel, Sara McLanahan, Marta Tienda, and Jeanne Brooks-Gunn. For a complete list of coinvestigators see Chapter 2. The study was initiated with funding from the Ford Foundation and is now funded by the National Institute for Child Health and Human Development and a consortium of foundations including the Robert Wood Johnson Foundation and the Hogg Foundation. See Chapter 2 for a complete list of funders. For more information on this initiative see http://crcw.princeton.edu/fragilefamilies/index.html on-line.

4. Jodie Roth is the primary author of this section of Chapter 12. The principal investigator for PSID-CDS is Jacquelynne Eccles. Coinvestigators are Jeanne Brooks-Gunn, Frank Stafford, and Greg Duncan. Funding for the Child Development Supplement was provided primarily by the National Institute of Child Health and Human Development (NICHD); additional funding was provided by the William T. Grant Foundation, the Annie E. Casey Foundation, the U.S. Department of Agriculture, and the U.S. Department of Education. For more information, see http://www.isr.umich.edu/src/child-development/home.html on-line.

5. Contact information: Karen Tourangeau, Westat, 1650 Research Boulevard, Rockville, MD 20850; (301) 251-1500.

6. Primary research questions are taken from Ingels, 1997, Appendix N. In addition to these questions, there are a number of secondary questions, not printed here because of space limitations. Secondary research questions include the effects of many of the above constructs on outcomes such as child development and parent involvement, and variation in the above constructs according to children's age, sex, race, and ethnicity.

7. See Conlisk and Watts (1969) for a similar approach. Duncan and Raudenbush (2001) present a similar justification (maximizing variance) for the utility of cross-national studies. For a textbook discussion, see Groves (1989).

CHAPTER 13

Synthesis: Issues and Imperatives in Research on Early Childhood Development

ALLISON SIDLE FULIGNI AND JEANNE BROOKS-GUNN

In this volume we have described 28 large-scale research initiatives focusing on young children. Together, these studies represent well over 140,000 families and children. They include studies tracking development longitudinally across the early childhood years in large and nationally representative samples; studies assessing the importance of different environmental contexts of child development (such as child care settings and neighborhood and community settings); and studies evaluating the effects of early intervention programs for certain populations of families (such as those who are economically disadvantaged, at risk for child abuse and neglect, and children with diagnosed disabilities).

When viewed as a whole, this group of initiatives highlights the growing interest among researchers on the trajectories of development that begin early in life and the contexts and environments that may influence these trajectories. The studies also illustrate the growing concern among policy makers and advocates that many children are experiencing these early years in conditions that are well short of optimal. Many of the studies represent attempts to document the negative effects of growing up in poverty, as well as the potential benefit of policies and programs aimed toward poor children and families. In fact, 7 of the 28 studies described are large-scale studies of early childhood development, including assessments of contexts of development, such as child care and school settings (the NICHD Study of Early Child Care; the Cost, Quality, and Child Outcomes [CQO] Study; and the Early Childhood Longitudinal Study—Birth and Kindergarten Cohorts [ECLS-B,

ECLS-K]), unmarried families (Fragile Families and Child Wellbeing Study), and neighborhoods and communities (the Project on Human Development in Chicago Neighborhoods [PHDCN]; the Los Angeles Family and Neighborhood Study [L.A. FANS]). Eleven of the studies are evaluations of early intervention programs or demonstrations, including early childhood education interventions for low-income children[1] (the Early Head Start [EHS] Research and Evaluation Project, the National Head Start/Public School Early Childhood Transition Demonstration Study, the Head Start Family and Child Experiences Survey [FACES]); family support programs (the Comprehensive Child Development Project [CCDP], the National Even Start Evaluation, and the National Evaluation of Family Support Programs [NEFSP]); interventions for children with disabilities (the National Early Intervention Longitudinal Study[NEILS]); antipoverty programs (New Hope Child and Family Study); and parenting-focused interventions (the Nurse-Family Partnership, Healthy Families America, and Healthy Steps for Young Children). Finally, eight of the studies were designed to evaluate the effects of policies on children and families. These include studies of children's experiences in the child welfare system (Consortium for Longitudinal Studies in Child Abuse and Neglect [LONGSCAN] and the National Study of Child and Adolescent Well-Being [NSCAW]) and studies of the impacts of welfare reform and job-training programs (the National Evaluation of Welfare-to-Work Strategies—Child Outcomes Study [NEWWS-COS], the New Hope Child and Family Study, Welfare, Children and Families: A Three City Study, the Project on State-Level Child Outcomes, Assessing the New Federalism (ANF)—National Survey of America's Families [NSAF], and Los Angeles FANS).

In this chapter, we discuss this set of initiatives collectively, describing the innovations and strengths it brings to developmental research, and highlighting issues to be considered in these and future investigations. First, we describe the theoretical backgrounds that many of the studies have in common and the sophisticated research questions that may be addressed in such studies. Next, we highlight some of the unique qualities of the initiatives, and describe some of the specific ways they are advancing the field, by including fathers, qualitative methods, siblings, and children with special needs. We conclude by considering some issues limiting the initiatives here, and recommend directions for continued work in the area of early childhood developmental research.

THEORETICAL UNDERPINNINGS

Although the research questions pertaining to the well-being of young children and families may differ, these studies share some general theoretical underpinnings. First, they all view the experiences of young children as important determinants of their ongoing development and consider early experiences in multiple contexts of children's lives, including home environments, neighborhood and community environments, and child care settings. The ecological developmental perspective of Bronfenbrenner (e.g., Bronfenbrenner & Morris, 1998) is well represented in the theoretical designs of many of the studies, which consider multiple proximal and distal settings and their interactions when assessing influences on development. Among the studies that are evaluations of intervention programs, ecological and transactional theories (e.g., Sameroff, 1983) are also dominant, with the effects of interventions posited to be partially dependent upon the interactions between legislative, policy, and community contexts and program designers, as well as the interactions between program staff and program participants (Berlin, O'Neal, & Brooks-Gunn, 1998).

Economic perspectives on development, namely resource theories, are evidenced in a few of the programs: the Panel Study of Income Dynamics—Child Development Supplement (PSID-CDS) examines the resources allocated to children from family, school, neighborhood/ community, and larger societal systems; and the Fragile Families study examines contributions of fathers in terms of economic support as well as input of psychological and time resources. Additionally, studies of the impacts of reform policies (NEWWS-COS; Welfare, Children and Families; and New Hope) consider that policy changes may have effects on children that are both economic (through changes in family employment and income patterns) as well as non-economic (through changes in parental psychological well-being and child care environments).

By investigating the potential contributions of multiple sources of influence affecting child development, these studies have the ability to assess processes and pathways involved in developmental change. The evaluation studies described here have gone beyond traditional impact studies that make simple program versus nonprogram comparisons, to assess mechanisms by which change may or may not be occurring (for a discussion, see Berlin, O'Neal, & Brooks-Gunn, 1998). These studies are making special efforts to measure program processes, including the amount and intensity of services families receive, and to tie these factors into assessments of program impacts. For instance, the NEWWS-COS includes process measures of program operations, staff, and case files, to assess the nature, quality, and dosage of activities and services. The EHS Research and Evaluation Project includes detailed use of program process information in its evaluation, and uses evaluation information to feed back into its continuous program improvement activities. In the NEFSP, each individual program evaluation is designed based on the theoretical approach of that program, so that hypotheses are tested on a program-specific basis.

Similarly, the studies that do not evaluate intervention effects are also able to test detailed pathways of influence on development. For instance, studies of impacts of welfare reform policies can determine how the relationships between policy change and child outcomes are affected by such mediating factors as improved home environments, improved parental self-efficacy, or increased parental work-related stress. Many studies are collecting the information needed to consider how socioeconomic factors such as family income, maternal education, and neighborhood structural features may influence children's well-being by assessing their influences on potential family, child care, and neighborhood mediating factors (for a discussion, see Fuligni & Brooks-Gunn, 2000).

UNIQUE QUALITIES OF INITIATIVES

While all of these studies may share some broad conceptual underpinnings regarding the importance of early experiences and the multiple contexts that affect early development, individually they introduce many unique qualities for large-scale studies. For example, some of the studies include large samples of populations that have not previously been well-represented in the literature on child development, such as children across multiple statuses of child protection (LONGSCAN), children born out of wedlock (Fragile Families), young children with diagnosed disabilities (NEILS), and large or nationally representative samples of young children followed longitudinally and assessed in multiple settings (ECLS-B, ECLS-K, and PSID-CDS). The studies that focus on particular settings (such as child care and neighborhood studies) are providing important new information by including extensive measurement of the settings of interest, and focusing on their interplay with family factors and child characteristics. Their longitudinal nature allows for examination of a dynamic system, and the relative importance of timing and duration of different experiences on child outcomes.

Qualitative Methods

A unique feature of many of these studies is the marriage of qualitative methods within large-scale, quantitative designs. Using such approaches adds richness to data that might otherwise be restricted to self- or other-reports in survey format. Qualitative methods may supplement quantitative measures, serving to verify or enhance these reports. For instance, many of the studies are using qualitative observational measures of child-parent inter-actions, such as the Nursing Child Assessment Teaching Scale and other struc-tured or semistructured interactions that are videotaped and coded for various dimensions of interaction quality (CCDP; EHS Research and Evaluation Project; NEWWS-COS; Welfare, Children and Families; and PHDCN). Rich observational measures of child care settings are being employed, not only in the studies that are designed with specific child care questions (the NICHD Study of Early Child Care, the CQO Study), but also in studies focused on other main research questions (Head Start FACES; Welfare, Children and Families; Project on State-Level Child Outcomes; and PHDCN). New meth-odologies are being used for the qualitative assessment of neighborhood and community settings, including videotaped neighborhood observations (PHDCN), ethnography (Welfare, Children and Families), and reports from neighborhood experts (PHDCN and L.A. FANS). Finally, time diary meth-odology is being employed to assess both family life (Welfare, Children and Families and PSID-CDS) and school settings (PSID-CDS).

Fathers

Many of the studies profiled in this volume represent advances in develop-mental research in that they collect data from reporters that are not often included in such studies. For instance, several studies have made a point of including fathers as respondents. The EHS Research and Evaluation Project has targeted subsets of fathers to illustrate characteristics of biological and social fathers in the communities served by Early Head Start, to examine their involvement with their children, and to describe ways that the programs seek to involve fathers in program activities and children's lives. Fathers or father figures in the child's life are also interviewed in the LONGSCAN study and the Welfare, Children and Families study, and both residential and nonresi-dential biological fathers are contacted in Fragile Families, ECCLS-B, and PSID-CDS. In most other studies, fathers are only included when they are identified as the child's primary caregiver; otherwise, information about fathers is obtained from the primary caregiver (generally the mother). Inter-viewing fathers and father figures in studies of child development helps cap-ture the child's relationship with these men from a perspective other than that of the mother and provide a richer portrait of the child by including reports from another person who has a relationship with the child.

Siblings

Another methodological feature that is beginning to emerge in large-scale developmental research is the inclusion of data from siblings. Inclusion of siblings enables investigators to control for unmeasured family characteristics when estimating effects on development. Both the PSID-CDS and the New Hope evaluation collected data on up to two children in the family within the age range of the study, and Healthy Families America used nonprogram participant siblings as comparison groups in some of the individual evaluations. The L.A. FANS study collected data on up to two randomly selected children per household, a design which will potentially result in the inclusion of sibling pairs with varying degrees of relatedness (such as full siblings, half-siblings, step-siblings, and foster-siblings).

Children with Special Needs

As Hebbeler and Spiker illustrated in Chapter 11, including children with special needs in large-scale studies of early development can be costly and difficult. Therefore, many so-called nationally representative studies have not adequately represented the population of children with special needs, who could be as numerous as 5% of children under age 3. Only one study, NEILS, is designed to specifically address issues of development and services among young children with disabilities. Some of the other studies profiled in this volume have made various attempts to include children with disabilities in their samples. For instance, the ECLS-K makes every effort to include children with a wide range of disabilities by making necessary accommodations in data collection procedures. Both the Early Head Start evaluation and the Head Start FACES study include assessments of how well the programs are serving their disabled participants. The Welfare, Children and Families study includes a subsample of families with a disabled child in the comparative ethnographic study. Other studies, such as the NEWWS-COS and the CQO Study, include children with disabilities to the extent that they naturally appear in their sample, but do not make any modifications to data collection procedures to accommodate special needs. Thus we are seeing increased attention to the needs of these children, but ongoing research will need to focus on the developmental trajectories and needs of children with disabilities.

FUTURE DIRECTIONS

The individual profiles for the studies described in this volume list the central research questions that are being investigated in these studies. Findings reported from these initiatives will be of value to researchers, practitioners, and policy makers. As we have described, the studies break new ground in many ways by incorporating new measures, new methodologies, and new populations. The understanding of young children's development in many diverse contexts will be enhanced by the findings from these studies. Additionally, practitioners concerned with providing useful services to children and families will benefit from the lessons learned in the evaluations described here. Policy makers will have a stronger knowledge base from which to make crucial legislative decisions based on the findings from the large-scale developmental studies as well as the results of evaluations of policy changes and intervention programs.

The extensive scope of information collected on the children and families in these studies also makes these samples rich sources for secondary data analysis. Almost all of the studies described here will have publicly available data archives, enabling researchers to explore numerous questions of development in contexts including neighborhood and community settings, child care settings, diverse family structures, and diverse socioeconomic backgrounds. Some of the studies have released their data files to the public (e.g., CCDP, Even Start, and PSID-CDS). Others have released data from early waves and will continue to release data as they become available (e.g., the NICHD Study of Early Child Care, the CQO Study, PHDCN, NEWWS-COS, Assessing the New Federalism—NSAF, and LONGSCAN). Researchers from multiple disciplines will be able to take advantage of these data to explore additional questions of interest to policy makers, developmental scientists, practitioners, and child advocates.

Despite elaborate design planning, none of these studies is without some limitations. Most of the investigations have gone to great lengths to minimize design factors that might limit the applicability or generalizability of their findings by including large samples (often nationally representative or from multiple sites), including multiple measures of constructs from multiple respondents, and using measures that have been previously validated (or going through extensive measure-design to create new instruments as needed). Nevertheless, limitations do exist for each of the studies we have described. Primary limitations have to do with the generalizability of the samples. Many studies, although employing large samples and collecting rich data, are not nationally representative or focus on a single city (e.g., PHDCN and L.A. FANS); are representative only of children from certain populations (e.g., children born in large cities as in Fragile Families; people impacted by welfare reform legislation as in NEWWS-COS; and children in center-based child care as in the CQO Study); or have multiple sites for data collection, but do not represent the national population (NICHD Study of Early Child Care and the CQO Study).

Among the studies that are evaluations of intervention programs, additional limitations often have to do with methods of assessing the impacts of the programs. Random assignment to program or control groups is often a difficult part of the design of evaluations. Such problems affect the evaluation of the Head Start Transition study (randomization is at the site level); Even Start evaluation (only a small sample of programs was involved in a randomized experiment); and the Healthy Families America and the NEFSP (few sites used random assignment). Furthermore, variation in levels of program implementation can blur program impacts, which may affect findings in studies such as NEWWS-COS (for which the passage of the 1996 welfare reform package may affect implementation), Healthy Steps (which reports uneven program implementation across sites), and CCDP and other interventions which do not assess program implementation or quality.

A review of the extensive measures used in these studies of child development and the contexts in which development occurs reveals that most studies assessing child well-being over time are taking a multifaceted view of child development and including measures of cognitive and linguistic development, achievement, social development, and emotional development. Some studies include measures of physical development as well. It is important to note that the expanded focus on social and emotional development in studies focusing on school readiness as an important outcome is relatively new. Early studies of intervention programs seeking to improve children's school readiness focused almost exclusively on measures of cognitive ability.

We now see an emerging trend toward broader definitions of child well-being among investigators interested in school readiness and child health alike. For instance, the Goal One Technical Planning Group (1993) has defined school readiness as including the following five dimensions: physical well-being and motor development, social and emotional development, approaches toward learning, language usage, and cognition and general knowledge. Similarly, child health is sometimes divided into four broad categories: physical health, emotional well-being and behavioral competence, cognitive and linguistic competence, and social competencies (McCormick & Brooks-Gunn, 1989). Thus scholars and policy makers from a variety of disciplines have converged on broadening their definitions of child well-being: Educators have begun to consider physical and emotional health; health scholars include emotional health, communication, and relationships; and psychologists include more than cognitive, social, and emotional aspects of development (Fuligni & Brooks-Gunn, 2000).

Within such a framework of child well-being, many of the studies described here are somewhat limited in their evaluation of the physical health status of children. There are notable exceptions. Some studies, especially those focusing on low-income families, assess usage of preventive health care and/ or immunization rates (e.g., CCDP, EHS Research and Evaluation Project, NEFSP, and New Hope). Some studies include global measures of health status (usually a question or set of questions asked of the parent rating child's overall health; e.g., EHS, Head Start Transition Study, and NEWWS-COS).

Some include more detailed assessments of multiple health conditions and activity limiting conditions (e.g., PSID-CDS, LONGSCAN, NICHD Study of Early Child Care, PHDCN, ECLS-B, and ECLS-K). Some evaluation studies included no measures of child health (Even Start, Head Start FACES, and CQO Study). The studies that do assess the multiple domains of child well-being, with assessments of cognitive, linguistic, emotional, behavioral, social, physical, and health constructs, offer a truly comprehensive view of child development and the opportunity to assess the impacts of a variety of early experiences on all of these areas of development.

NOTE

1. The U.S. Department of Health and Human Services has also recently announced plans to conduct a National Head Start Impact Study, utilizing random assignment and a national sample of Head Start sites (HHS RFP 282-00-0022).

References

Abbott-Shim, M., & Sibley, A. (1987). *Assessment profile for early childhood programs.* Atlanta, GA: Quality Assist.

Abbott-Shim, M., & Sibley, A. (1993). *Assessment profile for homes with young children—research version.* Atlanta, GA: Quality Assist.

Abbott-Shim, M., Sibley, A., & Neel, J. (1992). *Assessment profile for early childhood programs—research version.* Atlanta, GA: Quality Assist.

Aber, J. L., Brooks-Gunn, J., & Maynard, R. (1995). Effects of welfare reform on teenage parents and their children. *The Future of Children, 5*(2), 53–71.

Aber, J. L., Gephart, M., Brooks-Gunn, J., Connell, J., & Spencer, M. B. (1997). Neighborhood, family, and individual processes as they influence child and adolescent outcomes. In J. Brooks-Gunn, G. J. Duncan, & J. L. Aber (Eds.), *Neighborhood poverty: Vol. 1. Context and consequences for children* (pp. 44–61). New York: Russell Sage Foundation.

Abt Associates. (1996). *National evaluation of family support programs: Design report.* Cambridge, MA: Author.

Achenbach, T. M. (1978). The child behavior profile: I. Boys aged 6–11. *Journal of Consulting and Clinical Psychology, 46,* 478–488.

Administration on Children, Youth, and Families (ACYF), Head Start Bureau. (1995). *Charting our progress: Development of the Head Start Program Performance Measures.* Washington, DC: Administration on Children, Youth, and Families.

Alexander, K. L., & Entwisle, D. R. (1996). Schools and children at risk. In A. Booth & J. F. Dunn (Eds.), *Family-school links: How do they affect educational outcomes?* (pp. 67–88). Mahwah, NJ: Erlbaum.

Arnett, J. (1989). Caregivers in day-care centers: Does training matter? *Journal of Applied Developmental Psychology, 10,* 541–552.

Bailey, D. B., Aytch, L. S., Odom, S. L., Symons, F., & Wolery, M. (1999). Early intervention as we know it. *Mental Retardation and Developmental Disabilities Research Reviews, 5,* 11–20.

Bailey, D. B., McWilliam, R. A., Darkes, L. A., Hebbeler, K., Simeonsson, R. J., Spiker, D., & Wagner, M. (1998). Family outcomes in early intervention: A framework for program evaluation and efficacy research. *Exceptional Children, 64,* 313–328.

Bailey, D. B., Simmeonsson, R. J., Buysse, V., & Smith, T. (1993). Reliability of an index of child characteristics. *Developmental Medicine and Child Neurology, 35,* 806–815.

Bandura, A. (1977). *Social Learning Theory*. Englewood Cliffs, NJ: Prentice-Hall.

Bandura, A. (1986). *Social foundations of thought and action: A social cognitive theory*. Englewood Cliffs, NJ: Prentice-Hall.

Barnard, K. E. (1978). *Nursing Child Assessment Satellite Training learning resource manual*. Seattle: University of Washington, School of Nursing.

Barnard, K. E. (1994). *NCAST: Nursing Child Assessment Satellite Training: Teaching Scale, birth to three years*. Seattle, WA: University of Washington.

Barnard, K. E. (1998). Developing, implementing, and documenting interventions with parents and young children. *Zero to Three, 18*(4), 23–29.

Barnes, H. V., Goodson, B. D., & Layzer, J. I. (1995). *Review of research on supportive interventions for children and families* (Vol. 1). Cambridge, MA: Abt Associates.

Barnes-McGuire, J., & Reiss, A. (1993, November). *Systematic social observation manual: Project on Human Behavior in Chicago Neighborhoods* (Report prepared for Foundation for Child Development). Boston: Author.

Barnett, W. S. (1995). Long-term effects of early childhood programs on cognitive and school outcomes. *The Future of Children, 5*(3), 25–50.

Bavolek, S. J. (1984). *Adult Adolescent Parenting Inventory*. Park City, UT: Family Development Resources.

Baydar, N., & Brooks-Gunn, J. (1991). Effects of maternal employment and child-care arrangements on preschoolers' cognitive and behavioral outcomes: Evidence from the children of the National Longitudinal Survey of Youth. *Developmental Psychology, 27*, 932–945.

Bayley, N. (1969). *Bayley Scales of Infant Development*. San Antonio, TX: The Psychological Corporation.

Bayley, N. (1993). *Bayley Scales of Infant Development—Second edition (BSID-II)*. San Antonio, TX: The Psychological Corporation.

Beecroft, E., Cahill, K., & Goodson, B. D. (2002). *The impacts of welfare reform on children: The Indiana welfare reform evaluation*. Cambridge, MA: Abt Associates.

Belsky, J. (1988). The "effects" of infant day care reconsidered. *Early Childhood Research Quarterly, 3*, 235–272.

Belsky, J. (1990). Parental and nonparental child care and children's socioemotional development. *Journal of Marriage and the Family, 52*, 885–903.

Benasich, A. A., Brooks-Gunn, J., & Clewell, B. C. (1992). How do mothers benefit from early intervention programs? *Journal of Applied Developmental Psychology, 13*, 311–362.

Berlin, L. J., Brooks-Gunn, J., & Aber, J. L. (2001). Promoting early childhood development through comprehensive community initiatives. *Children's Services: Social Policy, Research, and Practice, 1*, 1–24.

Berlin, L. J., Brooks-Gunn, J., McCarton, C., & McCormick, M. C. (1998). The effectiveness of early intervention: Examining risk factors and pathways to enhanced development. *Preventive Medicine, 27*, 238–245.

Berlin, L. J., Brooks-Gunn, J., Spiker, D., & Zaslow, M. J. (1995). Examining observational measures of emotional support and cognitive stimulation in black and white mothers of preschoolers. *Journal of Family Issues, 16*(5), 664–686.

Berlin, L. J., O'Neal, C. R., & Brooks-Gunn, J. (1998). What makes early intervention programs work? The program, its participants, and their interaction. *Zero to Three, 18*, 4–15.

Bianchi, S. M. (2000). Maternal employment and time with children: Dramatic change or surprising continuity? *Demography, 37*(4), 401–414.

Black, M. M., Dubowitz, H., Hutcheson, J., Berenson-Howard, J., & Starr, R. H., Jr. (1995). A randomized clinical trial of home intervention among children with failure to thrive. *Pediatrics, 95*(6), 807–814.

Black, M. M., Howard, D., Kim, N., & Ricardo, I. B. (1998). Primary interventions to prevent violence among African-American adolescents from low-income communities. *Aggression and Violent Behavior, 3*, 17–33.

Blau, D. M. (1991). *The economics of child care*. New York: Russell Sage Foundation.

Bloom, D., Kemple, J. J., Morris, P., Scrivener, S., Verma, N., & Hendra, R. (2000). *FTP: Final results of Florida's initial time-limited welfare program*. New York: Manpower Demonstration Research Corporation.

Boller, K., Sprachman, S., & the Early Head Start Research Consortium. (1998). *The Child-Caregiver Observation System instructor's manual*. Princeton, NJ: Mathematica Policy Research.

Booth, A. (Ed.). (1992). *Child care in the 1990s: Trends and consequences*. Hillsdale, NJ: Erlbaum.

Bos, H., Huston, A., Granger, R., Duncan, G., Brock, T., & McLoyd, V. (1999). *New Hope for people with low incomes: Two-year results of a program to reduce poverty and reform welfare*. New York: Manpower Demonstration Research Corporation.

Bowlby, J. (1969). *Attachment and loss: Vol. 1. Attachment*. New York: Basic Books.

Boyce, C. A., Hoagwood, K., Lopez, M. L., & Tarullo, L. B. (2000). The Head Start Mental Health Research Consortium: New directions for research partnerships. *Behavioral Disorders, 26*(1), 7–12.

Brady-Smith, C., Brooks-Gunn, J., Waldfogel, J., & Fauth, R. (2001). Work or welfare? Assessing the impacts of recent employment and policy changes on very young children. *Evaluation and Program Planning, 24*, 409–425.

Brick, J. M., Flores-Cervantes, I., & Cantor, D. (1999, March). *No. 8: 1997 NSAF response rates and methods evaluation*. Washington, DC: Urban Institute. Available on-line: http://newfederalism.urban.org

Brick, P. D., Kenney, G., McCullough-Harlin, R., Rajan, S., Scheuren, F., & Wang, K. (1999, July). *No. 1: National Survey of America's Families: Survey methods and data reliability*. Washington, DC: Urban Institute. Available on-line: http://newfederalism.urban.org

Bricker, D., & Squires, J. (1999). *Ages and Stages Questionnaire: A parent-completed child-monitoring system* (2nd ed.). Baltimore: Paul H. Brookes.

Briggs, X. S., & Mueller, E. (with Sullivan, M. L.). (1997). *From neighborhood to community: Evidence on the social effects of community development*. New York: New School for Social Research, Graduate School of Management and Urban Policy, Community Development Research Center.

Brock, T., Doolittle, F., Fellerath, V., & Wiseman, M. (1997). *Creating New Hope: Implementation of a program to reduce poverty and reform welfare.* New York: Manpower Demonstration Research Corporation.

Bronfenbrenner, U. (1979). *The ecology of human development: Experiments by nature and design.* Cambridge, MA: Harvard University Press.

Bronfenbrenner, U. (1986). Ecology of the family as a context for human development: Research perspectives. *Developmental Psychology, 22*(6), 723–742.

Bronfenbrenner, U. (1993). Ecological systems theory. In R. Wozniak & K. Fisher (Eds.), *Specific environments: Thinking in contexts* (pp. 3–44). Hillsdale, NJ: Erlbaum.

Bronfenbrenner, U., & Crouter, A. C. (1983). The evolution of environmental models in developmental research. In P. H. Mussen (Series Ed.) & W. Kessen (Vol. Ed.), *Handbook of child psychology: Vol. 1. History, theory, and methods* (4th ed., pp. 357–414). New York: Wiley.

Bronfenbrenner, U., & Morris, P. A. (1998). The ecology of developmental processes. In W. Damon (Series Ed.) & R. M. Lerner (Vol. Ed.), *Handbook of child psychology: Vol. 1. Theoretical models of human development* (5th ed., pp. 993–1028). New York: Wiley.

Brooks-Gunn, J. (1995a). Children in families in communities: Risk and intervention in the Bronfenbrenner tradition. In P. Moen, G. H. Elder, Jr., & K. Luscher (Eds.), *Examining lives in context: Perspectives on the ecology of human development* (pp. 467–519). Washington, DC: American Psychological Association.

Brooks-Gunn, J. (1995b). Strategies for altering the outcomes for poor children and their families. In P. L. Chase-Lansdale & J. Brooks-Gunn (Eds.), *Escape from poverty: What makes a difference for children?* (pp. 87–117). New York: Cambridge University Press.

Brooks-Gunn, J., Berlin, L. J., Aber, J. L., Carcagno, G. J., & Sprachman, S. (1996). *Moving from welfare to work: What about the family?* Princeton, NJ: Mathematica Policy Research.

Brooks-Gunn, J., Berlin, L. J., & Fuligni, A. S. (2000). Early childhood intervention programs: What about the family? In J. P. Shonkoff & S. J. Meisels (Eds.), *Handbook of early childhood intervention* (2nd ed., pp. 549–588). New York: Cambridge University Press.

Brooks-Gunn, J., Berlin, L. J., Leventhal, T., & Fuligni, A. (2000). Depending on the kindness of strangers: Current national data initiatives and developmental research. *Child Development, 71*(1), 257–268.

Brooks-Gunn, J., Burchinal, M., & Lopez, M. (2001). *Enhancing the cognitive and social development of young children via parent education in the Comprehensive Child Development Program.* Manuscript submitted for publication.

Brooks-Gunn, J., & Duncan, G. J. (1997). The effects of poverty on children. *The Future of Children, 7*(2), 55–71.

Brooks-Gunn, J., Duncan, G., & Aber, J. L. (Eds.). (1997a). *Neighborhood poverty: Vol. 1. Context and consequences for children.* New York: Russell Sage Foundation.

Brooks-Gunn, J., Duncan, G., & Aber, J. L. (Eds.). (1997b). *Neighborhood poverty: Vol. 2. Policy implications in studying neighborhoods.* New York: Russell Sage Foundation Press.

Brooks-Gunn, J., Duncan, G., Klebanov, P. K., & Sealand, N. (1993). Do neighborhoods influence child and adolescent development? *American Journal of Sociology, 99*(2), 353–395.

Brooks-Gunn, J., Duncan, G., Leventhal, T., & Aber, J. L. (1997). Lessons learned and future directions for research on the neighborhoods in which children live. In J. Brooks-Gunn, G. Duncan, & J. L. Aber (Eds.), *Neighborhood poverty: Vol. 1. Context and consequences for children* (pp. 279–297). New York: Russell Sage Foundation Press.

Brooks-Gunn, J., Fuligni, A. S., Barth, M. C., & Young, K. T. (1997). *Helping children take healthy steps: Abstracts of selected articles on early childhood interventions.* New York: The Commonwealth Fund.

Brooks-Gunn, J., Gross, R. T., Kraemer, H. C., Spiker, D., & Shapiro, S. (1992). Enhancing the cognitive outcomes of low birthweight, premature infants: For whom is the intervention most effective? *Pediatrics, 89*, 1209–1215.

Brooks-Gunn, J., Han, W. J., & Waldfogel, J. (2002). Maternal employment and child cognitive outcomes in the first three years of life: The NICHD Study of Early Child Care. *Child Development, 73*(4), 1052–1072.

Brooks-Gunn, J., Klebanov, P. K., & Liaw, F. (1995). The learning, physical, and emotional environment of the home in the context of poverty: The Infant Health and Development Program. *Children and Youth Services Review, 17*, 251–276.

Brooks-Gunn, J., Klebanov, P. K., Liaw, F. R., & Spiker, D. (1993). Enhancing the development of low birthweight, premature infants: Changes in cognition and behavior over the first three years. *Child Development, 64*(3), 736–753.

Brooks-Gunn, J., McCarton, C. M., Casey, P. H., McCormick, M. C., Bauer, C. R., Bernbaum, J. C., et al. (1994). Early intervention in low birthweight, premature infants: Results through age 5 years from the Infant Health and Development Program. *Journal of the American Medical Association, 272*, 1257–1262.

Brooks-Gunn, J., Phelps, E., & Elder, G. H. (1991). Studying lives through time: Secondary data analyses in developmental psychology. *Developmental Psychology, 27*(6), 899–910.

Brooks-Gunn, J., Smith, J., Berlin, L., & Lee, K. (in press). Familywork: Welfare changes, parenting, and young children. In G. K. Brookins (Ed.), *Exits from poverty.* New York: Cambridge University Press.

Brown, P., & Richman, H. A. (1997). Neighborhood effects and state and local policy. In J. Brooks-Gunn, G. J. Duncan, & J. L. Aber (Eds.), *Neighborhood poverty: Vol. 2. Policy implications in studying neighborhoods.* New York: Russell Sage Foundation.

Bryant, D. M., & Maxwell, K. (1997). The effectiveness of early intervention for disadvantaged children. In M. J. Guralnick (Ed.), *The effectiveness of early intervention* (pp. 23–46). Baltimore: Brookes.

Burchinal, M. R., Campbell, F. A., Bryant, D. M., Wasik, B. H., & Ramey, C. T. (1997). Early intervention and mediating processes in cognitive performance of children of low-income African American families. *Child Development, 68*, 935–954.

Butterfield, P. M. (1996). The Partners in Parenting Education program: A new option in parent education. *Zero to Three, 17*, 3–10.

Cabrera, N., Tamis-LeMonda, C. S., Bradley, R. H., Hofferth, S., & Lamb, M. E. (2000). Fatherhood in the twenty-first century. *Child Development, 71*, 127–136.

Caldwell, B. M., & Bradley, R. H. (1984). *Home Observation for Measurement of the Environment*. Little Rock: University of Arkansas.

Campbell, F. A., & Ramey, C. T. (1994). Effects of early intervention on intellectual and academic achievement: A follow-up study from low-income families. *Child Development, 65*, 684–698.

Carnegie Corporation of New York. (1994). *Starting points: Meeting the needs of our youngest children*. New York: Author.

Cassidy, J., & Asher, S. (1992). Loneliness and peer relations in young children. *Child Development, 63*, 350–365.

Caughy, M., DiPietro, J. A., & Strobino, D. M. (1994). Day-care participation as a protective factor in the cognitive development of low-income children. *Child Development, 65*(2), 457–471.

Caughy, M., Miller, T., Genevro, J., Huang, K., & Nautiyal, C. (2001, April). *The effects of Healthy Steps on discipline strategies of parents with toddlers*. Poster presented at the biennial meeting of the Society for Research in Child Development, Minneapolis, MN.

Chase-Lansdale, P. L., & Brooks-Gunn, J. (Eds.). (1995). *Escape from poverty: What makes a difference for children?* New York: Cambridge University Press.

Chase-Lansdale, P. L., Coley, R. L., Lohman, B. J., & Pittman, L. D. (2002). *Welfare reform: What about the children?* (Policy Brief 02-1) [On-line]. Available: http://www.jhu.edu/~welfare/ 19382_Welfare_janO2 .pdf

Chase-Lansdale, P. L., Gordon, R., Brooks-Gunn, J., & Klebanov, P. K. (1997). Neighborhood and family influences on the intellectual and behavioral competence of preschool and early school-age children. In J. Brooks-Gunn, G. Duncan, & J. L. Aber (Eds.), *Neighborhood poverty: Vol. 1. Context and consequences for children* (pp. 79–118). New York: Russell Sage Foundation Press.

Chase-Lansdale, P. L., Mott, F. L., Brooks-Gunn, J., & Phillips, D. (1991). Children of the NLSY: A unique research opportunity. *Developmental Psychology, 27*(6), 918–931.

Cherlin, A. J. (1995). Policy issues of child care. In P. Chase-Lansdale & J. Brooks-Gunn (Eds.), *Escape from poverty: What makes a difference for children?* (pp. 121–137). New York: Cambridge University Press.

Child Trends. (1999). *Children and welfare reform: A guide to evaluating the effects of state welfare reform policies*. Washington, DC: Author.

Clarke-Stewart, K. A. (1987). Predicting child development from child care forms and features: The Chicago study. In D. Phillips (Ed.), *Quality in child care: What does research tell us?* (pp. 21–42). Washington, DC: National Association for the Education of Young Children.

Coie, J. D., Watt, N. F., West, S. G., Hawkins, J. D., Asarnow, J. T., Markman, J. J., et al. (1993). The science of prevention: A conceptual framework and some directions for a national research program. *American Psychologist, 4*, 1013–1022.

Coleman, J., Hoffer, T., & Kilgore, S. (1981). *Public and private schools: An analysis of High School and Beyond, a national longitudinal study for the 1980's* (NCES No. 82230). Washington, DC: National Center for Education Statistics.

Committee on Ways and Means. (1998). *Overview of entitlement programs: 1998 Green Book.* Washington, DC: U.S. Government Printing Office.

Conger, R. D., Ge, X., Elder, G. H., Lorenz, F. O., & Simons, R. L. (1994). Economic stress, coercive family process, and development problems of adolescents. *Child Development, 65*, 541–561.

Congressional Research Service. (1992). *Selected brief facts about poverty and welfare among urban families with children.* Washington, DC: Author.

Conlisk, J., & Watts, H. (1969). A model for optimizing experimental designs for estimating response surfaces. Proceedings for the Social Statistics Section, *American Statistical Association*, 150–56.

Connell, J. P., & Kubisch, A. C. (Eds.). (in press). *Applying a theories of change approach to the evaluation of comprehensive community initiatives: Progress, prospects, and problems.* Washington, DC: Aspen Institute.

Connell, J. P., Kubisch, A. C., Schorr, L. B., & Weiss, C. H. (Eds.). (1995). *New approaches to evaluating community initiatives: Concepts, methods, and contexts.* Washington, DC: Aspen Institute.

Consortium for Longitudinal Studies (Ed.). (1983). *As the twig is bent. . . . Lasting effects of preschool programs.* Hillsdale, NJ: Erlbaum.

Consulting Services and Research, Inc. (CSR). (1997). *Process evaluation of the Comprehensive Child Development Program.* Washington, DC: Author.

Corbett, T. J. (1995). Welfare reform in Wisconsin: The rhetoric and the reality. In D. F. Norris & L. Thompson (Eds.), *The politics of welfare reform* (pp. 19–54). New York: Sage.

Cost, Quality, and Child Outcomes (CQO) Study Team. (1995). *Cost, quality, and child outcomes in child care centers: Technical report.* Denver: University of Colorado at Denver.

Cost, Quality, and Child Outcomes (CQO) Study Team. (1999). *The children of the Cost, Quality, and Outcomes Study go to school: Executive summary.* Chapel Hill: University of North Carolina at Chapel Hill, Frank Porter Graham Child Development Center. Available on-line: http://www.fpg.unc.edu/~NCEDL/PAGES/ cqes.htm

Currie, J. M., & Thomas, D. (1995). Does Head Start make a difference? *The American Economic Review, 85*(3), 341–364.

Danziger, S., & Gottschalk, P. (1986). *How have families with children been faring?* (Discussion Paper No. 801–86). Madison: Institute for Research on Poverty, University of Wisconsin—Madison.

Daro, D. A., & Harding, K. A. (1999). Healthy Families America: Using research to enhance practice. *The Future of Children, 9*(1), 152–176.

Denton, K., & West, J. (2002). *Children's reading and mathematics achievement in kindergarten and first grade* (NCES No. 2002-125). Washington, DC: U.S. Department of Education, National Center for Education Statistics.

Desai, S., Chase-Lansdale, P. L., & Michael, R. T. (1989). Mother or market? Effects of maternal employment on the intellectual ability of 4-year-old children. *Demography, 26*(4), 545–561.

DeTemple, J. M., & Tabors, P. O. (2000). *Predicting maternal-child literacy functioning at early school age: Findings from an observational study of welfare mothers and their young children.* Manuscript submitted for publication.

Diamond, A., & Taylor, C. (1996). Development of an aspect of executive control: Development of the abilities to remember what I said and to "Do as I say, not as I do." *Developmental Psychobiology, 29*, 315–334.

Dombro, A. L., Colker, L. J., & Dodge, D. T. (1997). *The Creative Curriculum for Infants and Toddlers.* Washington, DC: Teaching Strategies.

Duncan, G. J., & Brooks-Gunn, J. (Eds.). (1997). *Consequences of growing up poor.* New York: Russell Sage Foundation.

Duncan, G. J., Brooks-Gunn, J., & Klebanov, P. K. (1994). Economic deprivation and early-childhood development. *Child Development, 65*(2), 296–318.

Duncan, G. J., Connell, J., & Klebanov, P. K. (1997). Conceptual and methodological issues in estimating causal effects of neighborhoods and family conditions on individual development. In J. Brooks-Gunn, G. J. Duncan, & J. L. Aber (Eds.), *Neighborhood poverty: Vol. 1. Context and consequences for children* (pp. 219–250). New York: Russell Sage Foundation.

Duncan, G. J., & Morgan, N. J. (1985). The Panel Study of Income Dynamics. In G. H. Elder, Jr. (Ed.), *Life course dynamics: Trajectories and transitions, 1968–1980* (pp. 50–71). Ithaca, NY: Cornell University Press.

Duncan, G. J., & Raudenbush, S. W. (2001). Getting context right in quantitative studies of child development. In A. Thornton (Ed.), *The well-being of children and families: Research and data needs* (pp. 356–383). Ann Arbor: University of Michigan Press.

Duncan, G. J., Yeung, W. J., Brooks-Gunn, J., & Smith, J. R. (1998). How much does childhood poverty affect the life chances of children? *American Sociological Review, 63*, 406–423.

Dunn, L. M., & Dunn, L. M. (1981). *Peabody Picture Vocabulary Test—Revised (PPVT-R).* Circle Pines, MN: American Guidance Service.

Durkheim, E. (1897). *Suicide* (J. Spaulding & G. Simpson, Trans.). New York: Free Press.

Earls, F., & Buka, S. L. (1997, March). *Project on Human Development in Chicago Neighborhoods: Technical report.* Rockville, MD: National Institute of Justice.

Eckenrode, J., Ganzel, B., Henderson, C. R., Smith, E., Olds, D. L., Powers, J., et al. (2000). Preventing child abuse and neglect with a program of nurse home visitation: The limiting effects of domestic violence. *Journal of the American Medical Association, 284*, 1385–1391.

Edmonds, L. (1999, June). *A national agenda for birth defect research and prevention.* Paper presented at the Part C Data Systems Meeting, Washington, DC.

Eggbeer, L. (1995). Expanding the boundaries of pediatric primary care to support the development of infants, toddlers, and their families. *Zero to Three, 16*(1), 1–7.

Ehrle, J. L., & Moore, K. A. (1999). *1997 NSAF benchmarking measures of child and family well-being* (Methodology Report No. 6). [On-line]. Available: http://newfederalism.urban.org/nsaf/ methodology_rpts/Methodology_6.pdf

Eissa, N., & Liebman, J. B. (1996). Labor supply response to the Earned Income Tax Credit. *Quarterly Journal of Economics, 112*(2), 605–637.

Elder, G. H., Jr. (1998). The life course and human development. In W. Damon (Series Ed.) & R. M. Lerner (Vol. Ed.), *Handbook of child psychology: Vol 1. Theoretical models of human development* (5th Ed., pp. 939–992). New York: Wiley.

Emlen, A. (1997, February 19). *Quality from a parent's point of view: A place at the table for the child-care consumer.* Paper presented at Innovations in Child Care Consumer Education, Leadership Forum, Child Care Bureau, Washington, DC.

Entwisle, D. R., & Alexander, K. L. (1994). Entry into school: The beginning school transition and educational stratification in the United States. *Annual Review of Sociology, 19*, 401–423.

Entwisle, D. R., Alexander, K. L., & Olson, L. S. (1997). *Children, schools, and inequality.* Boulder, CO: Westview Press.

ERIC/OSEP Special Project at ERIC Clearinghouse on Disabilities and Gifted Education. (1998, Spring). State-wide assessment programs: Including students with disabilities. *Research Connections in Special Education, 2*, 1–5.

Farran, D. (2000). Another decade of intervention for children who are low income or disabled: What do we know now? In J. P. Shonkoff & S. J. Meisels (Eds.), *Handbook of early childhood intervention* (2nd ed., pp. 510–548). New York: Cambridge University Press.

Featherman, D. L., Spenner, K. T., & Tsunematsu, N. (1988). Class and the socialization of children: Constancy, change, or irrelevance? In E. M. Hetherington, R. M. Lerner, & M. Perlmutter (Eds.), *Child development in life-span perspective* (pp. 1–57). Hillsdale, NJ: Erlbaum.

Feil, E. G., & Becker, W. C. (1993). Investigation of a multiple-gated screening system for preschool behavior problems. *Behavioral Disorders, 19*(1), 44–53.

Feil, E. G., Walker, H. M., & Severson, H. H. (1995). The Early Screening Project for young children with behavior problems. *Journal of Emotional and Behavioral Disorders, 3*(4), 194–202.

Feil, E. G., Walker, H., Severson, H., & Ball, A. (2000). Proactive screening for emotional/behavioral concerns in Head Start preschools: Promising practices and challenges in applied research. *Behavioral Disorders, 26*(1), 13–25.

Field, T. (1991). Quality of infant day-care and grade school behavior and performance. *Child Development, 62*, 863–870.

Florian, L. (1995). Part C early intervention program: Legislative history and the intent of the law. *Topics in Early Childhood Special Education, 15*, 247–262.

Fox, N., & Fein, G. (Eds.). (1990). *Infant day care: The current debate.* New York: Ablex.

Friedlander, D., Riccio, J., & Freedman, S. (1993). *GAIN: Two-year impacts in six countries.* New York: Manpower Demonstration Research Corporation.

Fraker, T. M., Ross, C. M., Stapulonis, R. A., Olsen, R. B., Kovac, M. D., Dion, M. R., & Rangarajan, A. (2002). *The evaluation of welfare reform in Iowa: Final impact report*. Princeton, NJ: Mathematica Policy Research.

Fuchs, E., & Thompson, J. P. (1996). Urban community initiatives and shifting federal policy: The case of the empowerment zones. In A. J. Kahn & S. B. Kamerman (Eds.), *Children and their families in big cities: Strategies for service reform* (pp. 230–255). New York: Columbia University School of Social Work, Cross-National Studies Program.

Fuligni, A. S., & Brooks-Gunn, J. (2000). The healthy development of young children: SES disparities, prevention strategies, and policy opportunities. In B. D. Smedley & S. L. Syme (Eds.), *Promoting health: Intervention strategies from social and behavioral research* (pp. 170–216). Washington, DC: National Academy Press.

Fuligni, A. S., & Brooks-Gunn, J. (2002). Meeting the challenges of new parenthood: Responsibilities, advice, and perceptions. In N. Halfon, K. T. McLean, & M. A. Schuster (Eds.), *Child rearing in America: Challenges facing parents with young children* (pp. 83–115). New York: Cambridge University Press.

Fuller, B., Kagan, S. L., Caspary, G., Cohen, N., French, D., Gascue, L., et al. (2000). *Remember the children: Mothers balance work and child care under welfare reform (Wave 1 findings)*. Berkeley: University of California, Graduate School of Education, PACE.

Fuller, B., Kagan, S. L., Loeb, S., Carroll, J., Kreicher, G., McCarthy, J., Cook, G., Carrol, B., Chang, Y., & Sprachman, S. (2002). *New lives for poor families? Mothers and young children move through welfare reform* [On-line]. Available: http://www-gse.berkeley.edu/research/PACE/pace_new_release html.

Furstenberg, F. F., Brooks-Gunn, J., & Morgan, S. P. (1987). *Adolescent mothers in later life*. New York: Cambridge University Press.

Furstenberg, F. F., Cook, T. D., Eccles, J. S., Elder, G. H., & Sameroff, A. J. (1999). *Neighborhood Scales*. Philadelphia: University of Pennsylvania, Population Studies Center; and Boulder, CO: University of Colorado, Institute of Behavioral Science.

Furstenberg, F. F., & Harris, K. M. (1992). The disappearing American father? Divorce and the waning significance of biological parenthood. In S. J. South & S. E. Tolnay (Eds.), *The changing American family: Sociological and demographic perspectives*. Boulder, CO: Westview Press.

Furuno, S., O'Reilly, K. A., Hosaka, C. M., Inatsuka, T. T., Zeisloft-Falbey, B., & Allman, T. (1992). HELP Checklist—Hawaii Early Learning Profile. In J. J. Kramer & J. C. Conoley (Eds.), *The eleventh mental measurements yearbook* (pp. 373–375). Lincoln, NE: University of Nebraska—Lincoln, Buros Institute of Mental Measurements.

Galinsky, E., Howes, C., Kontos, S., & Shinn, M. (1994). *The Study of Children in Family Child Care and Relative Care: Highlights of findings*. New York: Families and Work Institute.

Gallagher, J. J., Harbin, G., Eckland, J., & Clifford, R. M. (1994). State diversity and policy implementation. In L. J. Johnson, R. J. Gallagher, M. J. La Montagne,

J. B. Jordan, J. J. Gallagher, P. L. Hutinger, & M. B. Karnes (Eds.), *Meeting early intervention challenges: Issues from birth to three* (pp. 235–250). Baltimore: Brookes.

Garbarino, J. (1990). The human ecology of risk. In S. J. Meisels & J. P. Shonkoff (Eds.), *Handbook of early childhood intervention* (pp. 78–96). New York: Cambridge University Press.

Garber, H. L. (1988). *The Milwaukee Project: Preventing mental retardation in children at risk*. Washington, DC: American Association on Mental Retardation.

Garfinkel, I. (1992). *Assuring child support*. New York: Russell Sage Foundation.

Garfinkel, I., & McLanahan, S. (1986). *Single mothers and their children: A new American dilemma*. Washington, DC: Urban Institute.

Garfinkel, I., McLanahan, S., Meyer, D., & Seltzer, J. (Eds.). (1998). *Fathers under fire: The revolution in child support enforcement*. New York: Russell Sage Foundation.

Garfinkel, I., McLanahan, S., & Robins, P. (Eds.). (1992). *Child support assurance: Design issues, expected impacts, and political barriers as seen from Wisconsin*. Washington, DC: Urban Institute.

Garfinkel, I., McLanahan, S., & Robins, P. (Eds.). (1994). *Child support and child wellbeing*. Washington, DC: Urban Institute.

General Accounting Office. (1998). *Supplemental Security Income: SSA needs a uniform standard for assessing childhood disability*. Washington, DC: Author.

Gennetian, L. A., & Miller, C. (2000). *Reforming welfare and rewarding work: Final report on the Minnesota Family Investment Program: Vol. 2. Effects on children*. New York: Manpower Demonstration Research Corporation.

Gilliam, W. S. (2000). On over-generalizing from overly-simplistic evaluations of complex social programs: In further response to Goodson, Layzer, St. Pierre, & Bernstein. *Early Childhood Research Quarterly, 15*(1), 67–74.

Gilliam, W. S., Ripple, C. H., Zigler, E. F., & Leiter, V. (2000). Evaluating child and family demonstration initiatives: Lessons from the Comprehensive Child Development Program. *Early Childhood Research Quarterly, 15*(1), 40–60.

Goal One Technical Planning Group. (1991). The Goal One Technical Planning subgroup report on school readiness. In National Education Goals Panel (Ed.), *Potential strategies for long-term indicator development: Reports of the technical planning subgroups* (Report No. 91-0, 1-18). Washington, DC: National Education Goals Panel.

Goal One Technical Planning Group. (1993). *Reconsidering children's early development and learning: Toward shared beliefs and vocabulary* (Draft report to the National Education Goals Panel). Washington, DC: National Education Goals Panel.

Gomby, D. S., Culross, P. L., & Behrman, R. E. (1999). Home visiting: Recent program evaluations—analysis and recommendations. *The Future of Children, 9*(1), 4–26.

Goodson, B. D., Layzer, J. I., St. Pierre, R. G., & Bernstein, L. S. (2000). Good intentions are not enough: A response to Gilliam, Ripple, Zigler, & Leiter. *Early Childhood Research Quarterly, 15*(1), 61–66.

Goodson, B. D., Layzer, J. I., St. Pierre, R. G., Bernstein, L. S., & Lopez, M. (2000). Effectiveness of a comprehensive five-year family support program on low-income children and their families: Findings from the Comprehensive Child Development Program. *Early Childhood Research Quarterly, 15*(1), 5–39.

Greenberg, M. T., Lengua, L. J., Coie, J. D., & Pinderhughes, E. E. (1999). Predicting developmental outcomes at school entry using a multiple-risk model: Four American communities. *Developmental Psychology, 35*(2), 403–417.

Greenberg, M. T., Levin-Epstein, J., Hutson, R., Ooms, T., Schumacher, R., Turetsky, V., et al. (2000). *The 1996 welfare law: Key elements and emerging reauthorization issues*. Washington, DC: Center for Law and Social Policy.

Greenberger, E., & Goldberg, W. A. (1989). Work, parenting, and the socialization of children. *Developmental Psychology, 25*(1), 22–35.

Groves, R. M. (1989). *Survey errors and survey costs*. New York: Wiley.

Groves, R. M., & Wissoker, D. (1999, March). *No. 7: Early nonresponse studies of the 1997 National Survey of America's Families*. Washington, DC: Urban Institute. Available on-line: http://newfederalism.urban.org

Grusec, J. E. (1992). Social learning theory and developmental psychology: The legacies of Robert R. Sears and Albert Bandura. *Developmental Psychology, 28*(5), 776–786.

Gueron, J. M., & Pauly, E. (1991). *From welfare to work*. New York: Russell Sage Foundation.

Gunnar, M. R. (1998). Quality of early care and buffering of neuroendocrine stress reactions: Potential effects on the developing human brain. *Preventative Medicine, 27*, 208–211.

Guralnick, M. J. (Ed.). (1997). *The effectiveness of early intervention*. Baltimore: Brookes.

Guyer, B., Caughy, M., & McLearn, K. T. (1998, July). *Children and families in an era of rapid change: Creating a shared agenda for researchers, practitioners, and policy makers*. Paper presented at Head Start's Fourth National Research Conference, Washington, DC.

Guyer, B., Hughart, N., Strobino, D., Jones, A., Scharfstein, D., & the Healthy Steps Evaluation Team. (2000). Assessing the impact of pediatric-based developmental services on infants, families, and clinicians: Challenges to evaluating the Healthy Steps Program. *Pediatrics, 105*(3), 1–10.

Gyamfi, P., Brooks-Gunn, J., & Jackson, A. P. (2001). Associations between employment and financial and parenting stress in low-income single black mothers. *Women and Health, 32*(1/2), 119–135.

Hamilton, G., Brock, T., Farrell, M., Friedlander, D., & Harknett, K. (1997). *Evaluating two welfare-to-work program approaches: Two-year findings on the Labor Force Attachment and Human Capital Development programs in three sites*. Washington, DC: U.S. Department of Health and Human Services, Administration for Children and Families, and Office of the Assistant Secretary for Planning and Evaluation.

Hamilton, G., Freedman, S., Gennetian, L., Michalopoulos, C., Walter, J., Adams-Ciardello, D., Gassman-Pines, A., McGroder, S., Zaslow, M., Brooks, J., &

Ahluwalia, S. (2001). *National Evaluation of Welfare-to-Work Strategies: How effective are different welfare-to-work approaches? Five-year adult and child impacts for eleven programs.* Washington, DC: U.S. Department of Health and Human Services, Administration for Children and Families and Office of the Assistant Secretary for Planning and Evaluation, and U.S. Department of Education.

Harbin, G. L., Kochanek, T. T., McWilliam, R. A., Gallagher, J. J., Shaw, D., Tocci, L., et al. (1998). *Implementing federal policy for young children with disabilities: How are we doing?* Chapel Hill, NC: Early Childhood Research Institute on Service Utilization.

Harms, T., & Clifford, R. M. (1989). *Family Day Care Rating Scale.* New York: Teachers College Press.

Harms, T., & Clifford, R. M. (1990). *Early Childhood Environment Rating Scale.* New York: Teachers College Press.

Harms, T., Clifford, R. M., & Cryer, D. (1998). *Early Childhood Environment Rating Scale—Revised Edition.* New York: Teachers College Press.

Harms, T., Cryer, D., & Clifford, R. M. (1990). *Infant/Toddler Environment Rating Scale.* New York: Teachers College Press.

Harrington, D., Black, M. M., Starr, R. H., Jr., & Dubowitz, H. (1998). Child neglect: Relation to child temperament and family context. *American Journal of Orthopsychiatry, 68*(1), 108–116.

Harris, S. R. (1997). The effectiveness of early intervention for children with cerebral palsy and related motor disorders. In M. J. Guralnick (Ed.), *The effectiveness of early intervention* (pp. 327–347). Baltimore: Brookes.

Hauser, R. M., & Mossell, P. A. (1985). Fraternal resemblance in educational attainment and occupational status. *American Journal of Sociology, 91,* 650–673.

Haveman, R., & Wolfe, B. (1994). *Succeeding generations: On the effects of investments in children.* New York: Russell Sage Foundation.

Hayes, C. D., Palmer, J. L., & Zaslow, M. J. (Eds.). (1990). *Who cares for America's children? Child care policy for the 1990s.* Washington, DC: National Academy Press.

Head Start Bureau. (1996). *Head Start children's entry into public school: An interim report on the National Head Start–Public School Early Childhood Demonstration Study.* Washington, DC: U.S. Department of Health and Human Services.

Head Start Bureau. (1998). *Head Start Performance Measures: Second progress report.* Washington, DC: U.S. Department of Health and Human Services.

Healthy Steps for Young Children Program. (1997). *Survey of parents with young children* [On-line]. Available: http://www.healthysteps.org/page1-survey-highlights.html

Hebbeler, K. (1997). A system in a system: Sociopolitical factors and early intervention. In S. K. Thurman, J. R. Cornwell, & S. R. Gottwald (Eds.), *Contexts of early intervention: Systems and settings.* Baltimore: Brookes.

Hebbeler, K., Blackorby, J., McKenna, P., Gerlach-Downie, S., & Clayton, S. (1997). *Inclusion of students with disabilities in the Early Childhood Longitudinal Study: Issues and recommendations.* Menlo Park, CA: SRI International.

Hebbeler, K., Spiker, D., Wagner, M., Cameto, R., & McKenna, P. (1999). *State-to-state variation in early intervention system*. Menlo Park, CA: SRI International.

Hebbeler, K., & Wagner, M. (1998). *The National Early Intervention Longitudinal Study (NEILS) design overview*. Menlo Park, CA: SRI International.

Hebbeler, K., Wagner, M., Spiker, D., Scarborough, A., Simeonsson, R., & Collier, M. (2001). *National Early Intervention Longitudinal Study: A first look at the characteristics of children and families entering early intervention services*. Menlo Park, CA: SRI International.

Helburn, S., & Howes, C. (1996). Child care cost and quality. *The Future of Children, 6*, 62–82.

Hiatt, S. W., Sampson, D., & Baird, D. (1997). Paraprofessional home visitation: Conceptual and pragmatic considerations. *Journal of Community Psychology, 25*, 77–93.

Hill, C. R., & Stafford, F. P. (1985). Lifetime fertility, child care, and labor supply. In F. T. Juster & F. P. Stafford (Eds.), *Time, goods, and wellbeing* (pp. 471–492). Ann Arbor: University of Michigan Survey Research Center.

Hill, M. (1992). *The Panel Study of Income Dynamics: A user's guide* (Guides to major social science databases, Vol. 2). Newbury Park, CA: Sage.

Hirschi, T. (1969). *Causes of delinquency*. Berkeley: University of California Press.

Hofferth, S. L. (1985). Children's life course: Family structure and living arrangements in cohort perspective. In G. H. Elder (Ed.), *Life course dynamics: Trajectories and transitions, 1968–1980* (pp. 75–112). Ithaca, NY: Cornell University Press.

Hofferth, S. L. (1991). Comments on the importance of child care costs to women's decision making. In D. M. Blau (Ed.), *The economics of child care*. New York: Russell Sage Foundation.

Hofferth, S. L. (1998). *Healthy environments, healthy children: Children in families. A report on the 1997 Panel Study of Income Dynamics Child Development Supplement*. Ann Arbor, MI: Institute for Social Research.

Hofferth, S. L., Brayfield, A., Deich, S., & Holcomb, P. (1991). *National child care survey, 1990*. Washington, DC: Urban Institute.

Hofferth, S. L., Davis-Kean, P. E., Davis, J., & Finkelstein, J. (1997). *The Child Development Supplement to the Panel Study of Income Dynamics: 1997 user's guide* (Chapter 1). Ann Arbor, MI: Institute for Social Research, Survey Research Center.

Hofferth, S. L., & Sandberg, J. (2000). *Changes in American children's time, 1981–1997*. Ann Arbor, MI: Institute for Social Research.

Hofferth, S. L., & Sandberg, J. (2001). How American children spend their time. *Journal of Marriage and the Family, 63*(2), 295–308.

Hoffman, L., & Youngblade, L. (1999). *Mothers at work: Effects on children's wellbeing*. Cambridge, UK: Cambridge University Press.

Hogan, D. P., Msall, M. E., Rogers, M. L., & Avery, R. C. (1997). Improved disability population estimates of functional limitation among American children aged 5–17. *Maternal and Child Health Journal, 1*, 203–216.

Hojat, M. (1990). Can affectional ties be purchased? Comments on working mothers and their families. *Journal of Social Behavior and Personality, 5*, 493–502.

Hollenbeck, K., Tindal, G., & Almond, P. (1998). Teacher's knowledge of accommodations as a validity issue in high-stakes testing. *Journal of Special Education, 32,* 175–183.

Howes, C. (1980). Peer Play Scale as an index of complexity of peer interaction. *Developmental Psychology, 16*(4), 371–372.

Howes, C. (1997). Children's experiences in center-based child care as a function of teacher background and adult:child ratio. *Merrill-Palmer Quarterly, 43,* 404–425.

Howes, C., & Stewart, P. (1987). Child's play with adults, toys, and peers: An examination of family and child care influences. *Developmental Psychology, 23*(3), 423–430.

Hughart, N., & Healthy Steps Evaluation Team. (2002, February 1). *Healthy Steps phase three, year five—final report: The Healthy Steps for Young Children Program national evaluation.* [On-line]. Available: http://www.healthysteps.org

Hyson, M. C., Hirsh-Pasek, K., & Rescorla, L. (1990). An observation instrument based on NAEYC's Guidelines for developmentally appropriate practices for 4- and 5-year-old children. *Early Childhood Research Quarterly, 5,* 475–494.

Infant Health and Development Program (IHDP). (1990). Enhancing the outcomes of low-birth-weight, premature infants: A multisite randomized trial. *Journal of the American Medical Association, 263,* 3035–3042.

Ingels, S. J. (1997). *Early Childhood Longitudinal Study: Preliminary study design report.* Chicago: National Opinion Research Center.

Jackson, A. P., Brooks-Gunn, J., Huang, C., & Glassman, M. (2000). Single mothers in low-wage jobs: Financial strain, parenting, and preschoolers' outcomes. *Child Development, 71*(5), 1409–1423.

Jackson, A. P., Tienda, M., & Huang, C. (2001). Capabilities and employability of unwed mothers. *Children and Youth Services Review, 23,* 327–351.

Kagan, S. L. (1991a). Examining profit and non-profit child care: An odyssey of quality and auspices. *Journal of Social Sciences Issues, 47,* 87–104.

Kagan, S. L. (1991b). Moving from here to there: Rethinking continuity in transitions in early care and education. In B. Spodek & O. Saracho (Eds.), *The yearbook in early childhood education* (Vol. 2, pp. 132–151). New York: Teachers College Press.

Kagan, S. L. (1992). Readiness, past, present, and future: Shaping the agenda. *Young Children, 48*(1), 48–53.

Kagan, S. L. (1996). America's family support movement: A moment of change. In E. F. Zigler, S. L. Kagan, & N. W. Hall (Eds.), *Children, families, and government: Preparing for the twenty-first century* (pp. 156–170). New York: Cambridge University Press.

Kagan, S. L., & Pritchard, E. (1996). Linking services for children and families: Past legacies, future possibilities. In E. F. Zigler, S. L. Kagan, & N. W. Hall (Eds.), *Children, families, and government: Preparing for the twenty-first century* (pp. 378–393). New York: Cambridge University Press.

Kagan, S. L., & Weissbourd, B. (Eds.). (1994). *Putting families first: America's family support movement and the challenge of change.* San Francisco: Jossey-Bass.

Kahn, A. J., & Kamerman, S. B. (Eds.). (1996). *Children and their families in big cities: Strategies for service reform.* New York: Columbia University School of Social Work, Cross-National Studies Program.

Kaiser, A. P., Hancock, T. B., Cai, X., Foster, E. M., & Hester, P. P. (2000). Parent-reported behavior problems and language delays in boys and girls enrolled in Head Start classrooms. *Behavioral Disorders, 26*(1), 26–41.

Karoly, L. A., Greenwood, P. W., Everingham, S. S., Hoube, J., Kilburn, M. R., Rydell, C. P., et al. (1998). *Investing in our children: What we know and don't know about the cost and benefit of early childhood interventions.* Santa Monica, CA: RAND.

Kauffman, J. M., & Brigham, F. J. (Eds.). (2000). Assessing and addressing problems in children enrolled in Head Start [Special Issue]. *Behavioral Disorders, 26*(1).

Kaufman, A. S., & Kaufman, N. L. (1981). *Kaufman Assessment Battery for Children (K-ABC).* Circle Pines, MN: American Guidance Service.

Kennedy, E. M. (1993). The Head Start Transition Project: Head Start goes to elementary school. In E. F. Zigler & S. J. Styfco (Eds.), *Head Start and Beyond: A national plan for extended childhood intervention.* New Haven, CT: Yale University Press.

Kenney, G., Dubay, L., & Haley, J. (2000, October). *Snapshots of America's families II: Health insurance, access, and health status of children.* Washington, DC: Urban Institute.

Kenney, G., Scheuren, F., & Wang, K. (1999, February). *No. 16: National Survey of America's Families: Survey methods and data reliability* (pp. IA.1–IA.10). Washington, DC: Urban Institute. Available on-line: http://newfederalism.urban.org

Kindlon, D. J., Brooks-Gunn, J., Brennan, B., Selner-O'Hagan, M. B., & Earls, F. (1999). *Differential item functioning of the HOME inventory among cultural and economic groups.* Manuscript in preparation.

Kindlon, D. J., Wright, B. D., Raudenbush, S. W., & Earls, F. (1996). The measurement of children's exposure to violence: A Rasch analysis. *International Journal of Methods in Psychiatric Research, 6,* 161.1–161.8.

Kisker, E. E., Love, J. M., & Raikes, H. (with Boller, K., Paulsell, D., Rosenberg, L., Coolahan, K., & Berlin, L. J.). (1999). *Leading the way: Characteristics and early experiences of selected Early Head Start programs: Vol. 1. Cross-site perspectives.* Washington, DC: U.S. Department of Health and Human Services.

Kisker, E. E., Maynard, R. A., Rangarajan, A., & Boller, K. (1998). *Moving teenage parents into self-sufficiency.* Princeton, NJ: Mathematica Policy Research.

Kisker, E. E., Rangarajan, A., & Boller, K. (1998). *Moving into adulthood: Were the impacts of mandatory programs for welfare-dependent teenage parents sustained after the programs ended?* Princeton, NJ: Mathematica Policy Research.

Kitzman, H. J., Cole, R., Yoos, H. L., & Olds, D. (1997). Challenges experienced by home visitors: A qualitative study of program implementation. *Journal of Community Psychology, 25,* 95–109.

Kitzman, H., Olds, D. L., Henderson, C. R., Hanks, C., Cole, R., Tatelbaum, R., et al. (1997). Effect of prenatal and infancy home visitation by nurses on pregnancy outcomes, childhood injuries, and repeated childbearing: A randomized controlled trial. *Journal of the American Medical Association, 278*, 644–652.

Kitzman, H., Olds, D. L., Sidora, K., Henderson, C. R., Hanks, C., Cole, R., et al. (2000). Enduring effects of nurse home visitation on maternal life course. *Journal of the American Medical Association, 283*, 1983–1989.

Klebanov, P. K., Brooks-Gunn, J., Chase-Lansdale, L., & Gordon, R. (1997). Are neighborhood effects on young children mediated by features of the home environment? In J. Brooks-Gunn, G. Duncan, & J. L. Aber (Eds.), *Neighborhood poverty: Vol. 1. Context and consequences for children* (pp. 119–145). New York: Russell Sage Foundation Press.

Klebanov, P. K., Brooks-Gunn, J., & Duncan, G. J. (1994). Does neighborhood and family poverty affect mothers' parenting, mental health, and social support? *Journal of Marriage and the Family, 56*(2), 441–455.

Klebanov, P. K., Brooks-Gunn, J., McCarton, C., & McCormick, M. C. (1998). The contribution of neighborhood and family income to developmental test scores over the first three years of life. *Child Development, 69*(5), 1420–1436.

Klebanov, P. K., Brooks-Gunn, J., & McCormick, M. C. (2001). Maternal coping strategies and emotional distress: Results of an early intervention program for low birth weight young children. *Developmental Psychology, 37*(5), 654–667.

Kochanska, G., Murray, K. T., & Coy, K. C. (1997). Inhibitory control as a contributor to conscience in childhood: From toddler to early school age. *Child Development, 68*, 263–277.

Kochanska, G., Murray, K. T, Jacques, T. Y., Koenig, A. L., & Vandegeest, K. (1996). Inhibitory control in young children and its role in emerging internalization. *Child Development, 67*, 490–507.

Korfmacher, J., Kitzman, H., & Olds, D. (1998). Intervention processes as predictors of outcomes in a preventive home-visitation program. *Journal of Community Psychology, 26*, 49–64.

Korfmacher, J., O'Brien, R., Hiatt, S., & Olds, D. (1999). Differences in program implementation between nurses and paraprofessionals providing home visits during pregnancy and infancy: A randomized trial. *American Journal of Public Health, 89*, 1847–1851.

Kornhauser, R. (1978). *Social sources of delinquency*. Chicago: University of Chicago Press.

Kotch, J. B., Browne, D., Dufort, V., Winsor, J., & Catellier, D. (1999). Predicting child maltreatment in the first four years of life from characteristics assessed in the neonatal period. *Child Abuse and Neglect, 23*, 305–319.

Kovacs, M. (1982). *Children's Depression Inventory*. New York: Multi-Health Systems.

Kubisch, A. C. (1996). On the term community: An informal contribution. In A. J. Kahn & S. B. Kamerman (Eds.), *Children and their families in big cities: Strategies for service reform* (pp. 256–260). New York: Columbia University School of Social Work, Cross-National Studies Program.

Kupersmidt, J. B., Bryant, D., & Willoughby, M. T. (2000). Prevalence of aggressive behaviors among preschoolers in Head Start and community child care programs. *Behavioral Disorders, 26*(1), 42–52.

Kupersmidt, J., Griesler, P. C., DeRosier, M. E., Patterson, C. J., & Davis, P. W. (1995). Childhood aggression and peer relations in the context of family and neighborhood factors. *Child Development, 66*(2), 360–375.

Lally, J. R. (1995). *Program for Infant/Toddler Caregivers* [Videotape modules and manuals]. Sacramento: California Department of Education.

Layzer, J. I., Goodson, B., Bernstein, L., & Price, C. (2001). *National evaluation of family support programs, final report: Vol. A. The meta-analysis.* Cambridge, MA: Abt Associates.

Layzer, J. I., Goodson, B., Creps, C., Werner, A., & Bernstein, L. (2001). *National evaluation of family support programs: Vol. B. Research studies, final report.* Cambridge, MA: Abt Associates.

Layzer, J. I., Goodson, B., & Moss, M. (1993). *Life in preschool: Final report. Vol. 1.* Cambridge, MA: Abt Associates.

Lazar, E. P., & Michael, R. T. (1988). *Allocation of income within the household.* Chicago: University of Chicago Press.

Lazar, I., & Darlington, R. B. (1982). Lasting effects of early education: A report from the Consortium for Longitudinal Studies. *Monographs of the Society for Research in Child Development, 47,* 2–4.

Leach, P. (1994). *Children first: What our society must do—and is not doing—for our children today.* New York: Knopf.

Lee, V. E., Brooks-Gunn, J., Schnur, E., & Liaw, F. (1990). Are Head Start effects sustained? A longitudinal follow-up comparison of disadvantaged children attending Head Start, no preschool, and other preschool programs. *Child Development, 61,* 495–507.

Lee, V. E., & Loeb, S. (1995). Where do Head Start enrollees end up? One reason why preschool effects fade out. *Educational Evaluation and Policy Analysis, 17,* 62–82.

Lee, V. E., Loeb, S., & Lubeck, S. (1998). Contextual effects of prekindergarten classrooms for disadvantaged children on cognitive development: The case of Chapter 1. *Child Development, 69*(2), 479–494.

LeMenestrel, S. M., Tout, K., McGroder, S. M., Zaslow, M., & Moore, K. (1999). *An overview and synthesis of the Project on State-Level Child Outcomes.* Washington, DC: Child Trends.

Lerman, R., & Sorensen, E. (1997, March). *Father involvement with their nonmarital children: Patterns, determinants, and effects on their earnings.* Paper prepared for the annual meeting of the Population Association of America, Washington, DC.

Leventhal, T., & Brooks-Gunn, J. (2000). The neighborhoods they live in: Effects of neighborhood residence on child and adolescent outcomes. *Psychological Bulletin, 126*(2), 309–337.

Leventhal, T., & Brooks-Gunn, J. (in press). Changing neighborhoods and child well-being: Understanding how children may be affected in the coming century. *Advances in Life Course Research.*

Leventhal, T., Brooks-Gunn, J., & Kamerman, S. B. (1997). Communities as place, face, and space: Provision of services to poor, urban children and their families. In J. Brooks-Gunn, G. J. Duncan, & J. L. Aber (Eds.), *Neighborhood poverty: Vol. 2. Policy implications in studying neighborhoods* (pp. 182–205). New York: Russell Sage Foundation.

Leventhal, T., Brooks-Gunn, J., McCormick, M. C., & McCarton, C. M. (2000). Patterns of service use in preschool children: Correlates, consequences, and the role of early intervention. *Child Development, 71*, 800–817.

Levine, D. B., & Bryant, E. C. (1997). *An examination of alternative approaches to selecting a sample of new births.* Paper prepared for the National Center for Education Statistics, Office of Educational Research and Improvement, U.S. Department of Education.

Lewit, E. M., & Baker, L. S. (1995). School readiness. *The Future of Children, 5*(2), 128–139.

Liaw, F. R., & Brooks-Gunn, J. (1993). Patterns of low birth weight children's cognitive development and their determinants. *Developmental Psychology, 29*(6), 1024–1035.

Liaw, F. R., & Brooks-Gunn, J. (1994). Cumulative familial risks and low birthweight children's cognitive and behavioral development. *Journal of Clinical Child Psychology, 23*(4), 360–372.

Liaw, F. R., Meisels, S. J., & Brooks-Gunn, J. (1995). The effects of experience of early intervention on low birth weight, premature children: The Infant Health and Development Program. *Early Childhood Research Quarterly, 10*, 405–431.

Linver, M., Brooks-Gunn, J., & Kohen, D. (1999). Parenting behavior and emotional health as mediators of family poverty effects upon young low-birthweight children's cognitive ability. *Annals of the New York Academy of Sciences, 896*, 376–378.

Lopez, M. L. (Chair). (1999, December). *Findings from the Head Start Mental Health Research Consortium.* Symposium conducted at the Division for Early Childhood 15th annual International Conference on Children with Special Needs, Washington, DC.

Lopez, M. L. (Chair). (2000, June). *Recent Findings from the Head Start Mental Health Research Consortium.* Symposium conducted at Head Start's Fifth National Research Conference, Washington, DC.

Lopez, M. L., & Boyce, C. (Chairs). (2002, June). *Findings from the Head Start Mental Health Research Consortium.* Symposium conducted at Head Start's Sixth National Research Conference, Washington, DC.

Lopez, M. L., Tarullo, L. B., Forness, S. R., & Boyce, C. A. (2000). Early identification and intervention: Head Start's response to mental health challenges. *Early Education and Development, 11*(3), 265–282.

Love, J. M., Aber, L., & Brooks-Gunn, J. (1994). *Strategies for assessing community progress toward achieving the first national educational goal.* Princeton, NJ: Mathematica Policy Research.

Love, J. M., Kisker, E. E., Ross, C. M., Schochet, P. Z., Brooks-Gunn, J., Boller, K., Paulsell, D., Fuligni, A. S., & Berlin, L. J. (2001). *Building their futures: How Early Head Start programs are enhancing the lives of infants and toddlers in low-income families.* Washington, DC: U.S. Department of Health and Human Services.

Love, J. M., Kisker, E. E., Ross, C. M., Schochet, P. Z., Brooks-Gunn, J., Paulsell, D., Boller, K., Constantine, J., Vogel, C., Fuligni, A. S., & Brady-Smith, C. (2002). *Making a difference in the lives of infants and toddlers and their families: The impacts of Early Head Start.* Washington, DC: U.S. Department of Health and Human Services.

Maccoby, E. E. (1992). The role of parents in the socialization of children: An historical overview. *Developmental Psychology, 28*(6), 1006–1017.

Maggenheim, E. (1990, October). *Barriers to entry into the child care industry.* Paper presented at the 12th annual Research Conference, Association for Public Policy Analysis and Management, San Francisco.

Markowitz, C. (1998, June). *Have professional recommendations and consumer demand altered pediatric practice regarding child development?* Paper presented at the meeting of the Association of Health Services Research, Washington, DC.

Marsiglio, W., & Day, R. (1997, March). *Social fatherhood and paternal involvement: Conceptual, data, and policymaking issues.* Paper presented at the Conference on Fathering and Male Fertility: Improving Data and Research, Bethesda, MD.

Mathematica Policy Research, Inc. (1995). *A proposal for the Early Head Start Research and Evaluation Project.* Princeton, NJ: Mathematica Policy Research.

Maynard, R., Boehnen, E., Corbett, T., Sandefur, G., & Mosley, J. (1998). Changing family formation behavior through welfare reform. In R. Moffit (Ed.), *Welfare, the family, and reproductive behavior* (pp. 134–176). Washington, DC: National Academy Press.

Maynard, R., Nicholson, W., & Rangarajan, A. (1993). *Breaking the cycle of poverty: The effectiveness of mandatory services for welfare-dependent teenage parents.* Princeton, NJ: Mathematica Policy Research.

McCabe, L. A., Hernandez, M., Lara, S., & Brooks-Gunn, J. (2000). Assessing preschoolers' self-regulation in homes and classrooms: Lessons from the field. *Behavioral Disorders, 26*(1), 53–69.

McCabe, L. A., Rebello-Britto, P., Hernandez, M., & Brooks-Gunn, J. (2003). *Games children play: Observing young children's self-regulation across laboratory, home, and school settings.* Manuscript in preparation.

McCartney, K., & Phillips, D. (1988). Motherhood and child care. In B. Birns & D. Hays (Eds.), *The different faces of motherhood* (pp. 157–183). New York: Plenum.

McCarton, C., Brooks-Gunn, J., Wallace, I., Bauer, C., Bennett, F., Bernbaum, J., et al. (1997). Results at eight years of intervention for low birthweight premature infants: The Infant Health and Development Program. *Journal of the American Medical Association, 227,* 126–132.

McCormick, M. C., & Brooks-Gunn, J. (1989). Health care for children and adolescents. In H. Freeman & S. Levine (Eds.), *Handbook of medical sociology* (pp. 347–380). Englewood Cliffs, NJ: Prentice-Hall.

McCurdy, K., & Daro, D. (2001). Parent involvement in family support programs: An integrated theory. *Family Relations: Journal of Applied Family and Child Studies, 50*(2), 113–121.

McDonnell, L. M., McLaughlin, M. J., & Morison, P. (Eds.). (1997). *Educating one and all: Students with disabilities and standards-based reform*. Washington, DC: National Academy Press.

McGrew, K. S., Thurlow, M. L., & Spiegel, A. N. (1993). An investigation of the exclusion of students with disabilities in national data collection programs. *Education Evaluation and Policy Analysis, 15*, 339–352.

McGroder, S. M., Zaslow, M. J., Moore, K., & Brooks, J. (2002). *Impacts of a mandatory welfare-to-work program on children at school entry and beyond: Findings from the NEWWS Child Outcomes Study*. Washington, DC: Child Trends.

McGroder, S. M., Zaslow, M. J., Moore, K. A., Hair, E. C., & Ahluwalia, S. K. (2002). The role of parenting in shaping the impacts of welfare-to-work programs on children. In J. Borkowsky & C. Ramey (Eds.), *Parenting and your child's world: Influences on academic, intellectual, and social-emotional development*. Mahwah, NJ: Erlbaum Associates.

McGroder, S. M., Zaslow, M. J., Moore, K. A., & LeMenestrel, S. M. (2000). *National Evaluation of Welfare-to-Work Strategies: Impacts on young children and their families two years after enrollment: Findings from the Child Outcomes Study*. Washington, DC: U.S. Department of Health and Human Services and U.S. Department of Education.

McGurk, H., Caplan, M., Hennessy, E., Martin, S., & Moss, P. (1993). Controversy, theory and social context in contemporary day care research. *Journal of Child Psychology and Psychiatry, 34*, 3–23.

McKey, R. H., Condelli, L., Ganson, H., Barrett, B. J., McConkey, C., & Plantz, M. C. (1985). *The impact of Head Start on children, families, and communities* (DHHS Publication No. OHDS 85–31193). Washington, DC: U.S. Government Printing Office.

McLanahan, S., & Sandefur, G. (1994). *Growing up with a single parent*. Cambridge, MA: Harvard University Press.

McLean, L. K., & Cripe, J. W. (1997). The effectiveness of early intervention for children with communication disorders. In M. J. Guralnick (Ed.), *The effectiveness of early intervention* (pp. 349–428). Baltimore: Brookes.

McLearn, K. T., Zuckerman, B. S., Parker, S., Yellowitz, M., & Kaplan-Sanoff, M. K. (1998). Child development and pediatrics for the twenty-first century: The Healthy Steps approach. *Journal of Urban Health: Bulletin of the New York Academy of Medicine, 75*, 704–723.

McLoyd, V. C. (1990). The impact of economic hardship on black families and children: Psychological distress, parenting, and socioemotional development. *Child Development, 61*(2), 311–346.

McLoyd, V. C. (1998). Children in poverty: Development, public policy, and practice. In W. Damon (Editor-in-Chief) & I. E. Sigel & K. A. Renninger (Eds.), *Handbook of child psychology: Vol. 4. Child psychology in practice* (5th ed., pp. 135–208). New York: Wiley.

Meyer, D. (1998). Effects of child support on the economic status of nonresident fathers. In I. Garfinkel, S. McLanahan, D. Meyer, & J. Seltzer (Eds.), *Fathers under fire: The revolution in child support enforcement.* New York: Russell Sage Foundation.

Miller, C., Knox, V., Gennetian, L. A., Dodoo, M., Hunter, J. A., & Redcross, C. (2000). *Reforming welfare and rewarding work: Final report on the Minnesota Family Investment Program. Vol. 1. Effects on adults.* New York: Manpower Demonstration Research Corporation.

Milner, J. (1986). *Child Abuse Potential Inventory.* DeKalb, IL: Psytec.

Minkovitz, C., Strobino, D., Hughart, N., Scharfstein, D., Guyer, B., & the Healthy Steps Evaluation Team. (2001). Early effects of the Healthy Steps for Young Children Program. *Archives of Pediatric and Adolescent Medicine, 155*(4), 470–479.

Moore, K. A. (1995). *Births to unmarried mothers: United States, 1980–92. Report to Congress on out-of-wedlock childbearing.* Washington, DC: U.S. Department of Health and Human Services.

Moore, K. A., Hatcher, J. L., Vandivere, S., & Brown, B. V. (2000, October). *Snapshots of America's families II: Children's behavior and well-being.* Washington, DC: Urban Institute.

Moore, K. A., Zaslow, M. J., Coiro, M. J., Miller, S., & Magenheim, E. (1995). *How well are they faring? AFDC families with preschool-aged children in Atlanta at the outset of the JOBS evaluation.* Washington, DC: U.S. Department of Health and Human Services, Office of the Assistant Secretary for Planning and Evaluation.

Morris, P. A., Huston, A. C., Duncan, G. J., Crosby, D. A., & Bos, J. M. (2001). *How welfare and work policies affect children: A synthesis of research.* New York: Manpower Demonstration Research Corporation.

Nash, J. M. (1997, February 3). Fertile minds. *Time, 149,* 48–56.

National Center for Children in Poverty. (1996). *One in four: America's youngest poor.* New York: Author.

National Center for Children in Poverty. (1997). *Young children in poverty fact sheet* [On-line]. Available: http://cpmcnet.columbia.edu/dept/nccp/ycpf.html

National Education Goals Panel. (1998). *The National Education Goals report: Building a nation of learners, 1998.* Washington, DC: U.S. Government Printing Office.

National Research Council. (1993). *Understanding child abuse and neglect.* Washington, DC: National Academy Press.

NICHD Early Child Care Research Network (ECCRN). (1992). *The NICHD Study of Early Child Care: A comprehensive longitudinal study of young children's lives.* (ERIC Document Reproduction Service No. ED 353 087)

NICHD Early Child Care Research Network (ECCRN). (1996). Characteristics of infant child care: Factors contributing to positive caregiving. *Early Childhood Research Quarterly, 11*(3), 269–306.

NICHD Early Child Care Research Network (ECCRN). (1997a). Child care in the first year of life. *Merrill-Palmer Quarterly, 43*(3), 340–360.

NICHD Early Child Care Research Network (ECCRN). (1997b). The effects of infant child care on infant-mother attachment security: Results of the NICHD Study of Early Child Care. *Child Development, 68*(5), 860–879.

NICHD Early Child Care Research Network (ECCRN). (1997c). Familial factors associated with the characteristics of nonmaternal care for infants. *Journal of Marriage and the Family, 59,* 389–408.

NICHD Early Child Care Research Network (ECCRN). (1998a). Early child care and self-control, compliance, and problem behavior at twenty-four and thirty-six months. *Child Development, 69*(4), 1145–1170.

NICHD Early Child Care Research Network (ECCRN). (1998b). Relations between family predictors and child outcomes: Are they weaker for children in child care? *Developmental Psychology, 34*(5), 1119–1128.

NICHD Early Child Care Research Network (ECCRN). (1999a). Child care and mother-child interaction in the first three years of life. *Developmental Psychology, 35*(6), 1399–1413.

NICHD Early Child Care Research Network (ECCRN). (1999b). Child outcomes when child care center classes meet recommended standards for quality. *American Journal of Public Health, 89,* 1072–1077.

NICHD Early Child Care Research Network (ECCRN). (1999c). Chronicity of maternal depressive symptoms, maternal sensitivity, and child functioning at 36 months. *Developmental Psychology, 35*(5), 1297–1310.

NICHD Early Child Care Research Network (ECCRN). (2000). The relation of child care to cognitive and language development: Results from the NICHD Study of Early Child Care. *Child Development, 71*(4), 960–980.

O'Connor, S. (1991). *ASQ: Assessing school-age child care quality.* Wellesley, MA: Wellesley College, Center for Research on Women.

Olds, D. L., Eckenrode, J., Henderson, C. R., Kitzman, H., Powers, J., Cole, R., et al. (1997). Long-term effects of home visitation on maternal life course and child abuse and neglect: Fifteen-year follow-up of a randomized trial. *Journal of the American Medical Association, 278,* 637–643.

Olds, D., Henderson, C. R., Cole, R., Eckenrode, J., Kitzman, H., Luckey, D., et al. (1998). Long-term effects of nurse home visitation on children's criminal and antisocial behavior: 15-year follow-up of a randomized controlled trial. *Journal of the American Medical Association, 280,* 1238–1244.

Olds, D. L., Henderson, C. R., Kitzman, H. J., Eckenrode, J. J., Cole, R. E., & Tatelbaum, R. C. (1999). Prenatal and infancy home visitation by nurses: Recent findings. *The Future of Children, 9*(1), 44–65.

Olds, D., Henderson, C., Tatelbaum, R., & Chamberlin, R. (1986). Preventing child abuse and neglect: A randomized trial of nurse home visitation. *Pediatrics, 78,* 65–78.

Olds, D., & Kitzman, H. (1993). Review of research on home visiting for pregnant women and parents of young children. *The Future of Children, 3*(3), 53–92.

Olds, D., Kitzman, H., Cole, R., & Robinson, J. (1997). Theoretical foundations of a program of home visitation for pregnant women and parents of young children. *Journal of Community Psychology, 25,* 9–25.

Olds, D. L., Robinson, J., O'Brien, R., Luckey, D. W., Pettitt, L. M., Henderson, C. R., Ng, R. K., Sheff, K. L., Korfmacher, J., Hiatt, S., & Ayelet, T. (2002).

Home visiting by paraprofessionals and by nurses: A randomized controlled trial. *Pediatrics, 110*(3), 486–496.

Oppenheimer, V. (1973). Demographic influences on female employment and the status of women. In J. Huber (Ed.), *Changing women in a changing society* (pp.184–189). Chicago, IL: University of Chicago.

Oppenheimer, V. (1982). *Work and family: A study in social demography.* New York: Academic Press.

The Ounce of Prevention Fund. (1993). *Beethoven's Fifth: The first five years of the Center for Successful Child Development—Executive summary.* Chicago: The Ounce of Prevention Fund.

Pascoe, J. M., Loda, F. A., Jeffries, V., & Earp, J. A. (1981). The association between mothers' social support and provision of stimulation to their children. *Developmental and Behavioral Pediatrics, 2,* 15–19.

Pearlin, L. I., Menaghan, E. G., Lieberman, M. A., & Mullan, J. T. (1981). The stress process. *Journal of Health and Social Behavior, 22*(4), 337–356.

Peddle, N., & Wang, C. (2001, August). *Current trends in child abuse prevention, reporting and fatalities: The 1999 fifty-state survey* (Working Paper No. 808). Chicago: National Center on Child Abuse Prevention Research, Prevent Child Abuse America. Available on-line: http://www.preventchildabuse.org/research _ctr/reports.html

Peisner-Feinberg, E., & Burchinal, M. (1997). Relations between preschool children's child care experiences and concurrent development: The Cost, Quality, and Child Outcomes Study. *Merrill-Palmer Quarterly, 43,* 451–477.

Phillips, D., McCartney, K., & Scarr, S. (1987). Child-care quality and children's social development. *Developmental Psychology, 23*(4), 537–543.

Phillips, D., Mekos, D., Scarr, S., McCartney, K., & Abbott-Shim, M. (1995). *Paths to quality in child care: Structural and contextual influences in children's classroom environments.* Unpublished manuscript.

Phillips, D., Voran, M., Kisker, E., Howes, C., & Whitebook, M. (1994). Child care for children in poverty: Opportunity or inequity? *Child Development, 65*(2), 472–492.

Pianta, R. C. (1992). *Student-Teacher Relationship Scale.* Charlottesville: University of Virginia.

Posner, J. K., & Vandell, D. L. (1994). Low-income children's after school care: Are there beneficial effects of children's social and academic adjustment? *Child Development, 65,* 440–456.

Powell, D. R. (1995). *Enabling young children to succeed in school.* Washington, DC: American Educational Research Association.

Primus, W., & Porter, K. (1998). *Strengths of the safety net: How the EITC, Social Security, and other government programs affect poverty.* Washington, DC: Center on Budget and Policy Priorities.

Project on Human Development in Chicago Neighborhoods (PHDCN). (1997). *The Project on Human Development in Chicago Neighborhoods: Intricate pathways.* Chicago: Author.

Quint, J., Bos, J., & Polit, D. (1997). *New Chance: Final report on a comprehensive program for young mothers in poverty and their children.* New York: Manpower Demonstration Research Corporation.

Radloff, L. S. (1977). The CES-D Scale: A self-report depression scale for research in the general population. *Applied Psychological Measurement, 1*(3), 385–401.

Ramey, C. T., Bryant, D. M., Wasick, B. H., Sparling, J. J., Fendt, K. H., & LaVange, L. M. (1992). The Infant Health and Development Program for low birthweight, premature infants: Program elements, family participation, and child intelligence. *Pediatrics, 3,* 454–465.

Ramey, C. T., & Ramey, S. L. (1998). Early intervention and early experience. *American Psychologist, 53,* 109–120.

Ramey, C. T., Ramey, S. L., Gaines, K. R., & Blair, C. (1995). Two-generation early intervention programs: A child development perspective. In S. Smith (Ed.), *Advances in Applied Developmental Psychology: Vol. 9. Two-generation programs for families in poverty: A new intervention strategy* (pp. 199–228). Norwood, NJ: Ablex.

Ramey, S. L., & Ramey, C. T. (1992). Early educational intervention with disadvantaged children—To what effect? *Applied and Preventive Psychology, 1,* 131–140.

Ramey, S. L., & Ramey, C. T. (1999). Early experience and early intervention for children "at risk" for developmental delay and mental retardation. *Mental Retardation and Developmental Disabilities Research Reviews, 5*(1), 1–10.

Raudenbush, S. W. (1997, March). Hierarchical linear models and growth models. In F. Earls & S. L. Buka (Eds.), *Project on Human Development in Chicago Neighborhoods: Technical report* (pp. 90–95). Rockville, MD: National Institute of Justice.

Raudenbush, S. W., & Sampson, R. J. (1999). "Econometrics": Toward a science of assessing ecological settings, with application of HLM. *Sociological Methodology, 29,* 1–41.

Reichman, N., & McLanahan, S. S. (1998). *Self-sufficiency, parenting adequacy, and child wellbeing: Lessons from New Chance, the Teenage Parent Demonstration, and LEAP* (Working paper No. 98-16). Princeton, NJ: Bendheim-Thoman Center for Research on Child Wellbeing, Princeton University.

Rendall, M. S., Clarke, L., Peters, H. E., Ranjit, N., & Verropoulou G. (1997, March). *Incomplete reporting of male fertility in the United States and Britain.* Paper presented at the annual meeting of the Population Association of America, Washington, DC.

Repetti, R. L., Mathews, K. A., & Waldron, I. (1989). Employment and women's health: Effects of paid employment on women's mental and physical health. *American Psychologist, 44,* 1394–1401.

Reynolds, A. J., Mann, E., Miedel, W., & Smokowski, P. (1997). The state of early childhood intervention: Effectiveness, myths and realities, new directions. *Focus, 19*(1), 5–11.

Riccio, J., Friedlander, D., & Freedman, S. (1994). *GAIN: Benefits, costs, and three-year impacts of a welfare-to-work program.* New York: Manpower Demonstration Research Corporation.

Richman, N., Stevenson, J., & Graham, P. J. (1975). Prevalence of behavior problems in three-year-old children: An epidemiological study in a London borough. *Journal of Child Psychology and Psychiatry, 16*, 277–288.

Riemer, D. (1988). *The prisoners of welfare: Liberating America's poor from unemployment and lower wages.* New York: Praeger.

Rimm-Kaufman, S. E., Pianta, R. C., & Cox, M. J. (2000). Teachers' judgments of problems in the transition to kindergarten. *Early Childhood Research Quarterly, 15*(2), 147–166.

Robins, L. N. (1966). *Deviant children grow up: A sociological and psychiatric study of sociopathic personality.* Baltimore: Williams and Wilkins.

Roid, G. H., & Miller, L. J. (1995, 1997). *Leiter International Performance Scale—Revised.* Wood Dale, IL: Stoelting.

Rosenthal, R., & Vandell, D. L. (1996). Quality of care at school-aged care programs: Regulatable features, observed experiences, child perspectives, and parent perspectives. *Child Development, 67*, 2434–2445.

Ross, C., & Kirby, G. (2000, June). *A study of infant care under welfare reform.* Paper presented at the Administration on Children and Families Research Conference, Arlington, VA.

Royce, J. M., Darlington, R. B., & Murray, H. W. (1983). Pooled analyses: Findings across studies. In Consortium for Longitudinal Studies (Ed.), *As the twig is bent. . . . Lasting effects of preschool programs* (pp. 411–460). Hillsdale, NJ: Erlbaum.

Runyan, D. K., Curtis, P. A., Hunter, W. M., Black, M. M., Kotch, J. B., Bangdiwala, S., et al. (1998). LONGSCAN: A consortium for longitudinal studies of maltreatment and the life course of children. *Aggression and Violent Behavior, 2*(3), 275–285.

Russell, B., Leonard, M., & Scheuren, F. (1999, March). *No. 11: 1997 NSAF child public use file codebook.* Washington, DC: Urban Institute.

Safer, N. D., & Hamilton, J. L. (1993). Legislative context for early intervention services. In W. Brown, S. K. Thurman, & L. F. Pearl (Eds.), *Family-centered early intervention with infants and toddlers: Innovative cross-disciplinary approaches.* Baltimore: Brookes.

Sameroff, A. J. (1983). Developmental Systems: Contexts and evolutions. In P. H. Mussen (Series Ed.) & W. Kessen (Vol. Ed.), *Handbook of child psychology: Vol.1. History, theory, and methods* (4th ed., pp. 237–294). New York: Wiley.

Sameroff, A. J., & Seifer, R. (1983). Familial risk and child competence. *Child Development, 54*(5), 1254–1268.

Sampson, R. J. (1992). Family management and child development: Insights from social disorganization theory. In J. McCord (Ed.), *Advances in criminological theory* (Vol. 3, pp. 63–93). New Brunswick, NJ: Transaction.

Sampson, R. J. (1997). Collective regulation of adolescent misbehavior: Validation results from eighty Chicago neighborhoods. *Journal of Adolescent Research, 12*(2), 227–244.

Sampson, R. J., & Groves, W. B. (1989). Community structure and crime: Testing social disorganization theory. *American Journal of Sociology, 94*(4), 774–780.

Sampson, R. J., & Laub, J. H. (1993). *Crime in the making: Pathways and turning points through life*. Cambridge, MA: Harvard University Press.

Sampson, R. J., Morenoff, J. D., & Earls, F. (1999). Beyond social capital: Spatial dynamics of collective efficacy for children. *American Sociological Review, 64*(5), 633–660.

Sampson, R. J., & Raudenbush, S. W. (1999). Systematic social observation of public spaces: A new look at disorder in urban neighborhoods. *American Journal of Sociology, 105*(3), 603–651.

Sampson, R. J., Raudenbush, S. W., & Earls, F. (1997, August 15). Neighborhoods and violent crime: A multilevel study of collective efficacy. *Science, 277*, 918–924.

Sandberg, J., & Hofferth, S. L. (2000). *Changes in children's time with parents, U.S. 1981–1997*. Unpublished manuscript.

Scarr, S. (1992). Developmental theories for the 1990's: Development and individual differences. *Child Development, 63*, 1–19.

Scarr, S., Eisenberg, M., & Deater-Deckard, K. (1994). Measurement of quality in child care centers. *Early Childhood Research Quarterly, 9*, 131–151.

Schaefer, E. S., & Edgerton, M. (1985). Parent and child correlates of parental modernity. In I. E. Sigel (Ed.), *Parental belief systems: The psychological consequences for children* (pp. 287–318). Hillsdale, NJ: Erlbaum.

Schaefer, E. S., Edgerton, M., & Aaronson, M. (1978). *Classroom behavior inventory*. Unpublished rating scale, University of North Carolina, Chapel Hill.

Schweinhart, L. J., Barnes, H. V., Weikart, D. P., Barnett, W. S., & Epstein, A. S. (1993). *Significant benefits: The High/Scope Perry Preschool Study through age 27*. Ypsilanti, MI: High/Scope Press.

Selner-O'Hagan, M. B., Kindlon, D. J., Buka, S. L., Raudenbush, S. W., & Earls, F. J. (1998). Assessing exposure to violence in urban youth. *Journal of Child Psychology and Psychiatry and Allied Disciplines, 39*, 215–224.

Selner-O'Hagan, M. B., Leventhal, T., Brooks-Gunn, J., Bingenheimer, J. B., & Earls, F. J. (2001). *Constructing a longitudinal assessment of the home environment across childhood: A refinement of the HOME inventory*. Manuscript submitted for publication.

Seltzer, J. (1994). Consequences of marital dissolution for children. *Annual Review of Sociology, 20*, 235–266.

Serna, L., Nielsen, E., Lambros, K., & Forness, S. (2000). Primary prevention with children at risk for emotional or behavioral disorders: Data on a universal intervention of Head Start classrooms. *Behavioral Disorders, 26*(1), 70–84.

Shaw, C., & McKay, H. (1942). *Juvenile delinquency and urban areas: A study of rates of delinquency in relation to differential characteristics of local communities in American cities*. Chicago: University of Chicago Press.

Shonkoff, J. P., Hauser-Cram, P., Krauss, M. W., & Upshur, C. C. (1992). Development of infants with disabilities and their families. *Monographs of the Society for Research in Child Development, 57* (6, Serial No. 230).

Shonkoff, J. P., & Meisels, S. J. (Eds.). (2000). *Handbook of early childhood intervention* (2nd ed.). New York: Cambridge University Press.

Shonkoff, J. P., & Phillips, D. A. (Eds.). (2000). *From neurons to neighborhoods:*

The science of early child development. Washington, DC: National Academy of Sciences.

Shore, R. (1997). *Rethinking the brain: New insights into early development*. New York: Families and Work Institute.

Silverstein, L. (1991). Transforming the debate about child care and maternal employment. *American Psychologist, 46*, 1025–1032.

Smeeding, T. M. (1995). An interdisciplinary model and data requirements for studying poor children. In P. L. Chase-Lansdale & J. Brooks-Gunn (Eds.), *Escape from poverty: What makes a difference for children?* (pp. 291–298). New York: Cambridge University Press.

Smith, J. R., Brooks-Gunn, J., & Jackson, A. (1997). Parental employment and children. In R. Hauser, B. Brown, & W. Prosser (Eds.), *Indicators of children's well-being* (pp. 279–308). New York: Russell Sage Foundation.

Smith, J. R., Brooks-Gunn, J., & Klebanov, P. K. (1997). Consequences of living in poverty for young children's cognitive and verbal ability and early school achievement. In G. J. Duncan & J. Brooks-Gunn (Eds.), *Consequences of growing up poor* (pp. 132–189). New York: Russell Sage Foundation.

Smith, J. R., Brooks-Gunn, J., Klebanov, P., & Lee, K. (2000). Welfare and work: Complementary strategies for low-income mothers? *Journal of Marriage and the Family, 62*, 808–821.

Smith, R. M. (Ed.). (1997, Spring/Summer). Your child from birth to three [Special issue]. *Newsweek*, 4–97.

Smith, R. M. (Ed.). (2000, Fall/Winter). Your child [Special edition]. *Newsweek*, 4–88.

Smith, S. (1995). Two-generation programs: A new intervention strategy and directions for future research. In P. L. Chase-Lansdale & J. Brooks-Gunn (Eds.), *Escape from poverty: What makes a difference for children?* (pp. 299–314). New York: Cambridge University Press.

Sparling, J. J., Lewis, I. S., Ramey, C. T., Wasik, B. H., Bryant, D. M., & LaVange, L. M. (1991). Partners: A curriculum to help premature, low birthweight infants get off to a good start. *Topics in Early Childhood Special Education, 11*, 36–55.

Spiker, D., Ferguson, J., & Brooks-Gunn, J. (1993). Enhancing maternal interactive behavior and child social competence in low birth weight, premature infants. *Child Development, 64*, 754–768.

Spiker, D., & Hopmann, M. (1997). The effectiveness of early intervention for children with Down Syndrome. In M. J. Guralnick (Ed.), *The effectiveness of early intervention* (pp. 271–305). Baltimore: Brookes.

SRI International. (1999). *Special Education Elementary Longitudinal Study (SEELS): Revised timeline and data collection, sample, and analysis plans*. Menlo Park, CA: Author.

St. Pierre, R. G., Gamse, B., Alamprese, J., Rimdzius, T., & Tao, F. (1998). *Even Start: Evidence from the past and a look to the future*. Washington, DC: U.S. Department of Education, Planning and Evaluation Service.

St. Pierre, R. G., & Layzer, J. I. (1999). Using home visits for multiple purposes: The Comprehensive Child Development Program. *The Future of Children, 9*(1), 134–152.

St. Pierre, R. G., Layzer, J. I., & Barnes, H. V. (1995). Two-generation programs: Design, cost, and short-term effectiveness. *The Future of Children, 5*(3), 76–93.

St. Pierre, R. G., Layzer, J. I., Goodson, B. D., & Bernstein, L. S. (1997). *National impact evaluation of the Comprehensive Child Development Program: Final report*. Cambridge, MA: Abt Associates.

St. Pierre, R. G., McLaughlin, J., Price, C., Layzer, J., Obeidallah, D., & Leherr, K. (2000). *National evaluation of the Comprehensive Child Development Program: Second cohort*. Cambridge, MA: Abt Associates.

St. Pierre, R. G., Ricciuti, A., Tao, F., Creps, C., Kumagawa, T., & Ross, W. (2000). *Third national Even Start evaluation: Interim report*. Washington, DC: U.S. Department of Education, Planning and Evaluation Service.

St. Pierre, R. G., Swartz, J., Gamse, B., Murray, S., Deck, D., & Nickel, P. (1995). *National evaluation of the Even Start family literacy program*. Washington: U.S. Department of Education.

Starfield, B. (1991). Innovative ways to study primary care using traditional methods. In P. G. Norton & M. Stewart (Eds.), *Primary care research: Traditional and innovative approaches. Research methods for primary care* (Vol. 1, pp. 26–39). Newbury Park, CA: Sage.

Starfield, B. (1992). Child and adolescent health status measures. *The Future of Children, 2*(2), 25–29.

Staveteig, S., & Wigton, A. (2000, October). *Snapshots of America's families II: Key findings by race and ethnicity*. Washington, DC: Urban Institute.

Stipek, D., Daniels, D., Galuzzo, D., & Milburn, S. (1992). Characterizing early childhood education programs for poor and middle-class children. *Early Childhood Research Quarterly, 7*, 1–19.

Sugland, B. W., Zaslow, M. J., Smith, J. R., Brooks-Gunn, J., Coates, D., Blumenthal, C., et al. (1995). The Early Childhood HOME Inventory and HOME–Short Form in differing racial/ethnic groups: Are there differences in underlying structure, internal consistency of subscales, and patterns of prediction? *Journal of Family Issues, 16*(5), 632–663.

Sullivan, M. L. (1993). *More than housing: How community development corporations go about changing lives and neighborhoods*. New York: New School for Social Research, Graduate School of Management and Urban Policy, Community Development Research Center.

Sumner, G., & Spietz, A. (Eds.). (1994). *NCAST Caregiver/Parent–Child Interaction teaching manual*. Seattle, WA: University of Washington, Nursing Child Assessment Satellite Training (NCAST).

Tanfer, K., & Mott, F. (1997, June). *The meaning of fatherhood for men*. Paper prepared for the Conference on Fathering and Male Fertility: Improving Data and Research, Bethesda, MD.

Tao, F., Gamse, B., & Tarr, H. (1998). *Second national evaluation of the Even Start family literacy program: Final report*. Washington, DC: U.S. Department of Education, Planning and Evaluation Service.

Tao, F., Swartz, J., St. Pierre, R., & Tarr, H. (1997). *National evaluation of the*

Even Start family literacy program: 1995 interim report. Washington: U.S. Department of Education.

Tarullo, L. (Chair). (2000, April). *Recent Findings from the Head Start Mental Health Research Consortium.* Symposium conducted at the 27th Annual Training Conference of the National Head Start Association, Washington, DC.

Tienda, M. (1991). Poor people and poor places: Deciphering neighborhood effects on poverty outcomes. In J. Haber (Ed.), *Macro-micro linkages in sociology* (pp. 244–262). Newberry, CA: Sage.

Tietze, W., Cryer, D., Bairrao, J., Palacios, J., & Wetzel, G. (1996). Comparisons of observed process quality in early child care and education programs in five countries. *Early Childhood Research Quarterly, 11,* 447–475.

Urban Institute. (1999, March). *1997 Snapshots of America's families.* Washington, DC: Author.

U.S. Advisory Board on Child Abuse and Neglect (U.S. ABCAN). (1990). *Child abuse and neglect: Critical first steps in response to a national emergency.* Washington, DC: Author.

U.S. Advisory Board on Child Abuse and Neglect (U.S. ABCAN). (1995). *A nation's shame: Fatal child abuse and neglect in the United States.* Washington, DC: Author.

U.S. Bureau of Labor Statistics. (1997). *Current Population Survey.* Washington, DC: U.S. Department of Commerce.

U.S. Census Bureau. (1999). *Statistical abstract of the United States, 1999,* Table 660. Washington, DC: U.S. Government Printing Office.

U.S. Department of Education. (1997). *To assure the free appropriate public education of all children with disabilities: Nineteenth annual report to Congress on the implementation of the Individuals with Disabilities Education Act.* Washington, DC: U.S. Government Printing Office.

U.S. Department of Education. (1998). *To assure the free appropriate public education of all children with disabilities: Twentieth annual report to Congress on the implementation of the Individuals with Disabilities Education Act.* Washington, DC: U.S. Government Printing Office.

U.S. Department of Health and Human Services. (1993). *Creating a 21st century Head Start: Final report of the advisory committee on Head Start quality and expansion.* Washington, DC: U.S. Government Printing Office.

U.S. Department of Health and Human Services. (1994). *Statement of the advisory committee on services for families with infants and toddlers* (DHHS Publication No. 1994-615-032/03062). Washington, DC: U.S. Government Printing Office.

U.S. Department of Health and Human Services, National Center for Child Abuse and Neglect. (1996). *Child abuse and neglect case-level data 1993* (Working Paper No. 1). Washington, DC: U.S. Government Printing Office.

Vaillant, G. E. (1983). *The natural history of alcoholism.* Cambridge, MA: Harvard University Press.

Vandell, D. L., & Wolfe, B. (2000). *Child care quality: Does it matter and does it need to be improved?* (Special Report No. 78). Madison: University of Wisconsin, Institute for Research on Poverty.

Vanderwood, M., McGrew, K. S., & Ysseldyke, J. E. (1998). Why we can't say much about students with disabilities during educational reform. *Exceptional Children, 64*, 359–379.

Vandivere, S., Moore, K. A., & Zaslow, M. (2000, October). *Snapshots of America's families II: Children's family environment.* Washington, DC: Urban Institute.

Ventura, S. J., Bachrach, C. A., Hill, L., Kaye, K., Holcomb, P., & Koff, E. (1995). *The demography of out-of-wedlock childbearing* (Report to Congress on Out-of-Wedlock Childbearing). Washington, DC: Department of Health and Human Services.

Vidal, A. C. (1992). *Rebuilding communities: A national study of urban community development corporations.* New York: New School for Social Research, Graduate School of Management and Urban Policy, Community Development Research Center.

Wagner, M. M., & Clayton, S. L. (1999). The Parents as Teachers program: Results from two demonstrations. *The Future of Children, 9(1),* 91–115.

Waite, L. (1995). Does marriage matter? *Demography, 32,* 483–508.

Walker, J. R. (1991). Public policy and the supply of child care services. In D. M. Blau (Ed.), *The economics of child care.* New York: Russell Sage Foundation.

Waller, M. (1997). *Redefining fatherhood: Paternal involvement, masculinity, and responsibility in the "other America."* Unpublished doctoral dissertation, Princeton University, Princeton, New Jersey.

Wang, C. T., & Daro, D. (1998). *Current trends in child abuse reporting and fatalities: The results of the 1997 Annual Fifty State Survey.* Chicago: Prevent Child Abuse America.

Ware, A. M., Brady, C. L., O'Brien, C., & Berlin, L. (1998). *Early Head Start Research and Evaluation Project: 14-month child-parent interaction rating scales for the three bag assessment.* Unpublished coding system, Teachers College, Columbia University.

Warr, P., & Parry, G. (1982). Paid employment and women's psychological well-being. *Psychological Bulletin, 91,* 498–516.

Waters, E., & Deane, K. (1985). Defining and assessing individual differences in attachment relationships: Q-methodology and the organization of behavior in infancy and early childhood. In I. Bretherton & E. Waters (Eds.), *Growing points of attachment theory and research* (pp. 41–65). Chicago: Monographs for the Society for Research in Child Development.

Wechsler, D. (1974). *Wechsler Intelligence Scale for Children–Revised* (WISC-R). San Antonio, TX: Psychological Corporation.

Weinfield, N. S., Ogawa, J. R., & Egeland, B. (2002). Predictability of observed mother-child interaction from preschool to middle childhood in a high-risk sample. *Child Development, 73(2),* 528–543.

West, J., Denton, K., & Germino Hauksen, E. (2000). *America's kindergartners* (NCES No. 2000-070). Washington, DC: U.S. Department of Education, National Center for Education Statistics.

West, J., Denton, K., & Reaney, L. (2001). *The kindergarten year* (NCES No. 2001-023). Washington, DC: U.S. Department of Education, National Center for Education Statistics.

White, B. (1985). *The first three years of life* (Rev. ed.). New York: Prentice-Hall.

Whitebook, M., Howes, C., & Phillips, D. (1989). *Who cares? Child care teachers and the quality of care in America: Executive summary National Child Care Staffing Study.* Oakland, CA: Child Care Employee Project.

Whitebook, M., Howes, C., & Phillips, D. A. (1990). *Who cares? Child care teachers and the quality of care in America: Final report, National Child Care Staffing Study.* Oakland, CA: Child Care Employee Project.

Wilson, J. B., Ellwood, D. T., & Brooks-Gunn, J. (1995). Welfare-to-work through the eyes of children: The impact on parenting of movement from AFDC to employment. In P. L. Chase-Lansdale & J. Brooks-Gunn (Eds.), *Escape from poverty: What makes a difference for children?* (pp. 63–86). New York: Cambridge University Press.

Wilson, W. J. (1987). *The truly disadvantaged: The inner city, the underclass, and public policy.* Chicago: University of Chicago Press.

Wiseman, M. (1996). Welfare reform in the United States: A background paper. *Housing Policy Debate, 7*(4), 595–648.

Wolpin, K. I. (1987). *Handbook of the national longitudinal surveys of labor market experience.* Columbus: Ohio State University, Center for Human Resource Research.

Women's and Children's Health Policy Center. (1999a). *Healthy Steps: Phase three, year two final report: The Healthy Steps for Young Children Program National Evaluation, V1* (1). Baltimore: Johns Hopkins University School of Public Health, Department of Population and Family Health Sciences, Women's and Children's Health Policy Center.

Women's and Children's Health Policy Center. (1999b). *Healthy Steps: Phase three, year two final report: The Healthy Steps for Young Children Program National Evaluation, V1* (2). Baltimore: Johns Hopkins University School of Public Health, Department of Population and Family Health Sciences, Women's and Children's Health Policy Center.

Woodcock, R. W., & Johnson, M. B. (1989, 1990). *Woodcock-Johnson Psycho-Educational Battery—Revised.* Itasca, IL: Riverside.

World Health Organization. (1978). *Primary health care* (Report of the International Conference on Primary Health Care, Alma Ata, USSR). Geneva: Author.

World Health Organization. (1980). *International classification of impairments, disabilities, and handicaps.* Geneva: Author.

Yeung, J., Linver, M., & Brooks-Gunn, J. (2001). *How money matters for young children's development: Human capital and family process.* Manuscript submitted for publication.

Yeung, J. W., Sandberg, J. F., Davis-Kean, P. E., & Hofferth, S. L. (2001). Children's time with fathers in intact families. *Journal of Marriage and the Family, 63*(1), 136–154.

Yoshikawa, H. (1995). Long-term effects of early childhood programs on social outcomes and delinquency. *The Future of Children, 5*(3), 51–75.

Yoshikawa, H., & Knitzer, J. (1997). *Lessons from the field: Head Start mental health strategies to meet changing needs.* New York: National Center for Children in Poverty, Columbia University School of Public Health, and American Orthopsychiatric Association.

Young, K. T., Davis, K., Shoen, C., & Parker, S. (1998). Listening to parents: A national survey of parents with young children. *Archives of Pediatrics and Adolescent Medicine, 152,* 255–262.

Ysseldyke, J., & Olsen, K. (1999). Putting alternate assessments into practice: What to measure and possible sources of data. *Exceptional Children, 65,* 175–185.

Zaslow, M. J., & Eldred, C. A. (Eds.). (1998). *Parenting behavior in a sample of young mothers in poverty: Results of the New Chance Observational Study.* New York: Manpower Demonstration Research Corporation.

Zaslow, M. J., & Emig, C. A. (1997). When low-income mothers go to work: Implications for children. *The Future of Children, 7*(1), 110–115.

Zaslow, M. J., Mariner, C. L., Moore, K. A., & Oldham, E. (1998). *Exploratory measures of parenting developed for the JOBS Descriptive Study* (Methods Working Paper No. 98.6). Washington, DC: Child Trends.

Zaslow, M. J., McGroder, S. M., Cave, G., & Mariner, C. (1999). Maternal employment and measures of children's health and development among families with some history of welfare receipt. *Research in the Sociology of Work, 7,* 233–259.

Zaslow, M. J., McGroder, S. M., Moore, K. A., & LeMenestrel, S. M. (2000, June). *Summary report for National Evaluation of Welfare-to-Work Strategies: Impacts on young children and their families two years after enrollment: Findings from the Child Outcomes Study.* Washington, DC: U.S. Department of Health and Human Services and U.S. Department of Education.

Zaslow, M. J., Moore, K. A., Morrison, D. R., & Coiro, M. J. (1995). The Family Support Act and children: Potential pathways of influence. *Children and Youth Services Review, 17,* 231–249.

Zaslow, M. J., Tout, K., Smith, S., & Moore, K. A. (1998). Implications of the 1996 welfare legislation for children: A research perspective. *Social Policy Report, 12*(3), 1–34.

Zedlewski, S. R. (2000, October). *Snapshots of America's families II: Family economic well-being.* Washington, DC: Urban Institute.

Zigler, E. (1973). Project Head Start: Success or failure? *Learning, 1,* 43–47.

Zigler, E. (1998). By what goals should Head Start be assessed? *Children's Services: Social Policy, Research, and Practice, 1*(1), 5–17.

Zigler, E. F., & Styfco, S. J. (Eds.). (1993). *Head Start and beyond: A national plan for extended childhood intervention.* New Haven, CT: Yale University Press.

Zigler, E. F., & Styfco, S. J. (1996). Head Start and early childhood intervention: The changing course of social science and social policy. In E. F. Zigler, S. L. Kagan, & N. W. Hall (Eds.), *Children, families, and government: Preparing for the twenty-first century.* New York: Cambridge University Press.

Zill, N. (1995). National surveys as data resources for public policy research on poor children. In P. L. Chase-Lansdale & J. Brooks-Gunn (Eds.), *Escape from poverty: What makes a difference for children?* (pp. 272–290). New York: Cambridge University Press.

Zill, N., Resnick, G., McKey, R. H., Clark, C., Connell, D., Swartz, J., et al. (1998). *Head Start Program Performance Measures: Second progress report.* Washington, DC: Administration on Children, Youth, and Families.

Zuckerman, S., Haley, J., & Holahan, J. (2000, October). *Snapshots of America's families II: Health insurance, access, and health status of nonelderly adults.* Washington, DC: Urban Institute.

About the Editors and the Contributors

Jeanne Brooks-Gunn is the Virginia and Leonard Marx Professor of Child Development and Education at Teachers College, Columbia University. She is the first director of the National Center for Children and Families, which was founded in 1992, at Teachers College. In addition, she has directed the Adolescent Study Program at Teachers College and the College of Physicians and Surgeons, Columbia University, and is Co-Director of the Institute for Child and Family Policy at Columbia University. Dr. Brooks-Gunn's specialty is policy-oriented research focusing on family and community influences upon the development of children and youth. Her research centers on designing and evaluating interventions aimed at enhancing the well-being of children living in poverty and associated conditions. Author of over 340 published articles and 14 books, she has received the Distinguished Contributions to Research in Public Policy Award (2001) from the Committee on Public Interest of the American Psychological Association and the Urie Bronfenbrenner Award for her lifetime contribution to developmental psychology in the areas of science and society from Division 7 of the American Psychological Association (2001). She has been awarded the Vice President's National Performance Review Hammer Award for her participation in the Federal Interagency Forum on Child and Family Statistics, National Institute for Child Health and Human Development Research Network (1998). She has been awarded the Nicholas Hobbs Award from the American Psychological Association Division of Children, Youth, and Families for her contribution to policy research for children (1997) and also has received the John B. Hill Award from the Society for Research on Adolescence for her lifetime contribution to research on adolescence (1996). In 1988, she received the William Goode Book Award from the American Sociological Association for her book *Adolescent Mothers in Later Life* (coauthored with Drs. Furstenberg and Morgan). Dr. Brooks-Gunn is a National Fellow at Harvard University's Inequality and Social Policy Program, a visiting scholar at the Office of Population Research at Princeton University, a member of the Children's Roundtable at the Brookings Institute, and a senior research affiliate for the Joint Center for Poverty Research at Northwestern University/University of Chicago. She received her

BA from Connecticut College in 1969, her EdM from Harvard Graduate School of Education in 1970, and her PhD in human learning and development from the University of Pennsylvania in 1975.

Allison Sidle Fuligni has been a research scientist at the National Center for Children and Families (NCCF) at Teachers College, Columbia University, since 1996. She has recently joined the Center for the Improvement of Child Care Quality at UCLA. She received her doctorate in developmental psychology from the University of Michigan. Before joining the NCCF, she was a research associate at the Families and Work Institute in New York City, and an adjunct assistant professor of psychology at New York University. At the NCCF, Dr. Fuligni served as project director of the Early Head Start Research and Evaluation Project, a collaboration with Mathematica Policy Research, Inc. She also served as project coordinator for Columbia University's Head Start Quality Research Center. This project involved the design of an intervention to improve the quality of Head Start centers, as well as an evaluation of the intervention's effects on children's developmental outcomes. Her current research topics include patterns of child care use and quality of child care settings, the impact of early childhood intervention programs, the transition to parenthood, patterns of shared caregiving in two-parent families, and applications of this work to workplace and social policies to support working and low-income parents.

Lisa J. Berlin is a research scholar at the Center for Child and Family Policy at Duke University. Her work focuses on early development and on programs and policies for young children and their families. She is especially concerned with early child maltreatment. Dr. Berlin served as a member of the national evaluation team for the Early Head Start Research and Evaluation Project, a multisite, longitudinal, randomized evaluation of approximately 3,000 low-income families. She is currently working on a multidisciplinary, community-wide child abuse prevention initiative in Durham, North Carolina. Dr. Berlin received her PhD in human development and family studies from the Pennsylvania State University in 1994.

Christy Brady-Smith, is a research scientist at the National Center for Children and Families, Teachers College, Columbia University. Her research interests focus on parenting, early employment, child care, and early intervention among low-income families with young children. She is part of the national evaluation team of the Early Head Start Research and Evaluation Project, a national, 17-site, longitudinal evaluation of some of the first federally funded Early Head Start programs for low-income infants and toddlers, and their families. She is currently involved in the follow-up study of Early Head Start as children enter preschool and kindergarten and is also a collaborator on the qualitative addition to the Fragile Families study in New York City. Prior to attending graduate school, she was a teacher and principal at an elementary school in Tegucigalpa, Honduras. Dr. Brady-Smith attended Wheaton College for her undergraduate studies in psychology and graduated with honors. She earned her doctorate in developmental psychology from Teachers College, Columbia University. During her doctoral studies, she was awarded a Spencer Research Training Grant, a Harvey Fellowship from the Mustard Seed Foundation, and the Columbia University Public Policy Fellowship.

Donna Bryant is a senior scientist at the Frank Porter Graham Child Development Institute at the University of North Carolina at Chapel Hill and a research professor in the School of Education. She co-directs the National Center for Early Development and Learning, based at UNC–CH and funded by the Office of Educational Research and Improvement. Dr. Bryant's PhD is in experimental psychology from UNC–CH. She has directed several studies of early intervention and prevention for children at risk for developmental disabilities, recently focusing on Head Start. Current Head Start projects include membership in the Head Start Quality Research Consortium and a study of mental health interventions for teachers and parents of children with problems of aggression. She was a primary investigator on Project CARE, the Infant Health and Development Program, and the Head Start Transition Demonstration Project. Along with colleagues at the Frank Porter Graham Child Development Institute, she has conducted statewide studies of North Carolina's kindergarten and public preschool programs and of Smart Start, North Carolina's initiative to enhance child care and family services. She has authored many papers and chapters on early intervention and early childhood education and is a coauthor of two books, one on home visiting and another on early intervention.

Natasha Cabrera received her PhD in educational psychology from the University of Denver and her master's degree from the University of Toronto. Dr. Cabrera joined the National Institute of Child Health and Human Development as a Society for Research in Child Development Fellow; she had an Expert Appointment in child development and was the coordinator of the Science and Ecology of Early Development program, the cofacilitator of the Family and Child Well-Being Research Network, and the coordinator of fatherhood research and welfare studies. She is now an assistant professor at the University of Maryland, College Park. Dr. Cabrera's research interests include fatherhood, child care, Head Start, policy, the normative development of low-income children, and the interface between policy and research.

Greg Duncan is a professor of education and social policy and a faculty associate in the Institute for Policy Research at Northwestern University. He is director of the Northwestern University/University of Chicago Joint Center for Poverty Research. Duncan received a PhD in economics in 1974 from the University of Michigan. He was awarded an honorary Doctor of the University of Essex degree in 1999 and was elected to the American Academy of Arts and Sciences in 2001. Much of Duncan's career has been spent at the University of Michigan on the Panel Study of Income Dynamics data collection project. That project has conducted annual interviews with a large, representative set of families all around the country for nearly 30 years. It has become a major source of information about poverty and welfare dynamics in the United States. Duncan joined the faculty at Northwestern University in 1995. Duncan's own research has focused on issues of economic mobility, both within and across generations. He is the author of *Years of Poverty, Years of Plenty*, a 1984 book that documented the surprising degree of economic mobility in the United States and the coeditor (with Jeanne Brooks-Gunn) of *Consequences of Growing Up Poor*, a 1997 book about the impact of poverty on child development. More recently, his research has focused on how welfare reform affects families and children.

Phyllis Gyamfi received her undergraduate degree in psychology and journalism from the University of Miami, where she worked on numerous studies, including one on black youth and school desegregation; she received her master's degree and doctorate in developmental psychology from Teachers College, Columbia University. Dr. Gyamfi's dissertation examined the implications of the Welfare Reform Law of 1996 on single black mothers and their children. This work received the Outstanding Research Award of the Society for Social Work and Research and the first-place award in a graduate research paper competition under the auspices of the American Psychological Association. Dr. Gyamfi also won two dissertation fellowships on the basis of this work: one from the Woodrow Wilson Fellowship Foundation, and the other from the American Association of University Women. Dr. Gyamfi's research interests include social policy issues such as welfare reform, family and child poverty, ethnic and racial socialization, and immigration and acculturation. Currently, she is working at ORC Macro in Atlanta, Georgia, as a research scientist. At ORC Macro, Dr. Gyamfi is working on the National Evaluation of the Comprehensive Community Mental Health Services for Children and their Families Program. Her primary responsibilities include the System-of-Care Assessment portion of the evaluation, which examines whether programs have been implemented according to system-of-care program theory and assesses the development of systems and how the needs of children and families in the program are served; she also develops measures for the qualitative assessment of how these systems work and links these assessments to children's outcome data.

Kathleen Hebbeler is a program manager in the Center for Education and Human Services at SRI International in Menlo Park, California. She conducts research in several areas related to the health and well-being of children and youth, with much of her research focused on children and youth with disabilities. Currently, Dr. Hebbeler is directing the National Early Intervention Longitudinal Study (NEILS), which is examining services and outcomes for almost 3,400 children with disabilities in early intervention programs around the country. She recently completed overseeing the design of the Pre-Elementary Education Longitudinal Study (PEELS), which will follow children who began receiving special education as 3- through 5-year-olds. Both NEILS and PEELS are part of the U.S. Department of Education's program of longitudinal studies of children and youth with disabilities. Dr. Hebbeler served as an advisor on disability issues to the national evaluation of Early Head Start and has assisted the Early Childhood Longitudinal Study—Birth Cohort in a similar capacity. She directed a design component of the Early Childhood Longitudinal Study—Kindergarten Cohort that addressed issues for children with disabilities, including oversampling, measurement of disability, and accommodations to the direct assessment. Her other current research includes the use of community building as a strategy for improving children's health and well-being and the effectiveness of out-of-school programs for improving academic achievement. Dr. Hebbeler has written extensively and presented at numerous national meetings on policy and programs for children. Previously, she worked for the U.S. Department of Education, the National Association of State Directors of Special Education, and the evaluation department in a large suburban school district. She received her doctorate in human development and family studies from Cornell University.

Janis Kupersmidt is an associate professor of psychology at the University of North Carolina at Chapel Hill. She received her graduate degree in clinical child psychology from Duke University and completed her clinical internship at Yale University School of Medicine. She taught at the University of Virginia for three years before joining the faculty of UNC–CH in 1988. She was a William T. Grant Faculty Scholar and has served as a principal investigator or co–principal investigator on many projects funded by NIMH or Head Start. Her research interests include treatment of preschool aggression, peer rejection in childhood, social cognition and delinquency, and coping with peer-related stressors.

Tama Leventhal, a developmental psychologist, is a research scientist at the National Center for Children and Families. She received her doctorate (with distinction) from Columbia University in 1999, where she was also a graduate fellow at the National Center for Children and Families. She was a summer fellow in Putting Children First (a research fellowship in child and family policy) and held a Columbia University Public Policy Fellowship. Dr. Leventhal's research interests are in linking developmental research with social policy regarding children, youth, and families, particularly low-income families with children. Her work has focused on understanding how neighborhood contexts affect child and family well-being.

Lisa McCabe is a cooperative extension associate in early care and education at Cornell University's Early Childhood Program. Her current work focuses on applied research and outreach in the area of early childhood education and development. Dr. McCabe has also worked as a research scientist at the National Center for Children and Families, Teachers College, Columbia University, where she specialized in policy-oriented research focusing on early childhood education and emotional development. In addition, she has been a child care provider for infants and toddlers and a research assistant for the Child Care Action Campaign, an advocacy organization in New York City. Dr. McCabe received both her MA (1995) and PhD (1999) in human development from Cornell University.

Sara McLanahan is a professor of sociology and public affairs at Princeton University. She directs the Bendheim-Thoman Center for Research on Child Wellbeing and is an associate in the Office of Population Research. She received her PhD in sociology from the University of Texas at Austin. Her research interests include family demography, poverty and inequality, and social policy. She teaches courses on poverty and family policy. She is coauthor of (with Gary Sandefur) *Growing Up with a Single Parent* and (with Irwin Garfinkel) *Single Mothers and Their Children* and the coeditor of (with Irwin Garfinkel) *Fathers Under Fire*, (with Irwin Garfinkel and Jennifer L. Hochschild) *Social Policies for Children*, and (with Irwin Garfinkel and Philip K. Robins) *Child Support and Child Well-Being*. She has served on the boards of the American Sociological Association and the Population Association of America, for which she will serve as President-Elect 2003 and President 2004.

The **NICHD Early Child Care Research Network** is a team of investigators that has planned and implemented the NICHD Study of Early Child Care and Youth Development, a natural history longitudinal study of the development of children born across the United States in 1991 and followed up from early infancy through middle childhood. The National Institute of Child Health and Human Development funds the work of the team through a co-operative agreement mechanism that calls for scientific collaboration between grantees and NICHD staff.

Colleen R. O'Neal is a child clinical psychologist and is currently a National Institute of Mental Health postdoctoral fellow in mental health statistics at New York University. Her research is focused on resilient processes among children and families. She received her PhD in clinical psychology from Long Island University in Brooklyn, New York. As a graduate student, she received a predoctoral National Research Service Award from the National Institute of Mental Health.

Kerry Richter is a demographer and social researcher, holding a PhD in sociology from the University of Wisconsin. From 1988 to 1993, she was a Rockefeller Fellow and assistant professor at the Institute for Population and Social Research at Mahidol University in Thailand, where she did research on migration, child care, and old age security. After serving as a Mellon Postdoctoral Fellow and adjunct assistant professor at the Population Research Institute of Pennsylvania State University, she joined Child Trends in Washington, DC, in 1996. While at Child Trends, she did research on adolescent development, motivations for adolescent pregnancy, and the impact of national policies on children and youth. Since 1997 she has worked for Population Services International (PSI), which implements social marketing programs for HIV/AIDS prevention, family planning, and other health issues in over 50 countries. She is currently the regional research director for PSI/Asia in Bangkok.

Jodie Roth is a research scientist at the National Center for Children and Families at Teachers College, Columbia University. She received her PhD from the Combined Program in Education and Psychology at the University of Michigan in 1995. She is interested in how programs and institutions affect adolescents' development. Her research currently focuses on how prevention and youth development programs in schools and the community can promote healthy adolescent development.

Donna Spiker is the program manager of the Early Childhood Program in SRI International's Center for Education and Human Services. Dr. Spiker is a nationally known developmental psychologist with extensive experience in research on the efficacy of early intervention and early childhood programs and services, mother-child interaction, and young children with disabilities. She is currently a co–project director of the Statewide Data Collection and Evaluation of First 5 California-Funded Programs (programs and services for children from the prenatal period to age 5, with the goal of improving the health, development, well-being, and school readiness of California's young children and their families). She also is a co–principal investigator of the National Early Intervention Longitudinal Study (NEILS), a national study of infants and toddlers and their families who have received early intervention services (birth to age 3). In earlier work at Stanford University, she served as the deputy director of the Infant Health and Development Program (IHDP), a landmark national randomized study of early intervention and services for low–birth weight infants and their families, and as the clinical director of the Stanford Autism Genetics Project. Dr. Spiker has authored more than 60 articles and book chapters about issues of development, assessment, and program evaluation for infants and young children. She also is a coeditor (with Ruth Gross and Christine Haynes) of *Helping Low Birth Weight, Premature Babies: The Infant Health and Development Program.* Dr. Spiker was named a fellow of the American Psychological Association for her contributions to research on early intervention and developmental disabilities. She received her PhD in child development from the University of Minnesota in 1979.

Martha Zaslow is a developmental psychologist. At Child Trends, a nonpartisan, nonprofit research organization that focuses on research and statistics on children and families, she is the vice president for research. Her research takes an ecological perspective, considering the contributions of different contexts to the development of children in low-income families, including the family, child care, and policy contexts. In studying the role of the family, Dr. Zaslow has focused especially on parenting, carrying out observational studies of mother-child interaction in samples of families with a history of receiving welfare. In studying child care, Dr. Zaslow's work has focused on use of child care by families receiving welfare, on nonstandard work hours and child care among working poor families, and on strategies to improve child care quality. In the policy context, she has studied the impacts on children of different welfare reform policies. She is participating in evaluations of state-level early childhood initiatives aimed at improving children's school readiness in South Carolina and California. She received her PhD in developmental psychology from Harvard University.

Index